The
PSYCHOLOGY
of
WOMEN

Second Edition

MICHELE A. PALUDI

Prentice Hall   *Upper Saddle River, New Jersey   07458*

Library of Congress Cataloging-in-Publication Data

Paludi, Michele Antoinette.
  The psychology of women / Michele A. Paludi.—2nd ed.
    p. cm.
  Includes bibliographical references and index.
  ISBN 0-13-040963-4
  1. Women—Psychology.   I. Title.

HQ1206 .P29 2001
305.4—dc21

                         2001021418

VP Editorial Director: Laura Pearson
Executive Editor: Stephanie Johnson
Managing Editor (editorial): Sharon Rheinhardt
Sr. Managing Editor: Mary Rottino
Production Liaison: Fran Russello
Project Manager: Karen Berry/Pine Tree Composition
Prepress and Manufacturing Buyer: Tricia Kenny
Art Director: Jayne Conte
Cover Designer: Bruce Kenselaar
Cover Image Credit: Hannah Foote, "Baltimore Album Applique Quilt," 1850. From Collection America Hurrah
  Antiques.
Director of Marketing: Beth Gillett Mejia

This book was set in 10.5/14 Clearface by Pine Tree Composition, Inc., and was
printed and bound by R.R. Donnelley & Sons Company. The cover was printed by Phoenix Color Corp.

© 2002, 1998 by Pearson Education, Inc.
Upper Saddle River, New Jersey 07458

Printed in the United States of America
10 9 8 7 6 5 4 3 2 1

ISBN 0-13-040963-4

Pearson Education Ltd., *London*
Pearson Education Australia Pty, Limited, *Sydney*
Pearson Education Singapore, Pte. Ltd.
Pearson Education North Asia Ltd., *Hong Kong*
Pearson Education Canada, Ltd., *Toronto*
Pearson Educación de Mexico, S.A. de C.V.
Pearson Education—Japan, *Tokyo*
Pearson Education Malaysia, Pte. Ltd.
Pearson Education, Upper Saddle River, New Jersey

In Memory of

Antoinette Rose Peccichio Paludi

My Mother and My Best Friend

Contents

II Development Across the Life Cycle   66

3 Physical Development Across the Female Life Cycle   66

4 Theoretical Perspectives on Women's Personalities and Mental Health **102**

5 Women's Health Issues **149**

8 Women and Intimate Relationships 247

9 Career Psychology of Women 270

Preface

I have always considered the first day of the Psychology of Women course to be one of the most important days of the semester. During this first meeting, we sit in a circle. I spend time describing the format of the course, readings, requirements, and my own background in psychology and in the psychology of women. I then ask participants in the course to introduce themselves, to share their goals for the course, and to comment on one thing they like about the course so far (from reading the syllabus and hearing my opening comments) and one thing about which they are unsure (e.g., the format for the essays and paper).

This first-day format provides an opportunity for students to convey concerns about discussing the topics covered in courses in the psychology of women. These concerns especially apply to emotionally laden topics such as racial discrimination, date rape, and incest. There are both hopes and worries about participating in a course identified as "feminist" in content and process. As participants have commented during the first class:

- *I am looking forward to discussing the psychology of women—is there psychological research on ethnic minority women? I haven't had much of this information in my other psychology classes.*

- *I like sitting in a circle so I can see everybody and hear what they have to say. I don't talk too much, though; I hope I don't have to tell a lot about myself in here.*

- *Some of the topics on your syllabus make me anxious. I've experienced some of the things—they've happened to me.*

- *Isn't a course on the psychology of women discriminating against men? Shouldn't there be a psychology of men course?*

- *I plan to go to grad school in psychology—I hope this course will be relevant to my future career in clinical psych.*

- *I think there shouldn't be a psychology of women course—all of the information you have here should be taught in personality, social psych, developmental, and clinical psych.*

These comments reflect a great deal of excitement about devoting an entire course to women's lives and realities. They also reflect considerable doubt about the necessity of such a course, the benefits of the course, and the value of such a course for a future career in psychology. I believe the comments I hear on the first day of the course also reflect statements students have heard from their mates, friends, and family members: that the course is radical, or is a place to devalue men, or is not rigorous. I also hear many descriptions of women in this first meeting:

- *Women get into graduate schools and get jobs nowadays—there's no more sex discrimination.*
- *If women married accommodating husbands, they would be able to have it all.*
- *Infants need their mothers—women who use day care for their infants probably didn't really want children in the first place.*
- *Many women don't support the women's movement—not only men put women down, you know.*

Hearing such views about women in the psychology of women course is helpful to all participants in the class. These comments offer insight into the types of socialization experiences that place less value on women and femininity. The comments also suggest to me that feminism can facilitate new relationships among people and that the classroom is an important place for this to occur. I have found it most important to express to students in this first meeting my definition of feminism and how I incorporate this definition in facilitating the psychology of women course.

As I mention in this first meeting, *feminism derivatively means womanism.* Feminism thus means valuing women in and of themselves. This valuing is unconditional. Women are valued not solely for the work they produce; not solely for the services they provide their employer, family, partners, and friends; not according to some externally imposed set of requirements. Women are valued for their autonomy, caring, health care, relationships, commitment to children, nurturing of friends, education, love of family, and sexuality. Feminism connotes valuing the diversity among women around the world—acknowledging their similarities and appreciating their distinctiveness.

Thus, the term *feminist* refers to an individual who believes in economic, social, and political equality of women and men and thus favors the social and legal changes that are necessary to achieve equality.

The goals I have for the psychology of women course center around these components of feminism. My presentations, grading, and class discussions are all guided by the following feminist frameworks:

- A psychology of women course should deal with women and treat women as the norm. A non-Eurocentric perspective on women should be presented.

- A psychology of women course should identify the women of psychology—the contributions by historical and contemporary women psychologists.

- A psychology of women course should facilitate students making connections between their own experiences and the psychological theories and research findings.

- Information in a psychology of women course should encourage participants to critically analyze all subareas in psychology for their portrayal of women.

I would like to discuss each of these feminist frameworks in more detail. They provide the major guidelines for the organization of this book.

FRAMEWORKS FOR STUDYING THE PSYCHOLOGY OF WOMEN

- *A psychology of women course should deal with women and treat women as the norm. A non-Eurocentric perspective on women should be presented.*

Throughout much of psychology, an androcentric view of human behavior has assumed that men were the normative population and women were studied in order to determine how they compared with male standards (Bronstein & Quina, 1988; Makosky & Paludi, 1990; Paludi, Paludi, & Doyle, in press). Theories and research on morality (Kohlberg, 1966) and achievement motivation (McClelland, Atkinson, Clark, & Lowell, 1953) were based on boys and men only. Nearly 50 percent of the research on aggression has been conducted using boys or men only; 10 percent has used girls or women, and 40 percent has used both sexes. This 50 percent is higher than the percentage of male-only research in psychology in general (McKenna & Kessler, 1977). Naomi Weisstein (1971) made a persuasive case that many psychologists have allowed their personal biases about women to color their research endeavors. She concluded:

Until psychologists begin respecting evidence and until they begin looking at the social contexts within which people move, psychology will have nothing to say of substance to offer in this task of discovery. I do not know what immutable differences exist between men and women apart from differences in their genitals; perhaps there are some other unchangeable differences; probably there are a number of irrelevant differences.

But it is clear that until social expectations for men and women are equal, until we provide equal respect for both men and women, our answers to this question will simply reflect our prejudices. (p. 222)

Thus, a psychology of women course makes up for the problems in the psychology curriculum that have typically omitted women from theoretical perspectives and research, distorted their experiences to fit into a male-based structure, and trivialized their experiences or dismissed them as silly. In recent years, many psychologists have noted that a Eurocentric bias has existed in psychology in general and in the psychology of women as well. Integrating the scholarship on race and ethnicity into the psychology of women course adds an important dimension: It provides more understanding of the psychology of all women. Women's experiences are extremely diverse, yet women are frequently described collectively. And ethnic minority women differ among themselves as much as do white women.

In this book, I will discuss ways in which socialization practices of girls and women differ by class, race, sexual orientation, religion, and ethnicity. Rosita Daskal Albert (1988) has described several advantages in placing culture in the psychology curriculum. I have found these advantages to be especially useful in the psychology of women course:

1. We can obtain information that is not available in one's own culture.

2. We can obtain information about the incidence of a psychological issue in a different culture.

3. Values that are common to a certain cultural group can be discussed.

4. The generalizability of psychological research can be assessed by looking at research from several cultures.

In our study of cultural influences on the psychology of women, we have noted the following: Asian American women must deal with gender and racial oppression (Root, 1995). They must resolve the conflict between a traditional Asian focus on women's subservience versus the U.S. emphasis on equality in relationships between women and men.

Many Chicanas have a marked lack of power in the occupational, educational, economic, and political arenas. They may experience considerable stress, given their culture's emphasis on family values and the high incidence of single motherhood. There is a reported high incidence of depression among Chicanas (Vasquez & Baron,

1988). Child care accounts for the largest share of women's household labor, and there are only a few countries that offer alternative child care facilities. Families with many children place excessive demands on women's work, contributing to their increased stress.

As another example, Ferron's (1997) research suggested that compared to U.S. adolescent girls, French girls believe that an ideal body is impossible to attain; they believe their physical appearance is predetermined and cannot be modified through will power or courage. U.S. adolescent girls were more likely than French girls to engage in behaviors that are harmful to their health, including unbalanced diets.

Additional examples of cultural similarities and distinctiveness are described in this book as well.

• *A psychology of women course should identify the women of psychology—the contributions by historical and contemporary women psychologists.*

Acknowledging the role of women in the field of psychology allows us to discover women psychologists and their contributions to the discipline. We also reconstruct as models, the careers and family experiences of several women. Many of you who are reading this are preparing for a career in psychology, and these experiences can be related to your own strategies for establishing professional and personal identities.

Women psychologists are featured in this book. They have shared their research and clinical experiences and have provided us with some information about their educational and work experiences in a variety of subareas in psychology. I invite you to write to them about your own career goals.

• *A psychology of women course should facilitate participants making connections between their own experiences and the psychological theories and research findings.*

Throughout our discussions in this book, I encourage you to use a "life review" of your gender-role socialization.

In this text, you will find several examples of affective learning. At the end of each chapter is a group of Chapter Review Questions, which deal with the information presented in the chapter. They ask you to consider your views about women, feminism, your own gender-role socialization, and ways you can work on integrating feminism into your everyday life. In addition, there are some experiential exercises for you to complete alone or with friends. The questions will bring concepts from the chapter and from class discussions under the scrutiny of your own experiences and evaluations. They provide ways of adding your own analyses to the concepts of the psychology of women course.

> • *Information in a psychology of women course should encourage participants to critically analyze all subareas in psychology for their portrayal of women.*

Another goal I have for you is to question the role of women and women's issues in other courses in the psychology curriculum. For example:

How often are experiments in psychology based on girls' and women's responses?

What is the ethnic and racial background of the research participants in the experiments being discussed?

Do research reports focus on similarities between women and men as well as differences?

Does the title or abstract of a research report make reference to the limitations of the study?

Are gender (as well as racial, class, ethnic, and sexual orientation) differences inaccurately magnified?

Are critiques of the masculine bias in theories of personality development presented?

Are family styles such as single parenting, lesbian parenting, gay parenting, and dual-earner parenting presented?

This text, as well as your psychology of women course, will expose you to new research on women. The psychology of women course stimulates research and publication about women's lives and realities. Thus, the psychology of women course legitimizes the discipline of the psychology of women. As psychologist Mary Roth Walsh (1985) suggested, the course also serves as a "catalyst for change" by revealing serious deficiencies in psychological research and theories relevant to gender, cultural, and ethnic issues.

Material developed for the psychology of women course can be introduced into other courses in the psychology curriculum, including statistics, experimental design, theories of personality, life-span development, social psychology, counseling and clinical psychology, health psychology, and vocational psychology (Bronstein & Quina, 1988). The psychology of women course provides psychologists with resources, perspectives, and techniques with which to balance their courses with respect to gender, race, ethnicity, sexual orientation, age, and class. *The psychology of women course can thus provide information for a psychology of all people.*

This has been my goal as I wrote this book. Thus, the text is organized in four major sections. Part I deals with the heritage of the field of the psychology of women. Part II addresses women's development across the life cycle, including women's health issues, women's sexuality and reproductive rights, and women's personalities. In Part III, we discuss women and social relationships, including communication styles, career development, and friendships and romantic relationships. Part IV addresses women as victims and survivors of sexual victimization.

Within each chapter, I discuss how that particular subarea in psychology traditionally portrays women and women's experiences, and I offer feminist correctives to these portrayals.

Taking an active part in the psychology of women course can be exhilarating; however, you may also feel uncomfortable with what you are reading, with what your professor is saying, with your relationships, or with your classmates. This anger, like other emotions you may experience in the psychology of women course, is normative, part of our development. I want to assure you that the anger will pass. You may find yourself acknowledging a variety of perspectives on an issue, and these perspectives may challenge your own thinking on the topic. I encourage you to keep a journal of your thinking about the course process and course content. In fact, at the end of this introduction, I have shared some suggestions for keeping a journal. Perhaps you'll see a developmental process unfolding throughout the semester. Nancy Downing and Kathleen Rousch (1985) suggested that individuals may proceed through five stages when confronted with feminist issues:

1. Passive acceptance

2. Revelation

3. Embeddedness/emanation

4. Synthesis

5. Active commitment

In the *passive acceptance* stage of your development in the course, you may find yourself and others saying that discrimination is no longer present in politics, economics, the family, or education. You may believe that traditional roles are advantageous. Some of the topics you'll be discussing may start you questioning these assumptions. It's OK to do so. You may never change your opinions, but you may start to question why you have held on to certain ideas for so long in the face of contrary evidence.

By discussing issues related to women's lives and realities, one common transition from the passive acceptance stage is *revelation*. You may start to remember how you in fact have been discriminated against because of your race, your sexual orientation, and/or your sex. You may begin to notice magazine advertisements that connote women as objects. You may remember being called certain derogatory names because you were overweight, had acne, wore braces. During this stage in your development in the psychology of women course, you may become quite angry with yourself. You may ask yourself why you have allowed these comments to be made, why you haven't noticed the racism and sexism in advertisements until now. These feelings of anger and guilt are to be expected. All of the participants in your class are going through a similar process.

When women in the class share their anger about these issues, you may find yourself wanting to spend time connecting with them, sharing your experiences, and asking them how they have handled their experiences. This stage is referred to as the *embeddedness/emanation* stage. Frequently, you will hear comments in class that suggest cautious interaction with men. These comments are not evidence of "man hating." Rather, they reflect women's and men's concerns about the power imbalance in North American culture.

The embeddedness/emanation stage is frequently replaced by the *synthesis* stage, in which statements are made acknowledging the discriminatory practices against women, especially ethnic women, aged women, women of the working class, lesbian women, and physically challenged women. In addition, you'll hear statements reflecting women's and men's transcendence of gender-role stereotypes. Women and men will be described as individuals, not members of the sex categories.

Finally, you'll notice the class reflecting the *active commitment* stage. You'll hear your classmates ask what other courses are available that deal with women's concerns, what the women's studies program is offering during the next semester, what types of independent studies and research in women's studies are available, and so on. Keeping a journal in the psychology of women class will help you to see the various stages of this developmental process in yourself and in other students. I encourage you to share the content of your journal entries with some members of your class.

I enjoy participating in courses in the psychology of women. I hope you will enjoy it too. And I hope you will find this book helpful in your study about the psychology of women. I invite you to send me your comments and suggestions about this book.

HOW TO KEEP A JOURNAL IN THE PSYCHOLOGY OF WOMEN COURSE

After each class discussion and/or reading, you may want to jot down your answers to the following items:

1. What was the value of this issue to you as a whole?

2. How would you describe the discussion about this topic to a friend?

3. Were any of the issues raised in class and/or in the readings emotionally painful for you? Why or why not?

4. What did you learn or relearn about yourself today?

5. What could you have done differently in preparing for this topic?

6. What could your professor have done differently in discussing this topic, to better meet your needs?

7. How are you feeling about the psychology of women course?

8. What have been the reactions of your friends to your taking the psychology of women course?

Michele A. Paludi

REFERENCES

Albert, R. D. (1988). The place of culture in modern psychology. In P. Bronstein & K. Quina (Eds.), *Teaching a psychology of people: Resources for gender and sociocultural awareness.* Washington, DC: American Psychological Association.

Bronstein, P., & Quina, K. (Eds.). (1988). *Teaching a psychology of people: Resources for gender and sociocultural awareness.* Washington, DC: American Psychological Association.

Downing, N., & Rousch, K. (1985). From passive acceptance to active commitment. *The Counseling Psychologist, 13,* 695–709.

Ferron, C. (1997). Body image in adolescence: Cross cultural research—Results of the preliminary phase of a quantitative survey. *Adolescence, 32,* 735–744.

Kohlberg, L. (1966). A cognitive-developmental analysis of children's sex role concepts and attitudes. In E. Maccoby (Ed.), *The development of sex differences.* Stanford, CA: Stanford University Press.

Makosky, V., & Paludi, M. (1990). Feminism and women's studies in the academy. In M. Paludi & G. Steuernagel (Eds.), *Foundations for a feminist restructuring of the academic disciplines.* New York: Haworth.

McClelland, D., Atkinson, J., Clark, R., & Lowell, F. (1953). *The achievement motive.* New York: Appleton-Century-Crofts.

McKenna, W., & Kessler, S. (1977). Experimental design as a source of sex bias in social psychology. *Sex Roles, 3,* 117–128.

Paludi, M., Paludi, C., & Doyle, J. (in press). *Sex and gender.* (5th ed.). New York: McGraw Hill.

Root, M. P. P. (1995). The psychology of Asian American women. In H. Landrine (Ed.), *Bringing cultural diversity to feminist psychology: Theory, research, and practice.* Washington, DC: American Psychological Association.

Vasquez, M., & Baron, A. (1988). The psychology of the Chicano experience: A sample course structure. In P. Bronstein & K. Quina (Eds.), *Teaching a psychology of people: Resources for gender and sociocultural awareness.* Washington, DC: American Psychological Association.

Walsh, M. R. (1985). The psychology of women course: A continuing catalyst for change. *Teaching of Psychology, 12,* 198–203.

Weisstein, N. (1971). Psychology constructs the female. In V. Gornick & B. Moran (Eds.), *Women in sexist society.* New York: New American Library.

Acknowledgments

I wish to thank Carmen Paludi, Jr. for his sage advice, nurturance, and support. You are an important presence in my life and in my work.

I also would like to thank my sisters, Rosalie Paludi and Lucille Paludi, for their support and guidance during my writing of this text.

I appreciate the insights of students in my classes on the psychology of women and the psychology of gender. You help show me the great accomplishments of women and the work we have yet to do. You have made me believe that all of you, in your individual ways, will continue to value women.

My appreciation is also extended to the following friends and colleagues who continue to nurture my spirit:

Fr. John Provost
Janice Guy
Paula Lundberg-Love
Darlene C. DeFour
Billie Dziech
Fr. Raphael Wanjohi

I also thank the team at Prentice Hall for working with me to make this second edition of *The Psychology of Women* a reality.

ONE

THE WOMEN OF PSYCHOLOGY AND THE PSYCHOLOGY OF WOMEN

IN WOMEN'S VOICES

No man can ever fully realize the feeling of isolation and repression which was the lot, up to thirty years ago, of those few active-minded women who were afflicted with an unnatural desire to aid in the accumulation of the world's store of exact knowledge.

Christine Ladd-Franklin, 1896

How to be a scholar, though married, is, to tell the truth, one of the most specific problems of the scholarship of women.

Mary Calkins, 1913

Woman's efforts to achieve independence and enlargement of her field of activities are continually met with skepticism which insists that such efforts should be made only in the face of economic necessity, and that they run counter to her inherent character and natural tendencies. Accordingly, all efforts of this sort are said to be without any vital significance for women, whose every thought should center upon the male or motherhood.

Karen Horney, 1934

We find it curious that psychological thought is still heavily influenced by such nineteenth-century theorists as Darwin, Marx, and Freud. As products of their era, they were primarily supportive of the status quo, of upper-class White male privilege with its limited knowledge of and marginal concern for women. If they were alive today, they would be astonished: What? You are still using those old books? Throw them away.

Rachel Hare-Mustin and Jeanne Marecek, 1990

Chapter Outline

Questions for Reflection

1. Why did you register to take a course on the psychology of women? What issues do you hope will be addressed in this course?

2. What women psychologists have you studied thus far in your psychology curriculum?

3. How do you define the term "feminism"? Do your friends hold a similar definition of this term?

4. Are you a feminist? Why or why not?

5. Why do you believe it is important to have courses on the the psychology of women?

6. Identify racially minority women psychologists you have studied thus far in your psychology curriculum.

7. Do you believe there should be a course on the Psychology of Men? Why or why not?

8. What kinds of comments have you received from friends and family regarding you taking a Psychology of Women course? Why do you believe you received these comments? How have you addressed these comments with your friends and family?

INTRODUCTION: UP WITH PSYCHOLOGY'S FOREMOTHERS

In 1974, psychologists Maxine Bernstein and Nancy Felipe Russo published an article in *The American Psychologist* about the contributions of women to psychology. The article was titled "The History of Psychology Revisited: Or, Up with Our Foremothers." In this article, they gave their readers the following quiz. I invite you to take this quiz as well.

1. Who were the first persons to use the term "projective technique" in print?

2. Who was the first person to develop child analysis through play?

3. Who developed the Cattell Infant Intelligence Test Scale?

4. What do the following have in common?

   Bender Gestalt Test, Taylor Manifest Anxiety Scale, Kent-Rosanoff Word Association Test, Thematic Apperception Test, Sentence Completion Method

5. The following are the last names of individuals who have contributed to the scientific study of human behavior. What else do these names have in common?

   Ausubel, Bellak, Brunswick, Buhler, Dennis, Gardner, Gibson, Glueck, Harlow, Hartley, Hoffman, Horowitz, Jones, Kendler, Koch, Lacey, Luchins, Lynd, Murphy, Premack, Rossi, Sears, Sherif, Spence, Staats, Stendler, Whiting, Yarrow

The answers to these questions are:

1. Lois Murphy and Ruth Horowitz

2. Hermine von Hug-Hellmuth

3. Psyche Cattell

4. A woman is either the senior author or the sole author of each work

5. They are the surnames of female social scientists

How did you do? Bernstein and Russo reported that their colleagues were unable to correctly answer any of these questions! They concluded from this finding that women psychologists must be *rediscovered*. Elizabeth Scarborough and Laurel Furumoto (1987) also voiced their concern about the history of psychology being a history of male psychology:

At the 1984 meeting of the American Psychological Association, we listened as a woman psychologist told an anecdote she offered as an example of the invisibility of the women in psychology's past. The incident was drawn from her own experience and dated back to the days when she was a student in a psychology course that dealt with the topic of perception. She recalled that among the classical theories covered in the course was one labeled the Ladd-Franklin theory of color vision, a theory that she assumed to be the work of Mr. Ladd and Mr. Franklin. Not until much later did she discover that the theory was, in fact, the contribution of a woman who after marriage used a hyphenated surname: Christine Ladd-Franklin. (p. 1)

Such anecdotes are common. I show the list of women psychologists presented in Table 1.1 to students in my courses on the psychology of women. Only two psychologists (Anna Freud and Maria Montessori) are familiar to them (even to senior psychology majors). How many women psychologists listed in Table 1.1 can you identify?

WOMEN PSYCHOLOGISTS: HIDDEN FROM VIEW

Why are so few students and professors familiar with the contributions of women to psychology? The psychological literature's treatment of women psychologists has kept them invisible. For example, Ludy Benjamin reported that in a 1974 review of autobiographies and biographies of individuals contributing to psychology, only 33 references to women psychologists were found, out of a total of 700 references. In 1976, Benjamin and Heider found that, out of 255 textbooks that dealt with women's lives and contributions, 9 contained information about women. Gwendolyn Stevens and Sheldon Gardner (1982) offered the following:

TABLE 1.1   *Women Psychologists: How Many Can You Identify?*

Anne Anastasi	Matina Horner	Brenda Milner
Sandra Bem	Karen Horney	Maria Montessori
Martha Bernal	Ruth Howard	Christiana Morgan
Inge Broverman	Ethel Puffer Howes	Inez Prosser
Mary Calkins	Barbel Inhelder	Pamela Trotman Reid
Mamie Phipps Clark	Dorothea Jameson	Maria Root
Nancy Datan	Mary Cover Jones	Carolyn Sherif
Helene Deutsch	Gwendolyn Keita	Millicent Shinn
June Etta Downey	Tracy Kendler	Janet Taylor Spence
Anna Freud	Melanie Klein	Thelma Thurstone
Eleanor Gibson	Beatrice Lacey	Leona Tyler
Florence Goodenough	Teresa LaFromboise	Barbara Wallston
Margaret Harlow	Christine Ladd-Franklin	Margaret Floy Washburn
Leta Stetter Hollingworth	Eleanor Maccoby	Helen Thompson Woolley

The histories written by psychology's academicians are neither accurate nor complete, neglecting as they do the most important contributions made by women. A few examples: They do not include Mary Calkins' theory of self nor her invention of the method of paired associates; they do not mention Christine Ladd-Franklin's developmental theory of color vision, nor Lillien Jane Martin's research on psychophysics, or Lillian Gilbreth's pioneer work in time/motion studies. Additionally, they fail to mention the monumentally important books of Margaret Washburn on animal behavior or Helen Flanders Dunbar's work in psychosomatic medicine, and they totally ignore Magda Arnold's comprehensive theory of emotions and Margaret Harlow's contribution to our understanding of the importance of tactile stimulation in mothering. (p. 6)

The number of women mentioned in published histories of psychology (as well as textbooks in introductory psychology) still remains very small, although there has been some improvement (Furomoto, 1985; Petersen & Kroner, 1992). Florence Denmark, a past president of the American Psychological Association, surveyed psychological textbooks (1994) for their treatment of women and gender-related issues (e.g., sexual harassment, feminist therapy, women and leadership). Denmark noted the absence of citation of women psychologists in twenty undergraduate psychology textbooks, as presented in Table 1.2. Denmark noted that, of all the textbooks reviewed, the abnormal psychology books gave the least recognition to the women psychologists identified.

Denmark also reported that the majority of the introductory psychology books discussed gender and socialization, violence against women, and gender roles. Denmark offered a summary of her content analysis, as presented in Table 1.3.

In 1991, several of my colleagues and I reviewed 33 textbooks that were in use in undergraduate and graduate statistics courses taught in psychology departments in the United States. Our review indicated that practically no references were made to women/girls, and those that we found were stereotypical in content. We read phrases such as:

. . . **math instructor**. . . . Since **he** has added a constant amount . . .

The **behavioral scientist** needs to draw **his** conclusions . . .

The basic requirements and primary objectives of the experiment are formulated by the **experimenter;** the **experimenter** may or may not be aware of the possible alternative approaches that can be followed in the conduct of **his** experiment . . .

The types of variables used in the textbooks to illustrate some statistical analyses included:

TABLE 1.2   *Denmark (1994) Review of Twenty Undergraduate Psychology Textbooks for Identifying Women Psychologists*

Psychologist of Note	Area of Psychology			
	General	Social	Developmental	Abnormal
Anne Anastasi	xx		xxx	
Martha Bernal		x		
Mary Calkins	xx			
Mamie Clark	xxx	xxx	xx	
Carol Gilligan	xxx	x	xxx	
Florence Goodenough		x		
Leta Hollingworth				
Karen Horney	xxx	xxx	xx	x
Christine Ladd-Franklin	x			
Maud Merrill	x		x	
Carolyn Sherif	x	xxx	x	
Janet Spence	xxx	xx	xxx	x
Clara Thompson	xx		xx	x
Leona Tyler	xx			
Margaret Washburn	xx			

xxx: Inclusion in at least 75% of texts.
xx: Inclusion in more than 50% but less than 75% of texts.
x: Inclusion in less than 50% of texts.
Source: American Psychologist (1994). Vol. 49, pp. 329–334. Copyright © 1994 by the American Psychological Association. Adapted with permission.

Women's dress size
Whether blond women "really have more fun"
Rank ordering of women in a beauty pageant contest

We also found that cartoons were commonly present in the statistics texts, with the intent of making the material more fun. But the cartoons depicted women as "dumb" in math or husbands as "henpecked." Quotes from "famous" statisticians were present (e.g., Karl Pearson, Sir Francis Galton, Sir Ronald Fisher). No quotes from "famous" women statisticians were present. Thus, girls and women were ex-

TABLE 1.3 *Denmark (1994) Analysis of Introductory Psychology Textbooks*

Gender-Related Topic	Area of Psychology			
	General	Social	Developmental	Abnormal
Gender bias in research	x			
Biological aspects of sex and gender	xx		xxx	x
Gender differences in mathematical ability	xx	xx		
Gender and socialization	xxx	xxx	xxx	
Feminist therapy	x			
Violence against women	xxx	xxx	x	x
Women and mental health	xx	x	xx	x
Women and achievement	xx	x	xxx	
Sexual harassment	x	xxx		
Social construction of gender		xx		
Gender schema	x	x	xxx	
Women and leadership	x	xx		
Gender sterotypes	xx	xxx	xxx	
Gender roles	xx	xxx	x	

xxx: Inclusion in at least 75% of texts.
xx: Inclusion in more than 50% but less than 75% of texts.
x: Inclusion in less than 50% of texts.
Source: American Psychologist (1994). Vol. 49, pp. 329–334. Copyright © 1994 by the American Psychological Association. Adapted with permission.

cluded from the discussion; when they were included, they were not viewed as contributing to statistics or to psychology.

The number of students who aspire to a career in psychology and therefore take a statistics course (and an introductory psychology course) is quite large. Both courses are typically entry-level in most psychology curricula. They are, therefore, the critical points at which students explore basic vocabulary and concepts in psychology. If women psychologists' contributions and gender-related topics are omitted from such entry-level courses, women and gender-related concerns may not be subsequently questioned; they will remain marginal, not central, to the field of psychology.

Most research has suggested that college women plan to integrate careers with raising children (Farmer, Wardop, & Rotella, 1999). Women express considerable concern about the general incompatibility between family demands and workplace demands, as well as the relative lack of provisions to ease women's integration of these roles (see Box 1.1). Sally Archer, for example, concluded from her research that young adult women are isolated in their decision making about careers and family life: "Perhaps the most surprising revelation was my discovery that none of these girls had had any career counseling during which potential family roles had been discussed in relationship to career goals, nor had this subject been discussed in family life courses" (1985, p. 312).

Career counselors and faculty must be aware that the choices women make concerning their careers may have been constrained by gender role stereotypes, discriminatory behavior, or math anxiety (Betz & Schifano, 2000; Juntunen, 1996). Career counselors can facilitate women's career development by restoring to women options that societal pressures have taken away from them (Betz, 1993). This process involves (a) encouraging students to make decisions that leave their options open until they are ready to reject them for appropriate reasons and (b) asking students how their beliefs about gender and women's roles influenced their career choices and then sharing with them the research on gender bias in education. Betz (1993) and Lupart and Barva (1998) recommend that counselors introduce young women to women role models, work with women to manage anxiety about a career, and provide active support and encouragement to women's efforts to develop skills and competencies.

We find this to hold true for girls and boys during childhood. Betz (1993) reported that the sex of a school administrator has a significant impact on children's gender role attitudes. Children who attended a school that was administered by a female principal held fewer gender stereotypes than peers who had a male principal.

Exposure to women psychologists (contemporary and historical) can contribute to women's self-concept development, self-definition in terms of feminism, and pursuit of career options. Thus, women psychologists may be role models for women students.

Reconstructing the Lives of Psychology's Foremothers

In response to the neglect of women's contributions to psychology and to the recognition that women's history has the potential to transform women's self-understanding, a subfield of **women's history in psychology** has evolved (Russo &

BOX 1.1
IN THEIR OWN VOICES

Adolescent and Young Adult Women Discuss Their Family and Career Options

If I have a career and a husband who doesn't want me to work, I'll do what I want. [Twelfth grader]

I wouldn't marry somebody who didn't understand how important my work was. [Twelfth grader]

It just wouldn't work out. . . . Usually men are not going to help you in any way. They'll come home, sit like my dad, and my mom is left doing everything. [Sixth grader]

I see no conflict between school or work and taking care of my kids. I'm a mother now and my mom or my sister, who has two kids of her own, take care of him. I'm tired at night and I don't get to do what I want for myself much, but my baby is more important anyway. [Twelfth grader]

I plan to be a nurse. I'll just take night shifts so I can be with my family during the day. [Sixth grader]

I want to work. You can't work and be a mother at the same time. [Eighth grader]

(Archer, 1985)

I would choose a male [mentor] if I found the female to lack interest in me. I might also choose a male if I perceived him to have a great deal of power in relation to the female. However, he would still have to have the warm, understanding, etc. personality for me to choose him over the female. [College student]

I might choose a male over a female as my mentor or role model for an academic career because I feel males can devote more time and energy to their work without being called selfish or a "bad" husband or father. However, I realize that as a woman who would like a family, I will have to deal with the conflict between spending time on my career and time with my family. I wish I had a female model for this, but I've yet to meet a woman who doesn't express some guilt or dissatisfaction about either spending too little or too much time developing her career. [College student]

A woman who has experienced the casualties of womanhood, who knows discrimination, harassment, fear of violence, and who overcomes through her action and spirit would be a much more likely role model than a man. [College student]

(Paludi, Waite, Hoewing-Roberson, & Jones, 1988)

Denmark, 1987). Gerda Lerner's model for doing women's history—**compensatory history, contribution history,** and **reconstruction history** has been used in this subfield in psychology. In compensatory history, the historian finds lost or overlooked women and places them back in the history. In contribution history, women's contributions to the field are noted. Finally, in reconstruction history, noting how the past is gendered, historians reconstruct history through the perspective of women, not men. As Lerner (1979) pointed out:

> Traditional history has been written and interpreted by men in an androcentric frame of reference; it might quite properly be described as the history of men. The very term "Women's History" calls attention to the fact that something is missing from historical scholarship. (p. xiv)

In 1969, women in psychology organized themselves and formed the **Association for Women in Psychology.** The **Division of the Psychology of Women,** within the American Psychological Association (APA), was formed in 1973 "to promote the research and study of women . . . to encourage the integration of this information about women with current psychological knowledge and beliefs in order to apply the gained knowledge to the society and its institutions" (Russo, 1984). The **Committee on Women in Psychology** was formed in 1973. The goal of this committee was to "function as a catalyst, by means of interacting with and making recommendations to the various parts of the Association's governing structure . . ." (Russo, 1984).

Both the Division of the Psychology of Women and the Committee on Women in Psychology have encouraged attention to the compensatory history and reconstruction history of women in psychology (see the box on p. 11).

One consequence of the work of the participants on these committees was rediscovering "lost" women psychologists and their contributions. Laurel Furumoto and Elizabeth Scarborough, for example (Furumoto & Scarborough, 1986; Scarborough & Furumoto, 1987), reconstructed the experiences of the **first generation of American women psychologists** as they lived and as they worked to establish their professional identities as psychologists. Furumoto and Scarborough reported that the first women psychologists were similar to their male peers in age and training. However, these women were less likely to achieve professional status equivalent to that of the men. High professional status in psychology was typically attained by unmarried women who were employed in colleges for women. Furumoto and Scarborough (1986) concluded that "certain gender-specific factors profoundly affected the women's experience: exclusion from important educational and employment opportunities, the responsibility of daughters to their families, and the marriage-

AN INTERVIEW WITH DR. NANCY FELIPE RUSSO

Dr. Nancy Felipe Russo was the first Administrative Officer for Women's Programs of the American Psychological Association (APA). A former member of the Subpanel on the Mental Health of Women of the President's Commission on Mental Health, she also chairs the National Coalition for Women's Mental Health. Author of numerous scientific, professional, and public policy articles, Dr. Russo is a recipient of the 1987 Distinguished Leader Award from APA's Committee on Women in Psychology.

Question: Can you describe your work on the heritage of women in psychology?

Dr. Russo's response: Lack of information about women's lives perpetuates devaluation of women and their contributions, implies that such neglect and oblivion are deserved, and promotes the stereotype that women's lives are irrelevant to public life. We have worked to correct that, and we view our correction of the historical record as challenging women's disadvantaged status in psychology and empowering women psychologists.

Our work has multiple roots, including our personal and professional experiences as well as the larger effort by feminists to develop new methods to more fully understand women's realities and experiences from women's points of view.

Our approach takes multiple forms. Our framework is dynamic, its critical assumption being that women's actions and activities both reflect and shape the larger social context. This is a major difference between our work and that of historians of women's history who have emphasized separate spheres for women and men.

Our work reflects feminist values. It also reflects the value placed on diversity, which is seen in our seeking out ethnic minority women psychologists so that their experiences shape the picture of psychology that we are constructing. Herein lie both the greatest disappointments and rewards in our approach, for racism in society prevented participation of ethnic minority women in the early years of the field. We take pride in the fact that it was our work that preserved the stories of the first black woman psychologist, Ruth Howard [Beckham] (1983), and the first Chicana to receive a PhD in psychology, Martha Bernal (1988), among other ethnic minority women. However, the fact that racism in society denied psychology the benefits of ethnic minority women's contributions to its early historical roots is a source of sadness to us. We are hoping that our work will promote changes in the field and encourage preservation of the contributions of the increasing numbers of contemporary ethnic minority women.

First experimental psychology laboratory in the United States in a women's college. Wellesley College. (Courtesy of Wellesley College Archives.)

versus-career dilemma" (p. 39). Margaret Washburn, for example, taught at Wells College and then at Vassar College for thirty-four years. In 1913, she wrote a letter of resignation from her position as review editor of the *Journal of Animal Behavior* to Robert Yerkes, its editor:

> I doubt if anyone else on the board is teaching eighteen hours a week, as I am. I simply must cut down my work somewhere. If I am ever to accomplish anything in psychology it must be done in the next five years, for as my parents get older, I shall have less and less command of my time. (Washburn, 1913, as cited in Scarborough & Furumoto, 1987)

Ethel Puffer taught at Radcliffe, Simmons College, and Wellesley College concurrently. The following letter, from the president of Smith College in 1908, indicated the negative impact marriage was believed to have on a woman's academic career:

> Dear Miss Puffer: If you really are disposed to think seriously of the position at Barnard I am sure it would be well for your friends in Cambridge to recommend you to President Butler, although I fear the rumor which reached me concerning your engagement may have also affected the recommendation which I myself sent, and that a candidate has already been selected to present to the trustees of Columbia at their next commencement. (Seelye, 1908)

Among the first women psychologists, each experienced discrimination in her attempts to earn a graduate degree. Christine Ladd-Franklin, Mary Calkins, and Margaret Washburn, for example, began their graduate studies in psychology as "special students" at Johns Hopkins, Harvard, and Columbia, respectively. The "special student" status reflected the exclusionary policies of those universities toward women.

For example, Mary Calkins (1863–1929) completed the requirements for her PhD from Harvard in 1895; she was refused this degree because she was a woman. Psychologist William James wrote the following note to one of Mary Calkins's classmates at Smith College:

> It was much the most brilliant examination for the PhD that we have had at Harvard. It is a pity, in spite of this, that she still lacks the degree. Your downtrodden but unconquerable sex is fairly entitled to whatever glory and credit may accrue to it from Miss Calkins's prowess. (To Dear Madam, June 29, 1895, reported in Scarborough & Furumoto, 1987, p. 46)

Mary Calkins was offered the PhD under the auspices of Radcliffe College in 1902, but she declined this offer because she believed it validated Harvard's refusal to recognize women's accomplishments. She wrote:

> I sincerely admire the scholarship of the three women to whom it is to be given and I should be very glad to be classed with them. I furthermore think it highly probable that the Radclife degree will be regarded generally as the practical equivalent of the Harvard degree and finally, I should be glad to hold the Ph.D. degree for I occasionally find the lack of it an inconvenience, and now that the Radcliffe degree is offered, I doubt whether the Harvard degree will ever be open to women. On the other hand, I still believe that the best ideals of education would be better served if Radcliffe College refused to confer the doctor's degree. You will be quick to see that, holding this conviction, I cannot rightly take the easier course of accepting the degree.

Portrait of Mary Whiton Calkins, 1863–1930. Partridge/Wellesley College. (Courtesy of Wellesley College Archives.)

Harvard granted women PhDs for the first time in 1963, nearly seventy-five years after women began taking graduate courses. To date, Harvard has not issued a PhD in honor of Mary Calkins. The university continues to state that they see "no reason to" award the degree.

In addition to **access discrimination,** the early women psychologists experienced **treatment discrimination.** Margaret Washburn (1871–1939) is credited with being the first woman to receive the PhD in psychology (in June 1904 from Cornell University) and to serve as president of the APA in 1921. She was excluded from membership in the society referred to as the "Experimentalists" and denied an academic position at a research university. As Elizabeth Scarborough and Laurel Furumoto (1987) pointed out:

> Given Washburn's reputation, had she been a man, she would certainly have been offered such an appointment. Given her interests, she would no doubt have welcomed such an offer. But at that time women were not considered for faculty posts in the psychology or philosophy departments at any major Eastern University. The exclusion of women from these positions apparently was not a matter of considering and then rejecting them; rather the idea of hiring women as regular faculty was simply not entertained. . . . At Vassar, Washburn was subject to the limitations experienced by all faculty at the women's colleges: heavy teaching loads, inadequate resources for research, expectations of considerable involvement in student affairs, and lack of stimulating collaboration with colleagues in one's own specialty area and advanced students. (p. 103)

Portrail of Margaret Washburn, 1871–1939. University of Akron. (The Unviersity of Akron, Archives of the History of American Psychology.)

Christine Ladd-Franklin (1847–1930) also experienced treatment discrimination.

When Ladd-Franklin was in her mid-60s she began writing to E.B. Tichener concerning his exclusion of women from the "Experimentalists." In 1912 she wrote:

> I am particularly anxious to bring my views up, once in a while, for hand-to-hand discussion before experts, and just now I have especially a paper which I should like very much to read before your meeting of experimental psychologists. I hope you will not say nay! (Scarborough & Furumoto, 1987, p. 125)

In response to Tichener's argument that women were not allowed at these meetings because they could not tolerate masculine activities such as smoking, Ladd-Franklin responded:

> Have your smokers separated if you like (tho I for one always smoke when I am in fashionable society), but a scientific meeting is a public affair, and it is not open to you to leave out a class of fellow workers without extreme discourtesy. (Scarborough & Furumoto, 1987, p. 125)

Ladd-Franklin never gained membership in this club.

Portrait of Chrinstine Ladd-Franklin. (Courtesy of the American Psychological Association.)

The contributions of the first women psychologists were lost. Mary Calkins founded the psychological laboratory at Wellesley College in 1891, invented the paired associate technique, and created a theoretical perspective of self-psychology that brought her recognition in psychology and philosophy (Furumoto, 1980). She was also the first woman president of the APA in 1905. Her experiences and contributions to psychology have been essentially omitted and trivialized in the history of psychology, however. As Gwendolyn Stevens and Sheldon Gardner (1982) wrote:

> Mary Whiton Calkins was a great psychologist; one of the few women recognized as such, and one who has been poorly treated by history. . . . Her major contribution to her science . . . her invention of the experimental procedure she called the method of right associates, is now credited to someone else and even appears in textbooks under a different name than the one she had bestowed upon it. Her general theory of psychology, which she developed over so many years and which was so controversial then, is dismissed today as unscientific, inconsequential, or unoriginal. (p. 88)

Devaluation of Women: Past and Present

The **masculine bias** inherent in the definition of career advancement for the first generation of U.S. psychologists helps to explain why the contributions of women were omitted, distorted, and trivialized. Mary Calkins, for example, spent her entire academic career at Wellesley College. Women faculty members at Wellesley had certain advantages because it was an all-women's educational community (Palmieri, 1983), but there were career disadvantages as well. Because Calkins was not on a faculty at a *university* (the center of professional activity during this stage of psychology's history), she was limited in her research productivity. In addition, she was never able to mentor graduate students who were doing PhD research; she was thus not considered influential in the training of the next generation of psychologists. The definition of success, therefore, eliminated women psychologists who were on the faculty at women's colleges, where no graduate programs existed.

Furthermore, there existed a **devaluation of women** psychologists' work (Doyle & Paludi, 1997). Women psychologists have traditionally preferred person-oriented and service-oriented subfields of psychology: school psychology, counseling, clinical, and developmental psychology rather than perception, learning, and motivation. However, academic/experimental psychology has been viewed as more prestigious than applied psychology. Part of the masculine bias inherent in this view stems from the belief that experimental psychology requires greater intelligence and competence than social, clinical, school, or developmental psychology. This stereotype exists to this day. Courses in social psychology, developmental psychology, and the psychology of women are not typically viewed to be as rigorous as courses in learning, statistics, or experimental psychology. As Gwendolyn Stevens and Sheldon Gardner (1982) pointed out with respect to early women psychologists:

> The women . . . are generally brilliant, productive professionals. As a group they would appear to be brighter and more ambitious than male psychologists. They became leaders, not because of the politics or "old boy" friendships which permeate the story of men in psychology but because of brilliantly original work and sheer competence. The history of psychology is replete with shameful examples of men's being advanced over women who demonstrated superior competence and achievement. (p. 45)

Thus, the first generation of women psychologists and women themselves were devalued. Research on women's career development (also see Chapter 9) suggests that men are less likely than women to hold liberal views about women's roles and their degree of career commitment. This indifference to women in academic settings alone, however, may undermine women's commitment to their professional careers (Juntunen, 1996; Pattatucci, 1998; Reskin, 1998).

Like the first generation of U.S. men psychologists, their contemporaries are rated higher than women in performing certain tasks and in job qualifications. Similarly, women receive lower recognition and economic rewards for their work than men, and lower prestige, knowledge, and expertise are attributed to them as well.

Thus, because women are expected to conform to the gender-role stereotypes, their lack of conformity may be negatively evaluated (e.g., Farmer et al., 1999; Moyer, Salovey, & Casey-Cannon, 1999; Vincent, Peplau, & Hill, 1998).

In one of the first empirical studies of the devaluation of women academicians, Lynn Fidell (1976) reported that academic departments of psychology discriminate in hiring on the basis of sex. She asked chairpersons of psychology departments in the United States to "judge [their] current impression about the chances of [a woman or man] getting an offer for a full-time position." They were asked to indicate the desirability of the woman or man candidate on a scale from totally unacceptable to highly desirable and to indicate at what rank the individual should be offered a position (e.g., lecturer, assistant professor, full professor). Fidell found that (1) the distributions of level of appointment were higher for men than for women, (2) only men were offered full professorships, and (3) men received more positions leading to tenure.

However, even when women conform to gender-role stereotypes, their performance may well be devalued (Lupart & Barva, 1998; Vincent et al., 1998). Phyllis Bronstein and her colleagues (Bronstein, Black, Pfennig, & White, 1986) reviewed letters of recommendation written for women and men who applied for a faculty position at the University of Vermont. They reported that men, in their letters of recommendation for women applicants, described the woman's family responsibilities as a burden. For men applicants, however, a family life was presented as an asset.

GATEKEEPERS OF WOMEN'S CAREERS

Frequently, the individuals who make such judgments about women's work are termed **gatekeepers.** A gatekeeper, in this context, is an individual who keeps women out of various careers or limits their advancement. Graduate school professors who believe that women have no place in their particular profession can be especially powerful gatekeepers (Betz & Schifano, 2000). Gatekeepers often don't see themselves as prejudiced against women per se. They rationalize that their resistance to women in the profession is based on "facts." To their way of thinking, women can never be as serious about a career as a man; even if women do enter the field, they'll leave once they start their families.

G. Stanley Hall, the first president of the APA, was a gatekeeper for many of the early women psychologists. In a presentation on coeducation, made to the American Academy of Medicine in 1906, Hall commented:

It [coeducation] violates a custom so universal that it seems to express a fundamental human instinct . . . girls . . . are attracted to common knowledge which all share, to the conventional, are more influenced by fashions, more imitative and lack the boy's intense desire to know, be, do something distinctive that develops and emphasizes his individuality. To be thrown on their own personal resources in sports, in the classroom, in nature study and elementary laboratory brings out the best in a boy, but either confuses or strains a girl. . . . Equal pay to the teachers of boys and girls is unfair. . . . Good teachers of boys should be paid more. . . . Sex distinctions should at this age be pushed to their utmost. Boys should be more masculine and girls more feminine. (cited in Scarborough & Furumoto, 1987)

Hall's beliefs—expressed in his presentations and writing—influenced hundreds of students and professors. Jo Freeman (1975) described the problem of gatekeepers as encountered by contemporary women graduate students:

"Any girl who gets this far has got to be a kook" one distinguished (male) member of the University of Chicago faculty told a female graduate student who had come to see him about being on her dissertation committee. This was just one of many such statements collected by women students at the University in the spring of 1969 to illustrate their contention that "some of our professors have different expectations about our performance than about the performance of male graduate students' expectations based not on our ability as individuals but on the fact that we are women." There were many others. They included:

"The admissions committee didn't do their job. There is not one good-looking girl in the entering class."

And most telling of all:

"I know you're competent and your thesis advisor knows you're competent. The question in our minds is are you really serious about what you're doing."

This was said to a young woman who had already spent five years and over $10,000 getting to that point in her PhD program. (pp. 194–195)

John Hogan and Virginia Sexton (1991), in their review of the treatment of women in the American Psychological Association, identified the fact that women did not attain high-level office, editorships, and significant committee posts at the same level as male colleagues. During one 51-year period studied, Hogan and Sexton found that no women were elected to the American Psychological Association presidency. The first woman president following this period was elected in 1972 (Anne Anastasi).

ETHNIC MINORITY WOMEN IN PSYCHOLOGY

Ethnic minority women have been more disadvantaged in psychology than White women, what Beale (1970) referred to as **double jeopardy** because of the minority women's participation in a culture that has valued neither women nor nonwhites. Maria de la Luz Reyes and John Halcon (1988) pointed out that ethnic minority individuals are tokens, and many gatekeepers operate under the "one-minority-per-pot" syndrome. These authors drew these conclusions about academia:

> We believe that implicit in this practice is a deep-seated belief that minorities are not as qualified as non-minorities. This conviction stems from an unspoken fear that the presence of more than one minority . . . in a mainstream, traditional department might reduce the department's . . . reputation. . . . Typically, consideration of minority candidates occurs only when there is pressure applied to diversify. . . . The limitation on minority hiring that is part of the "one-minority-per-pot" syndrome has the effect of restricting the career goal aspirations of Hispanics and other minority faculty. (pp. 305–315)

Historical information about ethnic minority women in psychology is scarce. The first African American woman to earn a doctoral degree was Inez Prosser, who received the EdD in educational psychology from the University of Cincinnati. Ruth Howard was the first African American woman to receive the PhD in psychology, and Martha Bernal was the first Chicana to receive the PhD in psychology.

MEET DR. STEPHANIE SHIELDS

Dr. Stephanie Shields is Professor of Psychology at the University of California, Davis. She has devoted considerable attention to the life of Leta Stetter Hollingworth. According to Dr. Shields:

Little did I realize when I "discovered" Leta Stetter Hollingworth, when I was a first-year graduate student, that nearly twenty years later I would participate in an exciting renaissance of interest in her life and work. At the time, I was much more struck with her prescient explorations into the psychology of women—she seemed the role model and exemplar many of us needed as a new generation of feminist psychologists challenged the social and scientific status quo. . . . Somehow I knew she was too important a figure in the study of the psychology of women ever to be lost again.

Sandra Graham (1992) analyzed the contents of six psychology journals [(1) *Developmental Psychology,* (2) *Journal of Applied Psychology,* (3) *Journal of Consulting and Clinical Psychology,* (4) *Journal of Counseling Psychology,* (5) *Journal of Educational Psychology,* and (6) *Journal of Personality and Social Psychology*] from 1970 to 1989 for the presence of empirical articles on African Americans. She reported that there was a declining representation of African American research in all of the journals she reviewed. Graham offered the following suggestions for reversing this decline:

> Much of what is needed will require major shifts in priorities of the research enterprise, such as greater access to training opportunities for minority scholars, enhanced funding initiatives for minority research, and more sensitivity to the diversity of paths that scholarship can follow, given the enormous complexity underlying the psychological study of ethnic minority populations. (p. 638)

The participation of Asian, Hispanic, and Native American women in psychology has received less attention than that of African American women. The APA has published a variety of directories and guides to assist ethnic minority students and faculty in meeting their career goals in psychology. A division of the APA, the **Society for the Psychological Study of Ethnic Minority Issues,** is devoted to ethnic awareness. The Society was established in 1987. Earlier, the **Office of Ethnic Minority Affairs** was established at the APA in Washington, DC, in 1980, and the **Board of Ethnic Minority Affairs** was appointed in 1981.

In 1968, the **Association of Black Psychologists** was established. The major objectives of this organization were to eradicate the myths regarding the psychology of African American women and men and to increase the representation of African American individuals in the discipline of psychology.

All of these organizations offer support and are aware of the needs of ethnic minority women students, faculty, and administrators. They help ease the isolation many ethnic minority women experience on college/university campuses (DeFour & Hirsch, 1990). As women have commented:

> It was pointed out to me that I was female and a minority and otherwise would not be at Stanford. Also [people said there was] no way I would pass qualifying exams, etc. . . . Several times, I nearly gave up because of this. I find that students (mostly white) seem to resist the intellectual and pedagogical authority of a black female professor.

> Sometimes I used to think that I was imagining this treatment of isolation. When I would talk to other black women about it and they would talk about it too—it was not just me, but I thought it was, at least for the first year. (Moses, 1988)

MEET DR. HOPE LANDRINE

Dr. Hope Landrine is an African American psychologist who does full-time research at the Public Health Foundation, City of Industry, California. She conducts interventions to improve the health of women, girls, and ethnic minorities. Recently, she edited *Bringing Cultural Diversity to Feminist Psychology*, published by the American Psychological Association. According to Dr. Landrine:

Bringing Cultural Diversity to Feminist Psychology is an edited volume that details how feminist psychology can begin to include and address the enormous ethnic and social class diversity that characterizes the population of women in America and in the world. For far too long, feminist psychology has consisted of writings by European American women to each other about themselves, and has excluded the experiences and needs of the women of color who constitute the majority of women in that world. That exclusion has diminished the relevance of feminist psychology to women, and thereby has diminished feminist psychology as a science and practice, to the detriment of all women. This book represents the beginning of the process of changing that, of elevating feminist psychology from the status of a mere fetish of White women of privileged class status, to that of a science and practice relevant and beneficial to all women. Thus, in this book, feminist psychology is about advocacy for working Black and Latino mothers whose lack of access to affordable child care soon will make welfare their only alternative; it is about enabling, educating and assisting White middle-class women in fighting sexual harassment and victimization; it is about providing services for southeast Asian immigrant women whose witnessing of the torture of their families in their home countries prior to immigration left them with hysterical blindness, now unable to see anything at all; it is about helping all women, no matter what their life circumstances, become what our lack of power prevents us from even imagining. The relevance and stature of feminist psychology are enhanced and empowered by embracing all women in this manner, and all women, everywhere, are similarly empowered by feminist psychology's embrace.

As Veronica Thomas and Shari Miles (1995) concluded:

Before feminist psychology can become culturally diverse and the psychology of Black women can be considered a specialty in the discipline, a number of changes are needed. There must be a genuine acknowledgment of Black female populations as an integral part of society, thereby worthy of a serious scientific attention. Because Black women are the most likely researchers of Black women, psychology departments must establish better recruiting and mentoring programs for them. . . . it is also important to have a cadre of Black female scholars that can take the research on the psychology of Black women to broader dimensions in years to come. (p. 324)

A similar sentiment was expressed at a National Multicultural Conference and Summit in 1999 that was hosted by three divisions of the American Psychological Association: Counseling Psychology, Society for the Psychology of Women, and Society for the Psychological Study of Ethnic Minority Issues (see Sue, Bingham, Porche-Burke, & Vasquez, 1999). Participants at this conference endorsed resolutions to implement cultural competence in all psychological endeavors. This conference, as well as guidelines for nonsexist research (see Chapter 2), help ensure that the study of psychology will truly be the study of all people.

THE FEMINIZATION OF PSYCHOLOGY

There has been considerable recognition of the importance of role models and mentors (see Chapter 9) in defining what individuals might possibly accomplish. The activities of women psychologists influence college and graduate women in specific life decisions. Psychologist Suzanna Rose (1986) edited a book titled *Career Guide for Women Scholars,* which has been a "paper mentor" for many psychologists. According to Rose:

> The aim in assembling this book was to focus on nontraditional advice that would help women graduate students and recent Ph.D.'s as they began their careers. Contributors were asked to reflect on advice in the category of "what I wish I'd known then," and to

---

MEET DR. MARIA ROOT

Dr. Maria Root is a clinical psychologist in private practice and clinical associate professor at the University of Washington.
According to Dr. Root:

I have . . . been working in the area of biracial and multiracial identity development. My interests and publications have focused on understanding the historical and community contexts within which attitudes toward racial mixing and racially mixed persons develop, the meaning of flexible and situational identity commonly experienced by racially mixed persons, and developmental differences that have implications for examining the "universal truth" of some of our identity models. These variables determine different attitudes toward different racial mixes, a preoccupation with White/people of Color mixes versus the mixing of two racial minority groups, and predict that the development of positive self-esteem will be a more complex task.

pass their ideas on to other women. The intent was to go beyond traditional advice, such as how to dress for success or how to learn academic gamesmanship. Instead, we gleaned from our experiences strategies that enabled us to survive and sometimes flourish in spite of the structure of the profession, discrimination, and academic unemployment. (p. xix)

Women psychologists portrayed in this collection discuss issues such as building a professional network, applying for academic jobs, career options in business and management, starting a private therapy practice, middle-aged women and career transitions, issues confronting lesbian scholars, and transitions and stresses for African American women scholars.

Bonnie Strickland, president of the APA in 1987, discussed the importance of this sharing of career survival strategies among women in psychology in her presentation to the Association for Women in Psychology. She acknowledged that women constitute about one-third of psychologists employed and over one-half of those earning PhDs in psychology each year. Strickland also noted that psychology is going to become the first science to be "feminized," in that it will have more women than men. This feminization means that women psychologists can open the field of psychology to provide answers to a set of research problems that did not come to light in traditional psychology and could not be solved by the **androcentric paradigm:** women's friendships with women, rape, sexual harassment, battered women, eating disorders, and sexism in psychotherapy, to name a few. The **feminization of psychology** means that research can be generated by examining the disparities between individual experiences/perceptions and existing theory (Makosky & Paludi, 1990). Moreover, the feminization of psychology means that women can bring nurturance, valuing, and respect for other individuals, which have not always been available in psychology (Strickland, 1987). This valuing extends to historical as well as contemporary women psychologists. As Russo and Denmark (1987) pointed out:

The more we study women's history, the more we appreciate the power of society's norms and institutions to affect the development of psychology as well as the career paths of individual psychologists. This knowledge is having an effect on the discipline. Led by women, both women and men are working to eliminate sex bias in psychology and to legitimize the study of women's experiences. (p. 296)

Feminism and Feminists in Psychology

For the next few minutes, read the following story, developed by psychologist Sue Rosenberg Zalk (described in Paludi, 1992):

You are at a social gathering talking to a small group of people you have just met. They all appear fairly educated, informed, and articulate. After some small talk about New York City's urban plight, the conversation turns to the accusations about gang rapes and the growing realization that such incidents may be more common than previously thought.

Everyone in the group agreed that it was scandalous although different motivations and explanations were attributed to the men's behavior. Finally, one of the men in the group laughed softly and stated "I know feminists will have a field day with this, but we can hardly generalize from the misdirected behavior of some boys trying to prove they are men, to the entire society."

The nods to his comment were interrupted by the voice of one of the women. In a slightly raised voice, she announced "I am a feminist, and you are greatly underestimating the social meaning and impact of their behavior." She proceeded to explain her position. A few other women added comments, but you were most impressed with how articulate she was and the thoughtfulness of her argument.

Here are some questions to answer about this story:

How closely do you think men listened to the woman's argument?
How seriously was she taken by the men?
How closely do you think the women listened to the woman's argument?
How seriously do you think she was taken by the women?
How assertive did the men think she was?
How assertive did the women think she was?
Do you think the men found her threatening?
Do you think it mattered that she began with the words "I am a feminist"?
Why do you think she began this way?

For the next few minutes consider whether your answers to these questions would have been different if the following sentence appeared in the story:

I am not a feminist, but you are greatly underestimating the social meaning and impact of their behavior.

Would your answers be different? Why or why not? Here's another consideration for you: Suppose that instead of a woman identifying herself as a feminist, a man identified himself as a feminist and made the comment. Would your answers be different now? Why or why not?

I typically use this exercise in my course on the psychology of women toward the beginning of the term. I consistently find differences in the way women and men respond to either a woman or a man who introduces himself or herself as a feminist or not as a feminist. For example, most students view the feminist woman as not being taken seriously by the men or the women at this social gathering. In addition, they view her as not being listened to, being very assertive by women and men, and not attractive. She is also perceived to be threatening to the men and not listened closely to at all.

Compare these responses to students' answers to the same questions when they were told the woman begins her statement with the words "I am not a feminist . . ." Students view this woman as being taken more seriously, not assertive, not threatening, and listened to.

For students who are asked to read the story and it is a man who states he is a feminist, they view him as not being listened to, not taken seriously, unassertive and not threatening. Responses from students who are asked to read the version with the man introducing his response with the words "I am not a feminist . . ." are typically more positive. He is perceived as being listened to more closely, taken more seriously, and seen as more attractive.

Now that you have read the story and common students' responses to this story, what words do you think of when you hear the word "feminist"?

If you are like most students taking their first course on the psychology of women you may think of the following words:

manhater
angry
militant
lesbian
unattractive

What does the word "feminism" mean? Feminism derivatively means *womanism,* that is, valuing women. Feminists believe that men and women should be valued equally; that men and women should be economically, politically, socially, and legally equal. Feminists also favor the social and legal changes that are necessary to achieve equality. Men as well as women are feminists (Lorber, 1998).

While most of us use the term "feminist" as a singular concept, in actuality there are different types of feminists. Lorber (1998) categorized feminists into three major categories: gender-reform feminists, gender-resistance feminists, and gender-rebellion feminists.

Gender-reform feminists emphasize similarities between women and men instead of focusing on differences between the sexes. Lorber includes the following in this category: liberal feminists, Marxist feminists, socialist feminists and development feminists. *Liberal feminists* deal with securing the same legal rights for men and women. *Marxist feminists* as well as *socialist feminists* view women's oppression as caused by economic dependence. Both of these feminisms emphasize the importance of increasing women's employment opportunities as well as increasing their salaries and working conditions. *Development feminists* focus on women in economically developing countries. This form of gender-reform feminism focuses on improving educational and work opportunities for women.

Gender-resistance feminists believe that formal legal rights alone will not end gender inequality. They believe that male dominance is too ingrained into social relations. They focus on how men and women are different—cognitively, socially, emotionally—and urge women to form women-centered organizations. The focus in on resisting the social order. Included in this category are radical feminists, lesbian feminists, psychoanalytic feminists, and standpoint feminists. *Radical* as well as *lesbian feminists* deal with the sexual exploitation of women by men, especially with respect to men's violence against women. *Psychoanalytic feminists* use Sigmund Freud's theory to explain gender inequality as a result of sex differences in personality development (see Chapter 4). *Standpoint feminists* examine all aspects of life—work, education, relationships, sexuality—from women's unique standpoint.

Gender-rebellion feminists look at the interrelationships among inequalities of sex, race, ethnicity, social class, and sexual orientation. Lorber includes the following types of feminists in this category: multiracial feminists, men feminists, social construction feminists, postmodern feminists, and queer theory. *Multiracial* and *men feminists* focus on how one's social locations with the stratification hierarchy provide advantages or disadvantages to men and women in different ways. *Social construction feminists* look at the ways individuals construct identities and labels through their interactions with others. *Postmodern feminists* and *queer theory* view sex and gender as social scripts; they rewrite the scripts as each situation presents itself.

Thus, as Lorber's classification systems suggests, there are several components of feminism. Many of these branches of feminism are not mutually exclusive. I wanted to provide you with a brief overview of the diversity of contemporary feminism. Because there is a plurality of feminist voices, younger women, men, and individuals of color find their own issues being addressed rather than ignored.

There are individuals who are uncomfortable with feminists. Many women do not want to use this label when describing themselves (Boxer, 1997; Goldner, 1994). They may avoid taking courses in women's studies or gender studies because of the fear of being labeled a feminist. Frequently, we hear students say "I am not a feminist but I believe men and women should be paid the same amount of money for identical work." Thus, students espouse feminist ideology, but reject the label feminist. Why do you believe this is so?

Why do you believe students reject the term while still embracing the ideology? Goldner's (1994) research provides some answers to this question. Her research noted that when women who hold feminist beliefs anticipate a negative reaction from their peers to the label "feminist," they will avoid using the term as a self-label. Goldner (1994) identified the media as a primary source of negative images of feminists. For example, newscasters, while discussing feminists, accompany their text with photos of women only, especially of women who have clenched fists and who are yelling. These women are predominantly shown as being alone, especially without men. Images such as these are rejected by many women college students who are in the throes of identity development, in which the peer group and peer approval are important to their sense of self-esteem and self-concept.

Another explanation to why women may reject the label "feminist" but embrace the ideology concerns women's need to view themselves as in control, as powerful, not as victims of injustice. They believe the term "feminist" implies a powerless position, which is something they reject (Rhode, 1997).

DeWitt (1996) has noted that younger women have become more involved in the feminist movement. This may be attributed to several national events that have highlighted gender inequality in education, the workplace, and victimization. These national events include the sexual assault trials of William Kennedy Smith and Mike Tyson, the sexual harassment case of Paula Jones, threats to repeal *Roe v. Wade* (see Chapter 6) and threats to affirmative action programs and policies.

Certainly, participating in courses on the psychology of women has had an impact on the number of women and men who work toward feminist causes (Harris, Melaas, & Rodacker, 1999; Highly, 1998; Lloyd, 1999). Research indicates that participation in feminist courses is positively correlated with more progressive gender role attitudes. I encourage you to reread the Preface of this text in which I discuss the stages of feminist identity development.

Ms. Magazine's December 1999/January 2000 issue was a celebration of the first 100 years of feminism. *Ms.* Magazine's editor, Marcia Ann Gillespie, stated the following with respect to the future of feminism:

So, what about tomorrow?

. . . throwing off the mountain of oppression that women have carried on our backs requires group action. Action that never has been and never should be taken up by women alone. We can't reform women's lives in isolation from men's. If not us, who will demand that the minimum wage do more than ensure that women workers remain poor? If not us, who will demand safe, affordable child care? If not us, who will push for wages for child care workers and teachers that are commensurate with the importance of the work they perform? . . . None of us can afford to take the rights and privileges we've struggled to obtain for granted. And progress for some women, gained on the backs of other women, is no progress at all. We have proven that women can do what men can, and men are discovering that women's work is not gender specific. But transformation is about something more profound than role reversal. What threatens the keepers of the status quo is not women taking on men's roles, it's people challenging the ways of the system itself. (pp. 81–82)

ENGENDERING PSYCHOLOGY

Florence Denmark (1994) has called for **"engendering psychology,"** that is, for the field of psychology to cultivate a discipline that is sensitive to issues of gender and diversity. As she noted:

Much of the psychology curriculum being taught is without a gender-balanced perspective. . . . I believe it is important that we present our students with material that is not biased in order that they may obtain an accurate view of the world and come to appreciate that society has been shaped by both women and men. . . . Part of our role as instructors is to make our students careful consumers of information, so that traditional female and male stereotypes can be eliminated. (p. 331)

In keeping with Gillespie's and Denmark's prescription, in the next chapter I will discuss methodological perspectives that psychologists have taken in order to study the psychology of women.

NEW TERMS

access discrimination

androcentric paradigm

Association of Black Psychologists

Association for Women in Psychology

Board of Ethnic Minority Affairs

Committee on Women in Psychology

compensatory history

contribution history

devaluation of women

Division of the Psychology of Women of the American Psychological Association

double jeopardy

engendering psychology

feminization of psychology

first generation of American women psychologists

gatekeeper

masculine bias

Office of Ethnic Minority Affairs

reconstruction history

Society for the Psychological Study
of Ethnic Minority Issues

treatment discrimination

women's history in psychology

CHAPTER REVIEW QUESTIONS

1. Cite some reasons why women psychologists have typically been hidden from view.

2. Distinguish among compensatory history, contribution history, and reconstruction history.

3. Discuss the goals of the following organizations and committees:

   Association for Women in Psychology

   Board of Ethnic Minority Affairs

   Committee on Women in Psychology

   Division 35 of the American Psychological Association

   Society for the Psychological Study of Ethnic Minority Issues

4. Discuss the access discrimination encountered by the first generation of American women psychologists in their pursuit of graduate degrees in psychology.

5. Summarize the literature on evaluations of women's performance.

6. Discuss Beale's concept of double jeopardy for ethnic minority women in psychology.

7. Discuss Strickland's comment that psychology will become "feminized."

8. To what does the term "engendering psychology" refer?

9. What kinds of feminisms have been identified? If you were to label yourself as a feminist, what category of feminist would you most likely use as the label?

SELECTED READINGS

Denmark, F. L. (1994). Engendering psychology. *American Psychologist, 49,* 329–334.

Scarborough, E., & Furumoto, L. (1987). *Untold lives: The first generation of American women psychologists.* New York: Columbia University Press.

Landrine, H. (Ed.). (1995). *Bringing cultural diversity to feminist psychology.* Washington, DC: American Psychological Association.

Lorber, J. (1998). *Gender inequality: Feminist theories and politics.* Los Angeles: Roxbury.

LEARNING MORE ABOUT . . .

Suggestions for Term Papers and Independent Studies Related to *The Women of Psychology and the Psychology of Women*

Gender comparisons for work opportunities in academia for nineteenth-century psychologists

Gender bias in history of psychology textbooks

Contributions of women psychologists to developmental psychology (or social psychology, or any other specialty)

Career/family dilemma in the lives of nineteenth-century women psychologists

Impact on female students' feminist identity development when they take a psychology of women course

TAKING ACTION . . .

on *The Women of Psychology and the Psychology of Women*

1. Look through your introductory psychology textbook and list classic experiments that are described. Jot down the experimenters' names that are associated with these experiments (e.g., Harlow's contact comfort studies, Sherif's Robbers' Cave experiment, the Taylor Manifest Anxiety Scale, Morgan and Murray's Thematic Apperception Test).

    For each name on the list, indicate whether the experimenter is female or male.

    How do you believe the use of surnames of psychologists may lead people to view researchers as male, especially if the research is in an area considered masculine?

    Help set up in the psychology department a bulletin board that depicts brief biographies of women psychologists, with accompanying pictures.

    By the way, here are the answers:

    Harlow: Margaret and Harry

    Sherif: Carolyn and Muzafer

    Taylor: Janet (Janet Taylor Spence)

    Morgan: Christiana Morgan and Henry Murray

2. Ask professors in the psychology department to identify their graduate school mentor. Also ask them to identify their mentor's mentor. Repeat this process until the professor does not know the answer. Note sex and race of these mentors. Display this genealogy for the psychology department.

REFERENCES

Archer, S. L. (1985). Career and/or family: The identity process for adolescent girls. *Youth and Society, 16,* 289–314.

Beale, F. (1970). Double jeopardy: To be black and female. In T. Cade (Ed.), *The black woman: An anthology.* New York: New American Library.

Benjamin, L. T., & Heider, K. I. (1976). History of psychology in biography: A bibliography. *JSAS Catalog of Selected Documents in Psychology, 4,* MS. 535.

Bernstein, M. D., & Russo, N. F. (1974). The history of psychology revisited: Or, up with our foremothers. *American Psychologist, 29,* 130–134.

Betz, N. (1993). Career psychology of women. In F. Denmark & M. Paludi (Eds.), *The psychology of women: A handbook of issues and theories.* Westport, CT: Greenwood.

Betz, N., & Schifano, R. (2000). Evaluation of an intervention to increase realistic self-efficacy and interests in college women. *Journal of Vocational Behavior, 56,* 35–52.

Boxer, S. (1997, December 14). One casualty of the women's movement: Feminism. *New York Times,* p. WK3.

Bronstein, P., Black, L., Pfennig, J., & White, A. (1986). Getting academic jobs: Are women equally qualified and equally successful? *American Psychologist, 41,* 318–322.

DeFour, D. C., & Hirsch, B. J. (1990). The adaptation of black graduate students: A social networks approach. *American Journal of Community Psychology, 18,* 489–505.

de la Luz Reyes, M., & Halcon, J. (1988). Racism in academia: The old wolf revisited. *Harvard Education Review, 58,* 299–314.

Denmark, F. L. (1994). Engendering psychology. *American Psychologist, 49,* 329–334.

DeWitt, K. (1996, February 5). New cause helps feminists appeal to younger women. *New York Times,* p. A10.

Doyle, J., & Paludi, M. (1997). *Sex and gender.* (4th ed.) New York: McGraw Hill.

Farmer, H., Wardrop, J., & Rotella, S. (1999). Antecedent factors differentiating women and men in science/nonscience careers. *Psychology of Women Quarterly, 23,* 763–780.

Fidell, L. S. (1976). Empirical verification of sex discrimination in hiring practices in psychology. In R. Unger & F. Denmark (Eds.), *Woman: Dependent or independent variable?* (pp. 779–782). New York: Psychological Dimensions.

Freeman, J. (1975). How to discriminate against women without really trying. In J. Freeman (Ed.), *Women.* Palo Alto, CA: Mayfield.

Furumoto, L. (1980). Mary Whiton Calkins (1863–1930). *Psychology of Women Quarterly, 5,* 55–67.

Furumoto, L. (1985). Placing women in the history of psychology course. *Teaching of Psychology, 12,* 203–206.

Furumoto, L., & Scarborough, E. (1986). Placing women in the history of psychology: The first American woman psychologists. *American Psychologist, 41,* 35–42.

Goldner, M. (1994). *Accounting for race and class variation in the disjuncture between feminist identity and feminist beliefs: The place of negative labels and social movements.* Paper presented at the Annual Meeting of the Americal Sociological Association, Los Angeles, CA.

Graham, S. (1992). Most of the subjects were white and middle class: Trends in published research on African Americans in selected APA journals, 1970–1989. *American Psychologist, 47,* 629–639.

Harris, K., Melaas, K., & Rodacker, E. (1999). The impact of women's studies courses on college students of the 1990s. *Sex Roles, 40,* 969–977.

Highly, K. (1998). The impact of women's studies on feminist identity development, sex-role egalitarianism, assertiveness, and self-esteem in college women. *Dissertation Abstracts International, 59* (1-B), 0417.

Hogan, J., & Sexton, V. S. (1991). Women and the American Psychological Association. *Psychology of Women Quarterly, 15,* 623–634.

Juntunen, C. (1996). Relationship between a feminist approach to career counseling and career self-efficacy beliefs. *Journal of Employment Counseling, 33,* 130–143.

Lerner, G. (1979). *The majority finds its past: Placing women in history.* New York: Oxford University Press.

Lloyd, K. B. (1999). Becoming and being feminist: An existential phenomenological study. *Dissertation Abstracts International,* 59 (9-A), 3674.

Lorber, J. (1998). *Gender inequality: Feminist theories and politics.* Los Angeles, CA: Roxbury.

Lupart, J., & Barva, C. (1998). Promoting female achievement in the sciences: Research and implications. *International Journal for the Advancement of Counseling, 20,* 319–338.

Makosky, V. P., & Paludi, M. A. (1990). Feminism and women's studies in the academy. In M. A. Paludi & G. A. Steuernagel (Eds.), *Foundations for a feminist restructuring of the academic disciplines.* New York: Haworth Press.

Moses, Y. (1988). *Black women in the academy.* Washington, DC: Project on the Status and Education of Women.

Moyer, A., Salovey, P., & Casey-Cannon, S. (1999). Challenges facing female doctoral students and recent graduates. *Psychology of Women Quarterly, 23,* 607–630.

Palmieri, P. (1983). Here was fellowship: A social portrait of the academic community at Wellesley College, 1895–1920. *History of Education Quarterly, 23,* 195–214.

Paludi, M. (1992). *The psychology of women.* Dubuque, IA: Brown.

Pattatucci, A. (Ed.). (1998). *Women in science: Meeting career challenges.* Thousand Oaks, CA: Sage.

Petersen, S., & Kroner, T. (1992). Gender biases in textbooks for introductory psychology and human development. *Psychology of Women Quarterly, 16,* 17–36.

Reskin, B. (1998). Bringing the men back in: Sex differentiation and the devaluation of women's work. In K. Myers et al. (Eds.), *Feminist foundations: Toward transforming sociology.* Thousand Oaks, CA: Sage.

Rhode, D. (1997). *Speaking of sex.* Cambridge, MA: Harvard University Press.

Rose, S. (Ed.). (1986). *Career guide for women scholars.* New York: Springer.

Russo, N. F. (1984). *Women in the American Psychological Association.* Washington, DC: Women's Program Office, American Psychological Association.

Russo, N. F., & Denmark, F. L. (1987). Contributions of women to psychology. *Annual Review of Psychology, 38,* 279–298.

Scarborough, E., & Furumoto, L. (1987). *Untold lives: The first generation of American women psychologists.* New York: Columbia University Press.

Seelye, L. (1908, April 29). *Letter to Ethel Puffer* (From the Morgan-Howes Paper). Schlesinger Library, Cambridge, MA.

Stevens, G., & Gardner, S. (1982). *The women of psychology: Pioneers and innovators.* Cambridge, MA: Schenkman.

Strickland, B. (1987, March). *The feminization of psychology.* Paper presented at the annual meeting of the Association for Women in Psychology, Denver, CO.

Sue, D., Bingham, R., Porche-Burke, L., & Vasquez, M. (1999). The diversification of psychology: A multicultural revolution. *American Psychologist, 54,* 1061–1069.

Thomas, V., & Miles, S. (1995). Psychology of black women: Past, present, and future. In H. Landrine (Ed.), *Bringing cultural diversity to feminist psychology.* Washington, DC: American Psychological Association.

Vincent, P., Peplau, L. A., & Hill, C. (1998). A longitudinal application of the theory of reasoned action to women's career behavior. *Journal of Applied Social Psychology, 28,* 761–778.

TWO

PERSPECTIVES ON RESEARCH METHODOLOGIES

IN WOMEN'S VOICES

The traditional psychological experiment never has yielded or entailed objective observations or brute behavioral data; rather, it always has entailed and yielded interpretations of interpretations of interpretations, each level of which is in part culturally determined and situated.

Hope Landrine, Elizabeth Klonoff, and Alice Brown-Collins

As larger numbers of women (and minority and poor people) have become involved in social science research and as more matters of concern to them become the objects of research, it has become harder for social scientists to sustain the illusion that knowledge is abstract and value-free . . . . Women scholars are particularly likely to reach this conclusion because we have been largely excluded from the processes through which knowledge is obtained.

Rhoda K. Unger

When psychologists publish research that compares the behavior of women and men, they face political as well as scientific issues . . . . Never before in the history of psychology has such a formidable body of scientific information encountered such a powerful political agenda. The results of this encounter should be instructive to all psychologists who believe that psychology should serve human welfare as it advances scientific understanding.

Alice Eagly

Academic psychology cannot maintain its integrity by continuing to allow ethnic minorities to remain so marginalized in mainstream research. In contemporary society, most of the population is not White and middle class. Neither should the subject populations in the journals of our discipline continue to be so disproportionately defined.

Sandra Graham

Chapter Outline

Questions for Reflection

1. After reading the definition of "feminist" provided in Chapter 1, to what do you believe the term "feminist research" refers?

2. Do you believe psychological research is value-free? Why or why not?

3. Do you believe the outcome of psychological research is influenced by the experimenter's sex? Age? Race? Why or why not?

4. Do you believe psychological research should focus on differences between women and men or on similarities?

5. Pretend you have been asked to design a research study that deals with the impact of employed mothers on their children's achievement in elementary school, social development, and cognitive development. Identify the participants for your study. Operationally define the following terms: employed mother, cognitive development, achievement, social development.

INTRODUCTION: PSYCHOLOGICAL RESEARCH: VALUE-FREE VERSUS VALUE-LADEN

In the Hollywood movie, "Sleepless in Seattle," there are two scenes devoted to discussing the book, *Backlash*, by Susan Faludi. Specifically, the characters played by Meg Ryan, Rosie O'Donnell, Tom Hanks, and Rita Wilson discuss the "man shortage" that causes women not to marry. Male characters in the movie cite the statistic that it's more likely for a woman to be killed by a terrorist than marry after 30 years of age. The female characters offer an alternative explanation (that actually Faludi discusses): that these so-called "research facts" were based on single research studies that were subsequently shown to be seriously flawed or entirely incorrect. Faludi's main message is that social science research about women's lives is slanted to make it appear that women have achieved equality with men and that this equality is not worth the price in terms of their relationships with men, children, and their colleagues at work.

"Sleepless in Seattle" thus raised our consciousness about the politics of research on women and men. Do you believe it is possible for the results of psychological research to be interpreted in ways that are not incorrect? Consider the following situation.

Pretend you are a student in a class on social psychology. The topic for today's class is "Research Methods." Your professor arrives to the class carrying a stopwatch, a needle with a small eye, a spool of thread, and a pair of small scissors. Your professor asks for five women students to come to the front of the classroom and thread a needle. Each woman has one trial, during which she is to (a) pick up the needle and thread, (b) thread the needle, (c) tie a knot in the end of the thread, (d) cut the knot off again, (e) take out the thread, and (f) replace the needle and thread on the desk.

Your professor tells each woman she did quite well. Your professor times the trials and obtains the average time it took for the five women to complete the task. Next, your professor asks five men in the class to do the same task. As each of the men approaches the front of the classroom, your professor indicates that he probably won't do well at this task, and thanks the men for their cooperation. After each of the men's trials, your professor makes consoling statements.

When your professor compares the average times, the women are quicker. Your professor then announces that this exercise was a test of fine motor aptitude, that women are clearly superior, and therefore only women should be allowed to be neurosurgeons.

What would you say in response to your professor's statement? Do you agree that this demonstration proves only women should be neurosurgeons? Why or why not?

This classroom demonstration was actually conducted by psychologist Vivian Parker Makosky a number of years ago at St. Lawrence University in New York State. As you may have expected, many objections were voiced by students in her class in response to the classroom demonstration and Dr. Makosky's interpretation of the findings:

You only asked five women—that's way too small a sample.
You encouraged women but discouraged the men!
Threading a needle is not the same as performing neurosurgery.
It's not fair to make that comparison!

One of the issues illustrated with this exercise was that the psychological research process is not value-free. Psychologists are just as likely to be influenced by their cultural beliefs, values, and expectations as is anyone else in society, and psychologists' biases act like screens that distort our perception of the world in which we live.

Few areas of inquiry have been so fraught with personal biases as the study of women. Helen Thompson Wooley's (1910) comment that "sentimental rot and drivel run riot in the study of women and men" was the first feminist challenge to psychology's methodology. Feminist psychologists have challenged the methodology in several areas, including achievement, psychotherapy, victimization, and cognitive development. In this chapter, we will discuss sources of biases that influence our views, and feminist correctives to these biases, including guidelines for conducting nonsexist psychological research. Let's begin our discussion with an overview of the scientific process psychologists use in conducting research.

SCIENTIFIC METHOD IN PSYCHOLOGY

A basic tenet of psychological research is its insistence on objectivity. The objective researcher is supposedly detached from her or his topic and, through the **scientific method,** observes, controls, measures, and analyzes external events as they happen and let the results speak for themselves (Paludi, Paludi, & Doyle, in press). Psychologists, as other scientists, typically use a single research paradigm that leads to studying human behavior from a linear, predetermined model:

Statement of the problem
Survey of the literature
Hypotheses
Design
Statistical analyses
Results
Conclusion

Patricia Campbell (1988) has indicated that these stages in the psychological research process are incomplete because (1) they do not encourage any modification in the ongoing research process, (2) the preselection of statistical analyses does not encourage using alternative analyses of the data, and (3) the stages overemphasize the search for differences and only define differences statistically (Campbell, 1988). We will discuss these critiques in more detail and will illustrate them with studies from a variety of subareas in psychology.

Experimenter Bias: Excluding Women from Psychological Research

Can psychological research be totally value-free? Because psychologists say they approach their topics without personal biases doesn't mean their research efforts are value-free. For the next few minutes, pretend you have been asked to design a research study that concerns "nurturant behavior." How would you operationally define "nurturance"? Identify the participants you would include in your study. Would you include men and women? Only women? Only men? Children? What ages would you study? What races? Would you consider research participants who are physically challenged?

If you browse through research articles on "nurturant behavior," you will find that psychologists have operationalized "nurturance" as the number of times a *mother* talks to or smiles at her baby while she is holding the child. This in fact is one example of "nurturant behaivor." There are others, however. Why do you believe researcher study babies' *mothers* in a study on "nurturant behavior"? Why do you believe researchers have typically omitted studying fathers in this area of research? The gender-role stereotype that links mothers with caregiving, or the stereotype that women and not men are "naturally" expected to perform nurturant activities, may have played important roles in the selection of participants.

Would you study women or men or both if you were asked to design a study on aggression? If you answered "men," is it because you associate men with aggression and women with being unaggressive? How would you study achievement? Would you include girls and women in your sample or would you study only boys and men? What if you were to study moral behavior? Do you believe you would include men and women in your sample? Why or why not?

As another example, pretend you are conducting research on parenting styles. Would you include the following groups in your sample: lesbian couples, fathers, nonmarried heterosexual couples, single women, or gay couples? Researchers who exclude these individuals are biasing the design, outcome, and interpretation of their research.

When research has been conducted on moral behavior, achievement, and aggression, psychologists have asked only one sex to participate in their research. For example, the classic theories and research on morality (e.g., Kohlberg, 1966) and achievement motivation (e.g., McClelland, Atkinson, Clark, & Lowell, 1953) were based on boys and men only. Men, more often than women, are the participants in psychological research (Rabinowitz & Sechzer, 1993; Wallston & Grady, 1985). In addition, in research on aggression, nearly 50 percent of the research was conducted using boys or men only, 10 percent using girls or women, and 40 percent using both sexes. This 50 percent is higher than the percentage of male-only research in psychology in general (Denmark, 1994; Rabinowitz & Sechzer, 1993). Thus, when psychologists have investigated a behavior they associate as being "masculine" they are less likely to include girls and women. Similarly, when psychologists study a topic they associate with "femininity," they are less likely to include boys and men as participants.

Thus, researchers are just as likely to be influenced by their cultural beliefs, values, and expectations as anyone else in society. Such bias is referred to as **experimenter bias** or **researcher bias.** Experimenter bias may cause a researcher to look at a problem in only one way, while avoiding other possibilities.

Research by Florence Denmark and her colleagues (Denmark, Sechzer, & Rabinowitz, 1992, 1993) suggests that most researchers in the behavioral and biomedical sciences fail to report the sex of their human participants and animal subjects. As Denmark (1994) summarized:

> . . . in large epidemiological studies of aging, cholesterol, intervention for heart disease, and so forth, we found that women were not invited to participate. . . . We found this omission to be true in AIDS-HIV infection research in which male-female differences have also largely been ignored despite the different progression of the disease among women and men. (p. 332)

ASKING QUESTIONS: INDICATIVE OF RESEARCHER BIAS

Researcher bias may also show itself in the way researchers phrase their questions. For example, requesting information about a participant's "marital status" denies lesbian and gay relationships as well as nonmarital heterosexual cohabitation. Even the types of questions a researcher asks may bias the results in favor of the researcher's hypothesis (Rosenthal, 1979). Omitting information about participants' sexual orientation, ethnicity, and age is also indicative of the researcher's biases. The questions we ask (and don't ask) and the way we ask them can determine the answers we find. If our questions are embedded with our personal bias, we are more likely to find answers that support our bias. This argument was expressed by Karen Briefer (1987), who pointed out that heterosexist bias has largely been unexamined in psychological research. She wrote:

> The problem is not one of explicit anti-gay prejudice, or even one of a lack of non-biased research. Heterosexist bias in recent work is found in more subtle forms: in the structuring of texts, use of language and grammatical constructions, through veiled anti-gay statements that imply undesirability, and through the omission of a lesbian/gay perspective entirely. . . . Negative attitudes toward homosexuality run deep, and are rooted in basic assumptions about women, men, and what constitutes "appropriate" sex-role [sic] behavior. But precisely because these attitudes run deep, and can be traced to such basic notions of what it means to be female or male, challenging heterosexism should become an important and explicitly acknowledged part of the task we have set for ourselves as feminists. (pp. 2–3, 13)

The race, age, sex, sexual orientation, socioeconomic class, and ethnicity of the researcher and participants should be considered when reviewing and conducting research. And Bill Bauer and I (Paludi & Bauer, 1979) reported sex-of-experimenter effects on the Draw-A-Person Test, a measure of individuals' gender-role identification (see Chapter 4). Jean Fankell-Hauser and I (Paludi & Fankell-Hauser, 1986) employed three women interviewers of different age cohorts in our cross-sectional study of women's achievement striving, so as to avoid age-of-experimenter effects in our research.

RESEARCHER BIAS EVIDENT IN MEASUREMENT TECHNIQUES

Much of the confusion surrounding the terms "femininity" and "masculinity" is caused by the vastly different definitions that have been offered (see Chapter 4). Researchers have not agreed on what they are measuring, nor have they derived a straightforward scale for the measurement of these constructs.

This confusion is perhaps best illustrated with a discussion of a widely used test of children's gender-role preferences, the **IT Scale for Children (ITSC),** developed by psychologist Daniel Brown in 1956. This is a projective test that uses a child-figure drawing, "IT," for which children are asked to make choices among drawings of feminine and masculine objects, figures, and activities. The assumption underlying the ITSC is that children will project themselves into the IT figure on the basis of their own gender-role preferences: a girl who prefers a feminine gender role will project such a preference to IT and will select predominantly (if not entirely) "feminine" activities, toys, and objects. However, research with the ITSC has found that girls (as well as boys) exhibit masculine preferences at all ages (D. Brown, 1956b).

This finding led several psychologists to conclude that girls perceive Western culture to be male oriented and to provide boys and men with advantages not afforded girls and women (see Paludi, 1981). Research with the ITSC, however, has suggested that several methodological problems regarding the test can explain the predominant findings. For example, the IT figure is not perceived by children to be sexually ambiguous but, instead, actually resembles a boy. Girls (and boys too) may select choices for the "male figure" rather than project their own choices onto IT (Paludi, 1981).

Support for this position comes from studies by Lansky and McKay (1963) and Thompson and McCandless (1970). These researchers asked children to complete the ITSC under standard conditions involving choices for the IT figure and also under conditions in which the choices were made for a concealed child named IT whose picture was hidden in an envelope. Both studies found that girls exhibited more feminine preference under the concealed, relative to the standard, conditions. In addition, Paludi (1981) pointed out that the majority of both sexes label the IT figure as a boy, while a majority of both label the concealed IT as their own sex.

A related issue concerns the fact that Brown defined gender-role preference in terms of his preconceived cultural standards of femininity and masculinity. It is more

---

MEET DR. DIANE HALPERN

Dr. Diane Halpern is Professor of Psychology at California State University, San Bernadino.

Question: What are your views on the development of gender differences in cognition?

Dr. Halpern's response: Gender differences in cognition is one of the most politically charged issues in psychology. Many psychologists fear that information about cognitive gender differences will be misused to justify discrimination and/or affirmative action based on sex. This fear is based on an unstated assumption that, if the truth were known, females would be found to be "less"—less smart, less able, or less of whatever it is society values. The data do not support this fear; there are sex-related differences in cognitive abilities, but differences are not deficiencies. If we find that society values the abilities associated with being male and devalues the abilities associated with being female, then it is time to rethink societal values instead of denying the existence of female-male differences.

meaningful, both theoretically and methodologically, to define the components of gender-role identity in terms of the modal response of individuals of the same age as those for whom the test is designed. Thus, when girls rejected "feminine" items in the ITSC, they may not have rejected the feminine role as they conceived of it.

Finally, the ITSC may be criticized on the basis that it is not ethnically sensitive, because the age at which components of gender-role identity become stable varies for girls and boys of different ethnic backgrounds and socioeconomic classes (Dill, Bradford, Prudent, Semaj, & Harper, 1975). Less stereotyped tests of children's gender-role preferences include those developed by Brinn and associates (Brinn, Kraemer, Warm, & Paludi, 1984) and Edelbrock and Sugawara (1978).

PSYCHOLOGY: A VALUE-LADEN SCIENCE

The question remains: What culturally influenced value system or set of biases can be singled out as infusing the so-called value-free science? Science is deeply embedded with our culture's all-pervasive antifeminine and androcentric worldviews (Keller, 1978). Even the language typically used in experimental procedures conveys the masculine-biased nature of the field. Terms like "subject," "manipulate," and "control" imply dominance, status, and power on the part of the researcher while placing the participant in a subordinate position. Darlene DeFour and I (DeFour & Paludi, 1988) reported that it is important to avoid the use of value-laden language so as not to legitimize negative stereotyping of ethnic minority women. For example, the labels used to describe various lifestyle choices depends on the socioeconomic class and/or ethnicity of the individual being discussed. Unmarried African American mothers have been described in the context of a "broken home," while single white mothers have been frequently discussed in the context of an "alternative" or "contemporary" lifestyle.

Psychologist Naomi Weisstein (1971) made a persuasive case that social scientists, especially male psychologists, have allowed their personal biases about women to bias their research endeavors. She concluded:

> Until psychologists begin respecting evidence and until they begin looking at the social contexts within which people move, psychology will have nothing to say of substance to offer in this task of discovery. I do not know what immutable differences exist between men and women apart from differences in their genitals; perhaps there are some other unchangeable differences; probably there are a number of irrelevant differences. But it is clear that until social expectations for men and women are equal, until we pro-

vide equal respect for both men and women, our answers to this question will simply reflect our prejudices. (p. 222)

In summary, psychology has given priority to the values of the white, heterosexual, middle-class men who have been its main researchers and professors.

STATISTICAL TREATMENT OF WOMEN'S RESPONSES

Psychologist Stephanie Shields (1975) reported that psychologists have considered women "as a special group" since the mid-nineteenth century. Researchers believed that they could distinguish between women's and men's brains in terms of differences in gross structure. The location of these differences varied according to the popular theory of the time. For example, when psychologists believed the frontal lobe was responsible for intelligence, men's frontal lobes were seen as larger than women's. When it became in vogue to consider the parietal lobe as the repository of intelligence, however, women's and men's frontal lobes were seen as equivalent, but women were now described as having smaller parietal lobes than men.

Thus, early research on the psychology of women was focused on "differences" and "similarities" between women and men; any direct discussion of women without comparisons to men was avoided. Leta Stetter Hollingworth, for example, devoted considerable research to investigating the **variability hypothesis:** the assertion that "women as a species are less variable among themselves than are men; all women are pretty much alike but men range enormously in their talents and defects" (1943, p. 114). This variability hypothesis, first discussed by Havelock Ellis, flourished in the early 1900s and was used to explain the greater frequency of men on lists of distinction, and a wider range of intelligence for men than for women.

From this variability hypothesis, psychologists derived implications about gender differences in perceptual-motor abilities and emotionality. Stephanie Shields (1975) pointed out that the variability hypothesis was used against women in the areas of social policies and education:

If this tendency to mediocrity was natural to the "fair" sex, as the variability hypothesis would hold true, then it would be wasteful of public and private resources to train or encourage women to high levels of achievement. (p. 6)

WELL-DOCUMENTED GENDER DIFFERENCES?

When research on gender is conducted, the emphasis is on differences rather than similarities. Even the term *gender similarities* may sound peculiar to researchers (Campbell, 1988). The overemphasis on differences provides confirmation of the stereotype that women and men are "opposite" and that the male is normative and the female is a deviation from the norm. Finding no difference after conducting a study may even cause a researcher to file the study's results away in a file drawer because the researcher believes there is little chance for publication (Rosenthal, 1979). The outcome is then a **publication bias** in the field of gender. One reason that so many early studies reported many gender differences may have been that, all too often, studies finding no differences were unceremoniously put away and forgotten in researchers' file drawers.

This focus on gender similarities and differences was used in the 1970s by psychologists Eleanor Maccoby and Carol Nagy Jacklin (1974). In their **voting method** of analysis, they tallied the number of research studies reporting statistically significant gender differences (in each direction), in addition to the number of studies reporting no gender differences. They then published their classic text, *The Psychology of Sex Differences,* in which they examined over 1,600 published studies encompassing a broad spectrum of human behavior, including cognitive functions, personality traits, and social behaviors. Their goal for this text was "to sift the evidence to determine which of the many beliefs about sex differences have a solid basis in fact and which do not" (p.vii). Their analyses revealed that many of the presumed gender differences were more myth than fact, whereas a few differences appeared to stand up.

Some of the studies reviewed by Maccoby and Jacklin (1974) and Jacklin (1989) point to several areas where there seem to be some gender differences with respect to specific abilities and to one personality trait:

Girls have greater verbal ability than boys.
Boys excel in visual-spatial ability.
Boys excel in mathematical ability.
Males are more aggressive than females.

Maccoby and Jacklin concluded that girls' verbal abilities mature more quickly than boys'. Girls' and boys' verbal abilities are similar during the early school years, but girls take the lead in high school and beyond. This results in girls having a better understanding of and fluency in the complexities of language, better spelling and creative writing abilities, and better comprehension of analogies.

Beginning in early adolescence, boys are better able to rotate an object in space. Boys also are better at picking out a simple design or figure that is embedded within a larger, more complex design (Baenninger & Newcombe, 1989). Again, beginning in adolescence, boys show a greater facility with math than do girls. However, in those studies that use verbal processes in mathematical questions, girls do better than boys; in those that require visual-spatial abilities, boys do better than girls.

Beginning in the early preschool years, boys are more physically aggressive than girls. Boys exhibit more mock fighting and other forms of aggression than girls do. Also, boys direct their aggression during these early years more toward other boys than toward girls. Males continue to be more aggressive than females throughout adolescence and the adult years.

Many of these conclusions have been challenged because, in many cases, Maccoby and Jacklin simply counted the studies that found a gender difference (no matter which sex the results favored) and compared them to those that did not. If there were more differences than similarities, Maccoby and Jacklin concluded a significant gender difference. Jeanne Block (1976) has argued that such a procedure is questionable. Many of the studies Maccoby and Jacklin reviewed contained relatively few participants, leading to the possibility of finding little or no gender differences with respect to the topic under study. Julia Sherman (1978) re-reviewed many of Maccoby and Jacklin's studies and found that, many times, the magnitude of the differences was quite small.

META-ANALYSIS AND THE PSYCHOLOGY OF WOMEN

Janet Hyde (1981) also reanalyzed Maccoby and Jacklin's verbal, quantitative, visual-spatial, and field articulation studies. She summarized her research in the following way:

> The main conclusion that can be reached from this analysis is that the gender differences in verbal ability, quantitative ability, visual-spatial ability, and field articulation reported by Maccoby and Jacklin (1974) are small. Gender differences appear to account for no more than 1%-5% of the population variance. . . . Generally, it seems that gender differences in verbal ability are smaller and gender differences in spatial ability are larger, but even in the latter case, gender differences account for less than 5% of the population variance. (pp. 894–896)

Hyde used **meta-analysis** to arrive at her conclusions. Meta-analysis is a statistical procedure that permits psychologists to synthesize results from several studies in order to measure the **magnitude of a difference.** It is a statistical method for conducting a literature review. Psychologists who use meta-analyses proceed in the following way:

1. They locate as many studies as they can on the particular topic of interest. They use computerized database searches in this phase of the analysis.

2. They perform a statistical analysis of the data reported in each of the journal articles or conference presentations. They then compute an effect size statistic, d, for each study. This d statistic explains the distance between the mean of the women's scores and the mean of the men's scores, in standard deviation units. This statistic also yields information about the variability of women's and men's scores, recognizing that each sex is not homogeneous.

3. They determine the average of the d statistics obtained from all the studies they reviewed and then analyze the variations in the values of d.

4. Finally, they group the studies into categories based on logical classifications (e.g., mathematical reasoning, arithmetic computation). They can then determine the gender difference based on the classifications assessed.

Meta-analytic studies have been conducted in a variety of areas, including self-esteem (Kling, Hyde, Showers, & Buswell, 1999), cognition (Hyde, 1981; Hyde & Linn, 1988), displaced aggression (Marcus, Pedersen, Carlson, & Miller, 2000), influenceability and conformity (Cooper, 1979), aggression (Eagly & Johnson, 1989), role conflict and job performance (Tubre & Collins, 2000), cheating attitudes and classroom cheating behavior (Whitley, Nelson, & Jones, 1999), achievement goal and intrisic motivation (Rawsthoren & Elliott, 1999); sexuality (Hyde & Oliver, 2000); and visual-spatial ability (Masters & Sanders, 1993). In their review of meta-analytic studies, Janet Hyde and Laurie Frost (1993) concluded that meta-analyses can advance the study of the psychology of women because they indicate not only whether there is a significant gender difference but also the magnitude of the gender difference.

Hyde and Frost (1993) suggested that meta-analyses can make feminist transformations in psychology by (a) demonstrating the extent to which gendered behavior is context-dependent and the product of feminine and masculine gender roles; (b) examining the intersections among sex, gender, race, ethnicity, and socioeconomic class; (c) providing data to counter stereotypical portrayals of the behavior of women and men; and (d) challenging stereotypic beliefs in only "differences" between the sexes and acknowledging "similarities" between women and men.

A criticism of meta-analytic techniques as well as the "voting method" concerns the belief that continued emphasis on gender differences and gender similarities encourages us to exaggerate those differences we do find (Rabinowitz & Sechzer, 1993). Similar to the early research that focused on differences in brain size, the tendency persists to use research data about women to formulate social policies that would be harmful to women (Eagly, 1995).

THE MEANING OF DIFFERENCE

One criticism of Maccoby and Jacklin's "voting method" points to the belief that continued emphasis on gender differences and gender similarities encourages us to exaggerate those differences we do find. A major problem with this perspective is that sex is treated as the explanation of rather than as the starting point for scientific investigation (Grady, 1981). Vivian Makosky and I (1990) suggested that psychologists may be creating the gender differences they report. This especially applies to research done with students in introductory psychology classes. The women who take introductory psychology are typically majoring in the social and behavioral sciences; the men are majoring in the natural and physical sciences. Thus, one part of the distribution in interests, abilities, and traits may be sampled for women, another for men.

There is still the tendency to use research data about women to formulate social policies that would be harmful to women—despite the fact that the focus is on viewing women as individuals separate from men. According to Rachel Hare-Mustin and Jeanne Marecek (1988), one consequence of focusing on difference is:

> . . . the tendency to view men and women as embodying opposite and mutually exclusive traits. Such a dichotomy seems a caricature of human experience. For example, to maintain the illusion of male autonomy at home and in the workplace, the contribution of women's work must be overlooked. Similarly, the portrayal of women as relational ignores the complexity of their experiences. Rearing children involves achievement, and nurturing others involves power over those in one's care. . . . Gender dichotomies are historically rooted in an era, now past, when the majority of women were not part of the paid labor force. . . . When gender is represented as dichotomized traits, the possibility that each includes aspects of the other is overlooked. (p. 459)

Proponents of the gender-as-difference perspective view differences between women and men as universal, enduring, and essential. Research along these lines has, therefore, as its goal reaffirming differences between women and men. This perspective can best be illustrated with the literature on moral reasoning.

Moral Reasoning: An Example of Exaggerating Differences Between Women and Men

Lawrence Kohlberg (1976) concluded that **moral reasoning** could be divided into six stages. Stage-one moral thinking is based on rewards and punishment. A girl who displays stage-one moral reasoning, for instance, obeys her parents and acts "good" to be rewarded or to avoid punishment. At stage-six moral reasoning, a person espouses a system of generalized ethical principles, such as living one's life according to universal moral principles.

Kohlberg's research has been criticized because it was predicated on boys' and men's responses only. Kohlberg concluded that his six moral stages adequately described the levels of moral reasoning for all people. Furthermore, Kohlberg argued that women's moral reasoning is less developed than men's.

Carol Gilligan's (1982) research is especially revealing in terms of the differences between women's and men's moral decision making. She views women's morality in terms of an **ethic of care.** She believes women see "life as dependent on connection, as sustained by activities of care, as based on a bond of attachment rather than a contract of agreement" (p. 57).

Kohlberg and Gilligan both used the following moral dilemma to test moral development. How would you resolve this dilemma?

In Europe, a woman was near death from a special kind of cancer. There was one drug that the doctors thought might save her. It was a form of radium that a druggist in the same town had recently discovered. The drug was expensive to make, but the druggist was charging ten times what the drug cost him to make. He paid $200 for the radium and charged $2,000 for a small dose of the drug. The sick woman's husband, Heinz, went to everyone he knew to borrow the money, but he could only get together about $1,000, which is half of what it cost. He told the druggist that his wife was dying, and asked him to sell it cheaper or let him pay later. But the druggist said, "No, I discovered the drug and I'm going to make money from it." Heinz got desperate and broke into the man's store to steal the drug for his wife. Should the husband have done that? (Kohlberg, 1963, pp. 18–19)

Both women and men (and girls and boys) typically want Heinz's wife to live. But girls' and women's solution is to "find some other way" besides stealing to get the drug. Girls and women see the dilemma in terms of how to gain the drug while preventing any negative consequences that may come from simply stealing it. Boys and men, on the other hand, opt for stealing it. They reason that life is more important than the druggist's demand to be paid a certain amount. Thus, women's moral reasoning revolves around the **"connectedness"** (Gilligan's term) between Heinz and his wife. Men, on the other hand, are more concerned about the unreasonableness of the druggist's demand.

Gilligan (1982) thus views women as relational-connected and men as rational and instrumental. She construes women's caring as an essential feminine attribute. However, political scientist Joan Tronto (1987) has argued that women's moral differences may be a function of their subordinate or tentative social position. According to Tronto:

> Even if an ethic of care could primarily be understood as a gender difference, however, the unsituated fact of moral difference between men and women is dangerous because it ignores the broader intellectual context within which "facts" about gender difference are generally received. Despite decades of questioning, we still live in a society where "man" stands for human and where the norm is equated with the male. Gender difference, therefore, is a concept that concerns deviation from the normal. Given the conservative nature of our perceptions of knowledge, evidence of a gender difference in and of itself is not likely to lead to the widespread questioning of established categories, such as Kohlberg's. Instead, it is likely to lead to the denigration of "deviation" associated with the female. (pp. 652–653)

When psychologists focus on why a gender difference exists in moral reasoning, we disregard the question of why domination exists. And there is a great deal of variability among women, due to ethnicity, age, class, stage in relationship, sexual orientation, stage in career development, and other cultural and social circumstances. Thus, focusing on gender differences ignores **within-group variability.** Furthermore, the overemphasis on differences provides confirmation of the stereotype that women and men are "opposite" and that the male is normative and the female is a deviation from the norm (Tronto, 1987).

Psychological Androgyny: An Example of Minimizing Differences Between Women and Men

Minimizing differences between women and men and focusing on similarities underlies the construct of **psychological androgyny** (see Chapter 4). Androgyny was initially considered an ideal personality pattern wherein a person combined the socially valued stereotypic characteristics associated with both femininity and masculinity. An androgynous person exhibits both feminine and masculine traits, depending on the situation. An androgynous woman could also show socially valued feminine and masculine traits when appropriate. According to the concept of androgyny, women were no longer expected or encouraged to restrict their behaviors to traditional gender-role-specific traits (Kaplan & Sedney, 1980). Sandra Bem (1977) and Jeanne Marecek (1978) prescribed androgyny as a liberating force, leading women to fuller lives.

However, Bernice Lott (1981) pointed out that although androgyny was an improvement over the view that femininity and masculinity were opposite and mutually exclusive ends of a personality dimension, the androgynous perspective still held that personality comprises feminine and masculine elements. The androgyny perspective implies the equivalence of femininity and masculinity; however, in fact, the masculine traits are more highly valued (Doyle & Paludi, 1995; see Chapter 3). Rachel Hare-Mustin and Jeanne Marecek (1988) noted that "when the idea of counterparts implies symmetry and equivalence, it obscures differences in power and social value. . . . Arguing for no differences between women and men, however, draws attention away from women's special needs and from differences in power and resources between women and men" (pp. 458, 460).

Androgyny ensures that attention is drawn away from women's unique needs and the power imbalance between women and men in this culture. Hare-Mustin and Marecek (1988) offered other examples:

> In a society in which one group holds most of the power, seemingly neutral actions usually benefit members of that group, as in no-fault divorce or parental leave. In Weitzman's research, no-fault divorce settlements were found to have raised men's standard of living 42% while lowering that of women and children 73%. Another example is the effort to promote public policies granting comparable parental leave for men and women. Such policies overlook the biological changes in childbirth from which women need to recuperate and the demands of breastfeeding, which are met uniquely by women. (p. 460)

TOWARD THE FUTURE: FEMINIST METHODOLOGIES

"Difference" is a problematic way to construe gender and the psychology of women. If differences are exaggerated (as is illustrated by the research on moral reasoning), the findings may serve as a basis for discrimination against women, who are "different." On the other hand, if actual differences (e.g., in wages) are ignored

---

MEET DR. JEANNE MARECEK

Dr. Jeanne Marecek teaches at Swarthmore College, where she is Professor and has been Department Chairperson. She was a founding member of the College's Women's Studies Program.

Question: What are some future concerns for feminist methodologies?

Dr. Marecek's response: Two central projects for feminist scholars are: (1) to understand and critique the way in which categories of gender, along with those of class and race, structure the distribution of power in society; and (2) to examine and interrupt the reproduction of gender in the everyday experiences of men and women, and in the structures and institutions of society. A key tool of feminist psychologists is skepticism about the discipline itself: How do the methods of psychology and its writing practices . . . limit what can be asked, what can be found, and what can be said within the field? How is the discipline embedded in culture and history? How does the knowledge produced by psychology serve to maintain the status quo in society and support the interests of those in power?

---

or minimized, women may also be discriminated against (e.g., through inadequate child support). Thus, in both the "gender-as-difference" model and the "minimizing difference" model, white, middle-class, heterosexual men and masculinity are the standards of comparison, the norm against which women and femininity are judged (Paludi et al., in press).

Feminist psychologists have suggested that researchers redefine the constructs typically used in studies of the psychology of women. For example, an ethic of care needs to be considered an alternative moral theory, not a complement to justice theories of moral reasoning; rejecting social programs as inappropriate to one's needs must be included in coping strategies for dealing with victimization, not viewed as an act of relinquishing control or helplessness; work needs to be redefined to include child care, housekeeping, and volunteer services; and power needs to be considered as a "capacity" rather than a "thing" word.

Feminist psychologists differ from nonfeminist psychologists in the theories we use, the ways we apply these theories to research problems, and the ways we believe knowledge is constructed. As we discussed in Chapter 1, there is *no one type* of feminist psychologist or feminist research methodology (Worell, 1996). Feminist psychologists use **qualitative data techniques** (e.g., interviews) as one way to correct the biases inherent in **quantitative methods;** many also use quantitative techniques (e.g., personality tests, achievement tests) (Barbour & Kitzinger, 1999;

Merrick, 1999; Unger, 1999; Wilkinson, 1999). One approach is not inherently more feminist than the other (Henwood, Griffin, & Phoenix, 1998).

Many feminist psychologists are advocating that we stop denying the role of values and recognize that scholarship that is not concerned with the larger society cannot adequately deal with reality (Makosky & Paludi, 1990; Unger, 1999; Wyche, 1999). For example, Bellah (1985) stated:

> Social science as public philosophy cannot be "value-free." It accepts the canons of critical, disciplined research, but it does not imagine that such research exists in a moral vacuum. . . . The analysts are part of the whole they are analyzing. In framing their problems and interpreting their results, they draw on their own experience and their membership in a community of research that is in turn located within specific traditions and institutions. (p. 38)

Feminist psychologists have identified the biases and underlying values in our research. Feminism has thus addressed whether research and theorizing on young, middle-class, white heterosexual men are indicative of people in general, and whether men are more worthy of investigation than women. Thus, feminist methodologies have been a direct response to the failure of psychology to present a comprehensive, inclusive, and affirmative investigation of human behavior (Worell, 1996).

Several psychologists have called for a new **value-laden approach to research**—a feminist orientation that will openly state one's heterosexist, androcentric, Eurocentric, and antifemale biases in the study of human behavior (Ceballo, 1999; Crawford & Kimmel, 1999; Jaffee, Kling, Plant, Ashby, & Hyde, 1999). Psychologist Mary Brown Parlee (1979) outlined the case for such an approach:

> One hallmark of feminist research in any field seems to be the investigator's continual testing of the plausibility of the work against her own experience. The historian, for example, asks what it was like to be a woman and what were women doing at that place and time, and then proceeds to find out—using her own experience both as a guide to formulating questions and as a preliminary way of evaluating the completeness of the results. The usual scholarly principles of reliability, consistency, logical inference, and the like are also used to evaluate the results, but the additional criterion of how does it accord with my own experience does enter into the work process. And similarly in other disciplines, including psychology. Feminist psychologists thus have as a priority finding the best possible version of the truth about the subject matter rather than adhering strictly to a particular method. (p. 130)

Laura Brown (1989) commented:

What does it mean for psychology if the experiences of being lesbian and/or gay male, in all the diversity of meanings that those experiences can hold, are taken as core and central to definitions of reality rather than as a special topic tangential to basic understandings of human behavior, particularly human interactions? After all, just as there is no American Psychological Association division on the psychology of men or white people, there is no special topic area called heterosexual studies in psychology. "Psychology," the official entity, values those experiences that are white, male, heterosexual, young, middle class, able-bodied, and North American; thus has the universe of "human behavior" been defined. "Special topics," including lesbian and gay issues, have traditionally been defined as of special interest only, not in the core curriculum in reality or emotionally. (pp. 445–446)

Feminist research insists that researchers become actively involved in the research process, taking the perspective of participants. Furthermore, by asking questions of the research participants during and after the study, one can gain additional information that might have been missed. Therefore, feminist researchers are not detached from the investigation but rather become an integral part of the whole research procedure (Unger, 1999; Wilkinson, 1999; Wyche, 1999).

MEET DR. MAUREEN McHUGH

Dr. Maureen McHugh is on the Psychology faculty at Indiana University of Pennsylvania, where she has also directed the Women's Studies Program. From 1979 to 1983, she cochaired a Committee on Establishing Guidelines for Nonsexist Research in Psychology.

Question: Can you discuss your work with the guidelines for nonsexist research?

Dr. McHugh's response: A version of [these guidelines] was eventually printed in *The American Psychologist* in August 1986. [This] article is important because it has the potential for reaching a wide audience of practicing psychologists. The article attempts to present—in a brief, accessible, and nonthreatening way—the critiques of psychology as sexist, examples of sexist research in psychology, and recommendations for conducting nonsexist research. We are encouraged that the article may help to educate a new generation of researchers as well as reeducate those already conducting psychological research. We have been told that the article has been used in research design courses on both an undergraduate and graduate level, and has been read in graduate seminars on contemporary issues in psychology.

THE PROCESS OF CHANGE

Linda Gannon and her colleagues (Gannon, Luchetta, Rhodes, Pardie, & Segrist, 1992) reported that, in 1970, 29 percent of the articles published in the *Journal of Personality and Social Psychology* used nonsexist language (see Chapter 7), but, in 1990, 99 percent of the articles used nonsexist terminology. This finding most likely reflects the fact that, beginning in 1983, the American Psychological Association's official *Publication Manual* required the use of nonsexist language in all APA journal articles. Similar findings were reported by Rebecca Campbell and Pamela Schram (1995) in their examination of 40 research methods textbooks in psychology and general social science for their use of nonsexist language.

Gannon and her colleagues (1992) also found that, in 1970, 42 percent of the articles published in the *Journal of Abnormal Psychology* were based on all-male samples whereas, in 1990, 20 percent of its articles were based on all-male samples. The process of change is slow, as evidenced by the fact that, by 1990, one in five research studies excluded women as participants.

Maureen McHugh and her colleagues (McHugh, Koeske, & Frieze, 1986) and Florence Denmark and her colleagues (Denmark, Russo, Frieze, & Sechzer, 1988) have offered suggestions for **nonsexist research,** including interpreting without bias, avoiding excessive confidence in traditional methods, and examining explanatory models. These suggestions are presented in Boxes 2.4 and 2.5.

This issue was summarized more recently by Hope Landrine and her colleagues (Landrine, Klonoff, & Brown-Collins, 1995):

1. Feminist psychologists can refer to human research participants as such and cease the use of the term *subjects.*

2. Feminist psychologists could pay research participants for their labor.

3. The American Psychological Association's Ethical Principles might include the statement that servitude as a research participant shall not be a contingency for receiving a degree or for a grade in a course (e.g., for extra credit). No matter how "educational" the researcher believes the experience of servitude to be, such arrangements decrease the voluntary nature of participation and thereby constitute unethical treatment of participants.

4. Feminist psychologists might assume that their interpretation (i.e., objective observations) of the behavior of research participants may differ significantly from the participants' meanings and intentions.

BOX 2.1
NONSEXIST GUIDELINES FOR PSYCHOLOGICAL RESEARCH

Avoiding Excessive Confidence in Traditional Methods

Carefully examine the underlying values and assumptions in all research and state them explicitly.

Encourage the use of alternative and nonexperimental research methodologies directed toward exploration, detailed description, and theory generation as well as experimental and quasi-experimental approaches designed for hypothesis testing.

Engage in ongoing debate about the strengths and weaknesses of all research techniques, focusing attention on the capacities and limitations of experimental and non-experimental research as procedures for studying processes and systems and for permitting generalizations to particular contexts.

When undertaking literature reviews, examine past research for both methodological rigor and unexamined sexism in procedure or interpretation.

Be aware of factors other than methodological soundness that may influence the publishability or distribution of results.

Remember that the convergence of established findings with experience and the convergence of results based on different methods adds to their credibility; divergence should prompt renewed study.

Examining Exploratory Models

Exercise care in the terminology employed to describe or explain results in order to avoid (1) confusing sex with gender, (2) confusing description with explanation, and (3) reducing complex or interactionist explanations to overly simple ones.

Consider all possible explanations for sex-related phenomena including social-cultural, biological, and situational factors.

Consider alternative explanations even if they have not been investigated.

Recognize that many consistently demonstrated sex-related behaviors may result from either consistent and pervasive cultural factors or biological factors. Often, empirical tests differentiating competing explanations are unavailable.

Become aware of, consider, and devise studies of alternative and more complex models of causation.

More detailed models that incorporate and specify relationships involving both physiological and sociocultural variables are needed.

Increased effort should be directed toward developing common terminologies and providing more elaborate tests of competing explanatory models.

Equal emphasis in publication should be given to findings of "sex similarities," rather than biasing journal policy toward findings of "sex differences."

Interpreting Without Bias

Carefully consider both the basis and the implications of the labels applied to individual traits and behaviors.

Make sure that the theoretical frameworks that form the body of psychological research are relevant to members of both sexes.

From M. McHugh, R. Koeske, & I. H. Frieze, "Issues to Consider in Conducting Nonsexist Psychological Research: A Guide for Researchers," *American Psychologist, 41:* 879–890. Copyright 1986 by the American Psychological Association. Reprinted by permission.

5. Feminist psychologists can regard studies that are based on African American, Latino, European American, Asian American, or Native American women and men as equally culturally saturated.

6. Feminist psychologists can define the presence of multiple control groups of people of color and of European Americans as the prototype of rigorous, experimental design. (p. 58)

One suggestion by Landrine and colleagues concerning paying research participants was incorporated in the 1992 version of the American Psychological Association's Ethical Principles.

Diane Halpern (1995) has provided researchers with a set of recommendations when planning, reading, and interpreting research. These recommendations include:

Are main effects being moderated by unidentified interactions? For example, is the main effect of gender or ethnicity really the effect of socioeconomic status on gender or ethnicity? Would the effects of gender, for example, change if different age groups had been included as subjects? What other variables are confounded with gender and ethnicity?

For example, African Americans in the United States take fewer college preparatory courses in high school than white students. Given the confounding of these variables, would at least part of the differences that are found be attributable to differential course-taking patterns?

Were tests of significance followed with effect size statistics? Were results that were not in accord with the researcher's worldview labeled as "small" and those

---

BOX 2.2
AVOIDING SEXISM IN PSYCHOLOGICAL RESEARCH

Research Methods

Problem: The selection of research participants is based on stereotypic assumptions and does not allow for generalizations to other groups.

Example: On the basis of stereotypes about who should be responsible for contraception, only females are looked at in studies of contraception.

Correction: Both sexes should be studied before conclusions are drawn about the factors that determine use of contraception.

Data Analysis

Problem: Gender differences are inaccurately magnified.

Example: Although only 24% of women were found to . . . fully 28% of the men. . . .

Correction: The results should include multiple descriptions of the data, such as means, standard deviations, and the amount of variance explained.

Conclusions

Problem: The title or abstract of an article makes no reference to the limitations of the study participants and implies a broader scope of the study than is warranted.

Example: A study purporting to be about "perceptions of the disabled" uses only blind white men.

Correction: Use more precise titles and clearly delineate sample selection criteria in the abstract.

Source: Based on F. Denmark, N. F. Russo, I. H. Frieze, & J. Sechzer, "Guidelines for Avoiding Sexism in Psychological Research: A Report of the Ad Hoc Committee on Nonsexist Research," *American Psychologist, 43:* 582–585. Copyright 1988 by the American Psychological Association.

---

that were in accord with the researcher's worldview described as "large" when they were, in fact, quite similar in size?

Are you careful to distinguish between research results and interpretations of research results? For example, the finding that women and men show different patterns of scores on the SATs does not necessarily mean that there are gender ability differences. All it does mean is at this time and with this test, there are "on the average" between-gender differences. Results of this sort indicate nothing about the cause of the differences.

Have you maintained an amiable skepticism? Do you scrutinize new research carefully and require independent replications before you are willing to place too much faith in the findings? (pp. 88–89)

The guidelines offered by McHugh and colleagues (1986), Denmark and colleagues (1988), Landrine and colleagues (1995), and Halpern (1995) provide the beginnings for an alternative approach to the study of human behavior. First and foremost, research is viewed as taking place within a well-defined cultural and social context, never totally free from the concerns and values of the larger society (Campbell & Schram, 1995; Worell, 1996). And, as Doyle and Paludi (1995) concluded:

We must keep in mind that sex and gender are topics laden with value judgments, assumptions and biases. Even when there are "large" gender differences, the differences within each sex are larger than the differences between women and men. Researchers may want to announce their particular biases openly so that others may know right from the start what those biases are. (p. 17)

NEW TERMS

connectedness

ethic of care

experimenter bias

IT Scale for Children (ITSC)

magnitude of gender differences

meta-analysis

moral reasoning

nonsexist research

psychological androgyny

publication bias

qualitative data techniques

quantitative data techniques

researcher bias

scientific method

value-laden approach to research

variability hypothesis

voting method

within-group variability

CHAPTER REVIEW QUESTIONS

1. Explain how gender-role stereotypes affect the outcome and interpretation of research.

2. Discuss the methodological biases inherent in the IT Scale for Children.

3. What is the variability hypothesis?

4. Discuss the differences between the voting method and meta-analysis procedures.

5. Why do psychologists focus on differences to explain gender?

6. Explain why defining gender as "minimizing difference" or "exaggerating difference" is problematic.

7. Cite some examples of how feminist research differs from nonfeminist research methodology.

8. Discuss Mary Brown Parlee's claim that "one hallmark of feminist research in any field seems to be the investigator's continual testing of the plausibility of the work against her own experience."

9. Discuss Stephanie Shields's comment that interpretation of facts has sometimes determined the facts themselves.

10. What are some feminist correctives to the following research biases: selection of research participants and reporting results?

SELECTED READINGS

Eagly, A. (1995). The science and politics of comparing women and men. *American Psychologist, 50,* 145–158.

Henwood, K., Griffin, C., & Phoenix, A. (Eds.). (1998). *Standpoints and differences: Essays in the practice of feminist psychology.* London: Sage Publications Ltd.

Special Issue of *Psychology of Women Quarterly,* "Innovations in Feminist Research," March, 1999, vol. 23.

LEARNING MORE ABOUT . . .

Suggestions for Term Papers and Independent Studies Related to *Research Methodologies*

Female versus male representation in psychological research

Importance of psychologists focusing on gender "comparisons" rather than "differences"

Interface of sexism and racism in psychological research methodologies

Use of meta-analytic techniques in research on *helping behavior* and/or *leadership styles*

TAKING ACTION . . .

on *Research Methodologies*

1. Browse through the latest issue of a psychological journal, for example:

   Psychology of Women Quarterly

   Sex Roles

   Developmental Psychology

   Journal of Personality and Social Psychology

   American Psychologist

   Journal of Experimental Psychology

   Educational Psychology

   Journal of Vocational Behavior

   Journal of Black Psychology

   Journal of Cross-Cultural Psychology

   Select one research article from the journal and answer the following questions:

   What volume of the journal did you select?

   What is the full citation of the article?

   What question, problem, or hypothesis did the author(s) investigate?

   Why did the author(s) believe this topic was important?

   How does (do) the author(s) say the topic relates to what has been published previously?

   Where was the study conducted?

   What instruments and techniques were used?

   Who was studied? Why?

   How did the author(s) summarize the observations?

   Did the findings turn out as anticipated? Why or why not?

   What biases have you found in this article? How would you recommend correcting them?

   Pretend you have been asked to do a follow-up study to the one you have read. What would you do? Why?

2. At your library, locate several issues of the same journal—some prior to 1983 and some subsequent to that year.

   Read a few of the articles that interest you. While reading the articles, jot down the number of times sexist and nonsexist language is used by the authors. For example, do the authors use "male" or "men" when describing both women and men research participants?

Compare your responses pre-1983 and post-1983. What are your results?

You should find that there are more examples of nonsexist language in the issues of the journal post-1983. Why?

Beginning in 1983, the American Psychological Association's official *Publication Manual* required the use of nonsexist language in all journal articles.

Linda Gannon and her colleagues (1992) found that, in 1970, for example, 29 percent of the articles in *Journal of Personality and Social Psychology* used nonsexist language as compared with 99 percent in 1990! Psychological researchers' behavior is most definitely impacted by institutional norms; in this case, the institution is the American Psychological Association.

REFERENCES

Baenninger, M., & Newcombe, N. (1989). The role of experience in spatial performance: A meta-analysis. *Sex Roles, 20,* 327–344.

Barbour, R., & Kitzinger, J. (Eds.). (1999). *Developing focus group research: Politics, theory and practice.* London: Sage.

Bellah, R. (1985). Creating a new framework for new realities: Social science as public philosophy. *Change,* 35–39.

Bem, S. L. (1977). On the utility of alternative procedures for assessing psychological androgyny. *Journal of Personality and Social Psychology, 31,* 634–643.

Block, J. (1976). Issues, problems, and pitfalls in assessing sex differences: A critical review of the *Psychology of Sex Differences. Merrill-Palmer Quarterly, 22,* 283–308.

Briefer, K. (1987, March). *Beyond sexism: Heterosexist bias in feminist psychology.* Paper presented at the meeting of the Association for Women in Psychology, Denver, CO.

Brinn, J., Kraemer, K., Warm, J., & Paludi, M. A. (1984). Sex role preferences in four age groups. *Sex Roles, 11,* 901–910.

Brown, D. (1956a). *The IT Scale for Children.* Missoula, MT: Psychological Test Specialists.

Brown, D. (1956b). Sex role preference in young children. *Psychological Monographs, 70* (Whole no. 421).

Brown, L. (1989). New voices, new visions. Toward a lesbian/gay paradigm for psychology. *Psychology of Women Quarterly, 13,* 445–458.

Campbell, P. B. (1988). *Rethinking research: Challenges for new and not so new researchers.* Washington, DC: U.S. Department of Education.

Campbell, R., & Schram, P. (1995). Feminist research methods: A content analysis of psychology and social science textbooks. *Psychology of Women Quarterly, 19,* 85–106.

Ceballo, R. (1999). Negotiating the life narrative: A dialogue with an African American social worker. *Psychology of Women Quarterly, 23,* 309–321.

Cooper, H. M. (1979). Statistically combining independent studies: A meta-analysis of sex differences in conformity research. *Journal of Personality and Social Psychology, 37,* 131–146.

Crawford, M., & Kimmel, E. (1999). Promoting methodological diversity in feminist research. *Psychology of Women Quarterly, 23,* 1–6.

DeFour, D. C., & Paludi, M. A. (1988, March). *Integrating the scholarship on ethnicity into the psychology of women course.* Paper presented at the meeting of the Association for Women in Psychology, Bethesda, MD.

Denmark, F. L. (1994). Engendering psychology. *American Psychologist, 49,* 329–334.

Denmark, F. L., Russo, N. F., Frieze, I. H., & Sechzer, J. (1988). Guidelines for avoiding sexism in psychological research: A report of the ad hoc committee on nonsexist research. *American Psychologist, 43,* 582–585.

Denmark, F. L., Sechzer, J., & Rabinowitz, V. C. (1992, August). *Gender, sex, and culture: Sources of bias in psychology.* Paper presented at the 100th Annual Convention of the American Psychological Association, Washington, DC.

Denmark, F. L., Sechzer, J., & Rabinowitz, V. C. (1993). Response to "Sex bias in psychological research: Progress or complacency?" *American Psychologist, 48,* 1093–1094.

Dill, J. R., Bradford, C., Prudent, S., Semaj, L., & Harper, J. (1975). Sex role preferences in black preschool children using a modification of the IT Scale for Children. *Perceptual and Motor Skills, 41,* 823–828.

Doyle, J., & Paludi, M. (1995). *Sex and gender: The human experience* (3rd ed.). Dubuque, IA: Brown.

Eagly, A. (1995). The science and politics of comparing women and men. *American Psychologist, 50,* 145–158.

Eagly, A., & Johnson, B. T. (1989). *Gender and leadership style: A meta-analysis.* Manuscript submitted for publication.

Edelbrock, C., & Sugawara, A. (1978). Acquisition of sex-typed preferences in preschool-aged children. *Developmental Psychology, 14,* 614–623.

Gannon, L., Luchetta, T., Rhodes, K., Pardie, L., & Segrist, D. (1992). Sex bias in psychological research: Progress or complacency? *American Psychologist, 4,* 389–396.

Gilligan, C. (1982). *In a different voice.* Cambridge, MA: Harvard University Press.

Gould, M. (1980). The new sociology. *Signs, 5,* 459–467.

Halpern, D. (1995). Cognitive gender differences: Why diversity is a critical research issue. In H. Landrine (Ed.), *Bringing cultural diversity to feminist psychology.* Washington, DC: American Psychological Association.

Hare-Mustin, R., & Marecek, J. (1988). The meaning of difference: Gender theory, postmodernism, and psychology. *American Psychologist, 43,* 455–464.

Henwood, K., Griffin, C., & Phoenix, A. (Eds.). (1998). *Standpoints and differences: Essays in the practice of feminist psychology.* London: Sage.

Hollingworth, H. (1943). *Leta Stetter Hollingworth.* Lincoln: University of Nebraska Press.

Hyde, J. (1981). How large are cognitive differences? *American Psychologist, 36,* 892–901.

Hyde, J., & Frost, L. (1993). Meta-analysis in the psychology of women. In F. L. Denmark & M. A. Paludi (Eds.), *Psychology of women: A handbook of issues and theories.* Westport, CT: Greenwood Press.

Hyde, J., & Linn, M. (1988). Gender differences in verbal ability: A metaanalysis. *Psychological Bulletin, 104,* 53–69.

Hyde, J., & Oliver, M. (2000). Gender differences in sexuality: Results from meta-analysis. In C. B. Travis, et al. (Eds.), *Sexuality, society, and feminism.* Washington, DC: American Psychological Association.

Jacklin, C. N. (1989). Female and male: Issues of gender. *American Psychologist, 44,* 127–133.

Jaffee, S., Kling, K., Plant, E., Ashby, S., & Hyde, J. (1999). The view from down here: Feminist graduate students consider innovative methodologies. *Psychology of Women Quarterly, 23,* 423–430.

Kaplan, A., & Sedney, M. (1980). *Psychology and sex roles: An androgynous perspective.* Boston: Little, Brown.

Keller, E. F. (1978). Gender and science. *Psychoanalysis and Contemporary Thought, 1,* 409–433.

Kling, K., Hyde, J., Showers, C., & Buswell, B. (1999). Gender differences in self-esteem: A meta-analysis. *Psychological Bulletin, 125,* 470–500.

Kohlberg, L. (1963). The development of children's orientations toward a moral order: Sequence in the development of human thought. *Vita Humana, 6,* 11–33.

Kohlberg, L. (1966). A cognitive-developmental analysis of children's sex role concepts and attitudes. In E. Maccoby (Ed.), *The development of sex differences.* Stanford, CA: Stanford University Press.

Kohlberg, L. (1976). Moral stages and moralization: The cognitive-developmental approach. In T. Lickona (Ed.), *Moral development and behavior.* New York: Holt, Rinehart and Winston.

Landrine, H., Klonoff, E., & Brown-Collins, A. (1995). Cultural diversity and methodology in feminist psychology: Critique, proposal, empirical example. In H. Landrine (Ed.), *Bringing cultural diversity to feminist psychology.* Washington, DC: American Psychological Association.

Lansky, L., & McKay, G. (1963). Sex-role preference of kindergarten boys and girls: Some contradictory results. *Psychological Reports, 13,* 415–421.

Lott, B. (1981). A feminist critique of androgyny: Toward the elimination of gender attributions for learned behavior. In C. Mayo & N. Henley (Eds.), *Gender and nonverbal behavior.* New York: Springer.

Maccoby, E. E., & Jacklin, C. N. (1974). *The psychology of sex differences.* Stanford, CA: Stanford University Press.

Makosky, V. P., & Paludi, M. A. (1990). Feminism and women's studies in the academy. In M. A. Paludi & G. A. Steuernagel (Eds.), *Foundations for a feminist restructuring of the academic disciplines.* New York: Haworth Press.

Marcus, A., Pedersen, W., Carlson, M., & Miller, N. (2000). Displaced aggression is alive and well: A meta-analytic review. *Journal of Personality and Social Psychology, 78,* 670–689.

Marecek, J. (1978). Psychological disorders in women: Indices of role strain. In I. Frieze, J. Parsons, P. Johnson, D. Ruble, & G. Zellman (Eds.), *Women and sex roles: A social psychological perspective.* New York: Norton.

Masters, M., & Sanders, B. (1993). Is the gender difference in mental rotation disappearing? *Behavior Genetics, 23,* 337–341.

McClelland, D., Atkinson, J., Clark, R., & Lowell, F. (1953). *The achievement motive.* New York: Appleton-Century-Crofts.

McHugh, M., Koeske, R., & Frieze, I. H. (1986). Issues to consider in conducting nonsexist psychological research: A guide for researchers. *American Psychologist, 41,* 879–890.

Merrick, E. (1999). "Like chewing gravel": On the experience of analyzing qualitative research findings using a feminist epistemology. *Psychology of Women Quarterly, 23,* 47–57.

Paludi, M. A. (1981). Sex role discrimination among girls: Effect on IT Scale for Children scores. *Developmental Psychology, 17,* 851–852.

Paludi, M. A., & Bauer, W. D. (1979). Impact of sex of experimenter on the Draw-A-Person Test. *Perceptual and Motor Skills, 40,* 456–458.

Paludi, M. A., & Fankell-Hauser, J. (1986). An idiographic approach to the study of women's achievement strivings. *Psychology of Women Quarterly, 10,* 89–100.

Paludi, M., Paludi, C., & Doyle, J. (in press). *Sex and gender* (5th ed.). New York: McGraw Hill.

Parlee, M. B. (1979). Psychology and women. *Signs, 5,* 121–133.

Rabinowitz, V., & Sechzer, J. (1993). Feminist perspectives on research methods. In F. Denmark & M. Paludi (Eds.), *Psychology of women: A handbook of issues and theories.* Westport, CT: Greenwood Press.

Rawsthoren, L., & Elliott, A. (1999). Achievement goals and intrinsic motivation: A meta-analytic review. *Personality and Social Psychology Review, 3,* 326–344.

Rosenthal, R. (1979). The "file drawer" problem and tolerance for null results. *Psychological Bulletin, 86,* 638–641.

Sherman, J. (1978). *Sex-related cognitive differences.* Springfield, IL: Thomas.

Shields, S. (1975). Functionalism, Darwinism, and the psychology of women: A study in social myth. *American Psychologist, 30,* 739–754.

Tronto, J. (1987). Beyond gender difference to a theory of care. *Signs, 12,* 644–663.

Tubre, C., & Collins, J. (2000). Jackson and Schuler (1985) revisited: A meta-analysis of the relationships between role ambiguity, role conflict, and job performance. *Journal of Management, 26,* 155–169.

Unger, R. (1999). Comments on "focus groups." *Psychology of Women Quarterly, 23,* 245–246.

Wallston, B., & Grady, K. (1985). Integrating the feminist critique and the crisis in social psychology: Another look at research methods. In V. O'Leary, R. Unger, & B. Wallston (Eds.), *Women, gender and social psychology.* Hillsdale, NJ: Erlbaum.

Weisstein, N. (1971). Psychology constructs the female. In V.Gornick & B.Moran (Eds.), *Women in sexist society.* New York: New American Library.

Whitley, B., Nelson, A., & Jones, C. (1999). Gender differences in cheating attitudes and classroom cheating behavior: A meta-analysis. *Sex Roles, 4,* 657–680.

Wilkinson, S. (1999). Focus groups: A feminist method. *Psychology of Women Quarterly, 23.*

Wooley, H. (1910). A review of the recent literature on the psychology of sex. *Psychological Bulletin, 7,* 335–342.

Worell, J. (1996). Opening doors to feminist research. *Psychology of Women Quarterly, 20,* 469–485.

Wyche, K. (1999). Teaching the psychology of women courses in another discipline: The case of African American studies. *Psychology of Women Quarterly, 22,* 69–76.

THREE

PHYSICAL DEVELOPMENT
ACROSS THE FEMALE
LIFE CYCLE

IN WOMEN'S VOICES

We have developed the proposition that the socialization of ethnic minority American girls may differ from that of White American girls because of a variety of factors. . . . Which of these groups represents "the American ideal," or the norm? Our response is all of them and none of them. All, because every American group must be included and represented in Americans' image, and none, because one alone is not adequate to convey the complexity of developing gender behavior in the context of family and community.

Pamela Trotman Reid, Calliope Haritos, Elizabeth Kelly, and Nicole Holland

Women who are not married by the age of thirty, married women of thirty-five without children, or women returning to school in their forties are likely to be viewed as being "off-time." Those who perceive themselves as being "off-time," that is, as deviating from the social clock, may experience both internal and external pressures to conform.

Claire Etaugh

In general, old women in our culture get little respect. They are often isolated, patronized, ignored. Most have been married and spent their lives and energies caring for husband and children. As they grow older, they find they have lost their main occupation and are ill-equipped to find a new career. Many realize they've received little emotional return for the long years of nurturing others. They've had little experience in dealing with the outside world. Some are even afraid to travel alone or to seek other new experiences. Their circle of friends has grown smaller, and because they grew up in an era when good nutrition and exercise weren't emphasized, their health has begun to deteriorate. Few have had the energy and daring to fight against prejudice.

Buffy Dunker

Chapter Outline

Questions for Reflection

1. Do you recall your own or a family member's menarche? What were the attitudes associated with menarche in your family?

2. What images do we see on television regarding menopausal women? Are these images positive? Negative? How do these images compare to your own experiences with menopausal women?

3. Do you believe there exists a double standard of aging in this society? Identify older women actresses who still get prime roles in Hollywood films. Now identify older men actors who still get prime roles in Hollywood films. Do you have the same number of men and women on your lists?

4. Have you known early and later maturing girls? What kinds of stresses did early or late maturation contribute to their lives?

5. Can you correctly name women's internal and external sexual organs? From where did you learn this information?

6. Pretend you have been asked to give a lecture to junior high school girls about puberty. What information would you provide these girls? What information would you omit at this time from your lecture? Cite the reasons for your answers.

INTRODUCTION: THE MEANING OF DEVELOPMENT

The development of girls into women is a *process*. This process includes a variety of interacting complex factors—involving psychological, physical, cognitive, and social domains—and continues throughout the life span. For example, we see growth as an infant girl becomes larger, more dexterous, and more coordinated in early and middle childhood. We see development during pubescence, when a girl's body grows into that of a woman. We see growth when adolescent girls think abstractly and hypothetically and no longer rely only on concrete experiences. Development is also evidenced in girls' and women's intellectual achievements.

In this chapter, I will discuss this developmental perspective in understanding girls and women. I define *development* as a combination of quantitative and qualitative growth that occurs over time (Paludi, 2001; Reid, Haritos, Kelly, & Holland, 1995; Reid & Paludi, 1993). This developmental approach to studying behavior is an attempt to establish the rules for the changes that may be observed over time. I will specifically focus on some issues in physical and cognitive development. We will continue this discussion in the next chapter, where I discuss socializing agents contributing to girls' and women's development across the life span. Here, we will address developmental discontinuities and continuities across the life span—in other words, the ways women change from childhood to adulthood and how certain behaviors remain constant. Let's begin with an overview of some issues in girls' and women's physical development.

ISSUES IN GIRLS' AND WOMEN'S PHYSICAL DEVELOPMENT

When a woman's ovum (the female reproductive cell, which has 23 single chromosomes) is fertilized by a sperm cell (the male reproductive cell, which has 23 single chromosomes), the result is expected to produce the **zygote,** which has a total of 46 chromosomes (23 pairs). Determination of sexual characteristics begins at conception. Of the 23 pairs, one pair determines the genetic sex of the offspring (Hyde & DeLamater, 1999; Rathus, 1988). The woman's ovum possesses an **X chromosome** for sex; the man's sperm cell may contain an X or a **Y.** When an X-bearing sperm cell fertilizes the X-bearing ovum, the genetic pattern is established for a female (XX).

This explanation of the development of sexual characteristics suggests that the male sperm cell controls the sex of the offspring and that chromosomes are the determinants of sexual characteristics (Hyde & DeLamater, 1999). The outcome of sex development, however, is also mediated by female viability and hormonal factors.

PRENATAL DEVELOPMENT

Female Viability

The environment through which the sperm cell must pass to reach the ovum is considered a factor in sex determination (Rathus, 1983). For example, genetic researchers have found that the X-bearing sperm appears more viable than the Y-bearing sperm. In addition, women who conceive during times when their vaginal environment is likely to be strongly acidic are more likely to have girls (Hyde & De-Lamater, 1999).

Hormonal Anomalies

The female pattern of development is the standard. Male development needs the secretion of male hormones from the testes to stimulate the growth and development of the male reproductive system. Female development occurs spontaneously, even in the absence of ovaries and their hormonal secretions (Rathus, 1988).

There are some chromosomal anomalies, however, that seriously affect genetically normal female fetuses. For example, **adrenogenital syndrome** is a hormonal abnormality that can develop from a variety of sources. One explanation concerns the fetus' adrenal cortices (Hyde & De Lamater, 1999). A fetus's adrenal glands produce a hormone called **cortisol,** which is similar to **androgen,** the male sex hormone. Female fetuses may have a defective adrenal cortex that produces an abundance of cortisol. This condition can affect its body much like an androgen.

A second explanation for adrenogenital syndrome has been linked to the fact that some women develop tumors on their adrenal glands or on their ovaries, which then produce too many androgens. If this condition develops during pregnancy, the excessive androgens may reach a female fetus via the bloodstream.

During the 1940s and 1950s, **progestin** was prescribed to help women who had histories of miscarriages maintain their pregnancies. Progestin is a synthetic drug that affected female fetuses much like androgen (Rathus, 1988). Psychologists Susan Baker and Anke Ehrhardt have reported their findings among girls with adrenogenital syndrome (Baker & Ehrhardt, 1978; Ehrhardt & Baker, 1978). The girls in their research (labeled as "male" at birth since they had a masculinized appearance despite having the normal sex chromosomes) were all treated soon after birth with cortisol, which prevented further masculinization of their bodies and allowed them to develop normal female secondary sex characteristics (to be discussed later). Thus, the outcome and extent of adrenogenital syndrome depend on the amount of the androgen substance that enters the fetus's bloodstream and the time at which the entry occurs (i.e., critical period). Various degrees of masculinization of the external sex structures can result.

Fetal Development

The **prenatal period** of development is the time that elapses between conception and birth. It averages about 266 days, or 280 days from the last menstrual period (see the discussion below). The prenatal period is divided into three stages: (a) the germinal period, (b) the embryonic period, and (c) the fetal period.

The **germinal period** is characterized by the growth of the zygote and the establishment of a linkage between the zygote and the woman's support system.

The **embryonic period** lasts from the end of the second week to the eighth week. This period is characterized by rapid growth, the establishment of a placental relationship with the woman, and the early structural appearance of all the major organs. Development begins with the brain and head areas and then works its way down the body. This growth trend is referred to as **cephalocaudal development.** The cells in the central portion of the embryo thicken and form a ridge that is referred to as the **primitive streak.** This streak divides the embryo into right and left halves and becomes the spinal cord. The tissues grow in opposite directions away from the axis of the primitive streak. This growth trend is referred to as **proximodistal development.**

The **fetal period** begins with the ninth week and ends with birth. This period is characterized by the continuous development of major organ systems, with the organs assuming their specialized functions.

Sex Chromosomal Abnormality

In the prenatal stage of development, as throughout life, there is an interaction between social and physical conditions. The sex chromosomes' contribution to fetal development is also important. In approximately 1 in every 10,000 infant girls, an abnormal sex chromosome pattern is found: The second X chromosome is either defective or missing (Hamerton et al., 1975; Powell & Schulte, 1999, Rovet & Buchanan, 1999). This condition is referred to as **Turner's syndrome.** Because the second sex chromosome directs the development of the gonadal tissue into functioning ovaries, girls with Turner's syndrome always develop a female body with either underdeveloped ovaries or no ovaries. Consequently, they will not menstruate at adolescence, nor will they develop breasts without hormonal treatment (Powell & Schulte, 1999). In effect, their bodies do not produce the estrogen necessary for the development of their secondary sex characteristics during adolescence. Administration of estrogen will contribute to breast growth. An artificial menstrual cycle may be produced by administering estrogen for three weeks followed by one week without this treatment (Golub, 1992). Estrogen treatment has been reported to be beneficial for girls' self-concept and self-esteem (Ehrhardt & Meyer Bahlberg, 1975) as well as memory (Ross & Zinn, 1999).

Girls with Turner's syndrome usually have a short stature, a weblike configuration around their neck, eyelid folds, and a shieldlike chest (Powell & Schulte, 1999). They show some impairment in visual-spatial ability but little or no impairment in intellectual ability. Some even have significantly above-normal IQ scores (Money, 1964).

Kagan-Krieger (1999) reported that the greatest stress for girls with Turner's syndrome was related to initiating and maintaining relationships with men. Kagan-Krieger noted that the lack of relationships for women with Turner's syndrome was related to their feeling isolated and having a lowered self-esteem. Doerholt, Noeker, Ranke, and Haverkamp (1999) reported that women with Turner's syndrome exhibited a more negative body image than women without Turner's syndrome. These women also reported less satisfaction with their emotional well-being.

This research suggests that women with Turner's syndrome have a more difficult time than most women in feeling accepted by a culture whose standards for attractiveness and beauty are elusive (Kimmell & Rudolph, 1998; see Chapter 5).

INFANCY AND CHILDHOOD

The life-stage of infancy extends from childbirth through toddlerhood—the second year of life. Although more males than females are conceived, many more males than females die before birth (Jacklin, 1989). Females experience fewer difficulties during the birth process and, consequently, have fewer birth defects. Carol Nagy Jacklin and Eleanor Maccoby (1982) reported that, even in unproblematic deliveries, the births of girls take an average of an hour less than the deliveries of boys. This shortened length of labor has been correlated with fewer problems in infancy. Girls are thus more viable than boys.

Research has supported this greater **female viability** even after birth. For example, women have an overall life expectancy that surpasses men at every decade of life, regardless of race (Jacklin, 1989; Strickland, 1988). Girls have fewer congenital disorders, are less likely to succumb to **sudden infant death syndrome (SIDS**; the death, while sleeping, of apparently healthy infants who cease breathing for unknown medical reasons), and are less prone to hyperactivity (Rathus, 1988). All of these findings suggest genetically determined strength.

Infant girls are more mature at birth than are infant boys. Girls have more advanced skeletal and neurological systems (Hutt, 1978). Between 2 years and 2½ years of age, girls continue to mature faster than boys. Girls' skeletal development at birth is approximately one month ahead of boys'. Development follows the cephalocaudal and proximodistal principles, progressing from the head region to the trunk and then to the leg region. Motor development also follows the cephalocaudal principle. Infants learn to control the muscles of their head and neck, then their arms and abdomen, and finally, their legs. Thus, infants learn to hold their head up before they can sit, and they learn to sit before they can walk. Their large-muscle control develops before their fine-muscle control.

The preschool life-stage characterizes children 3 to 5 years of age. At the beginning of the preschool period children weigh, on average 25 to 30 pounds and are approximately 36 inches tall. By the end of this life-stage, they weigh, on average, 46 pounds and are approximately 46 inches tall (Feldman, 1998). Average differences in height and weight between girls and boys increase during the preschool period. On average, preschool boys tend to be taller and weigh more than the average preschool girl. There is a great deal of overlap in these distributions, however (Rice, 1997). A sex difference has been noted in gross motor coordination among preschoolers, with boys, on average, having greater gross motor ability. This ability is a result of boys' muscle strength. Girls, on average, surpass boys in tasks that involve the coordination of their arms and legs (Cratty, 1979; Rice, 1997).

The years 6 to 11 characterize the middle childhood stage of the life cycle. In the United States, elementary school children grow in height approximately 2 to 3 inches per year. By age 11, the average girl is 4'10" tall and the average boy is 4'9.5" tall. This is the only time during the life cycle when girls are, on the average, taller than boys (Feldman, 1998). This sex difference is height reflects the slightly more rapid physical development of girls, who typically begin their growth spurt at 10 years. With respect to weight, the pattern during middle childhood is similar to that experienced for height (Feldman, 1998). Girls and boys gain approximately 5 to 7 pounds a year. Weight becomes redistributed; "baby fat" disappears and children's bodies become more muscular (Feldman, 1998). There is also considerable overlap in strength despite the fact that as a group, boys are physically stronger than girls (Feldman, 1998). We should note that differences in dietary customs and in affluence affect variations in height and weight for girls and boys (Story et al., 2000).

In middle childhood, boys are overrepresented among children who have speech, behavior, and learning disorders (Feingold, 1993). Approximately twice as many boys than girls exhibit articulatory errors; three times as many boys as girls stutter. The incidence of reading problems is almost five times more prevalent in boys than in girls (Feingold, 1993). In addition, mental retardation is higher among boys than girls. More boys than girls are autistic and hyperactive (Chen & Siegler, 2000).

Research has documented a sex difference in performance of motor tasks and that the advantage is for boys (e.g., Maccoby & Jacklin, 1974). This interpretation contradicts the fact that girls have more accelerated physical development. It is illogical that biological acceleration may be used as an explanation of girls' rapid acquisition of language skills and their ability to excel in fine motor activity remains. Bem (1981) noted that differences in motor performance appear to be influenced by both biological and environmental factors. Parents and teachers have low expectations for girls' motor peformance. Consequently, girls have a lower motivation than boys as well as lower performance levels for behaviors that have been societally defined as "appropriate" for boys (Hyde & DeLamater, 1999).

ADOLESCENCE AND YOUNG ADULTHOOD

The word "adolescence" is derived from the Latin verb, *adolescere,* which translates "to grow to maturity" or "to grow up." This life stage is a transitional stage or bridge between childhood and adulthood. Unlike the other stages of the life cycle we have highlighted thus far, adolescence (and adulthood) does not have a set range of ages associated with it. In addition, issues that individuals in their later teens must deal with (e.g., developing a vocational identity) are qualitatively different from those tasks younger adolescents face. Thus, as some theorists have suggested (e.g., Newman & Newman,1975), adolescence consists principally of two stages, early adolescence (ages 13–17) and late adolescence (ages 18–22).

The period of **adolescence** is marked by changes in physical development that are part of the passage from childhood to adulthood. These physical changes occur during the stage of development referred to as **pubescence,** which is the period of rapid growth that culminates in **puberty,** or sexual maturity and reproductive capacity. The age at which girls and boys begin this transitional stage and the amount of time taken to complete it varies from one individual to another. Just look at a photo from your junior high school yearbook. All of the students in your class were approximately the same age, yet they do not look like they are at all. Look at your classmates. Some of your peers were taller than you; others were shorter. Some looked "developed" for their age; others resembled younger children.

Pubescence technically begins when the **hypothalamus** (part of the upper brain stem) signals the pituitary gland to release the hormones known as **gonadotrophins.** This usually occurs during children's sleep a year or so before any of the physical changes associated with pubescence appear (Schowalter & Anyan, 1981).

Take a look back at the photo from your junior high school yearbook. The obvious physical differences among adolescents who are of an identical chronological age underscore an endocrinological issue: The hypothalamus does not signal the pituitary to release the gonadotrophins at the same time in every adolescent girl and boy. The exact factors that activate the hypothalamus have not been determined. However, researchers (e.g., Frisch, 1984; Tanner, 1962) have argued that the hypothalamus monitors the adolescent's body weight and releases the necessary hormones when the body is of sufficient weight.

In the United States, the age at which puberty is reached has steadily decreased, with the trend now leveling off (Adams, Montemayor, & Gullotta, 1996). Most adolescent girls in the United States begin pubescence at approximately 11 years of age and reach the end of their growth by age 17 years. Their growth spurt starts between 9.5 and 14.5 years. Girls grow fastest in height and weight at approximately 12 years of age. They reach 98 percent of their adult height at 16.25 years. Girls mature, on average, two years earlier than boys. As a group, boys are physically stronger, taller, and weigh more than girls after puberty (Rice, 1997).

During pubescence, girls' lymphatic tissues decrease in size; they lose vision because of rapid changes in their eyes between the ages of 11 and 14 years; and their facial structures change (Steinberg, 1999). Their hairline recedes, and their facial bones mature in such a way that the chin and nose become prominent (Steinberg, 1999). Adolescents' weight nearly doubles during pubescence; on average, girls weigh 25 pounds less than boys as a result of their lower proportion of muscle to fat tissue (Hyde & DeLamater, 1999). By the time they are 15 years old, girls have lost twenty deciduous teeth. The number of bone masses during pubescence drops from approximately 350 to less than 220 as a result of epiphyseal unions (Petersen & Taylor, 1980).

The sequence of events in the maturation of girls' sexual and reproductive anatomy is not universally predictable. Maturation does proceed in distinct developmental stages (Hyde & DeLamater, 1999; Katchadorian, 1977):

Growth of breasts
Growth of pubic hair
Body growth
Menarche
Underarm hair
Oil- and sweat-producing glands.

Girls who are better nourished mature earlier. Menarche is reached later in less developed countries than in more developed countries (Hyde & DeLamater, 1999).

Some of these stages in girls' maturation during pubescence will now be discussed in more detail.

Breast Development

During pubescence, girls produce significant estrogen to stimulate the growth of **adipose tissue** (fat) on their chest, thighs, hips, and upper arms. Breasts are primarily composed of adipose tissue; consequently, their size increases or decreases in accord with the amount of overall fat in a girl's body. An adolescent girl who loses 10 to 15 pounds will have smaller breasts as well as smaller hips, thighs, and abdomen. **Mammary glands** are milk- producing glands with ducts through which milk travels to the nipple during breastfeeding. The mammary glands do not mature fully until childbirth.

The breast consists of about fifteen to twenty clusters of mammary glands, each with a separate opening to the **nipple.** Occasionally, during pubescence, girls' breasts produce a milky substance. However, this is not milk; it is a cleansing liquid to keep the nipple's duct open.

As is indicated in Figure 3.1, during the 2 or 2½ years of pubescence, there is a distinct process to girls' breast development. In the initial stage of this sequence, the **areola** becomes thicker and darker. The areola is the area surrounding the nipple. It can range in color from light pink to very dark brown, depending on the amount of pigment in the girls' skin. In the next stage of this developmental sequence, the nipples mature. This is followed by the growth of the breast tissue. Breast size is genetically determined and cannot be augmented by physical exercise. Some exercises may increase the size of the **pectoral muscles** (underlying the breast tissue), and the breasts then appear to have a different shape. The amount of adipose tissue in the breasts can only be altered through gaining or losing weight. Figure 3.2 shows the internal structure of the breast.

FIGURE 3.1   *Stages of breast development in adolescent girls.*

1. Preadolescent flat appearance.
2. Small, raised breast bud.
3. General enlargement and raising of areola and breast.
4. Areola and nipple form contour separate from breast.
5. Adult breast with areola in same contour as breast.

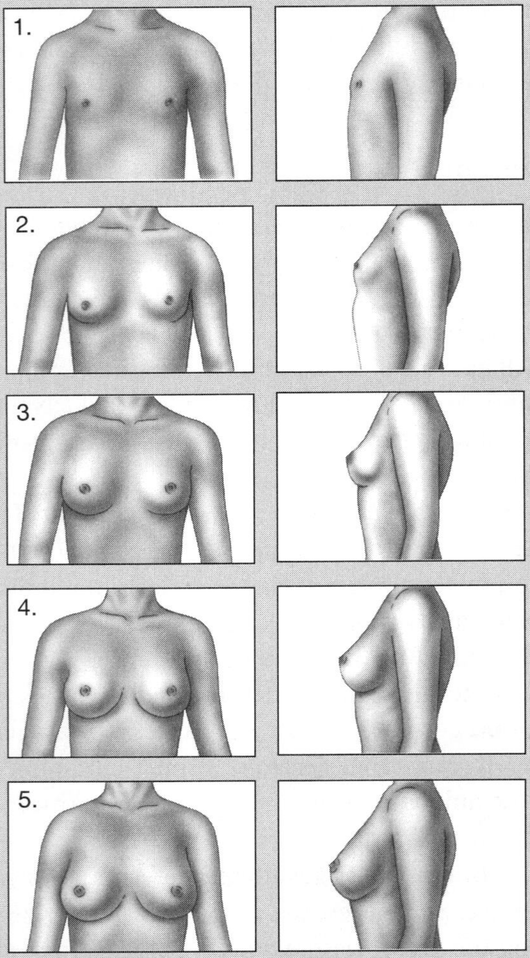

FIGURE 3.2   *The internal structure of the breast.*

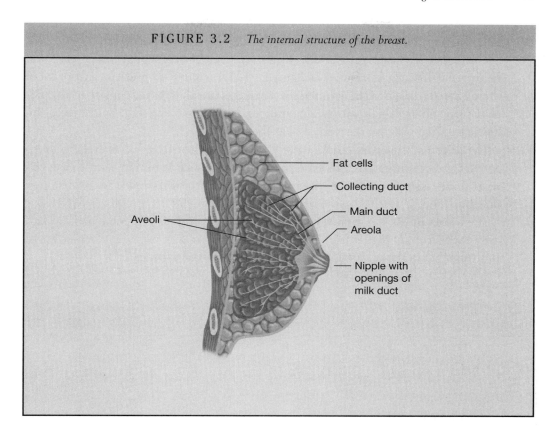

Fat cells

Collecting duct

Main duct

Areola

Aveoli

Nipple with openings of milk duct

Because adipose tissue retains water, the breasts become swollen and tender prior to and/or during menstruation, when women's bodies tend to retain fluid. The tenderness and swelling diminish at the completion of each menstrual period (to be discussed later). Normal breast tissue is somewhat lumpy. Nonetheless, adolescent girls (as well as adult women) must examine their breasts for unusual lumps that may be early signs of malignant growths. Women need to become familiar with their own breast tissue so they can more easily detect abnormal lumps. We will discuss this further in Chapter 5.

When breast tissue begins to grow, it usually develops at different rates in the two breasts. This process can contribute to girls' anxiety about the uneven appearance of their breasts. This anxiety is most likely nurtured by North America's cultural emphasis on the size of women's breasts. Adolescent girls worry about being big busted or flat chested. The size of women's breasts is in no way related to women's sexual enjoyment, the ability to breast-feed, or any health hazard.

Female Sex Organs

The female sex organs can be classified in two categories: the external organs and the internal organs (see Hyde & DeLamater, 1999). Figure 3.3 presents a diagram of women's external genitals. Women's **external sexual organs** consist of the clitoris, mons pubis, labia majora, labia minora, and vaginal opening. Collectively, the female external organs are referred to as the **vulva.**

The **clitoris** has a glans and a shaft. The glans of the clitoris is covered by a protective hood of skin referred to as the **prepuce.** The shaft is buried beneath the **clitoral hood,** a sheath of tissue that passes around the clitoris and is an extension of the labia minora.

The **mons pubis** is a rounded, fatty pad of tissue covered with pubic hair. It is located at the front of the female's body and lies on top of women's pubic bones. These come together in the center at a point called the **pubic symphysis.**

FIGURE 3.3   *Female external genitalia.*

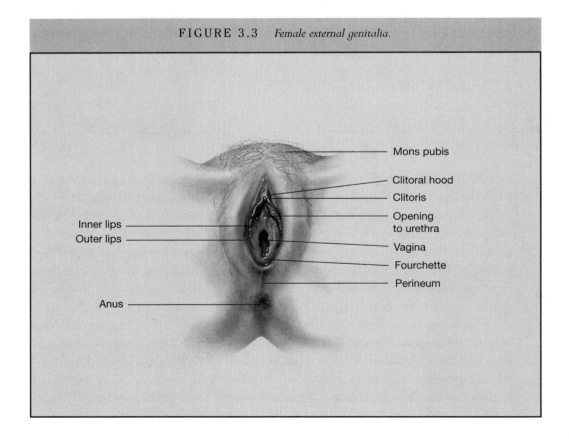

The **labia majora** (outer lips) are rounded pads of tissue lying across both sides of the vaginal opening. They are also covered with pubic hair. The **labia minora** (inner lips) are two hairless folds of skin lying between the labia majora and running along the edge of the vaginal opening. The labia minora come together in front, forming the clitoral hood.

The **hymen** is a thin membrane that, if present, is situated at the vaginal opening. The hymen has been taken as evidence of virginity. However, the absence of a hymen does not indicate that a woman has had vaginal intercourse. Some women are born without a hymen; other women may stretch their hymen themselves during masturbation; some women may stretch it in sports (Hyde & DeLamater, 1999).

Figure 3.4 illustrates women's **internal sexual organs:** the vagina, uterus, ovaries, and fallopian tubes. The **vaginal barrier** is about 8 to 10 centimeters (3 to 4 inches) long and tilts slightly backward from the bottom to the top (Hyde &

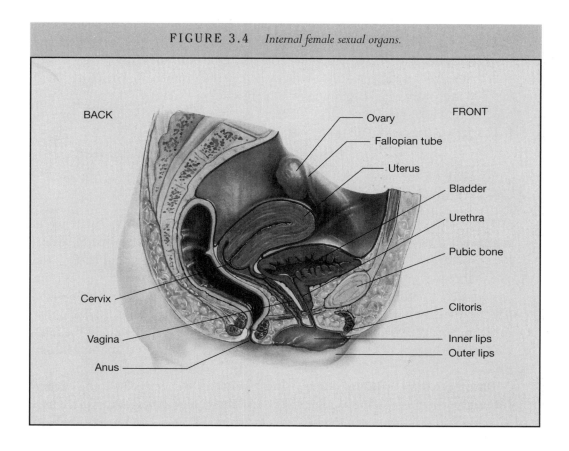

FIGURE 3.4 *Internal female sexual organs.*

DeLamater, 1999). At the bottom, it opens to the vaginal opening **(introitus).** At the top, it connects with the **cervix** (lower part of the uterus).

The walls of the **vagina** have three layers. The inner layer, referred to as the **vaginal mucosa,** is a mucous membrane. The middle layer is muscular; the outer layer forms a covering. The walls of the vagina are elastic and may expand to the extent necessary for sexual activity and childbirth.

The **uterus** is usually tilted forward and held in place by ligaments. The lower third of the uterus is the cervix, which opens into the vagina. The top is the **fundus;** the main part is the **body.** The uterus also consists of three layers. The inner layer, **endometrium,** is sloughed off during menstruation. The middle layer, the **myometrium,** is muscular. The outer layer, the **perimetrium** or serosa, forms the external cover of the uterus.

The **fallopian tubes,** also referred to as oviducts or uterine tubes, extend out from the sides of the upper end of the uterus. They are narrow and lined with hairlike projections, **cilia.**

The **ovaries** are two organs that lie on either side of the uterus. The ovaries produce ova (eggs) and they manufacture the female sex hormones, **estrogen** and **progesterone.** Within each ovary there are numerous **follicles.** A follicle is a capsule that surrounds an egg. It has been estimated that women are born with about 400,000 immature eggs. Beginning at puberty, one (or several) of the follicles matures during each menstrual cycle. When an egg has matured, the follicle moves to the surface of the ovary, bursts open, and releases the egg.

Physical and Psychological Reactions to Menarche and Menstruation

For adolescent girls, a significant aspect of this maturational experience is **menarche,** the first menstrual period. A menstrual cycle can be separated into four phases, each describing the state of the ova and follicles within that phase. The first phase of the menstrual cycle is called the **follicular phase.** It lasts from day 4 to day 14 after menstruation begins. (When counting the days of the cycle, day 1 is the first day of menstruation.) During the follicular phase, a follicle matures and enlarges. The end of this phase is signaled by the rupturing of the follicle and the release of the ovum. This second phase is known as the **ovulatory phase.**

During the third or **luteal phase,** reddish-yellow cells, referred to as the **corpus luteum,** form in the ruptured follicle. The last phase, **menstruation,** represents a sloughing off of the inner lining (the endometrium) of the uterus, which had been

MEET DR. DIANE RUBLE

Question: Is menarche a traumatic experience?

Dr. Ruble's response: The results of our research . . . suggest that girls experience a mixture of reactions to menarche. They are anxious about knowing what to do, about possible hassle and embarrassment, and about the developmental implications of "becoming a woman." Few of the girls spontaneously described their reactions in unambiguously positive or negative terms, and less than 20% of the girls used only negative terms (e.g., scared, bothered, upset) when asked to describe their reactions. The most frequently mentioned negative aspect about beginning to menstruate was the hassle—for example, carrying supplies or messiness.

Thus, although menarche may be initially disruptive, it does not appear to be traumatic for most girls. It may be traumatic for some girls, however, particularly those who have received no advance preparation. Autobiographical accounts describe the terror of girls who had never been told about menstruation and perceive themselves as bleeding to death. Fortunately, most girls in our culture are at least somewhat prepared for menarche.

building up in preparation for nourishing a fertilized egg. The **menstrual fluid** contains cervical mucus, vaginal secretions, cells, mucus, and degenerated endometrial particles, in addition to blood.

How are these phases regulated? The hypothalamus regulates the level of hormones in the bloodstream. When the level of estrogen drops too low, the hypothalamus signals the pituitary. The pituitary, in turn, releases **follicle-stimulating hormone (FSH)** into the bloodstream, which carries it to an ovary to stimulate the follicles to maturity. In addition, FSH signals the ovaries to increase their production of estrogen. Increased levels of estrogen stimulate the development of the endometrium in order to receive a fertilized egg. In addition, estrogen signals the pituitary to stop producing FSH. The pituitary does begin, however, to produce **luteinizing hormone (LH).** The LH then suppresses all development in all of the follicles except for one. Thus, only one ovum reaches maturity. The follicle releases the ovum at approximately day 14 of the menstrual cycle. This process is referred to as **ovulation.**

Occasionally, at the time of ovulation, women experience pain known as ***mittelschmerz*** ("middle pain"). Although the follicle has been abandoned by the egg, it forms into the corpus luteum, which secretes estrogen and progesterone. The higher level of progesterone inhibits the production of additional LH. The low level of LH is interpreted by the body as an indication that the corpus luteum can no longer be maintained. Consequently, it decomposes. Because the corpus luteum no longer exists, estrogen and progesterone production falls rapidly. The endometrium can no longer be maintained, so it is sloughed off and passes through the vagina as menstrual flow. This is considered day 1 of the menstrual cycle. The low level of estrogen then signals the hypothalamus, and the process repeats itself.

The biology of the menstrual cycle can cause a variety of responses. These include menstrual pain, premenstrual syndrome, and individuals' reactions to premenstrual and menstrual women. Let's look at each of these issues.

Menstrual Problems.   Most adolescents' and adult women's menstrual cycles are approximately 28 days long, with menstruation lasting approximately four or five days. During the first year or two of menstruation, women's cycles are often irregular. (This does not guarantee contraceptive security, however. Once ovulation begins, there is always a possibility of pregnancy.)

Shortly after menarche, adolescent girls may miss a period altogether. This condition is referred to as **amenorrhea** (Lauder et al., 1999; Powers, 1999). Amenorrhea may be caused by illness, athletic training, dietary changes, medication, stress, or excessive weight loss (perhaps resulting from anorexia) (Frisch, 1984; Gunn & Petersen, 1984). Occasionally, girls experience **menorrhagia,** in which an excessively heavy and prolonged menstrual flow leads to a temporary state of anemia. During the first few years of menstruation, adolescents may be less likely to become pregnant because their ovaries fail to release an egg into the fallopian tubes.

An **anovulatory period** refers to a menstrual cycle during which the ovaries failed to release an egg, despite the fact that menstruation occurred. Because the reproductive system is approaching maturity during adolescence, amenorrhea, menorrhagia, or anovulatory periods are not causes for alarm (Gunn & Petersen, 1984).

Girls and women often report menstrual pain or **dysmenorrhea,** which includes painful cramps in the abdominal region, lower back pain, and headache (Vogeltanz, Sigmon, & Vickers, 1998). Diane Ruble and Jeanne Brooks-Gunn (1982) reported that three-fourths of adolescent girls experience dysmenorrhea each month. Menstrual pain is not psychological. The contractions of the uterus that cause menstrual pain seem to be encouraged by **prostaglandins**—substances produced in high concentrations as menstruation approaches. Prostaglandins cause smooth muscle to contract and can affect the size of the blood vessels. The high levels of prostaglandins cause intense uterine contractions, which, in turn, choke off some of the uterus' supply of oxygen-carrying blood. Prostaglandins also cause greater sensitivity in nerve endings. Thus, the uterine contractions, lack of oxygen, and heightened nerve sensitivity produce cramping.

Antiprostaglandin drugs have been prescribed for the relief of cramps. The key drug, **mefenamic acid,** is sold with brand names such as Ponstel and Motrin. In addition to antiprostaglandin drugs, oral contraceptives have been found to be helpful for some women. Diet changes, exercises, aspirin, herbal teas, and heat have also been found to be effective.

The Premenstrual Syndrome. The term **premenstrual syndrome (PMS),** first described by Frank (1931), has been used to refer to a variety of symptoms that may occur a few days prior to menstruation. These symptoms include headaches, tenderness of the breasts, swelling, acne, and premenstrual tension (i.e., depression, irritability, lethargy) (Bailey & Cohen, 1999; Roca, Schmidt, & Rubinow, 1999).

A considerable amount of controversy has surrounded PMS. Researchers have failed to agree on the characteristics of PMS (Chrisler, 1997), and the lack of a definition makes it difficult to investigate women's symptoms carefully. PMS is also controversial because some experts report that all women experience the syndrome, and others state that PMS doesn't even exist—that it is a myth (Chrisler, 1997). Still other researchers report that prescribed images of mensturation suggest to women how they "should" feel during their menstrual cycle.

Some researchers point to fluid retention, brain changes, or a decrease in progesterone levels during the premenstrual period as possible factors in negative moods (Dalton, 1964; Janowsky, Berens, & Davis, 1973). Others, however, point out that stress-producing social factors—being fired from one's job or getting a divorce—may play a decisive role in PMS symptoms (Parlee, 1993). Whatever the causes for PMS, few can deny that the culturally defined negative social attitudes about menstruation can seriously influence a woman's perceptions of her own bodily states, as the research by Marvan and Escobedo (1999) and Chrisler and Zittel (1998) suggests.

For example, Marvan and Escobedo (1999) asked women to view a videotape that described menstrual cycle (control group) or a videotape that described premenstrual syndrome and its negative consequences in women's lives (experimental group). Marvan and Escobedo reported that for women in the control group, there were no differences in premenstrual symptoms reported before and after watching the video. Women who viewed the video on premenstrual syndrome, however, reported significantly more severe premenstrual syndrome after they watched the video.

Research does indicate that some women have mild to severe mood swings that are related to their menstrual cycles. The data simply demonstrate a correlation between cycle phase of hormone levels and mood (Chrisler, 1997). From this correlation, it is unwarranted to infer that hormones actually cause or influence mood.

Research on the relationship of moods to menstrual cycle has suggested that the mood change is related to women's attitudes about menstruation (Parlee, 1993). Carol Nagy Jacklin (1989) summarized the literature on hormones and behavior in the following way:

> A word of warning: Correlations between hormones and behavior are typically interpreted as cases in which the biological causes the psychological. It fits our predispositions to assume that hormones cause behavioral outcomes. The hormone system is an open system. Much more empirical work is needed before the direction of the causal arrows are understood. (p. 130)

Certainly, research that has included men as participants has provided another view to the literature on cycles and mood changes. McFarlane and Williams (1994), for example, studied 60 women and 10 men for 12 to 18 weeks, during which time they obtained daily mood data. McFarlane and Williams matched mood ratings against information about menstrual cycles, lunar cycles, and days of the week. They reported that two-thirds of the men and women exhibited cycles in their moods. The mood cycles varied by individual; few of them matched any premenstrual anxiety.

In many cultures and many religions, menstruating women are seen as unclean (Chrisler & Zittel, 1998). The words of Leviticus 15:19–33 speak most clearly of this belief. Women's position in all of the books of the Bible depends on the following rules in Leviticus:

> And if a woman have an issue, and her issue in her flesh be blood, she shall be put apart seven days: and whosoever toucheth her shall be unclean until the even.
>
> And every thing that she lieth upon in her separation shall be unclean: every thing also that she sitteth upon shall be unclean.
>
> And whosoever toucheth her bed shall wash his clothes, and bathe himself in water, and be unclean until the even. . . .
>
> And if any man lie with her at all, and her flowers be upon him, he shall be unclean seven days; and all the bed whereon he lieth shall be unclean. . . .
>
> Thus shall ye separate the children of Israel from their uncleanness; that they die not in their uncleanness, when they defile my tabernacle that is among them.
>
> This is the law of him that hath an issue, and of him whose seed goeth from him, and is defiled therewith. . . .

In Western culture, many women abstain from sexual intercourse during menstruation. Because all women have the same hormone cycles but the correlated psychological cycles are different, the latter must be influenced by cultural attitudes

(Huffnagel, 1999). Girls' and women's attitudes and feelings about menarche are most important (Golub, 1992).

Brook Gunn and Anne Petersen (1984) reported that adolescent girls who have negative attitudes toward menstruation will experience the most depression and discomfort in their menstrual cycles. Adolescent girls with the most liberal attitudes about gender roles and sexuality will experience less menstrual pain than adolescent girls with more conservative attitudes. Research has also suggested that girls who reach menarche prior to age 12 years feel the most "abnormal" about menstruation.

Many adults, as well as the media, emphasize only the hygienic aspects of menstruation, thus perpetuating the belief that menstruation is unclean and should be hidden from others in an ashamed manner. Negative attitudes about menstruation have been found to be related to health problems. Adolescent girls, while attempting to rid their bodies of what they have been socialized to believe are unclean odors, will use vaginal deodorants, deodorized tampons, and douches. These products irritate their genital tissues and may create vaginal infections.

Early Versus Late Puberty.   The age at which puberty is reached has a considerable impact on girls' behavior during adolescence (Ge, Conger, & Elder, 1996; Swar & Richards, 1996) and generally poses a source of anxiety and embarrassment. These concerns affect the development of girls' and women's self-concept and identity.

For example, girls who mature early usually begin dating earlier and will more often express less self-confidence than girls who reach puberty at a later age. Early maturers also express dissatisfaction with their bodies, feel isolated from other girls their own age who haven't reached puberty, and make lower grades (Blyth, Simmins, & Zakin, 1985). In addition, early-maturing adolescent girls have imposed on them sexual responsibilities that they are not ready to accept, considering the fact that their intellectual, social, and emotional maturity lag behind their physical maturity. Longitudinal studies have reported that, by adulthood, early-maturing girls exhibit a high level of cognitive mastery and coping skills as a result of their role-taking experiences throughout adolescence (Livson & Peskin, 1980).

Adolescent girls who mature later tend to be more tense, have low self-esteem, and more actively seek attention than non-later-maturing girls. Once menarche is reached, however, these feelings of low self-esteem diminish (Brooks-Gunn, Newman, & Holderness, 1994; Lackovic-Grgin, Dekovic, & Opacic, 1994; Spencer, Dupree, & Swanson, 1998).

The advantages of early or late maturation depend on the communication that exists between adolescent girls and their adult caretakers. Girls who have had adults discuss with them the emotional and social ramifications of early or late puberty ad-

---

MEET DR. ANNE PETERSEN

Question: Can you summarize the research on girls' early and late puberty?

Dr. Petersen's response: Early, but not late, maturation appears to have negative effects for girls in the United States. Early maturation is related to poorer body image and more depression, effects that persist at least until age 17. It is also linked to earlier engagement in sex and "problem behaviors" (e.g., drugs, alcohol, delinquency). Late maturation confers, in general, no negative and some positive effects (e.g., better body image). These results are seen in other developed countries—except in Germany, where early maturers have a positive body image (presumably because in that country more zaftig shapes are still preferred).

Negative effects are exacerbated when (1) girls change schools (any change including beginning junior high or middle school) at the same time that they're going through puberty or (2) when there are significant simultaneous family changes (e.g., divorce). They are reduced with good, supportive relationships with parents; there is no effect of good peer relationships.

---

just more successfully to their physical maturation than girls whose families have less time to invest in such discussions (Spencer et al., 1998).

Dale Blyth and his colleagues (Blyth et al., 1985) pointed out the need to consider the school environment in relation to specific body image dimensions, especially a youth culture that supports an ideal of thinness in women. In the United States, girls are considered most feminine if they meet the cultural ideal (large breasts, but generally thin). Adolescent girls are commonly concerned about body size and image rather than health (Ferron, 1997). For example, Ferron (1997) found that compared to U.S. adolescent girls, French girls believe that an ideal body is impossible to attain; they believe their physique is predetermined. U.S. adolescent girls in Ferron's sample, however, were more likely than French girls to engage in behaviors that are harmful to their health, including engaging in anorexic and bulimic behaviors. Thus, U.S. adolescent girls reported being more concerned with the social appeal of their appearance (Ferron, 1997). We will address these issues in more detail in Chapter 5.

Adolescent girls do not typically view the normal developmental process of pubescence and puberty positively. The socializing agents contribute to adolescent girls' perceptions about their bodies. Pipher (1994), after examining the adjustment problems faced by adolescent girls searching for beauty, concluded that adolescent girls suffer psychologically from negative body image, lowered self-esteem, and achievement conflicts—all as a consequence of the culture's messages about women's bodies needing to be protected, made more beautiful, and preserved.

MIDDLE AND LATE ADULTHOOD

Unlike the periods of infancy and adolescence, there is no one biological or psychological event that signals the beginning of women's middle or later adulthood (Arnett, 2000). Developmental psychologists identify the life stage of adulthood as describing events that occur after age 20 until death. Some developmental psychologists have organized the life stage of adulthood into early or young adulthood (20 to 40 years), middle adulthood (40 to 65 years), older adulthood (65 to 85 years), and the old old or very old (85 years and older). There is, however, no empirical research to support universally applicable stages of adult development (Bee, 1996). Several events often occur during these years, including employment, child rearing, romantic relationships, retirement, and physical changes. These events or developmental tasks of middle and later adulthood do not occur in all individuals at the same time or in the same sequence. And these developmental tasks may not be experienced by all women in middle and late adulthood (Arnett, 2000).

Life Expectancy

The **life expectancy** for women is 79.2 years; for men, it is 73.0 years (U.S. Bureau of the Census, 1993). Life expectancy in the United States is approximately six years longer for white individuals than for people of color. For example, the equivalent life expectancy figures for African American women and men are 74.3 years and 65.6 years, respectively. The United States Census (1993) reported that life expectancies are shorter for Mexican Americans and Native Americans.

Among the very old, people of color have longer life expectancies than white individuals. This fact supports the theory that people of color who live to be very old exhibit hardiness (Clark, Maddox, & Steinhauser, 1993).

Because women generally live longer than men, the ratio of women to men increases with age. Older women significantly outnumber older men in most parts of the world. By the time women are 85 years old or older, there are 220 women to every 100 men (Bee, 1996).

Environmental and biological explanations have been offered to explain this sex difference in longevity. For example, hormonal and genetic factors increase women's resistance to certain diseases, including cardiovascular disease (Bee, 1996). Another contributing factor is the more frequent utilization of health services by women.

We will discuss women's health issues in more detail in Chapter 5. A brief overview of women's health problems is presented here. As we will discuss in Chapter 5, lung cancer surpasses breast cancer as the leading cause of cancer death for women. While more men than women die from pulmonary causes, there has been a leveling off in deaths of white men, whereas for white and African American women and African American men there has been an increase (Klonoff, Landrine, & Scott, 1995). In addition, women have a higher death rate than men for strokes since they live longer and are thus more likely to suffer cerebral accidents.

Breast cancer is the second leading cause of cancer deaths among women 35 and 55 years old (George, 2000; Meyerowitz, Bull, & Perez, 2000). Breast self-examination for breast lumps is used by only a fraction of the women who will benefit from it (George, 2000). Older women, who are at greater risk for breast cancer, are least likely to examine their breasts (Fulmore, 1999). The failure of women to use breast self-examination may result from women being discouraged from touching their bodies. This may be especially true for older women who were socialized in a cohort that discouraged self-touching (Paludi, Paludi, & Doyle, in press). Since the etiology of breast cancer is unknown, early detection is important to reduce mortality (George, 2000).

The number of women with Alzheimer's disease is twofold to threefold that of afflicted men (Laakso, Hallikainen, Haenninen, Partanen, & Soininen, 2000; Ott, Lampane, & Gambassi, 2000). Women are also more likely than men to be subject to chronic and disabling diseases, for example, diabetes, arthritis, and hypertension (Hayflick, 1994).

We should note, however, that the mortality rates for ethnic minority women are greater than for white women for all major causes of death (Klonoff et al., 1995). The death rate for men is higher than for women, but African American women *and* men have a higher death rate than white individuals do. For example, African American women are more prone to have heart disease, obesity, hypertension, nutritional deficiencies, and   digestive problems (e.g., gastritis, ulcers, and cirrhosis of the liver). And African American women in lower-income families have higher mortality rates from breast cancer and cervical cancer than are reported in the general population. With respect to breast cancer, research suggests dramatically differing survival rates by race, controlling for access to health care (Richardson, Landrine, & Marks, 1994).

Asian/Pacific Islander elderly women are prone to hypertension, tuberculosis, malnutrition, eye failure (from working in poorly lighted areas), and alcoholism. These conditions are related to poor housing and poverty. They are also less likely to use formal health care services (Bee, 1996).

The major health problems of Native Americans include tuberculosis, diabetes, liver disease, kidney disease, malnutrition, and hypertension. Many do not utilize health care services because they live in isolated areas with unreliable transportation and limited resources (Agree, 1987). Latinas suffer from cardiovascular conditions, obesity, arthritis, anemia, and hypertension. Marieskind (1980) noted that, through their work, they may be exposed to potentially harmful pesticides that put them at greater risk for health problems. In addition, many Latinas do not utilize health care services (Russo, Amaro, & Winter, 1987). Many ethnic minority women have less access to health services and may be exposed to more hazardous conditions at their jobs, in addition to having an inadequate water supply and poor sanitation (Marieskind, 1980).

Changes in Physical Appearance and Physiology

Women's physical appearance begins to change in midlife (Ausman & Russell, 1990; Bee, 1996; Etaugh, 1993). Women's hair becomes grayer and coarser. Their weight increases until approximately 50 years of age and declines thereafter. Adipose tissue becomes redistributed again, decreasing in the legs, lower arms, and face, while increasing in the buttocks, upper arms, and abdomen. Beginning in the fourth decade of life, the disks between the spinal vertebrae compress, resulting in a loss of height of 1 to 2 inches. Women's bones become more brittle and porous and may lead to the appearance of **"dowager's hump."** Wrinkles and age spots may develop (Bee, 1996; Hayflick, 1994). These changes that are associated with growing older do not necessarily translate into any direct effect on our health or daily functioning (Ausman & Russell, 1990).

In addition, our muscle tissue slowly declines in tone, flexibility, and strength. Our pulmonary, cardiovascular, and excretory systems become less efficient. Our joints become less flexible and more brittle. These physical changes are not necessarily incapacitating (Hayflick, 1994).

Menopause refers to the cessation of menstrual periods. It technically occurs when a woman has not menstruated for one year. Women may experience menopause very abruptly; other women may skip two periods, resume menstruating each month and then skip one or two cycles again. Most women experience menopause around their 50th year (Leiblum, 1990). The age range is very large, however. Women may experience menopause in their late 30s or their early 60s.

Although the term *menopause* is used to describe the cessation of menstruation, it more precisely refers to several years of physical changes, referred to as the **climacteric,** which lasts approximately fifteen years. During this transitional time, fertility decreases and several physical symptoms appear. For example, women experience **hot flashes**—feelings of intense heat in the face, neck, and upper chest that last for a few minutes at a time. Weight gain is also common during menopause (Leiblum, 1990). Some women have reported physical symptoms such as fatigue, headaches, tingling sensations, and dizziness (Leiblum, 1990). Not all women experience all of these symptoms, however; 16 to 80 percent of women are free of menopausal symptoms (Golub, 1992).

The major change during the climacteric is the aging of women's ovaries. During this time, the ovaries are less able to respond to two hormones—FSH and LH—produced by the pituitary glands. There is also a decline in the output of two products of the ovaries: ova and the sex hormones, progestogens and estrogens. The ovaries experience a decrease in follicle development, sex hormone secretion, and ovulation. The decline in estrogens and progestogens results in inadequate uterine stimulation, excess secretion of FSH and LH, and, consequently, the end of menstruation. As a result of the decline in estrogens, changes take place in sexual organs, including decreased vaginal lubrication, decreased vaginal size, and thinning of the vaginal epithelium. These changes may contribute to increased pain during vaginal intercourse. However, the decline in estrogens does not lower women's sexual desire, sexual interest, or ability to have orgasms.

In the 1960s, menopausal women were frequently prescribed large doses of estrogen in what was referred to as **estrogen-replacement therapy.** Physicians believed that menopausal symptoms, especially hot flashes, could be cured by supplying estrogen. Estrogen was also recommended to help prevent **osteoporosis**—an excessive loss of bone tissue, which results in the bones becoming thinner, brittle, and more porous (Golub, 1992). Fractures from osteoporosis are likely to occur and can result in death. Because women who received estrogen-replacement therapy were found to be more likely to develop endometrial and breast cancer than women not given estrogen (Seidler, 1984), most women do not receive estrogen for menopausal symptoms.

Penny Budoff (1983) has suggested that any danger of estrogen-replacement therapy is offset by combining estrogen with progestin or progesterone. Physicians recommend increased calcium intake and regular exercise to prevent osteoporosis.

Estrogen alleviates hot flashes, but they return when the estrogen-replacement therapy ceases (Voda & Eliasson, 1985). The drug etidronate, when combined with calcium, appears to be more effective than hormone therapy.

Attitudes Toward Menopause

The term *menopause* may be frightening for some women. Negative responses to a normative event in women's lives are perpetuated in the media and folklore. Menopausal women are frequently portrayed in television dramas as having intense mood swings or as being nervous, irritable, and unable to get along with friends and family.

Menopause is an important event in women's development. It may be experienced positively or with fear, depending on a variety of factors (Sommer et al., 1999). For example, some women have reported that menopause symbolizes unattractiveness and stagnation and, consequently, emptiness (Leiblum, 1990). For other women, menopause signifies a time to redirect one's energies and develop new skills. Many women go back to school or to work—or begin these pursuits for the first time in their lives. Some women may worry that menopause means the end of sexual expression (Im & Meleis, 2000). However, other women report that menopause is sexually liberating because it means that sexual intercourse and pregnancy are no longer related (Leiblum, 1990).

Neugarten (1973) interviewed 100 women who ranged in age from 45 to 55 years. The women were asked to discuss the aspects of middle adulthood that concerned them the most. Only 4 of the 100 women included menopause in their lists. Women's concerns included becoming a widow and becoming older, with little assistance from friends and family.

Neugarten also reported that women were more positive about their own experiences than when they were asked to rate other "women in menopause." They rated themselves as pleasant, calm, optimistic, healthy, happy, and useful. Typically, younger women have had more negative views of menopause than did middle-aged and older women (Etaugh, 1993).

Research has suggested that menopausal symptomatology is a product of culture as well as biology (Im & Meleis, 2000; Sommer et al., 1999). Rhoda Unger (1979) noted:

> Very few women of the Rajput class show any effect of menopause other than menstrual-cycle change—there is no depression, dizziness, or physical incapacitation. . . . In our culture, on the other hand, menopause is a time of punishment rather than reward. The woman has lost her youth without any compensating gain in status. The

"menopausal syndrome" appears to be a phenomenon largely limited to Western European and American women. In fact, one intriguing finding indicates that West African women increased in number of subjective menopausal symptoms in direct relation to the amount of contact they had with European women. (p. 407)

Some women do exhibit heightened psychological distress during menopause, but their behavior must not be attributed only to biological processes. Numerous changes in social roles occur in midlife, including confronting aging, coping with illness or death of a mate, separation or divorce, new marriage, new job, attending college or graduate school, difficult teenagers, and aging parents who require care (McKinlay, McKinlay, & Brambilla, 1987).

Double Standard of Aging

The research on women's experiences with menopause supports the belief that there is a **double standard of aging** (Sontag, 1979) in North American culture as well as in other societies (Etaugh, 1993). Aging in women alters the qualities of "femininity" in a culture: Attractiveness, desirability, reproductive capacity, and caring. The identical changes that take place as women and men age (e.g., graying hair, wrinkles) enhance "masculinity" but diminish "femininity" (Heilbrun, 1991). Because "masculinity" is identified with autonomy, independence, self-control, and competency, aging does not threaten these qualities. However, aging does threaten the qualities of "femininity" in our culture: attractiveness, desirability, reproductive capacity, and nurturance.

Concern with one's appearance is characteristic of middle-aged and older ethnic minority women as well as of white women (Alston & Rose, 1981). Older women thus lose their value because they are viewed as lacking both beauty and youth.

Carolyn Heilbrun (1991) has remarked that "signs of age come upon women in our society like marks of the devil in earlier times" (p. 56). Middle-aged and older women may strive to achieve the physique and facial features of younger women so as to be "accepted" by a culture that values young women's bodies (see Chapter 5). As Heilbrun noted:

We need to continue to alter the societal influences that lead women to be valued for only their youth and physical appearance. We must learn to move with confidence into a new, as yet unnamed, life. A life, birth and not death, where we live by what we do, not by how we look or who looks at us. In the disguise of age, we explore and then live in this new world. (p. 58)

NEW TERMS

adipose tissue

adolescence

adrenogenital syndrome

amenorrhea

androgen

anovulatory period

antiprostaglandin drugs

areola

body (of the uterus)

cephalocaudal development

cervix

cilia

climacteric

clitoral hood

clitoris

corpus luteum

cortisol

double standard of aging

dowager's hump

dysmenorrhea

embryonic period

endometrium

estrogen

estrogen-replacement therapy

external sexual organs

fallopian tubes

female viability

fetal period

follicles

follicle-stimulating hormone (FSH)

follicular phase

fundus

germinal period

gonadotrophins

hot flashes

hymen

hypothalamus

internal sexual organs

introitus

labia majora

labia minora

life expectancy

luteal phase

luteinizing hormone (LH)

mammary glands

mefenamic acid

menarche

menopause

menorrhagia

menstrual fluid

menstruation

mittelschmerz

mons pubis

myometrium

nipple

osteoporosis

ovaries

ovulation

ovulatory phase

pectoral muscles

perimetrium

premenstrual syndrome (PMS)

prenatal period

prepuce

primitive streak

progesterone

progestin   uterus
prostaglandins   vagina
proximodistal development   vaginal barrier
puberty   vaginal mucosa
pubescence   vulva
pubic symphysis   X chromosome
sudden infant death syndrome   Y chromosome
Turner's syndrome   zygote

CHAPTER REVIEW QUESTIONS

1. Discuss what is meant by greater female viability.

2. What is Turner's syndrome?

3. Outline the developmental stages of pubescence for girls.

4. Discuss the research concerning mood swings and performance during the menstrual cycle.

5. Discuss how the perception of body change is magnified by cultural factors.

6. Design an educational program about menarche for girls in junior high school. What topics would you include? Why?

7. What is PMS?

8. Distinguish between early and late puberty. What are the advantages and disadvantages of both for adolescent girls?

9. What charaterizes the climacteric for women?

10. Discuss the controversy surrounding menopausal women taking estrogen.

11. What recommendations can you make for women wishing to learn more about their physical health?

12. Offer suggestions for changing individual's perceptions about aging women.

SELECTED READINGS

Boston Women's Health Book Collective. (1996). *The new our bodies, ourselves: A book by and for women.* New York: Simon & Schuster.

Golub, S. (1992). *Periods: From menarche to menopause.* Newbury Park, CA: Sage.

Hyde, J. S., & DeLamater, J. (1999). *Understanding human sexuality.* New York: McGraw Hill.

LEARNING MORE ABOUT . . .

Suggestions for Term Papers and Independent Studies Related to *Physical Development Across the Female Life Cycle*

Ways to empower women about their gynecological health

Media portrayal of menopausal women

Relationship among hormonal fluctuations, mood changes, and performance

Feminist approaches to PMS

Ethnic differences in mortality and morbidity ratesw

TAKING ACTION . . .

on *Physical Development Across the Female Life Cycle*

A relative of yours knows you are taking a course on the psychology of women. She asks you to help her with the following situation. She picked up her preteen daughter from school, and her daughter raised the issue of watching a film about "growing up." Her daughter asked what her mother thinks will be covered in the video. Your relative postponed giving a response and now wants you to help her. How would you answer the mother's concerns?

1. She feels embarrassed about telling her daughter about the "facts of life."

2. She isn't sure what topics are appropriate for her discussion.

   Should she include:

   Menstruation?

   Intercourse?

   Biology of the menstrual cycle?

   Emotional components of menstruation?

   Lesbian and gay relationships?

3. She needs some advice about how to deal with her daughter if the girl is uncomfortable to be around the boys in her class following her viewing of the film.

REFERENCES

Adams, G., Montemayor, R., & Gullotta, T. (Eds.). (1996). *Psychosocial development during adolescence.* Thousand Oaks, CA: Sage.

Agree, E. M. (1987). *A portrait of older minorities.* Washington, DC: American Association of Retired Persons, Minority Affairs Initiative.

Alston, D., & Rose, N. (1981). Perceptions of middle-aged Black women. *Journal of General Psychology, 104,* 167–171.

Arnett, J. (2000). Emerging adulthood: A theory of development from the late teens through the twenties. *American Psychologist, 55,* 469–480.

Ausman, L., & Russell, R. (1990). Nutrition and aging. In E. Schneider & J. Rowe (Eds.), *Handbook on the biology of aging.* New York: Academic Press.

Bailey, J., & Cohen, L. (1999). Prevalence of mood and anxiety disorders in women who seek treatment for premenstrual syndrome. *Journal of Women's Health and Gender Based Medicine, 8,* 1181–1184.

Baker, S., & Ehrhardt, A. (1978). Prenatal androgen, intelligence, and cognitive sex differences. In R. Friedman (Ed.), *Sex differences in behavior.* Huntington, NY: Krieger.

Bee, H. (1996). *The journey of adulthood.* Upper Saddle River, NJ: Prentice Hall.

Bem, S. (1981). Gender schema theory: A cognitive account of sex typing. *Psychological Review, 88,* 354–364.

Blyth, D., Simmins, R. G., & Zakin, D. F. (1985). Satisfaction with body image for early adolescent females: The impact of pubertal timing within different school environments. Time of maturation and psychosocial functioning in adolescence: I[Special issue]. *Journal of Youth and Adolescence, 14,* 207–225.

Brooks-Gunn, J., Newman, D., & Holderness, C. (1994). The experience of breast development and girls' stories about the purchase of a bra. *Journal of Youth and Adolescence, 23,* 539–565.

Budoff, P. (1983). *No more hot flashes and other good news.* New York: Putnam.

Chen, Z., & Siegler, R. (2000). Intellectual development in childhood. In R. Sternberg (Ed.), *Handbook of intelligence.* New York: Cambridge University Press.

Chrisler, J. (1997). PMS as culture bound. In J. Chrisler, C. Golden, & P. Rozee (Eds.), *Lectures on the psychology of women.* New York: McGraw-Hill.

Chrisler, J., & Zittel, C. (1998). Menarche stories: Reminiscences of college students from Lithuania, Malaysia, Sudan, and the United States. *Health Care for Women International, 19,* 303–312.

Clark, D., Maddox, G., & Steinhauser, K. (1993). Race, aging, and functional health. *Journal of Aging and Health, 5,* 536–539.

Cratty, B. (1979). *Perceptual and motor development in infants and children.* Englewood Cliffs, NJ: Prentice Hall.

Dalton, K. (1964). *The premenstrual syndrome.* Springfield, IL: Thomas.

Doerholt, D., Noeker, M., Ranke, M., & Haverkamp, F. (1999). Body height, body image and general well-being in adult women with Turner's syndrome. In U. Eiholzer et al. (Eds.), *Growth, stature, and psychosocial well-being.* Seattle, WA: Hogrefe & Huber Publishers.

Ehrhardt, A., & Baker, S. (1978). Fetal androgens, human central nervous system differentiation, and behavior and social dominance in man. *Psychosomatic Medicine, 36,* 469–475.

Ehrhardt, A., & Meyer-Bahlberg, H. (1975). Psychological correlates of abnormal pubertal development. *Clinics in Endocrinology and Metabolism, 4,* 207–222.

Ellwood, M., & Stolberg, A. (1993). The effects of family composition, family health, parenting behavior and environmental stress on children's divorce adjustment. *Journal of Child and Family Studies, 2,* 23–36.

Etaugh, C. (1993). Psychology of women: Middle and older adulthood. In F. L. Denmark & M. A. Paludi (Eds.), *Psychology of women: A handbook of issues and theories.* Westport, CT: Greenwood Press.

Feingold, A. (1993). Cognitive gender differences: A developmental perspective. *Sex Roles, 29,* 91–112.

Feldman, R. (1998). *Child development.* Upper Saddle River, NJ: Prentice Hall.

Ferron, C. (1997). Body image in adolescence: Cross-cultural research-results of the preliminary phase of a quantitative survey. *Adolescence, 32,* 735–744.

Frank, R. (1931). The hormonal causes of premenstrual tension. *Archives of Neurology and Psychiatry, 26,* 1053–1057.

Frisch, R. (1984). Fatness, puberty, and fertility. In J. Gunn & A. Petersen (Eds.), *Girls at puberty.* New York: Plenum Press.

Fulmore, C. (1999). Applying cognitive-social theory of health protective behavior to breast self-examination. *Dissertation Abstracts International, 60* (3–B), 1300.

Ge, X., Conger, R., & Elder, G. (1996). Coming of age too early: Pubertal influences on girls' vulnerability to psychological distress. *Child Development, 67,* 386–400.

George, S. (2000). Barriers to breast cancer screening: An integrative review. *Health Care for Women International, 21,* 53–65.

Golub, S. (1992). *Periods: From menarche to menopause.* Newbury Park, CA: Sage.

Gunn, J., & Petersen, A. (Eds.). (1984). *Girls at puberty: Biological, psychological, and social perspectives.* New York: Plenum Press.

Hamerton, J., et al. (1975). A cytogenetic survey of 14,069 newborn infants. *Clinical Genetics, 8,* 223–243.

Hayflick, L. (1994). *How and why we age.* New York: Ballantine Books.

Heilbrun, C. (1991). *The last gift of time: Life beyond sixty.* New York: Dell.

Huffnagel, G. (1999). A cultural analysis of the evolution of menarche and menstruation: Implications for education. *Dissertation Abstracts International, 60* (6–A), 2256.

Hutt, C. (1978). Biological base of psychological sex differences. *American Journal of Diseases of Children, 132,* 170–177.

Hyde, J. S., & DeLamater, J. (1999). *Understanding human sexuality.* New York: McGraw Hill.

Im, E., & Meleis, A. (2000). Meanings of menopause to Korean immigrant women. *Western Journal of Nursing Research, 22,* 84–102.

Jacklin, C. N. (1989). Female and male: Issues of gender. *American Psychologist, 44,* 127–133.

Jacklin, C. N., & Maccoby, E. (1982). Length of labor and sex of offspring. *Journal of Pediatric Psychology, 7,* 355–360.

Janowsky, D., Berens, S., & Davis, J. (1973). Correlations between mood, weight, and electrolytes during the menstrual cycle: A reinangiotension-aldosterone hypothesis of premenstrual tension. *Psychosomatic Medicine, 35,* 143–154.

Kagan-Krieger, S. (1999). The struggle to understand oneself as a woman: Stress, coping and the psychological development of women with Turner Syndrome. *Dissertation Abstracts International, 59* (12–A), 4368.

Katchadorian, H. (1977). *The biology of adolescence.* San Francisco: Freeman.

Kimmel, E., & Rudolph, T. (1998). Growing up female. In K. Borman et al. (Eds.), *The adolescent years: Social influences and educational challenges.* Chicago, IL: The National Society for the Study of Education.

Klonoff, E., Landrine, H., & Scott, J. (1995). Double jeopardy: Ethnicity and gender in health research. In H. Landrine (Ed.), *Bringing cultural diversity to feminist psychology.* Washington, DC: American Psychological Association.

Laasko, M., Hallikainen, J., Haenninen, T., Partanen, K., & Soininen, H. (2000). Diagnosis of Alzheimer's disease: MRI of the hippocampus vs. delayed recall. *Neuropsychologia, 38,* 579–584.

Lackovic-Grgin, K., Dekovic, M., & Opacic, G. (1994). Pubertal status, interaction with significant others, and self-esteem of adolescent girls. *Adolescence, 29,* 691–700.

Lauder, T., Williams, M., Campbell, C., Davis, G., Sherman, R., & Pulos, E. (1999). The female athlete triad: Prevalence in military women. *Military Medicine, 164,* 630–635.

Leiblum, S. R. (1990). Sexuality and the midlife woman. *Psychology of Women Quarterly, 14,* 495–508.

Livson, N., & Peskin, H. (1980). Perspectives on adolescence from longitudinal research. In J. Adelson (Ed.), *Handbook of adolescent psychology.* New York: Wiley.

Maccoby, E., & Jacklin, C. N. (1974). *The psychology of sex differences.* Stanford, CA: Stanford University Press.

Marvan, M., & Escobedo, C. (1999). Premenstrual symptomatology: Role of prior knowledge about premenstrual syndrome. *Psychosomatic Medicine, 61,* 163–167.

Marieskind, H. (1980). *Women in the health care system . . . patients, providers, and programs.* St. Louis: Mosby.

McFarlane, J., & Williams, T. (1994). Placing premenstrual syndrome in perspective. *Psychology of Women Quarterly, 18,* 339–373.

McKinlay, J., McKinlay, S., & Brambilla, D. (1987). Health status and utilization behavior associated with menopause. *American Journal of Epidemiology, 125,* 110–121.

Meyerowitz, B., Bull, A., & Perez, M. (2000). Cancers common in women. In R. Eisler et al. (Eds.), *Handbook of gender, culture, and health.* Mahwah, NJ: Erlbaum.

Money, J. (1964). Two cytogenetic syndromes: Psychological comparisons: I. Intelligence and specific-factor quotients. *Journal of Psychiatric Research, 2,* 223–231.

Neugarten, B. (1973). A new look at menopause. In C. Tavris (Ed.), *The female experience.* Del Mar, CA: Communications/Research Machines.

Newman, B., & Newman, P. (1975). *Development through life.* Homewood, IL: Dorsey.

Ott, B., Lapane, K., & Gambassi, G. (2000). Gender differences in the treatment of behavior problems in Alzheimer's disease. *Neurology, 54,* 427–432.

Paludi, M. (Ed.). (2001). *Human development in multicultural contexts: A book of readings.* Englewood Cliffs, NJ: Prentice Hall.

Paludi, M., Paludi, C., & Doyle, J. (in press). *Sex and gender* (5th ed.). New York: McGraw Hill.

Parlee, M. B. (1993). Cyclicity. In F. L. Denmark & M. A. Paludi (Eds.), *The psychology of women: A handbook of issues and theories.* Westport, CT: Greenwood Press.

Petersen, A., & Taylor, B. (1980). The biological approach to adolescence. In J. Adelson (Ed.), *Handbook of adolescent psychology.* New York: Wiley.

Pipher, M. (1994). *Reviving Ophelia: Saving the selves of adolescent girls.* New York: Ballantine Books.

Powell, M., & Schulte, T. (1999). Turner syndrome. In S. Goldstein et al. (Eds.), *Handbook of neurodevelopmental and genetic disorders in children.* New York: The Guilford Press.

Powers, P. (1999). The last word: Athletes and eating disorders. *Eating Disorders: The Journal of Treatment and Prevention, 7,* 249–255.

Rathus, J. (1988). *Human sexuality.* New York: Holt, Rinehart and Winston.

Rathus, S. (1983). *Human sexuality.* New York: Holt, Rinehart and Winston.

Reid, P. T., Haritos, C., Kelly, E., & Holland, N. (1995). Socialization of girls: Issues of ethnicity in gender development. In H. Landrine (Ed.), *Bringing cultural diversity to feminist psychology.* Washington, DC: American Psychological Association.

Reid, P. T., & Paludi, M. A. (1993). Psychology of women: Conception to adolescence. In F. L. Denmark & M. A. Paludi (Eds.), *Psychology of women: A handbook of issues and theories.* Westport, CT: Greenwood Press.

Rice, F. (1997). *Child and adolescent development.* Upper Saddle River, NJ: Prentice Hall.

Richardson, J., Landrine, H., & Marks, G. (1994). Does psychological status influence cancer survival? In E. Lewis, C. Sullivan, & J. Barraclough (Eds.), *The psychoimmunology of human cancer: Mind and body in the fight for survival.* Oxford, England: Oxford University Press.

Roca, C., Schmidt, P., & Rubinow, D. (1999). A follow up study of premenstrual syndrome. *Journal of Clinical Psychiatry, 60,* 763–766.

Ross, J., & Zinn, A. (1999). Turner syndrome: Potential hormonal and genetic influences on the neurocognitive profile. In H. Tager-Flusberg, et al. (Eds.), *Neurodevelopmental disorders.* Cambridge, MA: The MIT Press.

Rovet, J., & Buchanan, L. (1999). Turner syndrome: A cognitive neuroscience approach. In H. Tager-Flusberg et al. (Eds.), *Neurodevelopmental disorders.* Cambridge, MA: The MIT Press.

Ruble, D., & Brooks-Gunn, J. (1982). A developmental analysis of menstrual distress in adolescence. In R. Freedman (Ed.), *Behavior and the menstrual cycle.* New York: Marcel Dekker.

Russo, N. F., Amaro, H., & Winter, M. (1987). The use of inpatient mental health services by Hispanic women. *Psychology of Women Quarterly, 11,* 427–442.

Schlesier-Stroop, B. (1984). Bulimia: A review of the literature. *Psychological Bulletin, 95,* 247–257.

Schowalter, J., & Anyan, W. (1981). *Family handbook of adolescence.* New York: Knopf.

Seidler, S. (1984, March/April). ERT: Drug company sales vs. women's health. *Network News,* p. 7.

Sommer, B., Avis, N., Meyer, P., Ory, M., Madden, T., Kagawa-Singer, M., Mouton, C., Rasow, N., & Adler, S. (2000). Attitudes toward menopause and aging across ethnic/racial groups. *Psychosomatic Medicine, 62,* 96.

Sontag, S. (1979). The double standard of aging. In J. Williams (Ed.), *Psychology of women: Selected readings.* New York: Norton.

Spencer, M., Dupree, D., & Swanson, D. (1998). The influence of physical maturation and hassles on African American adolescents' learning behaviors. *Journal of Comparative Family Studies, 29,* 189–200.

Steinberg, L. (1999). *Adolescence.* New York: McGraw Hill.

Story, M., Mays, R., Bishop, D., Perry, B, Taylor, G., Smyth, M., & Gray, C. (2000). 5-a-Day Power Plus: Process evaluation of a multicomponent elementary school program to increase fruit and vegetable consumption. *Health Education and Behavior, 27,* 187–200.

Strickland, B. (1988). Sex-related differences in health and illness. *Psychology of Women Quarterly, 12,* 381–399.

Swar, A., & Richards, M. (1996). Longitudinal effects of adolescent girls' pubertal development, perceptions of pubertal timing, and parental relations on eating problems. *Developmental Psychology, 32,* 636–646.

Tanner, J. (1962). *Growth at adolescence.* Oxford, England: Blackwell.

Travis, C. (1993). Women and health. In F. L. Denmark & M. A. Paludi (Eds.), *The psychology of women: A handbook of issues and theories.* Westport, CT: Greenwood Press.

Unger, R. (1979). *Female and male: Psychological perspectives.* New York: Harper & Row.

U.S. Bureau of the Census. (1993). *Statistical Abstract of the United States: 1993.* Washington, DC: U.S. Government Printing Office.

Voda, A., & Eliasson, M. (1985). Menopause: The closure of menstrual life. In S. Golub (Ed.), *Lifting the curse of menstruation.* New York: Haworth Press.

Vogeltanz, N., Sigmon, S., & Vickers, K. (1998). Feminism and behavior analysis: A framework for women's health research and practice. In J. Plaud et al. (Eds.), *From behavior theory to behavior therapy.* Boston: Allyn & Bacon.

FOUR

THEORETICAL PERSPECTIVES ON WOMEN'S PERSONALITIES AND MENTAL HEALTH

IN WOMEN'S VOICES

The ways of Native American women who choose to follow the healing path include the following: the way of the daughter, the way of the householder, the way of the mother, the way of the teacher, and the way of the wise woman.

Teresa LaFromboise, Sandra Bennett Choney, Amy James, and Paulette Running Wolf

~

So to see how it feels to be on the wrong end of the Freudian myth, as well as to exorcise its power with laughter once and for all, I propose that everyone in the psychology trade, male or female, plus male human beings in general—indeed, all of us in this Freudianized culture—imagine a profession and a society influenced by the work, even the worship, of the greatest, most written about, mythic, and fiercely defended thinker in the Western world: Dr. Phyllis Freud.

Gloria Steinem

~

As a feminist therapist, I am aware that our best work comes out of our experience as women working with women. Only if our theory remains close to and within the world of women can it be a truly woman-based theory. The viewpoint must be female rather than male, as it has usually been.

Hannah Lerman

~

As a feminist therapist, I had had ample opportunity to observe the negative synergy of trauma and silence, abuse and secrecy, that would lead women to feel and act crazy, when in fact it was mainly the context in which they were forced to operate that was pathological.

Laura S. Brown

Chapter Outline

Questions for Reflection

1. How did you learn what your culture expected in terms of "femininity" and "masculinity"?

2. What kinds of toys did you play with as a child? Were they considered "appropriate" for girls or boys?

3. In what ways you believe women and men treat children differently because of the children's biological sex?

4. From other psychology courses you have taken, what are Sigmund Freud's views about women's personality? Do you support these views? Why or why not?

5. Have you studied the contributions of Karen Horney to personality psychology?

6. Why do you believe more women then men are diagnosed with a mental illness?

7. Why do you believe ethnic minority women underutilize mental health services?

8. If you were asked to list personality characteristics you think of when you hear the word "woman," what terms would you include in your list? Explain why you would list these terms.

INTRODUCTION: GENDER-ROLE STEREOTYPES

For the next few minutes pretend your best friend's mother just called you to tell you that your best friend gave birth to her first child. You are so happy for your friend. What is the first question you ask of her mother? Chances are you asked about the sex of the baby: "Is it a boy or a girl?"

We tend to ask that question first—it serves to help guide our thinking about gifts, color of gifts, how to hold the baby, what is appropriate play with the baby, and so on.

In 1974, Jeffrey Rubin and his colleagues interviewed 30 pairs of parents in the first 24 hours after the birth of their children. Fifteen of the children were girls. While mothers held their infants during the 24-hour period, fathers only viewed their children through the hospital nursery window. Typically, fathers saw their newborn daughters as "softer, finer featured, more awkward, more inattentive, weaker, and more delicate." They saw their newborn sons as "firmer, larger featured, better coordinated, more alert, stronger, and hardier." They thus described day-old infants in terms of gender-role-related characteristics. No sex-related differences existed, however; infant girls and infant boys were identical with respect to birth weight, birth length, and neonatal activity scores! The fathers' *gender-role stereotypes* played an important part in why they viewed their newborn infants so differently.

What are gender-role stereotypes? First, stereotypes refer to individuals' thoughts and beliefs. They typically do not correspond with reality (Ashmore & DelBoca, 1981). A stereotype is a "picture in the head" not an accurate mirror of the real world. Stereotypes occur when people are classified by others as having something in common because they are members of a particular group or category of people. Gender stereotyping in particular is a psychological process that illustrates individuals' structured sets of beliefs about the personal attributes of males and females (Fiske, 1993; Fiske & Stevens, 1993; Paludi, Paludi, & Doyle, in press). When asked to think of "a woman," for example, individuals may think of "passive," "submissive," "caring," or "dependent."

Additional research supports the findings that adults' behavior is the result of stereotypes and does not accurately reflect infants' characteristics. Jerrie Will, Patricia Self, and Nancy Datan (1976), for example, asked mothers to play with a 6-month-old infant. Some mothers played with an infant who was wearing a pink dress and was called "Beth." Some mothers played with *the same infant* who was then dressed in a blue pants outfit and was named "Adam." (The infant was really a 6-month-old boy!) Toys were provided: a plastic fish, a doll, and a train.

When mothers were asked to play with "Beth," they offered "her" the doll. They offered "Adam" the train. The mothers thus offered different toys on the basis of their perception of the sex of the child. They even interacted differently with "Beth" and "Adam." Mothers who believed they were playing with a girl smiled more and held the baby closer to themselves than did mothers who believed they were playing with a boy. When the research was completed, the mothers were interviewed about parenting skills and the impact of the sex of the child on differential parenting techniques. All the mothers stated that parents should not treat infant girls and boys differently.

Adults studied by Carol Seavey, Phyllis Katz, and Sue Rosenberg Zalk (1975) also made differential responses to girls and boys. Individuals who believed they were playing with a girl remarked on the baby's fragility, softness, and roundness. Individuals who were not provided with a sex label of the baby inquired what the baby's sex was. Thus, both parents and nonparents confirmed the importance that individuals place on information about sex in relating to infants. Adults are uncomfortable without sex information (Paludi & Gullo, 1986). When it is available, adults use it as a guide for "appropriate" judgments and behaviors.

For example, infant girls receive more **distal stimulation** (i.e., looking and vocalizing), and infant boys receive more **proximal stimulation** (i.e., holding and touching) (Bem, 1993). Beverly Fagot (1988) suggested that parents want their daughters to be neat and orderly, or "feminine," in their behaviors, and want their sons to be rough and tough, or "masculine," in their behaviors. Discussions with parents of young children suggest a consensus that girls are expected to be verbal, compliant, physically weak, and clean (Basow, 1986).

In addition to holding stereotypic expectations, parents encourage sex-appropriate activities by proving children with sex-typed clothes and toys (Geer & Shields, 1996; Raag & Rackliff, 1998). Girls are typically given dolls, doll houses, and miniature household appliances. Boys are commonly given building blocks, sports equipment, and models of cars or trucks. Raag and Rackliff (1998) noted that preschool boys engaged in more stereotyped play when they perceived that their fathers would think playing with "girl toys" was bad. Idle, Wood, and Desmarais (1993) reported that parents spent the least amount of time with "feminine" toys in interacting with their children in day-care centers. In addition, parents preferred using "feminine" toys with their daughters and "masculine" toys with their sons.

Furthermore, parents engage in more "rescuing" behavior with girls, for example, assisting and accompanying girls more often than necessary. Parents' willingness to help girls has been related to the high levels of dependency in girls (Geer & Shields, 1996).

Parents continue shaping their children's gender roles through the kinds of chores they assign them; girls work inside the house; boys work outside (Antill,

Goodnow, Russell, & Cotton, 1996). Research has noted a greater flexibility and permissiveness in middle-class homes (regardless of race or ethnicity) that leads to the availability of a wider range of activity choices for girls and boys (Reid, Haritos, Kelly, & Holland, 1995).

Thus, adults modify their behavior toward an infant and child to fit the sex of the child (Karraker, Vogel, & Lake, 1995). They then make attributions about a child's personality, physical characteristics, and even adult occupation—all from knowing whether the child is a girl or a boy. The strongest influence on children's knowledge of gender roles occurs within the family; parents pass on in a covert as well as an overt manner their beliefs about men and women to their children (Bohannon & Blanton, 1999; Kimmel & Rudolph, 1998; Witt, 1997).

In this chapter we will address the influence of parents and other socialization agents on children's acquisition of a gender-role identity, one central aspect to their personality development. We will then discuss two prominent theories of personality, those of Erik Erikson and Sigmund Freud, noting the biases against women, especially ethnic minority women and lesbian women. We will extend our coverage on theories of personality development by discussing feminist correctives to these personality theories. Finally, we will address major concerns in women's mental health, including biases in diagnoses, the impact of poverty, and the influence of multiple roles in women's lives on their mental health.

GENDER-ROLE IDENTITY: MEASUREMENT FACT OR ARTIFACT?

The term **gender-role identity** is used to describe a developmental process that includes the following components: gender-role preference, gender-role identification, knowledge of sex-determined role standards, gender-role adoption, and gender-role orientation (Lynn, 1959). We will discuss each of these components, noting the measurement techniques commonly used to measure these components of gender-role identity.

Gender-Role Preference

Gender-role preference refers to individuals' desire to adopt the behavior associated with either women or men, or the perception of such behavior as preferable or more desirable (Brown, 1956b; Lynn, 1959). The **IT Scale for Children** (ITSC; Brown, 1956a, 1956b) has been used frequently to measure children's gender-role preferences. As we discussed in Chapter 2, the ITSC is a projective test that uses a child-figure drawing, named *IT,* for which children are asked to make choices among drawings of feminine and masculine objects, figures, and activities. Research with the ITSC, however, suggests that girls do not exhibit feminine preferences; rather, girls prefer masculine to feminine items. The most reasonable explanation for this finding concerns the masculine bias inherent in the IT figure. Children select toys, objects of clothing, and activities for the IT figure not on the basis of their gender-role preference but in response to their knowledge of sex-determined role standards (as we will subsequently discuss in this chapter). In addition, Daniel Brown, the developer of the ITSC, assumed all children in the 1950s (or even today, since the items have not been modified since 1956!) had a washing machine in their home, were white, played "tea," wore lipstick, and built model airplanes! In the third part of the test, children are asked to select one child (from four) they believe IT would most like to be. A "masculine" girl is portrayed as one who wears men's clothes, and a "feminine" boy is one who wears a dress. The "feminine" girl is drawn as white, stereotypically dressed and coiffed, and wearing heavy makeup. There is thus a connection made between gender-role preference and sexual orientation and whether one cross dresses, connections that should not be made since they are not based in empirical research.

Gender-Role Identification

For the next few minutes, draw a person—any kind of person you want, but not a stick figure or a cartoon figure. After you have completed your drawing, draw another person. If you drew a female first, now draw a male. If you drew a male first, now draw a female.

Question: For your first drawing, did you draw a woman or a man?

Gender-role identification is the incorporation of a feminine or masculine role and the actions characteristic of the behavior of a particular role. This component of gender-role identity has typically been measured with the **Draw-A-Person Test,** developed by Karen Machover in 1949. Machover hypothesized that individuals would draw a figure of their own sex as their first response to the examiner's directions to "draw a person." However, research suggested that many adolescent and adult women (Craddick, 1963) typically drew a man first. This finding prompted personality theorists to explain women's drawings as being evidence for their ambivalence regarding their gender-role identification, including a desire to be men. (As we will discuss later in this chapter, the penis envy explanation is always offered whenever women's experiences do not fit into the masculine-biased theories.)

However, William Bauer and I (Paludi & Bauer, 1979) found a significant relationship between the first figure drawn and the sex of the test's administrator. Most drawings women made of men were elicited by a man. When women administered the test, more drawings of women were obtained. Most of the early research with the Draw-A-Person Test was conducted by men. Their presence, not women's unconscious conflicts, contributed to the results. Yet this consideration did not appear in the literature until 1979—thirty years after the psychoanalytic interpretation gained prominence!

Knowledge of Sex-Determined Role Standards

For the next few minutes, imagine that you are about to meet a woman for the first time, and all you know about this person is that she is a woman. How would you describe her? Using the following scale, check off the degree to which each of the following items reflects what you think of this woman:

Very Dependent   Not at All Dependent
1 . . . 2 . . . 3 . . . 4 . . . 5 . . . 6 . . . 7 . . .

Not at All Aggressive   Very Aggressive
1 . . . 2 . . . 3 . . . 4 . . . 5 . . . 6 . . . 7 . . .

Emotionally Expressive   Not Emotionally Expressive
1 . . . 2 . . . 3 . . . 4 . . . 5 . . . 6 . . . 7 . . .

Not at All Talkative   Very Talkative
1 . . . 2 . . . 3 . . . 4 . . . 5 . . . 6 . . . 7 . . .

By completing these rating scales you have just indicated your knowledge of sex-determined role standards. **Knowledge of sex-determined role standards** refers to individuals' concepts and espousal of gender-role stereotypes of both femininity and masculinity. In one of the first research studies on knowledge of sex-determined role standards, psychologist Paul Rosenkrantz (1968) asked college women and men to examine a list of 122 bipolar items—for example, very aggressive versus not at all aggressive, and very dependent versus not at all dependent—on a seven-point scale similar to the ones you just completed.

Students rated women as emotionally expressive, talkative, concerned with security, dependent, and not at all aggressive! How do these results compare to your ratings? Men were seen as exhibiting a relative absence of these characteristics. In addition, the stereotypic characteristics for women and men fell into two broad categories or clusters: a **warmth-expressiveness cluster** for women, and a **competency cluster** for men.

Several researchers, however, have taken the position that knowledge of sex-determined role standards comprise more than only certain personality traits (Deaux & Lewis, 1983, 1984; Eagly, 1995; Helgeson, 1994; Ricciardelli & Williams, 1995). Specifically, Kay Deaux and Laurie Lewis (1984) suggested that:

> [A] number of separate components of gender stereotypes can be identified: specifically, traits, role behaviors, occupations, and physical appearance, each of which has a masculine and feminine version. Although no component is seen as the exclusive province of one sex or the other, masculine and feminine components are significantly more strongly associated with males and females, respectively. The like-sex components (e.g., male role behaviors and masculine traits) bear some relationship to one another, but correlational analysis suggests that they are best viewed as separate factors that can vary independently. (p. 992)

An important feature of this new **multicomponent approach** to gender-role stereotypes is the emphasis away from gender-centric analyses; people do not define the various gender-role stereotypic characteristics in terms of their being associated with only one sex and not the other.

Research has suggested that children are aware of their cultural definitions of femininity and masculinity at very young ages (e.g., Raag & Rackliff, 1998). According to these children, girls and women: cry a lot, are quiet, are afraid, are thankful, are gentle, are loving, and have good manners.

Gender-Role Adoption

Gender-role adoption refers to individuals' overt behavior that is characteristic of a given sex rather than of stated preferences per se. Gender-role adoption has been measured by observing individuals' behavior in their daily activities at home, school, and work, as well as in the research laboratory. Research has indicated that girls are more likely to imitate male models than boys are to imitate female models (Golombok & Fivush, 1994).

As we discussed in Chapter 2, psychologists Eleanor Maccoby and Carol Nagy Jacklin (1974) published *The Psychology of Sex Differences,* in which they suggested that many of the presumed gender differences were more myth than fact. For example, girls were *not* found to be more social than boys; research did *not* support the belief that girls are more suggestible than boys; and girls were *not* found to have lower self-esteem than boys. Finally, Maccoby and Jacklin found no support for the belief that girls are particularly affected by heredity, whereas boys are affected by environment.

Peer groups play an important role in children's gender role adoption (Hibbard & Buhrmaster, 1998). During middle childhood for example, children grow progressively more sensitive to the importance of their peer group. During adolescence, the peer group becomes more structured and organized than it was during childhood. The functions of a peer group for adolescents include emotional intimacy, social support, fun, companionship and understanding (Bukowski, Newcomb, & Hartup, 1996; Cotterell, 1993).

During middle childhood and adolescence, individuals' best friends are members of the same sex and race (Halle, 1999). Schools that work with breaking down children's stereotypes associated with females and males find that the children are less likely to engage in stereotyping and are more likely to adopt the toy choices and attitudes of members of the other sex (and races) (Halle, 1999).

In schools that do not work with children in breaking down gender-role stereotypes, girls and boys who select culturally defined "sex-appropriate" toys are more liked by their peers; they are also more likely to have other children play with them than children who do not choose "sex-appropriate" toys (Martin, 1989).

Children's adoption of play with same-sex peers emerges during the child's second and third years. This adoption grows stronger through middle childhood (Martin, Fabes, Evans, & Wyman, 1999). In fact, Servin and Bohlin (1999) found in their study of gender-role adoption of toys that 1-, 3-, and 5-year-old girls and boys adopt "sex-appropriate" toys from as early as 1 year of age. Similar results were obtained by Golombok and Fivush (1994). These researchers also reported that "feminine" toys become less interesting to girls and boys as the children get older.

Boys are typically criticized by their male peers for engaging in play with girls; girls do not receive the same treatment when they play with boys (Thorne, 1993). Thorne (1993) noted that many children engage in "borderwork," that is, they try to take part in the activities associated with the other sex. These children are seldom met with approval from their peers.

Toy stores and toy sections of department stores arrange the toys according to children's age as well as sex. Browse through the toy section of a store. You'll find "doctor's kits" for boys and "nurses' kits" for girls. You'll find toys for boys that involve use of action figures and superheroes. You'll then find toys for girls that involve household appliances and dolls. While you're browsing, check out the prices of toys for boys and girls. You'll most likely find that the toys for boys are more expensive.

You may also be interested in knowing that Mattel's Barbie PC, a "computer for girls" has half of the educational software that Hot Wheels PC (the "computer for boys") has.

Gender-Role Orientation

For the next few minutes, indicate how you would describe yourself (from 1 to 7, with 1 being not very true of you to 7 being very true of you), using the following personality characteristics.

Warm
Caring
Independent
Passive
Childlike
Dependent
Dominant
Nurturant
Immature

Gender-role orientation refers to individuals' self-definition as feminine or masculine. From the 1930s to the 1960s, most psychologists interested in personality development and the measurement of gender-role identity believed that the behaviors, attitudes, and interests generally associated with either femininity or masculinity were exclusive features of women and men. Thus, women and men were believed to differ in terms of their basic personality characteristics, and these characteristics were conceived of as opposites. A person would exhibit characteristics of femininity by a lack of competitiveness, by aggressiveness, by independence, and by the presence of warmth, nurturance, and passivity.

In terms of behavior, whatever a feminine person did, a masculine person didn't do. Characteristics considered masculine were seen as more socially valued than those considered feminine.

To test this assumption about gender-role orientation, large groups of women and men (typically, introductory psychology students) were given items to determine how they *differed* in their responses. Many psychologists noted problems with this approach to the measurement of gender-role orientation. One major concern was the heterosexism involved in the test construction. Psychologist Miriam Lewin (1984) noted, for example, that women who scored in the "masculine" direction on these tests were assumed to be lesbian and, therefore, in need of therapy for dealing with their problems in adjusting to the feminine role.

Researchers questioned whether femininity and masculinity were opposite sides of a single **bipolar continuum,** or whether they were **independent dimensions.**

Could women be feminine *and* masculine? Was women's gender-role orientation independent of their biological sex and sexual orientation? The **androgynous conception of femininity and masculinity** was introduced into psychology during the late 1960s and the 1970s in an effort to provide answers to these questions. According to this perspective, femininity was not thought to be composed of personality characteristics that were *opposites* of masculinity. Instead, the psychological characteristics of femininity and masculinity were viewed as comprising two independent dimensions that could be separate but could overlap as well (Marsh, Antill, & Cunningham, 1989).

In an attempt to measure androgyny, psychologist Sandra Bem (1974) developed a test called the **Bem Sex Role Inventory (BSRI).** The initial BSRI consisted of 60 socially desirable "feminine" (e.g., shy and warm), "masculine" (e.g., aggressive and self-reliant), and "neutral" (e.g., happy and sincere) adjectives. (A shorter version of the BSRI consists of 30 items, 10 in each of the categories.) On a 7-point scale (1—never or almost never true; 7—always or almost always true), individuals indicate the extent to which each item is true for them. The test gives separate femininity and masculinity scores that can be combined into one of four types:

1. *Androgynous*—High on both the feminine and masculine items.

2. *Feminine*—High on the feminine items and low on the masculine ones.

3. *Masculine*—Low on the feminine items and high on the masculine ones.

4. *Undifferentiated*—Low on both the feminine and masculine items.

As mentioned in Chapter 2, underlying the construct of androgyny is the assumption that we should minimize differences between women and men. However, although androgyny was an improvement over the view that femininity and masculinity were opposite and mutually exclusive ends of an important personality dimension, the androgynous perspective still held that personality comprises feminine and masculine elements. Although the androgyny perspective implies the equivalence of femininity and masculinity, the masculine traits are in fact more highly valued.

Linda Garnets and Joseph Pleck (1979) suggested that women (and men) transcend rather than merge prescribed gender-role characteristics. **Gender-role transcendence** suggests that people should transcend the traditional stereotypical feminine and masculine characteristics altogether. The same problem we pointed to with androgyny, however, is found in gender-role transcendence: attention is drawn away from women's unique needs and from the power imbalance between women and men in this culture. We will address this theme again as we discuss traditional theories of personality.

THEORIES OF PERSONALITY: VALUE-LADEN VERSUS VALUE-FREE

Psychologist Judith Worell (1990) suggested that theories of personality may be described as "traditional" when they reflect the following themes in their conception of human behavior: androcentrism, gendercentrism, ethnocentrism, and heterosexism. **Androcentrism** refers to the theories of personality that use boys and men as the prototype for humankind, and girls and women as variants on the dominant theme (Note that the ITSC is androcentric in that it uses a masculine figure as the prototype for a child). **Gendercentrism** in personality theories is evident when separate paths of life-span development are suggested for women and men as a result of the biological differences between them. **Ethnocentrism** refers to personality theories that assume identical development for all individuals across all racial, ethnic, and class groups. **Heterosexism** is evident in personality theories that assume that a heterosexual orientation is normative, but a lesbian (or gay) sexual orientation is deviant and worthy of change.

Let's illustrate these themes with two classic theories of personality, those of Erik Erikson and Sigmund Freud.

Erik Erikson's "Eight Stages of Man"

We discussed androcentrism somewhat in Chapter 2, when we addressed research methods in psychology. We noted that the theories on achievement motivation and moral development were based on boys and men only. In Chapter 9 we will note how the masculine-biased theories of achievement resulted in a poor fit between these theories and women's realities and experiences. Personality theories (as well as the theories of achievement motivation) view women as "less than" men in terms of intelligence, rationality, and morality, and in taking responsibility for their lives. The work of Erik Erikson is an example of an androcentric theory of personality (1963, 1968).

Erikson proposed a model of development that was based on his concept of the **"eight stages of man."** According to Erikson's model, development proceeds throughout life according to stages in which polarities determine the formation of an individual's personality. His theory stated that growth proceeds from conflict, and he cast each of his stages of development in terms of unique crises. The eight stages, accompanied by the ages and "successful outcomes" Erikson believed individuals achieved, are as follows:

1. Trust versus mistrust (birth–1); security and predictability.

2. Autonomy versus shame and doubt (2–3); self-control.

3. Initiative versus guilt (4–5); responsibility.

4. Industry versus inferiority (6–12); competence and self-esteem.

5. Identity versus role confusion (13–19); coherent sense of self.

6. Intimacy versus isolation (20–24); establishment of mature relationships.

7. Generativity versus stagnation (25–64); guiding the next generation.

8. Ego integrity versus despair (65–death); wisdom.

The fifth and sixth stages, **identity versus role confusion** and **intimacy versus isolation,** posed problems for Erikson as he attempted to understand how women's development fits his theory. Only late in Erikson's career did he publish the paper that represented his analysis of women's personality: "The Inner and the Outer Space: Reflections on Womanhood" (1963). Let's look at these two stages in more detail, to address the biases they represent.

In stage 5, identity versus role confusion, Erikson theorized that adolescents achieve a sense of personal identity either by embracing a philosophy of life and commitment to a career or by being confused and uncommitted to a career. In stage 6, intimacy versus isolation, individuals, according to Erikson (1963), must meet the following standards for development that is "healthy":

mutuality of orgasm

with a loved partner

of the opposite sex

with whom one is able and willing to share a mutual trust

and with whom one is able and willing to regulate the cycles of work, procreation, and recreation

so as to secure to the offspring, too, all the stages of a satisfactory development (p. 266)

Individuals who cannot develop a capacity for intimacy, according to Erikson, experience a sense of isolation, an inability to take chances with their identity by sharing true intimacy. Erikson described these individuals as self-absorbed and able to engage in interpersonal relationships on only a very superficial level.

Erikson questioned these stages for women's development. He reasoned that women defer dealing with the identity versus role confusion polarity until "they know whom they will marry and for whom they will make a home" (1968, p. 123). Several biases are inherent in this theory. For example, "normal" intimacy is translated as heterosexual intimacy, thus denying lesbian relationships and considering them "abnormal." In addition, Erikson viewed sexual relationships in terms of procreation. One result of this assumption about development is that women who choose voluntarily to remain childless also have been considered "abnormal."

Erikson's position suggests that women's identity is not defined by career commitment, as is men's, but rather by their commitment to the roles of wife and mother, and by their relationship to a man who will give them direction. Erikson's theory thus posits very important prescriptive guidelines or mandates for women: to be a wife and, especially, a mother.

This latter mandate is what Nancy Felipe Russo (1976) labeled the **motherhood mandate.** According to Russo:

> Characterizing motherhood as prescribed, however, does not adequately communicate the centrality of this behavior to the definition of the adult female. "Being pretty" is also prescribed, but one can compensate for not being pretty (by being a "good mother," for example). Motherhood is on a qualitatively different plane. It is a woman's *raison d'etre*. It is mandatory. The mandate requires that one have at least two children (historically as many as possible and preferably sons) and that one raise them "well." As long as this situation exists for the vast majority of women in Western society and the world in general, prohibitions may be eliminated and options widened, but change will occur only insofar as women are first able to fulfill their mandate of motherhood. (p. 144)

One of the first questions asked of newly married women is when they are going to have babies. Thus, being a mother is the central core of a woman's identity as a person. In addition, little girls are socialized according to this motherhood mandate. They are encouraged to play with dolls and are reinforced for doing so (Lott & Maluso, 1993). Lytton and Romney (1991) reviewed 172 studies of parents' socialization practices and concluded that there was a significant tendency for parents to encourage gender-typed activities in their daughters and sons. Doll play is believed to be an important way for little girls to learn nurturant behaviors that will transfer, in later years, to their caring for children. And, in adolescence, girls are considered to be very capable of handling baby-sitting responsibilities (Karraker et al., 1995).

This perspective is also illustrated in Erikson's first stage, trust versus mistrust. Erikson believed that if a mother acts in a loving and consistent way, the infant will develop a sense of basic trust. In contrast, a baby will develop a sense of basic mistrust if the mother is undependable and doesn't care for the infant. Mothers are assumed to be the sole caretakers and the cause of the child's problems in infancy and throughout life. Mothers are also assumed to be "natural" caretakers, not interested in a career in addition to or instead of providing care for children.

The **mommy track** is supportive of another of Erikson's views of women: the construction of women's lives and realities based on a theory of male development (androcentrism). This theory also is gendercentric in that women's role is restricted to their presumed biological readiness to be mothers and wives. Gendercentrism is also illustrated in Erikson's division of life goals between women and men as career versus intimacy, with intimacy not as valued as career. This theory is ethnocentric as well: Erikson believed that children will best develop when in the care of a nurturing, biological mother. This position disregards evidence, from a variety of cultures (even within the United States), suggesting that children socialized in lesbian families, in extended family arrangements, by dual-earner couples, or by single parents are well adjusted (see Gottfried, Gottfried, Bathurst, & Killian, 1999; Hoffman & Youngblade, 1999; Hyde, Klein, Essex, & Clark, 1995; see Chapter 9).

In fact, as research by Marjorie Hill (1988) suggested, lesbian mothers perceived their daughters and sons to be more similar in characteristics than did heterosexual mothers. Lesbian mothers held less stereotypic ideas relating to the feminine role. Daughters of employed mothers perceive women's role as involving freedom of choice and satisfaction (Betz & Schifano, 2000; Farmer, Wardrop, & Rotella, 1999; Juntunen, 1996; Lapan, Adams, Turner, & Hinkelman, 2000). Daughters of employed mothers also perceive a smaller difference between women and men in terms of warmth and expressiveness than do children of unemployed mothers (Reid & Paludi, 1993). Research also suggests that greater flexibility and permissiveness in middle-class homes (regardless of ethnicity) lead to the availability of a wider range of activity choices for girls. In many working-class homes, parents are more concerned that their daughters adhere strictly to stereotypic feminine behavior (Reid, et al., 1995; Reid & Paludi, 1993).

Sigmund Freud: "Anatomy Is Destiny"

Let's illustrate androcentrism, ethnocentrism, gendercentrism, and heterosexism in another personality theory—the psychoanalytic theory proposed by Sigmund Freud (1948). This theory clearly illustrates gendercentrism; personality development was posited separately for women and men as a result of the biological differences between them (specifically, the presence of a penis in men and the capability of women to bear children). Freud believed that young girls, when noticing they have vaginas, not penises, blame their mother for this anatomical difference. Freud believed girls develop **penis envy** and, consequently, a basic sense of inferiority. They resolve this "genital loss" by passively accepting it from a man and bearing children. Freud maintained that girls' identification with their mother only develops out of their competition for their father and a fear of losing their mother's love altogether. Freud viewed women as less ethical than men, as having a lesser sense of morality, and as being more influenced by emotions than by logical reasoning. Why? Because girls' identification process is never as strong as that of boys, and, as a result, girls have less well-developed consciences. Consequently, women are passive, emotional, masochistic, narcissistic, and in competition with other women for men's attention. According to Freud (1968):

> I cannot escape the notion . . . that for women the level of what is ethically normal is different from what it is in men. Their superego is never so inexorable, so impersonal, so independent of its emotional origins as we require it to be in men. Character traits which critics of every epoch have brought up against women—that they show less sense of justice than men, that they are less ready to submit to the great necessities of life, that they are more influenced in their judgments by feelings of affection or hostility—all these would be amply accounted for by the modification of their superego which we have already inferred. (p. 193)

Freud maintained that girls' and women's moral inferiority is due to the fact that they lack a penis. Because they do not have to worry about being castrated (in retaliation from their father for loving their mother), girls and women are not as motivated to become obedient rule-followers. As Judith Worell (1990) pointed out:

> [Women's] major goals are to acquire a husband and to have his baby. When they step out of this role and move into the spheres of men, either by seeking roles other than motherhood or by showing "masculine" characteristics such as assertiveness and ambition, they are clearly afflicted by a disorder called "penis envy." Thus the theory concludes that "anatomy is destiny" for women, and that they are doomed from early childhood by the developmental outcomes of their physical deficiencies. (p. 196)

Freud's theory is also ethnocentric. Many ethnic minority women, for example, view themselves not as the passive and submissive women Freud described, but as strong, independent, and self-reliant (Landrine, 1995). These positively valued characteristics, however, have been misnamed as deviant in black women, resulting in the *matriarchal structure* responsible for the alienation of black men. Freud viewed white male/female power structures as normative and thereby cast ethnic minority families in a deviant framework (Greene, 1986). Darlene DeFour and I (DeFour & Paludi, 1991) found that single white mothers are frequently described in the psychological literature as being in an alternative or contemporary lifestyle; the same family constellation for black women is described as a "broken home."

We need to recognize that what Freudian theory referred to as deviance in women may be instead a function of women's *socially constructed position* in their culture. Boys and men are more highly valued; they are seen as rational, logical, ethical, and moral. Kate Millett (1970) claimed that Freud's concept of penis envy was a transparent example of male egocentrism. Rather than celebrating women's ability to give birth, Freud interpreted it as an attempt to possess a substitute penis. According to Millett, "Freudian logic has succeeded in converting childbirth, an impressive female accomplishment . . . into nothing more than a hunt for a male organ" (p. 185).

NEEDED: FEMINIST PERSONALITY THEORIES

Many feminist psychologists, noting that omissions, distortions, and trivializations of women's realities and experiences are inherent in personality theories and measurement techniques, have been working on a **woman-based theory of personality.** All have suggested that a feminist theory should address questions from the perspective of the female experience.

This section discusses criteria for a woman-based theory of personality. We will begin with the work of a psychologist who initially presented this view, Karen Horney.

Karen Horney: Feminine Psychology

Karen Horney (see photo on p. 119) was trained in classic psychoanalytic theory with two Freudian analysts, Karl Abraham and Hans Sachs. Between 1923 and 1935, Horney published her critique of Sigmund Freud's psychosexual stages of development as they were believed to describe women. In discussing Freud's hypothesis of penis envy, Horney cautioned that it is a hypothesis, not a fact. She also pointed out: "Unfortunately little or nothing is known of psychically healthy women, or of women under different cultural conditions" (1973, p. 216). In her paper, "The Flight from Womanhood," Horney addressed the androcentric bias of Freudian theory. She illustrated this bias by comparing the analytic ideas of feminine development with the ideas that young boys have of girls and noted the "remarkable parallelism." This analysis is as follows:

1. For both sexes it is only the male genital which plays any part.

2. Sad discovery of the absence of the penis.

3. Belief of the girl that she once possessed a penis and lost it by castration.

4. Castration is conceived of as the infliction of punishment.

5. The girl regards herself as inferior. Penis envy.

6. The girl never gets over the sense of deficiency and inferiority and has constantly to master afresh her desire to be a man.

7. The girl desires throughout life to avenge herself on the man for possessing something she lacks.

Karen Horney (1885–1952).
(Corbis-Bettmann.)

The boy's ideas

1. Naive assumption that girls as well as boys possess a penis.

2. Realization of the absence of the penis.

3. Idea that the girl is a castrated, mutilated boy.

4. Belief that the girl has suffered punishment which also threatens him.

5. The girl is regarded as inferior.

6. The boy is unable to imagine how the girl can ever get over this loss or envy.

7. The boy dreads her envy.

(Horney, 1973, pp. 57–58)

Horney argued against the importance of penis envy and inferiority feelings for women. She also claimed that boys have intense envy of pregnancy, childbirth, and breastfeeding. Because boys cannot handle the belief that women are biologically superior to them, they transform this envy into its opposite: a belief in women's inferiority. Horney believed men expressed this bias in several ways, including denying women's worth, deprecating them and their work, and devaluing femininity.

In addition to questioning the androcentric bias inherent in Freud's theory, Horney called for examining the ethnocentric bias as well. She suggested that cross-cultural research would indicate whether masochism and penis envy were inherent in women's personality. She claimed that cultural factors were causative agents and that masochistic behaviors would appear in any culture in which women were, among other things:

> Restricted on the number of children they could bear; viewed as inferior to men; economically dependent on men; blocked from expressing sexuality; restricted to roles that are tied into family, religion, and charity.

Horney argued that when these conditions were present in a culture, women's "nature" would be described as weak, passive, emotional, and dependent. Whereas Freud argued that women were the result of the social conditions, Horney argued that the social conditions were the cause of women's behavior.

Laura Brown: Toward a Lesbian/Gay Paradigm for Psychology

Laura Brown (1989) proposed an alternative model for psychological theory based on the experiences of lesbian women and gay men. She suggested that three elements define a lesbian (and gay) reality: (a) **biculturalism,** (b) **marginality,** and (c) **normative creativity.**

Biculturalism refers to having dominant and minority cultures as part of one's family of origin. Developing a bicultural identity creates for lesbian women new ways of defining themselves—not in polarities, as Erikson theorized. According to Brown:

> A healthy resolution of such conflicts of identity is one that must eschew either/or perspectives on who one is and embrace what is "other" within oneself. Such a successful resolution of a bicultural identity may create a propensity to view things on continua rather than in polarized fashion. Being able to operate within grey areas and on middle grounds and balancing the demands of two divergent groups that are now internalized self-representations are characteristic of the experience of being gay or lesbian. (Brown, pp. 449–450)

Marginality refers to the view of lesbian women as "others" as not belonging to the dominant heterosexual culture. This view of lesbians has resulted in violence toward them and their children (see Chapter 10). Lesbian women and gay men, by not having any clear rules about how to live in a heterosexual culture, have had to be creative and make up the rules as they develop. Brown (1989) stated:

> Simply being lesbian or gay has been something we have had to invent for ourselves . . . since whatever roadmaps the dominant culture offered have been full of wrong turns and uncharted territories. This need to invent for ourselves has been equal parts terrifying and exhilarating. (p. 452)

Brown's discussion highlights the fact that women know more about women than men do; that lesbians know more about lesbian cultures than heterosexual men do. She demands that lesbians take the right to define lesbian relationships:

> The art, literature, and criticism of this century assume that there is an unconscious mind, that behavior is motivated and determined by early experiences, that there is an Oedipal struggle between father and son, that women do lack the objectivity bestowed by a successful resolution of the Oedipal conflict. Having internalized psychoanalytic thought in so many and subtle ways, and having learned to value the grandiose over the accurate, many feminist therapists, indeed most literate members of Western civilization, use psychoanalytic thinking as a standard against which the quality of other theories of human behavior can be measured. (Brown, 1984, p. 75)

A similar critique has been offered by psychologist Hannah Lerman.

Hannah Lerman: A Mote in Freud's Eye—From Psychoanalysis to the Psychology of Women

Hannah Lerman (1986) has dealt with the impact of psychoanalysis on psychological thinking about personality theory, especially as it is applied to women's experiences. According to Lerman:

> I do not believe that Freud's original theories served women well. I also do not believe that the modern revisions of psychoanalytic theory further the health and well-being of the modern woman. After the initial feminist rejection of Freudian concepts in the early 1970s, there has been reacceptance of his ideas by some as having validity and applicability to women. I am not in that group because I see the theory as so fundamentally flawed in its thinking about women that it cannot be repaired, however extensive the tinkering with it. . . . Assumptions about the inherent inferiority of women are embedded in the very core of psychoanalytic theory. (p. 6)

Lerman has offered several criteria for a woman-based theory of personality.

1. Clinical usefulness: The concepts of the personality theory must be translatable into what would take place in a therapy setting and what could be useful for women's experiences.

2. Encompassing the diversity and complexity of women and their lives: The concepts of personality theory must include a variety of women's issues as well as experiences of lesbian women, ethnic minority women, and disabled women.

3. Viewing women positively and centrally: The concepts of the personality theory should place high value on women and femininity and should view women as central, not marginal, to human development.

4. Arising from women's experience: The concepts of the personality theory must be woman-based, not androcentric, and must originate from the clients' perspective, not the therapists' perspective.

5. Remaining close to the data of experience: The personality theory must reflect women's realities without overgeneralizing to all women.

6. Recognizing that the internal world is inextricably intertwined with the external world: The personality theory must take into account the ways in which its value system operates on women's lives.

7. Not confining concepts by particularistic terminology or in terms of other theories: The concepts of the personality theory will be written in language that does not denigrate women's experiences and that addresses women's development across the life span.

8. Supporting feminist (or, at a minimum, nonsexist) modes of psychotherapy.

As Lerman concluded:

The women's movement in general, by emphasizing the patriarchal biases in our culture, has been forcing our society to pay some, although not nearly enough, attention to the particular circumstances of women's lives. We wish to fervently work toward a theoretical framework that can actively participate in the process of increasing our understanding of and our ability to improve the quality of our own lives as women and those of our clients. (Lerman, 1986, p. 16)

We will address these issues in the following section on women's mental health and well-being.

WOMEN'S MENTAL HEALTH

INTRODUCTION: THE CASE OF DORA REVISITED

In 1905, Sigmund Freud published a paper titled "Fragment of an Analysis of a Case of Hysteria." This "case of hysteria" is better known in psychology as the case of Dora (Cixous, 1976). Dora was an 18-year-old woman whose real name was Ida Bauer. She was brought to see Freud by her father, a former patient of Freud. Her parents were concerned about her recent behavior, which involved writing them a letter in which she had said "goodbye," with the implied intention of committing suicide. Dora also had a "nervous" cough, a history of fainting spells, headaches, and depression, all of which dated back to her childhood. Her "most troubling symptom" was "a complete loss of voice."

These symptoms were diagnosed as a "typical case of hysteria" by Freud, whose goal was to explain to Dora the sexual meanings of her symptoms. To Freud, the cause of these symptoms lay in the repressed content of her early sexuality. Freud believed that hysteria resulted from masturbatory fantasies, lesbian fantasies, and incestuous desires for one's father. Dora's family included her parents and a brother.

In the family context, her brother took their mother's side; Dora was aligned with her father. Dora was described by Freud as an attractive, "sharp-sighted" girl whose father had taken great pride in the "early growth of her intelligence." Freud wrote that Dora's "critical powers" and her "intellectual precocity" were from her father, since he perceived her mother to be "an uncultivated woman" who "was occupied all day long in cleaning the house with its furniture and utensils."

Dora's father was having an affair with Frau K., wife of a family friend, Herr K. Herr K. had attempted to have sex with Dora (the first time when she was 14 years old) and she felt that "she had been handed over to Herr K." by her father in exchange for Herr K.'s complicity in the adultery. Dora believed that her father "handed her over" to Freud because he feared she would discuss the affair. Her father hired Freud hoping for someone to "bring her to reason."

Freud believed Dora's account of why her father had brought her to see him: ". . . I came to the conclusion that Dora's story must correspond to the facts in every respect." He believed that Dora's father and Herr K. conspired against Dora: "[E]ach of the two men avoided drawing any conclusions from the other's behavior which would have been awkward for his own plans" (p. 35). However, Freud published the case (even though it was incomplete) because he thought it demonstrated the sexual origin of hysteria. As Elaine Showalter (1985) commented:

In his case history of Dora, if not in the actual treatment, Freud is determined to have the last word—he even has a postscript—in constructing his own "intelligible, consistent, and unbroken" account of her hysteria. He asserts his intellectual superiority to this bright but rebellious young woman. He uses his text to demonstrate his power to bring a woman to reason, and to bring reason to the mysteries of woman. (p. 160)

Showalter's passage suggests there is an alternative analysis of this case: Ida's perspective. What was it like for Ida to be a young woman in Vienna at the turn of the century? To have been sexually abused by a trusted family friend when she was a young adolescent? Ida believed she was caught in a web of deceit and betrayal. She was! Ida believed she was caught in a double bind. She was! The situation with her father, Freud, and Herr K.—all individuals in whom she had placed a great deal of trust—was ample cause for depression and suicidal ideas. As Juanita Williams (1983) commented: "Freud might have said to [Ida], 'You are right and they are wrong'" (p. 42). He did not, however, and she continued to have the pattern of symptoms throughout her adult life.

For Helene Cixous, the case of Dora describes the silencing of women who question the patriarchical assumptions: "Silence: silence is the mark of hysteria. The great hysterics have lost speech . . . their tongues are cut off and what talks isn't heard because it's the body that talks and man doesn't hear the body" (1981, p. 49).

Elaine Showalter (1985) also recognized that women's hysteria fits in well with patriarchy:

Hysteria is tolerated because in fact it has no power to effect cultural change; it is much safer for the patriarchal order to encourage and allow discontented women to express their wrongs through psychosomatic illness than to have them agitating for economic and legal rights. (p. 161)

Later in this chapter I will discuss feminist approaches to understanding women's adjustment and the charge that the mental health profession has conspired against women by setting standards for women that differ greatly from those set for men. In Chapter 10 we will also discuss the implications of this silencing of women—among them, the disbelief when women say they have experienced sexual victimization. Let us begin with a discussion of psychotherapists' attitudes about women and women's roles.

THERAPISTS' ATTITUDES TOWARD WOMEN: WOMEN DEVALUED

Although many of us may believe that therapy is an effective way of offering support to women, several feminist psychologists have voiced severe criticism of traditional psychotherapy and have warned that therapy may be hazardous to women's emotional well-being (Brown, 1995). These concerns over the dangers inherent in therapists' treatment of women grew out of research conducted by Inge Broverman and her colleagues (Broverman, Broverman, Clarkson, Rosenkrantz, & Vogel, 1970) on therapists' attitudes toward women and femininity.

Broverman and her research team asked 33 women and 46 men who were mental health practitioners to list, using a series of personality characteristics, the traits that best described a mature, healthy, and socially competent adult woman, adult man, or adult whose sex was not specified. They were asked to check off a series of descriptive bipolar characteristics that best described each person. The descriptive categories contained bipolar items such as the following:

Very subjective	Very objective
Very submissive	Very dominant
Not at all ambitious	Very ambitious
Very passive	Very active
Feelings easily hurt	Feelings not easily hurt

Broverman and her colleagues reported agreement in the way clinicians in their sample described the characteristics of adult men and adults in general (e.g., very direct, very logical, can make decisions easily, never cry), which differed from the characteristics assigned to adult women (e.g., very excitable in minor crises, more easily influenced, less adventurous, less independent, very illogical, very sneaky). There was considerable agreement among the women and men in the way they described the different persons. Broverman and her research team reported that the mental health practitioners had a **double standard for mental health.** The personality characteristics they equated with mental health in an adult were also applied to an adult man but not to an adult woman. Thus, a woman could not be simultaneously described as a healthy adult and a healthy woman: "[The] general standard of health is actually applied only to men, while healthy women are perceived as significantly less healthy by adult standards" (Broverman et al., 1970, p. 5).

The social value of being rational, independent, and a leader outweighs the desirability of being submissive, emotional, and conforming.

Phyllis Chesler, in her book *Women and Madness* (1972), shared her views on the predominantly male professions of clinical psychology and psychiatry:

> The ethic of mental health is masculine in our culture. This double standard of sexual mental health, which exists side by side with a single and masculine standard of human mental health, is enforced by both society and clinicians. Although the limited "ego resources," and unlimited "dependence," and fearfulness of most women is pitied, disliked, and "diagnosed," by society and its agent-clinicians, any other kind of behavior is unacceptable in women! (p. 69)

The perspectives offered by Broverman and Chesler were shared by many researchers. In addition, vocational counselors were found to evidence gender bias toward women's career aspirations (see Chapter 9). Sexist ideology accounted for the double standard for women's mental health as well as women's career opportunities. When records from actual therapy sessions between clients and therapists are analyzed, there appears to be substantial evidence for **therapist bias against women** (Lopez, Smith, Wolkenstein, & Charlin, 1993). Women are seen for longer periods of time in therapy, and they are given stronger prescriptive medications than men are (Albino, Tedesco, & Shenkle, 1990). Furthermore, research has indicated that married women have higher rates of admission to mental health facilities than married men (Russo & Green, 1993).

In addition to sexism in traditional psychotherapy, heterosexism in its practice (as well as in theory and research) has been prevalent. In theories of psychological development, a heterosexual orientation is viewed as normative; a lesbian orientation is viewed as deviant and worthy of change (Worell, 1990). Consequently, lesbian women have been ignored, deprecated, and considered mentally ill. As the editors of the Boston Lesbian Psychologies Collective (1987) pointed out:

> The overt and covert fear of lesbians in our society is conveyed to all of us at an early age and in many ways. Moreover, many of us are rewarded for staying in the closet. As a result, a lesbian must struggle with her desire to be authentic not only to herself, but also publicly and with her too-often contradictory desire to get along comfortably in the world. The lesbian must deal by herself, in couples, and in community with the homophobia we have all internalized. (pp. 9–10)

It is also important to acknowledge issues of **cultural sensitivity of psychotherapists** (Canino, 1982). Women's behavior that may not be understood by the mental health profession (and indeed labeled "bizarre") may be easily understood in its community context (Canino, 1982). In addition, ethnic minority women may underutilize mental health services because of a sense of stigma attached to seeking support for problems in living. Other women may have no information about available services or have differential access to mental health services (Landrine, 1995).

The publicity surrounding Broverman's and Chesler's work contributed to the lessening of sex bias among the therapeutic professions. Mary Smith (1980), for example, reported that greater bias was found in earlier studies than in later ones, suggesting that professionals apparently had become more aware of and/or sensitive to the issue of sex bias. Julia Sherman (1980) reported that women were less biased than men. This change may reflect the fact that women, more than men, participate in courses dealing with women and therapy during their graduate training, where discussions of sex bias in psychotherapy are held (Paludi et al., in press).

In support of this explanation, Sherman and her colleagues (Sherman, Koufacos, & Kenworthy, 1978) found that therapists lack preparation and information about women in general and were woefully uninformed about research on the psychology of women, especially in the areas of sexuality, pregnancy, and menopause. Sherman noted that older therapists and therapists with a Freudian orientation were more likely to be biased against women than were younger and non–Freudian-oriented therapists.

It is imperative that mental health practitioners consider their stereotypes and biases concerning women's socioeconomic status and how these biases may affect their diagnosis, the client-clinician relationship, and the outcomes for women. Graduate training programs in clinical and counseling psychology must teach students to be more sensitive to clients' sex, ethnicity, and class, and to become aware of their own hidden biases (Brown, 1995; Pope, Levenson, & Schover, 1979; Porter, 1995).

Such training must also emphasize the ethical principles of psychologists. The American Psychological Association (APA) specifies clearly that sexual relations with clients are unethical. Based on self-reports, more than 5 percent of male therapists reported having sex with women clients (Bouhoutsos, Holroyd, Lerman, Forer, & Greenberg, 1983; Holroyd & Brodsky, 1977). Research has indicated that power needs motivate the therapists to engage in this unethical conduct (Bouhoutsos, 1984).

ISSUES IN WOMEN'S MENTAL HEALTH

Because women's adjustment has thus been constructed based on male development, feminist therapists have called for new models of mental health that value women and femininity (Gilbert, 1999; Marecek & Kravetz, 1998b). Feminist therapists (e.g., Eichler & Parron, 1987) have identified five priority areas to meet this goal:

1. The diagnosis and treatment of mental disorders in women.

2. The stressors involved in poverty.

3. The stressors involved in multiple roles.

4. Mental health issues for older women.

5. The causes and mental health effects of violence against women.

We discussed issues related to women and aging in the last chapter. We will address violence against women in Chapter 10. In the following discussion we will deal with the three remaining priority research areas, beginning with the diagnosis and treatment of mental disorders in women.

Diagnosis and Treatment of Mental Disorders in Women

Women are diagnosed and treated for mental illness at a much higher rate than men (Dohrenwend & Dohrenwend, 1976; Russo & Green, 1993). Women are likely to be diagnosed as depressed, agoraphobic, and having an eating disorder (Handwerker, 1999; Rudolf & Priebe, 1999). Women generally exhibit behaviors that are self-critical, self-deprecating, and self-destructive (Handwerker, 1999).

This diagnostic labeling may result from the fact that women are more likely to exhibit behaviors that males are apt to label as mental illness; women, for example, have been socialized to express their emotions. A second explanation for this labeling concerns women's unequal social position and their experience of greater discrimination and violence (Cascardi, O'Leary, & Schlee, 1999; Gilbert, 1999; see Chapters 9 and 10).

Some women are more likely to be diagnosed and treated for mental illnesses (Handwerker, 1999). For example, married women have a higher rate of mental illness than married men; single women have a lower rate of mental illness than single men (Sheehan, 1999; Wu & DeMaris, 1996). Jeanne Marecek (1978) suggested that many married women experience a loss of status and independence as well as difficulties associated with being a mother, all of which can create severe stress and lead to emotional problems (see the later discussion of women's multiple roles). For many women, a large part of their self-identity is tied to their ability to successfully establish intimate relationships (see Chapter 8). When the relationships end, women may experience emotional problems as a consequence of regarding themselves as failures in terms of the cultural standards of femininity (Carnelley, Wortman, & Kessler, 1999; Murtagh, 1998).

Women who are single heads of household are at high risk for depression (Russo & Greene, 1993). The interface of gender, ethnicity, and race is particularly salient (Comas-Diaz, 1999; Lijtmaer, 1998; Torres & Han, 2000). Ginorio, Gutierrez, Cance, and Acosta (1995) reported a high risk of depression among Latinas, especially because of race discrimination and the conflicts between cultural expectations and achievement as minorities. In addition, LaFromboise, Choney, James, and Running Wolf (1995) cited depression as a major clinical problem of Native American women.

Sands (1998) noted that depression among adolescent girls is common and is an unattended problem. Sands noted that when societal and peer pressure becomes overwhelming for adolescent girls, depression may result. Root (1995) identified depression as a major issue for Asian adolescent girls, especially those who are immigrants and refugees who feel constrained in their new environment by lack of social networks and language barriers. In fact, researchers and theorists view the life stage of adolescence as more difficult than other life stages because of three major issues: (1) conflict with parents; (2) mood disruptions, and (3) risk behavior that may potentially harm themselves and others (Sands, 1998). The more likely adolescent girls experience negative life events associated with this life stage (e.g., low popularity with a peer group, poor school performance), the more they will experience mood disruptions and perhaps depression (Petersen et al., 1993). Furthermore, lesbian and gay adolescents have a two- to threefold risk of suicide and are at greater risk for depression as a consequence of homophobia, violence directed at them, and a culture that does not value their sexual orientation (Petersen et al., 1993).

Marcie Kaplan (1983a, 1983b) claimed that the various categories of mental illnesses listed in the APA's *Diagnostic and Statistical Manual of Mental Disorders (DSM-III;* 1980), which was used by mental health professionals to categorize the various symptoms associated with mental illnesses, contained "masculine-biased assumptions about what behaviors are healthy and what behaviors are crazy" (Kaplan, 1983a, p. 788). Categories for illnesses were arbitrarily defined by the psychiatric establishment to the detriment of women. Women who acted according to their social expectations were often thought of as disturbed. Simply being too "feminine" or not "feminine" enough seemed to be grounds for being considered disturbed (Chesler, 1972).

Not surprisingly, those who helped in the development of the *DSM-III* believed that Kaplan overstated her case by charging male bias in the diagnostic categories. Williams and Spitzer (1983) asserted that "strenuous efforts were made to avoid the introduction of male-biased assumptions" (p. 797). However, given our society's attitudes toward women and the underlying sexist ideology that permeates our social institutions, when women and men behave in ways that don't fit their prescribed gender roles, they may still be looked at very differently.

Feminist psychologists and psychiatrists challenged diagnoses proposed for the *DSM-III-R* (APA, 1987): paraphilic rapism, self-defeating personality disorder, and late luteal phase dysphoric disorder (the new psychiatric label for premenstrual syndrome) (Kupers, 1995; Sparks, 1985). Leonore Tiefer (1990) asked that diagnoses of sexual dysfunction be redefined because then-current definitions of sexual functioning were based on an implicit model of men's sexual gratification.

A few of the earlier concerns over gender bias appear to have been addressed in *DSM-IV* (APA, 1994). As Kupers (1995) concludes:

> The DSM-IV is definitely an improvement over previous editions. There is more participation by women in the work groups; Homosexuality has been deleted from the list of disorders as has DSM-III's Ego-Dystonic Homosexuality; the proposal to add Self-Defeating Personality has been defeated; and there are sections on racial and ethnic differences. . . . (p. 76)

Ivey and Ivey (1999) highlighted the need for psychologists to recognize that the DSM does not take into account a developmental perspective; that what is needed is a diagnostic manual that focuses on the client in social and historical contexts. A similar perspective was offered by Thakker, Ward, and Strongman (1999). These researchers noted that cross-cultural research indicates significant differences in the manifestation of symptoms of mental disorders across racial and ethnic groups. Guidelines such as these are important, as are modifications in the DSM to ensure all people are treated fairly by therapists (Busfield, 1996; Paludi et al., in press).

Poverty

Deborah Belle (1984) asked therapists and researchers to consider the impact of low income and ethnic minority membership on women's depressive symptomatology. Belle and her colleagues (Belle, Longfellow, Makosky, Saunders, & Zelkowitz, 1981) found that their sample of 42 urban low-income mothers had personally experienced 37 violent events and witnessed 35 stressful events to family and friends during the preceding 2 years. In addition, ethnic minority women may be immigrants to the United States and must adjust to a very different lifestyle. Research has indicated that inadequate housing, dangerous neighborhoods, and financial concerns are more serious stressors than acute crises (Brown, 1995).

A high proportion of individuals living below the poverty line are women living alone or women and their children. This fact, referred to as the **feminization of poverty,** is related to the increased proportion of women as heads of households, nonpayment of child support following a divorce, and lack of acceptable and affordable child care, which facilitate women's working at jobs that would make them self-sufficient (Belle, 1990).

Poverty also undermines the sources of social support for women that might otherwise buffer the effects of stress. Relatives, neighbors, and friends of low-income women are themselves often stressed. Thus, women are likely to experience a **contagion of stress:** stressful events occurring to others about whom they care are added to the stressors in their own lives. This fact contributes to low-income women being at greater risk for depression. As Belle (1990) noted:

> Women's coping strategies are constrained by poverty. To be poor generally means that one is frighteningly dependent on bureaucratic institutions such as the welfare system, the public housing authority, the health care system, and the courts. Poor women who must seek assistance from such systems often experience repeated failure that reflects no lack of imagination or effort on the women's part, merely the fact that a powerful institution declined to respond. Repeated instances of such failure, however, may lead to the (often veridical) perception that one is indeed powerless to remove the major stressors from one's life. (p. 387)

Multiple Roles and Women's Mental Health

Many employed mothers not only have to deal with the discrimination in their workplaces (see Chapter 9), but they also must contend with the workload of housekeeping and child rearing. Many women find themselves doing **double duty** in the workplace and at home, which contributes to their experiencing **role conflict** and **role overload** (Etaugh, 1993). And some women (research indicates predominantly white women) view the roles of mate and mother as incompatible with the role of paid worker (Mednick & Thomas, 1993). Ethnic minority women may also experience role conflicts stemming from the differences between the values of the dominant white culture and their own culture (Landrine, 1995). Hyde (1986), for example, suggested that employed African American women's decision to limit their family size is sometimes viewed by African American leaders as a form of racial genocide as well as disloyalty.

Ruth Anderson-Kulman and I (Anderson-Kulman & Paludi, 1986) asked employed mothers to address the interrelationships among their work and family roles. We assessed how factors associated with the mother's employment (e.g., part- or full-time), job satisfaction, and commitment to work influenced the family's cohesiveness and degree of conflict. We included single mothers in our sample and assessed the similarities and differences between single and married employed mothers.

The women surveyed worked predominantly in white-collar occupations and ranged in age from 20 to 42 years (mean age: 30 years). We found few differences between single and married women or between those who worked part-time or full-time. Job satisfaction among employed mothers was found to be predictive of family cohesion; that is, greater maternal job satisfaction was associated with greater cohesiveness among their families. Maternal role strain was also found to be associated with familial conflict. Less role strain among employed mothers was predictive of lower levels of family conflict.

The areas of conflict endorsed by the mothers indicated that managing the household and home cleaning were major sources of stress. In addition, a majority of women reported experiencing conflict about care of sick children. The most commonly reported problems among the mothers were child-related. Other problems included issues with time management, stress, and fatigue. The lack of available time appears to be most accentuated in areas related to self—community activities, reading, hobbies, and physical fitness.

The finding that greater job satisfaction was associated with lower levels of role strain among employed mothers suggests that psychologists must seek ways to enhance women's level of satisfaction with work, which, in turn, may be expected to promote positive coping among employed mothers and their families.

Personal belief systems about women's role as mothers also have a profound effect on women's achievement. In dual-earner families, women continue to assume most of the home and parental responsibilities (Atkinson & Blackwelder, 1993). Even in marriages among the more liberal professionals, **egalitarian role relations** in the workplace and the home are uncommon (Jacobsen & Edmondson, 1993).

Mothers spend the majority of their parenting time nurturing children, feeding them, comforting them, and so on. Fathers spend a great deal of their time with children in play. While fathers do contribute to child care (95 percent of fathers report that they do participate in child-care chores each day), they do less than mothers (Maume & Mullin, 1993; National Survey of Families and Households, 1988). Other research has noted that 30 percent of fathers with wives who are employed do three or more hours of daily child-care, while 74 percent of employed married mothers spend that amount of time in child-care activities. In addition, fathers tend to spend more time with sons than with daughters (Ishii-Kintz, 1994; Marsiglio, 1991). It is important to note that when fathers do participate in the care of preschoolers as well as older children, the quality of the parent-child relationship is enhanced (Lamb, 1997).

Thus, the demands of parenting continue to have a far more significant effect on the achievements and career paths of women than on those of men. Women—even adolescent and young adult women—assume that combining a career and a family is nearly impossible and a feat to be achieved only by "superwomen" (Betz, 1993; Farmer et al., 1999). A not-so-surprising result of these strongly held assumptions is a low marriage rate among professional women; a secondary result is the increasing prevalence of voluntary childlessness among professional couples (Betz, 1993).

Angela McBride (1990) also pointed out that:

> Combining work and family does not only mean juggling parenting and work outside the home. Increasingly, it means providing care for elderly parents and/or in-laws as well, and it is women who provide the bulk of this care. . . . The costs to caregivers are many. Responsibilities may cripple a woman's climb up the career ladder, while the burden of care (21–28 hours per week) can lead to emotional collapse, financial hardship, strained personal relationships, and declines in physical health. (p. 381)

Symptomatology associated with role conflict and role overload includes somatization, depression, obsessive compulsiveness, anxiety, discomfort, dissatisfaction, anger, and hostility. Women's role overload is affected by their *social support network,* coping style, and self-esteem, and by the centrality of each role to themselves (McBride, 1990).

Research on the impact of employed mothers on their children's development has generally found positive effects (Gottfried et al., 1999; Hoffman & Youngblade, 1999). Maternal employment has a positive influence on children and adolescents, particularly on daughters; they are more self-confident, achieve better grades in school and are more likely to pursue nontraditional careers than are daughters of mothers who are not employed (Caruso, 1996).

We will return to this issue again in Chapter 9.

THERAPEUTIC SUPPORT FOR WOMEN

These priority areas in understanding women's mental health have direct implications for psychotherapy for women. Several feminist therapies have therefore been instituted in the past several years to assist women in finding support for issues relating to victimization, aging, role conflict, and poverty.

For example, **consciousness-raising groups** (CR groups) are a powerful alternative or adjunct to traditional therapies (Reid et al., 1995; Worell, 1980). In a CR group, individuals meet in a group member's home. The groups usually are leaderless, or the members take turns being responsible for facilitating the session; this assures that no single member can act as an authority figure within the group. The main focus centers on the group members' feelings and self-perceptions. Women meet in a CR group to define their own experiences in terms of their own criteria. Thus, for many women, the CR group becomes a form of resocialization, a safe forum for rethinking traditional definitions of femininity.

Feminist therapies are based on a philosophical critique of society wherein women are seen as having less political and economic power than men have (Gammell & Stoppard, 1999; Gilbert, 1999). Another assumption is that the bases for women's personal problems are social, not personal. A major goal of feminist therapies is for women to learn to strive for and acquire economic and psychological independence. Feminist therapies generally accept the idea that society's definitions of gender roles and the devaluation of women and femininity must end (Marecek & Kravetz, 1998b).

Individual approaches to feminist psychotherapy vary in the importance they place on key issues (Gilbert, 1999). Three common concepts are: (a) recognition of the inequality of social and institutional power distributions, (b) integration of values into scientific study, and (c) a responsibility to advocate for change. (Russo & Green, 1993). Guidelines endorsed by feminist therapists have been outlined by Worell (1980):

1. Providing an egalitarian relationship with shared responsibility between counselor and client. The client is encouraged to trust her own judgment and to arrive at her own decisions. In contrast to many traditional counseling relationships, the client is never in a one-down position of having to accept counselor interpretations of her behavior or external prescriptions for appropriate living.

2. Employing a consciousness-raising approach. Women are helped to become aware of the societal restraints on their development and opportunities. Clients are helped to differentiate between the politics of the sexist social structure and those problems over which they have realistic personal control.

3. Helping women explore a sense of their personal power and how they can use it constructively in personal, business, and political relationships.

4. Helping women to get in touch with unexpressed anger in order to combat depression and to make choices about how to use their anger constructively.

5. Helping women to redefine themselves apart from their role relationships to men, children, and home; exploring women's fears about potential role changes that may alienate spouse and children, as well as coworkers and boss.

6. Encouraging women to nurture themselves as well as caring for others, thereby raising self-confidence and self-esteem.

7. Encouraging multiple skill development to increase women's competence and productivity. This may include assertiveness training, economic and career skills, and negotiation skills with important others who resist change. (pp. 480–481)

Hannah Lerman and Natalie Porter (1990) offered the following as guidelines for feminist therapists:

1. A feminist therapist increases her accessibility to and for a wide range of clients from her own and other identified groups through flexible delivery of services. When appropriate, the feminist therapist assists clients in accessing other services.

2. A feminist therapist is aware of the meaning and impact of her own ethnic and cultural background, gender, class, and sexual orientation and actively attempts to become knowledgeable about alternatives from sources other than her clients. The therapist's goal is to uncover and respect cultural and experiential differences.

3. A feminist therapist evaluates her ongoing interactions with her clientele for any evidence of the therapist's biases or discriminatory attitudes and practice. The feminist accepts responsibility for taking appropriate action to confront and change any interfering or oppressing biases she has.

4. A feminist therapist acknowledges the inherent power differentials between client and therapist and models effective use of personal power. In using the power differential to the benefit of the client, she does not take control of power that rightfully belongs to her client.

5. A feminist therapist discloses information to the client that facilitates the therapeutic process. The therapist is responsible for using self-disclosure with purpose and discretion in the interests of the client.

In February 2000, the Council of Representatives of the American Psychological Association adopted Guidelines for Psychotherapy with Lesbian, Gay, and Bisexual Clients. These guidelines include having psychologists' "strive to understand the ways in which social stigmatization (i.e., prejudice, discrimination, and violence) poses risks to the mental health and well-being of lesbian, gay, and bisexual clients." The guidelines, educational in their goal also advises psychologists that homosexuality and bisexuality are not indicative of any mental illness.

Feminist therapies with women who have been sexually victimized (see Chapter 10) have included additional guidelines. For example, Mary Koss (1990) recommended:

> [It] is very important that the counselor keep roles straight. . . . The clinician is not a judge and doesn't have to be concerned with whether [victimization] as legally defined has occurred. Likewise, the clinician is not an attorney. Clinicians should only help clients with their options, not advise them on their civil rights. . . . Also, clinicians must make clients aware that making a claim of psychological damages will require them to waive their right to confidentiality in the sessions and the treating therapist may be called to trial to present an assessment of the client. (p. 43)

To resolve the victimization caused by rape, incest, battering, or sexual harassment, shattered beliefs must be reformulated to assimilate the experience. Successful cognitive readjustment of beliefs includes a discovered ability to cope, learn, adapt, and become self-reliant, and it produces a greater sense of self-confidence, maturity, honesty, and strength. Koss (1990) and Quina (1996) pointed out that the cognitive readjustment process involves three themes: (a) the search for meaning: "Why did this happen to me?"; (b) attempts to gain mastery and control in one's life: "How can I prevent further victimization?"; and (c) attempts to promote self-enhancement: "Now that I have experienced this victimization, who am I?"

All of the feminist approaches enlighten women about their options and help women make more informed choices about dealing with their victimization and its effects. These techniques are useful in **empowering** women, who typically feel vulnerable and out of control because of the victimization process (Koss, 1990).

Feminist therapists believe that what has been called "mental illness" needs to be reconsidered (Gammell & Stoppard, 1999; Gilbert, 1999). Lynne Bravo Rosewater (1984) suggested that therapists should not concentrate on diagnosis per se, but rather on the implications of the diagnosis. She concluded:

> To treat the source of the problem, a policy change in the concept of our treatment modality is needed; it should look beyond the label given to a mental health problem to its consequence. If a woman is diagnosed as depressed, what assumptions underlie that label? Is it assumed that women are generally unhappy individuals? It is assumed that depressed individuals are hopeless? Is the appropriate remedy psychotherapy or chemotherapy or shock treatments?. . . A feminist analysis of depression sees it as originating from women's role in society. . . . A feminist treatment of depression, therefore, centers on an examination of the environmental impact on the woman in treatment, historically and currently. Depression may be viewed as a coping skill . . . or as a healthy reaction to an unjust situation. . . . The role expectations for women in our

society and whether a given role is right for any particular woman needs to be critically examined. Feminist therapy aids in the reevaluating and renegotiating of specific roles and the rules governing those roles. (pp. 272–273)

TO THE FUTURE

Karen Horney, Laura Brown, and Hannah Lerman have called upon personality theorists to redefine the constructs typically used in personality and psychotherapy so that women's lives and realities will be visible. Feminist psychologists are thus suggesting that **gender be conceptualized as a system of social relations.** To fully comprehend gender, we need to develop a perspective of the dialectics of ethnicity, sex, physical ability, gender role, class, age, and sexual orientation (Gammell & Stoppard, 1999; Gilbert, 1999). Conceptualizing gender in terms of status suggests that psychologists look to institutional or structural factors to explain women's and men's behavior rather than looking only within women or men themselves. As psychologist Rae Carlson (1972) concluded:

> Current theoretical orientations in personality . . . despite major controversies concerning the kinds of constructs and observations deemed relevant—are united in presenting a general, universalistic (and largely masculine) account of personality. Thus, the problems of accounting for feminine deviations from universal principles have been almost equally embarrassing to (and ignored by) all major theorists. A genuinely adequate theory of personality will need to draw from many existing formulations [of] those problems and insights which could provide a comprehensible view of total human functioning. (p. 29)

The theories of Brown and Lerman, among others, will be the link between understanding women from a patriarchal perspective and understanding them from a feminist one. The theories will also assist psychotherapists in placing value on women and femininity. We will address this issue in the next chapter, when we address women's physical health concerns.

NEW TERMS

androcentrism

androgynous conception of femininity and masculinity

Bem Sex Role Inventory (BSRI)

biculturalism

bipolar continuum

competency cluster

consciousness-raising groups

contagion of stress

cultural sensitivity of psychotherapists

distal stimulation

double duty

double standard for mental health

Draw-A-Person Test

egalitarian role relations

eight stages of man

empowerment

ethnocentrism

feminist therapies

feminization of poverty

gender as socially constructed

gendercentrism

gender-role adoption

gender-role identification

gender-role identity

gender-role orientation

gender-role preference

gender-role transcendence

heterosexism

identity versus role confusion

independent dimensions

intimacy versus isolation

IT Scale for Children

knowledge of sex-determined role standards

marginality

mommy track

motherhood mandate

multicomponent approach

normative creativity

penis envy

poverty

proximal stimulation

role conflict

role overload

therapist bias against women

warmth-expressiveness cluster

woman-based theory of personality

CHAPTER REVIEW QUESTIONS

1. Discuss the research on the impact of infant sex labeling on adults' interactions with infants.

2. Define the following terms and provide an example of each term in the personality theories of Erik Erikson and Sigmund Freud: *gendercentrism, heterosexism, ethnocentrism,* and *androcentrism.*

3. Discuss Erikson's theory about women's resolution of the "identity versus role confusion" and "intimacy versus isolation" stages.

4. Discuss what Nancy Felipe Russo means by the "motherhood mandate."

5. Comment on the political implications of the mommy track.

6. Explain how Freud's view of deviance in women may instead be a function of women's socially constructed position in their culture.

7. Define and provide examples of each of the following components of gender-role identity: *gender-role preference, gender-role adoption, gender-role orientation, knowledge of sex-determined role standards,* and *gender-role identification.*

8. To what does *psychological androgyny* refer? How is androgyny measured? Provide a critique of this construct.

9. What is *gender-role transcendence?* How is this concept similar to *psychological androgyny?*

10. Comment on the contributions made by Karen Horney to the field of women's personality development.

11. Discuss Laura Brown's views on integrating a lesbian/gay perspective in psychology. Design ways her work can be integrated in the psychology curriculum at your school.

12. Explain why Hannah Lerman believes that modern revisions of psychoanalytic theory do not further the understanding of women's personality development.

13. Discuss the research findings from the study conducted by Inge Broverman and her colleagues. Have these results been replicated?

14. Cite some examples of therapists' bias against women.

15. Offer some reasons why women are diagnosed and treated for mental illness at a much higher rate than men.

16. Discuss the goals of feminist therapies.

SELECTED READINGS

Comas-Diaz, L., & Greene, B. (1994). *Women of color: Integrating ethnic and gender identities in psychotherapy.* New York: Guilford.

Seu, I. B., & Heenan, M. C. (Eds.).(1998). *Feminism and psychotherapy: Reflections on contemporary theories and practice.* Thousand Oaks, CA: Sage.

LEARNING MORE ABOUT . . .

Suggestions for Term Papers Related to *Theoretical Perspectives on Women's Personalities and Mental Health*

Implications of Freudian theory for child sexual abuse cases

Relationship between gender role identity and stressful life events

Becoming visible: Women of color in theories of personality

TAKING ACTION . . .

on *Theoretical Perspectives on Women's Personalities and Mental Health*

Locate educational programs/support groups for women's mental health-related concerns that are present in your campus community.

Obtain a brochure/pamphlet from at least one of the programs you have identified.

Bring the educational material to your class to set on display for all students to view.

Have your college newspaper editor write a story about services available for women on campus.

REFERENCES

Albino, J., Tedesco, L., & Shenkle, C. (1990). Images of women: Reflections from the medical care system. In M. Paludi & G. Steuernagel (Eds.), *Foundations for a feminist restructuring of the academic disciplines.* New York: Haworth Press.

American Psychiatric Association. (1987). *Diagnostic and statistical manual for mental disorders* (3rd ed. rev.). Washington, DC: Author.

American Psychiatric Association. (1994). *Diagnostic and statistical manual of mental disorders* (4th ed.). Washington, DC: Author.

Anderson-Kulman, R., & Paludi, M. A. (1986). Working mothers and the family context: Predicting positive coping. *Journal of Vocational Behavior, 28,* 241–253.

Antill, J., Goodnow, J., Russell, G., & Cotton, S. (1996). The influence of parents and family context on children's involvement in household tasks. *Sex Roles, 34,* 215–236.

Ashmore, R., & DelBoca, F. (1981). Conceptual approaches to stereotypes and stereotyping. In D. Hamilton (Ed.), *Cognitive processes in stereotyping and intergroup behavior.* Hillsdale, NJ: Erlbaum.

Atkinson, M., & Blackwelder, S. (1993). Fathering in the 20th century. *Journal of Marriage and the Family, 55,* 975–986.

Basow, S. (1986). *Sex role stereotypes: Traditions and alternatives.* Monterey, CA: Brooks/Cole.

Belle, D. (1984). Inequality and mental health: Low income and minority women. In L. Walker (Ed.), *Women and mental health policy.* Beverly Hills, CA: Sage.

Belle, D. (1990). Poverty and women's mental health. *American Psychologist, 45,* 385–389.

Belle, D., Longfellow, C., Makosky, V., Saunders, E., & Zelkowitz, P. (1981). Income, mothers' mental health and family functioning in a low-income population. In American Academy of Nursing (Ed.), *The impact of changing resources on health policy.* Kansas City, MO: American Nurses Association.

Bem, S. L. (1974). The measurement of psychological androgyny. *Journal of Consulting and Clinical Psychology, 42,* 155–162.

Bem, S. L. (1993). *The lenses of gender: Transforming the debate on sexual inequality.* New Haven, CT: Yale University Press.

Betz, N. (1993). Women's career development. In F. L. Denmark & M. A. Paludi (Eds.), *The psychology of women: A handbook of issues and theories.* Westport, CT: Greenwood Press.

Betz, N., & Schifano, R. (2000). Evaluation of an intervention to increase realistic self-efficacy and interests in college women. *Journal of Vocational Behavior, 56,* 35–52.

Bohannon, J., & Blanton, P. (1999). Gender role attitudes of American mothers and daughters over time. *Journal of Social Psychology, 139,* 173–179.

Boston Lesbian Psychologies Collective. (Eds.). (1987). *Lesbian psychologies: Explorations and challenges.* Urbana: University of Illinois Press.

Bouhoutsos, J. (1984). Sexual intimacy between psychotherapists and clients: Policy implications for the future. In L. Walker (Ed.), *Women and mental health policy.* Beverly Hills, CA: Sage.

Bouhoutsos, J., Holroyd, J., Lerman, H., Forer, B., & Greenberg, M. (1983). Sexual intimacy between psychotherapists and patients. *Professional Psychology: Research and Practice, 14,* 185–196.

Broverman, I., Broverman, D., Clarkson, F., Rosenkrantz, P., & Vogel, S. (1970). Sex-role stereotypes and clinical judgments of mental health. *Journal of Consulting and Clinical Psychology, 34,* 1–7.

Brown, D. (1956a). *The IT Scale for Children.* Missoula, MT: Psychological Test Specialists.

Brown, D. (1956b). Sex role preference in young children. *Psychological Monographs, 70* (Whole No. 421).

Brown, L. (1984). Finding new language: Getting beyond analytic verbal shorthand in feminist therapy. *Women and Therapy, 3,* 73–75.

Brown, L. (1989). New voices, new visions. Toward a lesbian/gay paradigm for psychology. *Psychology of Women Quarterly, 13,* 445–458.

Brown, L. (1995). Cultural diversity in feminist therapy: Theory and practice. In H. Landrine (Ed.), *Bringing cultural diversity to feminist psychology.* Washington, DC: American Psychological Association.

Bukowski, W., Newcomb, A., & Hartup, W. (Eds.). (1996). *The company they keep: Friendships in childhood and adolescence.* New York: Cambridge University Press.

Busfield, J. (1996). *Men, women, and madness: Understanding gender and mental disorders.* New York: New York University Press.

Canino, G. (1982). The Hispanic woman: Sociocultural influences on diagnoses and treatment. In R. Becerra, M. Karno, & J. Escobar (Eds.), *The Hispanic: Mental health: Latina women in transition.* New York: Hispanic Research Center.

Carlson, R. (1972). Understanding women: Implications for personality theory and research. *Journal of Social Issues, 28,* 17–32.

Carnelley, K., Wortman, C., & Kessler, R. (1999). The impact of widowhood on depression: Findings from a prospective survey. *Psychological Medicine, 29,* 1111–1123.

Caruso, D. (1996). Maternal employment status, mother-infant interaction, and infant development. *Child and Youth Care Forum, 25,* 125–134.

Cascardi, M., O'Leary, K., & Schlee, K. (1999). Co-occurrence and correlates of postraumatic stress disorder and major depression in physically abused women. *Journal of Family Violence, 14,* 227–249.

Chesler, P. (1972). *Women and madness.* New York: Avon Books.

Cixous, H. (1976). *Portrait de Dora.* Paris: Editions des femmes.

Comas-Diaz, L. (1999). Feminist therapy with mainland Puerto Rican women. In L. Peplau et al. (Eds.), *Gender, culture, and ethnicity: Current research about women and men.* Mountain View, CA: Mayfield.

Cotterell, J. (1993). The relation of attachments and supports to adolescent well-being and school adjustment. *Journal of Adolescent Research, 7,* 28–42.

Craddick, R. (1963). The self image in the Draw-A-Person Test and self-portrait drawings. *Journal of Projective Techniques, 27,* 288–291.

Deaux, K., & Lewis, L. (1983). Assessment of gender stereotypes: Methodology and components. *Psychological Documents, 13,* 25 (ms. no. 2583).

Deaux, K., & Lewis, L. (1984). Structure of gender stereotypes: Interrelationships among components and gender label. *Journal of Personality and Social Psychology, 32,* 629–636.

DeFour, D. C., & Paludi, M. A. (1991). Integrating the scholarship on ethnicity into the psychology of women course. *Teaching of Psychology, 18,* 85–90.

Dohrenwend, B., & Dohrenwend, B. (1976). Sex differences and psychiatric disorders. *American Journal of Sociology, 81,* 1447–1454.

Eagly, A. (1995). The science and politics of comparing women and men. *American Psychologist, 50,* 145–158.

Erikson, E. (1963). *Childhood and society.* New York: Norton.

Erikson, E. (1968). *Identity: Youth and crisis.* New York: Norton.

Etaugh, C. (1993). Psychology of women: Middle and older adulthood. In F. L. Denmark & M. A. Paludi (Eds.), *Psychology of women: A handbook of issues and theories.* Westport, CT: Greenwood Press.

Fagot, B. (1988, November). *Gender role development in young children.* Paper presented at the Gender Roles Through the Life Span Conference, Muncie, IN.

Farmer, H., Wardrop, J., & Rotella, S. (1999). Antecedent factors differentiating women and men in science/nonscience careers. *Psychology of Women Quarterly, 23,* 763–780.

Fiske, S. (1993). Controlling other people: The impact of power on stereotyping. *American Psychologist, 48,* 621–628.

Fiske, S., & Stevens, L. (1993). What's so special about sex? Gender stereotyping and discrimination. In S. Oskamp & M. Costanzo (Eds.), *Gender issues in contemporary society.* Newbury Park, CA: Sage.

Freud, S. (1948). *Some psychological consequences of the anatomical distinction between the sexes.* In *Collected papers* (Vol. 5). London: Hogarth.

Freud, S. (1968). Femininity. In J. Strachey (Ed.), *The complete introductory lectures on psychoanalysis.* New York: Norton.

Gammell, D., & Stoppard, J. (1999). Women's experiences of treatment of depression: Medicalization or empowerment? *Canadian Psychology, 40,* 112–128.

Garnets, L., & Pleck, J. (1979). Sex role identity, androgyny, and sex role transcendence: A sex-role strain analysis. *Psychology of Women Quarterly, 3,* 270–283.

Geer, C., & Shields, S. (1996). Women and emotion: Stereotypes and the double bind. In J. Chrisler, C. Golden & P. Rozee (Eds.), *Lectures on the psychology of women.* New York: McGraw Hill.

Gilbert, L. (1999). Reproducing gender in counseling and psychotherapy: Understanding the problem and changing the practice. *Applied and Preventive Psychology, 8,* 119–127.

Ginorio, A., Gutierrez, L., Cauce, A., & Acosta, M. (1995). Psychological issues for Latinas. In H. Landrine (Ed.), *Bringing cultural diversity to feminist psychology.* Washington, DC: American Psychological Association.

Golombok, S., & Fivush, R. (1994). *Gender development.* Cambridge: Cambridge University Press.

Gottfried, A., Gottfried, A., Bathurst, K., & Killian, C. (1999). Maternal and dual-earner employment: Family environment, adaptations, and the developmental impingement perspective. In M. Lamb et al. (Eds.), *Parenting and child development in "nontraditional" families.* Mahwah, NJ: Erlbaum.

Greene, B. (1986). When the therapist is white and the patient is black: Considerations for psychotherapy in the feminist heterosexual and lesbian communities. *Women and Therapy, 5,* 41–46.

Halle, T. (1999). Implicit theories of social interactions: Children's reasoning about the relative importance of gender and friendship in social partner choices. *Merrill Palmer Quarterly, 45,* 445–467.

Handwerker, W. (1999). Cultural diversity, stress and depression: Working women in the Americas. *Journal of Women's Health and Gender Based Medicine, 8,* 1303–1311.

Helgeson, V. (1994). Prototypes and dimensions of masculinity and femininity. *Sex Roles, 31,* 653–682.

Hibbard, D., & Buhrmaster, D. (1998). The role of peers in the socialization of gender-related social interaction styles. *Sex Roles, 39,* 185–202.

Hill, M. (1988). Child-rearing attitudes of black lesbian mothers. In Boston Lesbian Psychologies Collective (Eds.), *Lesbian psychologies: Explorations and challenges.* Urbana: University of Illinois Press.

Hoffman, L. W., & Youngblade, L. (1998). Maternal employment, morale, and parenting style: Social class comparisons. *Journal of Applied Developmental Psychology, 19,* 389–413.

Holroyd, J., & Brodsky, A. (1977). Psychologists' attitudes and practices regarding erotic and non-erotic physical contact with patients. *American Psychologist, 32,* 843–849.

Horney, K. (1973). *Feminine psychology.* New York: Norton.

Hyde, J. (1986). *Half the human experience.* Lexington, MA: Heath.

Hyde, J., Klein, M., Essex, M., & Clark, R. (1995). Maternity leave and women's mental health. *Psychology of Women Quarterly, 19,* 257–285.

Idle, T., Wood, E., & Desmarais, S. (1993). Gender role socialization in toy play situations: Mothers and fathers with their sons and daughters. *Sex Roles, 28,* 679–691.

Ishii-Kuntz, M. (1994). Parental involvement and perception toward fathers' roles: A comparison between Japan and the United States. *Journal of Family Issues, 15,* 30–48.

Ivey, A., & Ivey, M. (1999). Toward a developmental diagnostic and statistical manual: The vitality of a contextual framework. *Journal of Counseling and Development, 77,* 484–490.

Juntunen, C. (1996). Relationship between a feminist approach to career counseling and career self-efficacy beliefs. *Journal of Employment Counseling, 33,* 130–143.

Kaplan, M. (1983a). A woman's view of *DSM-III. American Psychologist, 38,* 786–792.

Kaplan, M. (1983b). The issue of sex bias in *DSM-III:* Comments on the articles by Spitzer, Williams, and Kass. *American Psychologist, 38,* 802–803.

Karraker, K., Vogel, D., & Lake, A. (1995). Parents' gender stereotyped perceptions of newborns: The eye of the beholder revisited. *Sex Roles, 33,* 687–701.

Kimmel, E., & Rudolph, T. (1998). Growing up female. In K. Borman et al. (Eds.), *The adolescent years: Social influences and educational challenges.* Chicago, IL: The National Society for the Study of Education.

Koss, M. P. (1990). The women's mental health research agenda: Violence against women. *American Psychologist, 45,* 374–380.

Kupers, T. A. (1995). The politics of psychiatry: Gender and sexual preference in *DSM-IV. Masculinities, 3,* 597–605.

LaFromboise, T., Choney, S., James, A., & Running Wolf, P. (1995). American Indian women and psychology. In H. Landrine (Ed.), *Bringing cultural diversity to feminist psychology.* Washington, DC: American Psychological Association.

Lamb, M. (Ed.). (1997). *The role of the father in child development.* New York: Wiley.

Landrine, H. (Ed.). (1995). *Bringing cultural diversity to feminist psychology.* Washington, DC: American Psychological Association.

Lapan, R., Adams, A., Turner, S., & Hinkelman, J. (2000). Seventh graders' vocational interest and efficacy expectation patterns. *Journal of Career Development, 26,* 215–229.

Lerman, H. (1986). *A mote in Freud's eye: From psychoanalysis to the psychology of women.* New York: Springer.

Lerman, H., & Porter, N. (1990). *Feminist ethics in psychotherapy.* New York: Springer.

Lewin, M. (1984). Psychology measures femininity and masculinity: 2. From "13 gay men"— to the instrumental-expressive distinction. In M. Lewin (Ed.), *In the shadows of the past.* New York: Columbia University Press.

Lijtmaer, R. (1998). Psychotherapy with Latina women. *Feminism and Psychology, 8,* 538–543.

Lopez, S., Smith, A., Wolkenstein, B., & Charlin, V. (1993). Gender bias in clinical judgment: An assessment of the analogue method's transparency and social desirability. *Sex Roles, 28,* 35–45.

Lott, B., & Maluso, D. (1993). The social learning of gender. In A. E. Beall & R. J. Sternberg (Eds.), *The psychology of gender.* New York: Guilford Press.

Lynn, D. (1959). A note on sex differentiation in the development of masculinity and femininity. *Psychological Review, 64,* 126–135.

Lytton, H., & Romney, D. (1991). Parents' differential socialization of boys and girls: A meta-analysis. *Psychological Bulletin, 109,* 267–296.

Maccoby, E. E., & Jacklin, C. N. (1974). *The psychology of sex differences.* Stanford, CA: Stanford University Press.

Machover, K. (1949). *Personality projection: The drawing of the human figure.* Springfield, IL: Thomas.

Marecek, J. (1978). Psychological disorders in women: Indices of role strain. In I. Frieze, J. Parsons, P. Johnson, D. Ruble, & G. Zellman (Eds.), *Women and sex roles: A social psychological perspective.* New York: Norton.

Marecek, J., & Kravetz, D. (1998a). Power and agency in feminist therapy. In B. Seu & M. Heenan (Eds.), *Feminism and psychotherapy: Reflections on contemporary theories and practices.* Thousand Oaks, CA: Sage.

Marecek, J., & Kravetz, D. (1998b). Putting politics into practice: Feminist therapy as feminist praxis. *Women and Therapy, 21,* 17–36.

Marsiglio, W. (1991). Paternal engagement activities with minor children. *Journal of Marriage and the Family, 53,* 973–986.

Martin, C. (1989). Children's use of gender-related information in making social judgments. *Developmental Psychology, 25,* 80–88.

Martin, C., Fabes, R., Evans, S., & Wyman, H. (1999). Social cognition on the playground: Children's beliefs about playing with girls versus boys and their relations to sex segregated play. *Journal of Social and Personal Relationships, 16,* 751–771.

Maume, D., & Mullin, K. (1993). Men's participation in child care and women's work attachment. *Social Problems, 40,* 533–546.

McBride, A. (1990). Mental health effects of women's multiple roles. *American Psychologist, 45,* 381–384.

Mednick, M., & Thomas, V. (1993). Women and achievement. In F. L. Denmark & M. A. Paludi (Eds.), *The psychology of women: A handbook of issues and theories.* Westport, CT: Greenwood Press.

Millett, K. (1970). *Sexual politics.* New York: Doubleday.

Murtagh, A. (1998). The relationship of partners' intimacy behaviors to marital satisfaction and subclinical symptoms of depression in women. *Dissertation Abstracts International, 58* (12-B), 6818.

National Survey of Families and Households. (1988). *Married fathers with preschoolers.* Washington, DC: U.S. Government Printing Office.

Paludi, M. A., & Bauer, W. D. (1979). Impact of sex of experimenter on the Draw-A-Person Test. *Perceptual and Motor Skills, 40,* 456–458.

Paludi, M. A., & Gullo, D. F. (1986). Effect of sex label on adults' knowledge of infant development. *Sex Roles, 16,* 19–30.

Paludi, M., Paludi, C., & Doyle, J. (in press). *Sex and gender* (5th ed.). New York: McGraw Hill.

Petersen, A., Compas, B., Brooks-Gunn, J., Stemmler, M., Ey, S., & Grant, K. (1993). Depression in adolescence. *American Psychologist, 48,* 155–168.

Pope, K., Levenson, H., & Schover, L. (1979). Sexual intimacies in psychology training. *American Psychologist, 34,* 682–689.

Porter, N. (1995). Supervision of psychotherapists: Integrating anti-racist, feminist, and multicultural perspectives. In H. Landrine (Ed.), *Bringing cultural diversity to feminist psychology.* Washington, DC: American Psychological Association.

Quina, K. (1996). The victimizations of women. In M. Paludi (Ed.), *Sexual harassment on college campuses: Abusing the ivory power.* Albany: State University of New York Press.

Raag, T., & Rackliff, C. (1998). Preschoolers' awareness of social expectations of gender: Relationships to toy choices. *Sex Roles, 38,* 685–700.

Reid, P. T., Haritos, C., Kelly, E., & Holland, N. (1995). Socialization of girls: Issues of ethnicity in gender development. In H. Landrine (Ed.), *Bringing cultural diversity to feminist psychology: Theory, research and practice.* Washington, DC: American Psychological Association.

Reid, P. T., & Paludi, M. A. (1993). Psychology of women: Conception to adolescence. In F. L. Denmark & M. A. Paludi (Eds.), *Psychology of women: A handbook of issues and theories*. Westport, CT: Greenwood Press.

Ricciardelli, L., & Williams, R. (1995). Desirable and undesirable gender traits in three behavioral domains. *Sex Roles, 33,* 637–655.

Root, M. (1995). The psychology of Asian American women. In H. Landrine (Ed.), *Bringing cultural diversity to feminist psychology*. Washington, DC: American Psychological Association.

Rosenkrantz, P. (1968). Sex-role stereotypes and self-concepts in college students. *Journal of Consulting and Clinical Psychology, 32,* 287–295.

Rosewater, L. (1984). Feminist therapy: Implications for practitioners. In L. Walker (Ed.), *Women and mental health policy*. Beverly Hills, CA: Sage.

Rubin, J., Provenzano, F., & Luria, Z. (1974). The eye of the beholder: Parents' views on sex of newborns. *American Journal of Orthopsychiatry, 44,* 512–519.

Rudolf, H., & Priebe, S. (1999). Subjective quality of life in famale in-patients with depression: A longitudinal study. *International Journal of Social Psychology, 45,* 238–246.

Russo, N. F. (1976). The motherhood mandate. *Journal of Social Issues, 32,* 143–153.

Russo, N. F., & Green, B. (1993). Women and mental health. In F. L. Denmark & M. A. Paludi (Eds.), *Psychology of women: A handbook of issues and theories*. Westport, CT: Greenwood Press.

Sands, T. (1998). Feminist counseling and female adolescents: Treatment strategies for depression. *Journal of Mental Health Counseling, 20,* 42–54.

Seavey, C., Katz, P., & Zalk, S. R. (1975). Baby X: The effect of gender labels on adult responses to infants. *Sex Roles, 1,* 103–109.

Servin, A., & Bohlin, G. (1999). Do Swedish mothers have sex-stereotyped expectations and wishes regarding their own children? *Infant and Child Development, 8,* 197–210.

Sheehan, J. (1999). An analysis of the relationship between depression and the perception of available support in single and married women. *Dissertation Abstracts International, 59* (10-B), 5309.

Sherman, J. (1980). Therapist attitudes and sex role stereotyping. In A. Brodsky & R. Hare-Mustin (Eds.), *Women and psychotherapy*. New York: Guilford.

Sherman, J., Koufacos, C., & Kenworthy, J. (1978). Therapists: Their attitudes and information about women. *Psychology of Women Quarterly, 2,* 299–313.

Showalter, E. (1985). *The female malady: Women, madness and English culture, 1830–1980*. New York: Penguin.

Smith, M. (1980). Sex bias in counseling and psychotherapy. *Psychological Bulletin, 87,* 392–407.

Sparks, C. (1985). *Preliminary comment on the DSM-III proposed revision.* Bethesda, MD: Feminist Institute.

Thakker, J., Ward, T., & Strongman, K. (1999). Mental disorder and cross-cultural psychology: A constructivist perspective. *Clinical Psychology Review, 19,* 843–874.

Thorne, B. (1993). *Gender play: Girls and boys in school.* New Brunswick, NJ: Rutgers University Press.

Tiefer, L. (1990, August). *Gender and meaning in the DSM-III R sexual dysfunctions.* Paper presented at the meeting of the American Psychological Association, Boston.

Torres, S., & Han, H. (2000). Psychological distress in non-Hispanic white and Hispanic abused women. *Archives of Psychiatric Nursing, 14,* 19–29.

Will, J., Self, P., & Datan, N. (1976). Maternal behavior and perceived sex of infant. *American Journal of Orthopsychiatry, 46,* 135–139.

Williams, J. (1983). *Psychology of women: Behavior in a biosocial context.* New York: Norton.

Williams, J., & Spitzer, R. (1983). The issues of sex bias in DSM-III: A critique of "a woman's view of DSM-III" by Marcie Kaplan. *American Psychologist, 38,* 793–798.

Witt, S. (1997). Parental influence on children's socialization to gender roles. *Adolescence, 32,* 253–259.

Worell, J. (1980). New directions in counseling women. *Personnel and Guidance Journal, 58,* 477–484.

Worell, J. (1990). Women: The psychological perspective. In M. A. Paludi & G. Steuernagel (Eds.), *Foundations for a feminist restructuring of the academic disciplines.* New York: Haworth.

Wu, X., & DeMaris, A. (1996). Gender and marital status differences in depression: The effects of chronic strains. *Sex Roles, 34,* 299–319.

FIVE

WOMEN'S HEALTH ISSUES

IN WOMEN'S VOICES

Changes in the medical care establishment brought about by the women's movement have been primarily attitudinal. As women have become more informed health care consumers, the attitudes of physicians have begun to change. Women are demanding and, in many cases, receiving more information and respect from medical care professionals. These changes in the way services are delivered, as well as the challenge to the male-dominated hierarchical structure imposed by the growth of alternative health care systems, are legacies of the women's movement.

Judith Albino, Lisa Tedesco, and Cheryl Shenkle

We need freedom of choice to combat the health and mental health consequences of unintended and unwanted childbirth. . . . We need just laws and careful justice to protect women and children from abuse and violence. We need improved health care, at reasonable costs, for all of our citizens, especially women and the elderly who have been underserved in the past. We need continued and committed attention to women's concerns and child care across a broad range of public policies.

Bonnie Strickland

Feminist analyses of women's health reaffirm that "the personal is political." Often what might initially be viewed as biologically impersonal and objective is embedded in a social and political context. Thus, whether an Egyptian woman carries the burden of schistosomiasis, or an Indian woman suffers pesticide poisoning, or a homeless New York woman contracts HIV infection is shaped not only by access to medical care, but also by sociocultural factors.

Carol Travis

Chapter Outline

Questions for Reflection

1. Do you have annual physicals? Why or why not?

2. Do you or your women friends have annual gynecological exams?

3. Do you or your women friends and family members conduct monthly breast exams?

4. Are there health problems that are common in your family, e.g., diabetes, arthritis? If so, are you aware of diet and exercise approaches you can take to deal with being predisposed to these illnesses?

5. How is AIDS not spread? How is AIDS spread?

6. Do you diet excessively? Do your friends diet excessively?

7. What do you like about your physique? What would you like to change about your physique? Why?

8. Do you believe you have control over your body type? Or, do you believe your body type reflects genetics and there is nothing you can do to alter your physique?

9. What are the risks of drug use (including cigarette smoking and use of alcohol) on a developing fetus?

10. To what do you believe the term "feminist health care" refers?

INTRODUCTION: IMPACT OF MEDIA REPRESENTATION ON GIRLS' AND WOMEN'S SATISFACTION WITH THEIR BODIES

Before you begin reading this chapter, take out a pen and some paper. Now, list three things about your body that you like.

Why do you like these characteristics?

Next, list three things about your body that you dislike.

Why do you dislike these characteristics?

Do you believe your views are shaped by cultural definitions of beauty and attractiveness? Why or why not?

Do you believe you are:

Underweight?

Overweight?

At the right weight?

If you believe you are overweight, how many pounds do you believe you should lose?

Have you checked with a physician about the weight that's right for you? Why or why not?

Now flip through some magazines such as *Cosmopolitan, Vogue, Essence, Glamour*, and *Allure*. Notice the advertisement in these magazines. Do you see advertisements similar to the following:

Sexier, More Beautiful Breasts

Do Ugly Scars Embarrass You?

Permanent Hair Removal

I Went from a Size 16 to Size 4 Without Dieting

Do you believe there is sexism present in the magazine advertisements? Are there overweight women in the advertisements? If you do see overweight women in the ads, are the women portrayed with men? Are they smiling? Are they sitting alone? Are they with other overweight women?

Lanis and Covell (1995) reported that in North American culture, the sexually exploitative use of women in advertising has increased since 1970. Women rarely have a relationship to the product; they are shown in the advertisement only because of their physical attractiveness and sexuality. For example, women are depicted on the hoods of cars, not driving cars; they are depicted lying seductively next to a bottle of alcohol.

MRTW (1997) noted that an advertisement for Epson color printers exploited women sexually. In one of Epson's advertisements, a woman in a bathing suit is depicted. The accompanying copy tells us to look more closely: the woman is wearing the bathing suit at 360 DPI, a wet bathing suit at 720 DPI, a "painted on" bathing suit at 1440 DPI. Thus, a nude woman was used by Epson to supposedly demonstrate the quality of their printers.

We are all aware of media stereotypes, especially those found in women's magazines and on television. We formulate ideas about their roles in society from the media content. Children Now (1997) conducted a study of children aged 10 to 17 about their knowledge of women and men on television. Children and adolescents reported that men television characters act as leaders, play sports, want to be kissed or have sex. They identified the following behaviors common to women on television: Women worried about their appearance and weight, cried, and flirted. Sixty-nine percent of the girls and 40 percent of the boys indicated that they wanted to look like a television character. Perhaps more importantly, 31 percent of the girls and 22 percent of the boys actually altered their appearance to look more like a television character.

Additional research has indicated that girls and women feel inadequate when they compare themselves with the media portrayals of femininity (Kilbourne, 1999). They feel dissatisfied with their body, hair, teeth, weight, breast size, and height (Jackson, 1992; Wolf, 1991).

Certainly, this discussion does not mean that advertising causes eating disorders. However, the images of girls and women portrayed in advertisements does contribute to the self-hatred girls and women have toward their bodies. As Kilbourne (1999) noted, advertising promotes unhealthy and abusive attitudes about eating, attractiveness, and thinness for women.

Many adolescent girls believe they are too fat; very few boys, in comparison, feel this way. And adolescent girls perceive the normative physical developmental changes accompanying pubescence (see Chapter 3)—especially the redistribution of weight—as their gaining weight and needing to diet (Dyer & Tiggermann, 1996; Pipher, 1994).

Girls and women have usually been willing to harm themselves physically to achieve the elusive status of being "feminine" (Fallon, Katzman, & Wooley, 1994; Wiederman & Pryor, 2000). With beauty so prized and rewarded in our society, it is little wonder that many women seem so concerned with having a youthful and beautiful body. One way to do that is to stay thin. Consequently, women are on a never-ending cycle of dieting, visiting fitness centers daily or weekly, and working toward the "fashion model" look—a look that is tall, white, blond, middle to upper class, and bordering on emaciation (Kempa & Thomas, 2000; Striegel-Moore & Smolak, 2000; Thompson, Sargent, & Kemper, 1996). Why? Susan Brownmiller (1984) gives this answer:

Hippy or scrawny, busty or flat, the general principle governing the feminine body is not subject to change. How one looks is the chief physical weapon in female-against-female competition. Appearance, not accomplishment, is the feminine demonstration of desirability and worth. In striving to approach a physical ideal, by corsetry in the old days or by a cottage-cheese-and-celery diet that begins tomorrow, one arms oneself to fight the competitive wars. Feminine armor is never metal or muscle, but, paradoxically, an exaggeration of physical vulnerability that is reassuring (unthreatening) to men. Because she is forced to concentrate on the minutiae of her bodily parts, a woman is never free of self-consciousness. She is never quite satisfied, and never secure, for desperate, unending absorption in the drive for a perfect appearance—call it feminine vanity—is the ultimate restriction on freedom of mind. (pp. 50–51)

One answer to why women harm themselves in order to meet with society's approval concern the interface between achievement and femininity (see Chapter 9). For example, Brett Silverstein and colleagues (Silverstein, Perdue, Wolf, & Pizzolo, 1988) reported that some forms of eating disorders are related to women's beliefs that intellectual/professional achievement for women is a disadvantage. The strongest pattern of evidence for this hypothesis is related to the following conditions: (1) The women's parents had traditional sexist attitudes about women and women's roles; (2) the women's mothers were dissatisfied with their career choices; (3) the women's fathers viewed their wives as being unintelligent; and (4) the women's brother(s) was (were) treated as the most intelligent sibling(s) in the family.

Using items on their **Body-Self-Relations Questionnaire,** Linda Jackson, Linda Sullivan, and Ronald Rostker (1988) found that women who have an androgynous gender-role orientation as well as a feminine gender-role orientation regard their physical appearance as very important: "Women who are high in femininity may view an attractive physical appearance as an asset in interpersonal exchange, a domain that they consider important" (p. 440).

Laura Brown (1987) contends that women's fear of fat, distortions of body image, and poor self-feeding are consequences of the conflict between wanting to be healthy and adherence to the following male-biased rules governing women's behavior:

1. Small is beautiful.

2. Weakness of body is valued.

3. Women are forbidden to nurture themselves in a straightforward manner.

4. Women are forbidden to act powerfully in overt ways.

5. Women are valued only when they adhere unfailingly to the first four rules.

MEET DR. LINDA JACKSON

According to Dr. Jackson:

The major focus of my research on physical attractiveness is to demonstrate that attractiveness effects depend on gender. Of particular interest are the differential consequences of attractiveness for women and men in the workplace. Past research and theory suggest conflicting conclusions about attractiveness for women. On the one hand is the evidence that attractiveness is a liability for women in male-dominated occupations, a finding explicable from a sociocultural perspective. On the other hand is the evidence that attractiveness is an asset for women in the professional domain, a finding explicable from a sociobiological perspective. Future research is aimed at clarifying whether attractiveness is a professional asset or a liability for women, and why it is a more important consideration for women than men.

Brown has also reported that lesbian women are less likely to have eating disorders than women in general. She stated:

> Lesbians are at risk from fat oppression in different ways than are heterosexual women. A lesbian's own internalized homophobia is likely to determine the degree to which she fat-oppresses herself. The more a lesbian has examined and worked through her internalized homophobia, the less at risk she is to be affected by the rules that govern fat oppression. . . . Once having successfully begun to challenge the rule against loving women in a patriarchal and misogynist context, a woman may be more likely not to impose other such rules on herself, for example, conventions about attractiveness, size, and strength. (p. 299)

Thus, many women associate gaining weight with rejection by their friends—especially male friends and boyfriends. And several researchers have reported that overweight women are viewed negatively by others (as well as by themselves) (Rothblum, 1992). Rothblum reviewed the research on individuals' attitudes toward overweight women and found that (1) college students rate overweight women as less active, less intelligent, less hardworking, less successful, less athletic, and less popular than nonoverweight women; (2) when students are asked to rank categories of people as potential marriage partners, they report preferring to marry an embezzler, cocaine user, shoplifter, and blind woman before an overweight woman; (3) landlords are less likely to rent apartments and houses to overweight than nonoverweight women; and (4) physicians rate overweight women as weak-willed and awkward.

Women who are **overweight** (defined as weighing at least 20% more than the recommended weight on standardized charts) do not necessarily eat more than average-weight women (Fodor & Thal, 1984; Wooley & Wooley, 1980). And overweight women who do lose weight are very likely to gain the weight back. Women's metabolism changes a great deal after dieting, and they can function on fewer calories (Rodin, Silberstein, & Striegel-Moore, 1985). But rather than accept this biological fact, many women blame themselves for not having enough "will power" and "restraint" to stay slender. In women's own voices:

> I remember I used to be desperately hungry—but by eating I would be in some way failing.

> Just as the worker's ultimate weapon in his negotiation with management is his labor and the threat of its withdrawal, so my body was my ultimate and, to me, only weapon in my bid for autonomy. It was the only thing I owned, the only thing which could not be taken away from me. . . . I had discovered an area of my life over which others had no control. . . . What was going on in my body was as unreal, as devoid of meaning, as were the events in the outside world. The two were part of one whole, a whole of which "was no part." I had shrunk to a nugget of pure and isolated will whose sole purpose was to triumph over the wills of others and over the chaos ensuing from their conflicting demands.

Research by Ferron (1997) suggested that U.S. adolescents are more likely than French adolescents to believe that there are personal characteristics that will enable them to achieve a body that represents an image of perfection. These characteristics include will power, adherence to rules, courage, and self-confidence. Ferron reported that U.S. adolescent girls were more likely than French girls to engage in behaviors that are harmful to their health, including eating unbalanced diets and eating disorders (to be discussed next in this chapter). U.S. and French adolescent boys were mostly satisfied with their height and weight. However, 75 percent of the U.S. girls as compared with less than 25 percent of the French girls indicated they would be considerably happier in their lives if they had a "flawless body." Happiness was operationally translated into having more friends, an easier life, accepted by a peer group, and finding love.

This latter issue was commonly expressed by adolescent girls in Halpern and colleagues' (Halpern, Udry, Campbell, & Suchindran, 1999) research. Adolescent girls indicated that having a boyfriend was important to them and that slimness is an important factor in dating and popularity with boys. Halpern and colleagues also reported that for both African American and white adolescent girls, more body fat was associated with a lower probability of dating.

There has been empirical support for minority adolescent girls developing a higher incidence of eating disorders as they assimilate into white culture (Striegel-Moore, Schreiber, Lo, Crawford, Obarzanek, & Rodin, 2000). Adolescent girls associate gaining weight with rejection by their friends, especially male friends and potential dating partners.

Adjusting to a masculine-biased definition of feminine physical beauty can be hazardous to women's health (Davis, Claridge, & Fox, 2000; Wiederman & Pryor, 2000). Severe dieting can lead to death.

The direct and indirect media messages about women and their role in relationships—at work or with sexual partners—are destructive to girls' and women's health. Let's address this issue by first discussing weight problems and eating disorders.

WEIGHT PROBLEMS AND EATING DISORDERS

Anorexia Nervosa

Estimates suggest that approximately 1 percent of all women between the ages of 12 and 25 years suffer from this eating disorder (Smith, 1996). These percentages translate into approximately 260,000 women. The most likely age for the onset of anorexia nervosa is 12 to 18 years. **Anorexia nervosa** must be considered a serious **eating disorder** because 15 percent of anorexics die (Smith, 1996). Estimates suggest that women anorexics outnumber men by a 20:1 ratio (Smith, 1996), and there is an increasing incidence of anorexia nervosa among black adolescent and young adult women (Henriques, Calhoun, & Cann, 1996; Lask & Bryant-Waugh, 2000).

Anorexia nervosa among women is characterized by three common symptoms: (1) self-induced, severe weight loss; (2) **amenorrhea** (i.e., cessation of menstrual periods); and (3) an intense fear of losing control over eating and thus becoming fat (Garfinkel & Garner, 1982). **Lanugo**, a growth of downy hair on the body, is also present. This is part of the body's attempt to keep itself warm when so few calories are taken in by the anorexic.

The anorexic, unlike persons who go through the "normal ritual" of dieting to lose a pound or two, voluntarily induces a dramatic loss of body weight (i.e., 25% of original body weight) that can damage body organs and threaten life. Anorexics typically limit their caloric intake to 600 to 800 calories a day. Their thoughts are obsessively focused on eating and on food in general; Consequently, rituals surrounding eating develop.

Several psychosocial characteristics have been offered to explain anorexia, such as a distorted body image and an extreme concern with pleasing others (Jackson, 1992; Smith, 1996; Travis, 1993). However, there is no universally accepted theory about its onset. Often, anorexia occurs in response to a new situation where women may be judged by masculine-biased standards (e.g., starting a new job, dating, entering college, achievement, marriage). Our society's obsession with the "fashion model" look for women may lead some young women to develop an intense fear of gaining weight because they associate weight gain with rejection by others. Anorexics usually engage in denial; they insist that they have no problem with food and that they are not underweight. This denial prevents them from seeking psychotherapeutic support (Smith, 1996).

Bulimia

Initially, several researchers believed that **bulimia** was a subcategory of anorexia nervosa (Hinz & Williamson, 1987). However, bulimia is now classified as a separate eating disorder. Bulimia, or the **"binge-purge syndrome,"** has received considerable attention in the past several years (Boskind-White & White, 1986; Jackson, 1992; Schlesier-Stroop, 1984).

Bulimia is characterized by episodes of inconspicuous gross overeating (food binges) that typically last for an hour or two. The food is usually high in calories, soft, and sweet. The food binge stops when the woman experiences severe abdominal pain, goes to sleep, is interrupted, or engages in self-induced purging (e.g., vomiting or using laxatives). Although bulimic women, like anorexic women, have an abnormal concern with becoming fat, the bulimic differs from the anorexic in several ways. Generally, a bulimic is only slightly underweight or even maintains normal weight (Fairburn, 1981; Smith, 1996). Amenorrhea is not a usual feature among bulimics. Although both anorexics and bulimics have a morbid fear of becoming fat, the bulimic's weight fluctuates between weight loss and weight gain, whereas the anorexic loses weight to an extreme degree (Crandall, 1988).

Bulimia is a fairly common problem. Surveys of college populations have found a high incidence (13 to 67%) of undergraduate women engaging in bulimic behaviors. It is difficult to reliably estimate the number of bulimics because of the extreme secrecy surrounding the women's behavior. The bulimic's food binges and vomiting usually occur in private.

Adding to the problem is the bulimic's normal appearance in terms of body weight. Her eating habits in social situations also appear quite normal. Bulimia leads to medical complications involving the kidneys and intestines, as well as dental problems (because of the gastric acid in the vomited food).

Jackson (1992) offered the following conclusions concerning bulimics and nonbulimics:

1. Bulimics are more accepting of cultural standards of attractiveness and thinness and aspire to a thinner ideal than nonbulimics.

2. Bulimics score higher than nonbulimics on measures of need for approval and interpersonal sensitivity.

3. Bulimics have a more feminine gender-role orientation than do nonbulimics.

Developmental Considerations

Anorexia and bulimia have frequently been discussed in the context of adolescence and young adulthood, but we need to consider them as eating disorders affecting women of all ages (Smith, 1996). For women in midlife, the narrow standard of beauty and femininity can lead to a mourning over the loss of important years of youth (Hyde & DeLamater, 1999). As women grow older, many gain weight. Women's metabolism slows as they age; consequently, they require fewer calories. Women usually consume the same amount of food as before, however. Gaining weight in midlife and beyond may be especially hard to accept when women must deal simultaneously with a host of other bodily changes contributing to menopause (see Chapter 3).

Health problems, too, can lead to body changes, including weight gain. Women taking steroids (e.g., prednisone) for asthma, rheumatoid arthritis, or lupus gain weight; their faces become more rounded and puffy. Connective tissue diseases contribute to women's hands and feet becoming swollen.

McKinley (1999) interviewed middle-aged mothers and their young adult daughters. Her results suggested that both mothers and daughters internalized the cultural body standards. Mothers had lower levels of surveillance and body shame than daughters. In addition, mothers weighed more and were less satisfied with their weight than daughters. Restricted eating showed no age differences. Middle-aged women restricted their eating because of a fear of aging (Gupta, 1995). Thus, restricted eating is common for women in both age groups and is an expression of many anxieties related to traditional female socialization practices (Gupta, 1995). Furthermore, McKinley reported that among the mothers in her sample, those whose partners disapproved of their appearance had the lowest body esteem compared to those middle-aged women with no partners or who had partners who approved of their appearance. According to McKinley:

> As parents, we need to do more than reassure our daughters that they are attractive; we need to encourage them to evaluate themselves on other dimensions altogether . . . as long as women and society continue to evaluate women's worth in terms of how well they meet some arbitrary appearance standard, the lives of women of all ages will be negatively affected. (p. 768)

Eating disorders are becoming widespread problems in our society (Haworth-Hoeppner, 2000; Striegel-Moore & Smolak, 2000). It seems that as long as our society stresses thinness as a major criterion of beauty, we will have many women jeopardizing their physical well-being and having poor self-concepts. Ruth Snyder and Lynn Hasbrouck (1996) reported that women's identification with feminist values is associated with body satisfaction and feelings of effectiveness. And Christine Smith (1996) concluded:

> Beliefs about what is attractive or erotic vary from one culture to another and from one historical period to another. What is beautiful? In some cultures facial scarring is attractive; in others, drooping breasts. What is currently beautiful for women in Western culture? If one looks at the media . . . one sees models who are tall and very thin; they are wrinkle-free, and have small hips and waists, medium to large breasts, and European features. Women in Western cultures are constantly bombarded with images of this unrealistically slim, eternally young, ideal woman. (p. 91)

Educational campaigns to assist girls and women with developing healthier body images have been found to be beneficial for increasing girls' and women's knowledge about eating and eating disorders, unrealistic media images, and limits to control of body size and shape (Kilbourne, 1999).

SUBSTANCE ABUSE

Substance abuse is the use of alcohol or drugs to such an extent that normal functioning is impaired. Let's discuss abuse of cigarettes and alcohol and the resulting impact on women's concept of self and on the emotional and physical health of women and their children.

Smoking

Lung cancer now surpasses breast cancer as the leading cause of death for women (Waldron, 1995). Following World War II, a significant number of women began smoking, until the prevalence of smoking among women reached its peak in the late 1960s and early 1970s. Currently, adolescent and young adult women surpass men in beginning smoking (Hanson, 1994). Advertisements for cigarettes depict women smokers as glamorous, young, thin, liberated, and sophisticated. Consider the product names and slogans in these advertisements, for example, "You've come a long way, baby!" and "Virginia Slims." Research has suggested that adolescent women may be especially vulnerable to such advertisements in their search for an identity status (Kilbourne, 1999).

The nicotine obtained through cigarette smoking is an addicting agent. In addition to lung cancer, several diseases are attributed to cigarette smoking, for example, heart disease, strokes, cancer of the urinary tract, larynx, oral cavity, esophagus, kidney, pancreas, and uterus. Women who smoke are also likely to suffer from bronchitis, chronic sinusitis, emphysema, and severe hypertension.

Maternal health is also adversely affected by cigarette smoking. During pregnancy, nicotine retards the rate of fetal growth as well as increases the likelihood of spontaneous abortion, low birth weight, fetal death, and neonatal death (Hanson, 1994). Children of mothers who smoke have deficiencies in physical growth, intellectual development, and social-emotional development that are independent of other risk factors. These children are also at risk for respiratory disorders (Hanson, 1994; Waldron, 1995).

Alcohol

A look at alcohol advertisements reveals that drinking promises women sexiness, friendship, romance, a man, sophistication, beauty, and increased status (Kilbourne, 1999). The alcohol industry has taken advantage of the data on women's careers and changing roles, especially women's participation in paid employment, and has established an aggressive campaign directed toward women drinkers. Employed women have more opportunities to drink and have greater exposure to alcohol than nonemployed women (Wilsnack & Wilsnack, 1991).

However, unlike men, women are not likely to be met with approval when they drink (Ettorre, 1997). Ettorre (1997) noted: "[R]eal men drink, but nice girls don't" (p. 14). Traditional gender-role norms that exist in North American culture get expressed with respect to health concerns. Ettore's sentiment has been found to receive empirical support. For example, parents are more likely to provide their sons with opportunities to drink alcohol than they are their daughters (Barnes, Farrell, & Dintcheff, 1997).

Ettorre (1997) has also found a relationship between sex and sexual orientation with alcoholism. Lesbian women were more likely than heterosexual women to drink heavily and become alcoholics. One explanation offered by Ettore for this finding concerns the fact that bars have traditionally been safe places for lesbians and gay men; thus drinking plays a role in their social lives. Furthermore, homophobia is related to feelings of isolation and alienation for lesbians and gay men. They may drink heavily as a way to cope with alienation, violence, and oppression in their lives.

Women who drink excessively are at increased risk for heart attack, stroke, liver disease, muscle disease, gastrointestinal problems, and brain damage. Women's stomachs have almost none of the enzyme that helps digest alcohol prior to it getting into their bloodstream (Freeza, Padova, Pozzato, Terpin, Baraona, & Lieber, 1990). Consequently, more alcohol gets into their bloodstream than into men's, even when controlling for the amount of alcohol drunk relative to body size.

Women who consume an excessive amount of alcohol during pregnancy increase their baby's risk of being born with **fetal alcohol syndrome**, a pattern of irreversible abnormalities such as joint defects, mental retardation, and pre- and postnatal growth deficiencies. To date, no safe level of alcohol intake during pregnancy has been established.

Unlike women who smoke cigarettes, many women who drink alcohol do so privately, as a result of our culture's tendency to judge women harshly (especially in terms of their sexuality and ability to care for children) when they become dependent on alcohol (Corrigan & Butler, 1991; Gomberg, 1993). Consequently, women may hide their addiction rather than seek assistance with alcoholism (Travis, 1993). Some women may become addicted to **mood-altering drugs** prescribed by physicians who may misdiagnose their alcoholism as depression or anxiety (Albino, Tedesco, & Shenkle, 1990).

Many factors predispose a woman to become an alcoholic. These factors include a family history of alcoholism, incest, disruption in early family life, and a history of depression (Gomberg, 1993). Furthermore, there is an interrelationship among sex, race, and alcohol abuse. For example, Travis (1988) found that, among adolescent girls, Native Americans drank the most and African Americans drank the least; Latinas, whites, and Asians consumed intermediate amounts. Research also suggests that the death rate of Native American women from chronic liver disease and cirrhosis exceeds the rate of Native American, African American, Hispanic, Asian, and white men (LaFromboise, Choney, James, & Running Wolf, 1995). Teresa LaFromboise and her colleagues noted that alcoholism among Native American women has serious implications for the future of Native Americans as a people: "The incidence of fetal alcohol syndrome and fetal alcohol effect ranges from 1 in 552 births to 1 in 55 births, depending on the tribe and area of residence" (p. 203).

BREAST DISEASES

Breast cancer is the second leading cause of cancer deaths among women aged 35 and 55 (Helgeson, Cohen, Schultz, & Yasko, 2000). More than 100,000 women each year in the United States are diagnosed with breast cancer. The risk for women increases with age. Mortality rates from breast cancer are declining among women between 45 and 54. However, they are dramatically increasing for women over 55 years of age. (Helgeson et al., 2000).

According to the American Cancer Society, 1 in 8 women will develop breast cancer during her lifetime. Since the etiology of breast cancer is unknown, early detection is important to reduce mortality (George, 2000; Kline & Mattison, 2000). Increased education about breast cancer, cancer genetics, and personal risk for breast cancer is warranted since most women are not knowledgeable about these issues (Donovan & Tucker, 2000; McCaul & O'Donnell, 1998). Furthermore, the literature on breast cancer and other **breast diseases** has not been written at appropriate reading levels and is not culturally sensitive (Guidry, Fagan, & Walker, 1998). This factor may play an important part in why women are not as knowledgeable as they must be about breast cancer.

Certainly, most conditions that contribute to changes in women's breasts are not cancer (Donovan & Tucker, 2000). They are benign conditions, such as **fibrocystic condition** or **fibroadenomas.** Fibrocystic condition refers to the breast cells retaining fluid. Cysts often develop during ovulation and just prior to menstruation, when hormone levels change. Lumps will appear during these times, but they will decrease or disappear within a day or two after menstruation begins. This condition affects some women at menarche and others during their young adult years; it disappears at menopause for the majority of women. Research has indicated that fibrocystic condition is not a causative factor in breast cancer (Grady, 1988).

Fibroadenomas are lumps that do not fluctuate with the menstrual cycle. These lumps most often appear during women's teens or 20s, and they may interfere with circulation or distort the shape of the breast. When this occurs, they may be surgically removed. At menopause, fibroadenomas shrink, suggesting that they are a normal occurrence. There is no evidence to link fibroadenomas with breast cancer.

Breast self-examination for breast cancer (see Figure 5.1) is used by only a fraction of the women who might benefit from it. Research has also indicated that older women—who are at greater risk for breast cancer—most often do not exam-

FIGURE 5.1   *Three Methods of Breast Self-Examination*

1. Go through each section of the "clock" in turn, starting with the nipple at the center.
2. Examine in concentric circles, spiraling upward.
3. Examine in strips, starting at the top of the chest.

1.

2.
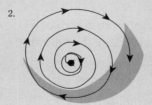

3.
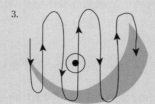

ine their breasts (Grady, 1988). The failure of women to use breast self-examination may result from their being discouraged from touching their bodies (Fulmore, 1999).

Mammograms help detect breast cancer in its early stages. They reveal cancers as small as one quarter inch in diameter. The American Cancer Society recommends that women get a **baseline** (i.e., initial) **mammogram** between the ages of 35 and 40 years. Mammograms should be repeated every year or two from ages 40 to 49 years and annually after the age of 50 years. Some women may not want to get **mammograms** because they fear the radiation, but the radiation used in mammograms is very low and thus safe.

Other women may not get mammograms because of the cost involved. There are facilities that offer free or low-cost mammograms as a preventive measure. Women who use these facilities must be certain that a qualified physician will review and evaluate the results.

Women typically underutilize mammographies, however, especially among older women breast cancer survivors (Kent, Howie, Fletcher, Newbury, & Hosie, 2000; Preston, Scinto, Grady, Schulz, & Petrillo, 2000; Schapira, McAuliffe, & Nattinger, 2000).

Educational campaigns have been successful in assisting women to get mammographies and in breast self-examination (e.g., Brown et al., 2000; Donovan & Tucker, 2000; Helgeson et al., 2000).

AIDS

For the next few minutes, take the following quiz.

True or False:

HIV/AIDS is transmitted through:
1. Contact with a pet
2. Shaking hands, hugging, or casual kissing
3. Sharing needles or other injection devices
4. Blood
5. Semen
6. Vaginal secretions
7. Using the same restrooms, water fountains, or telephones
8. Donating blood
9. Being bitten by an insect
10. Sharing dishes or eating utensils

The correct answers are:

1. F
2. F
3. T
4. T
5. T
6. T
7. F
8. F
9. F
10. F

How did you do on this quiz? From what source(s) have you obtained information about sexually transmitted diseases, including HIV? Are these sources reliable?

The World Health Organization Joint United Nations Program on HIV/AIDS (1999) reviewed how AIDS and HIV impacts on women, men, children, and adolescents worldwide, especially in developing nations. This report indicated that women are more adversely affected by HIV/AIDS than men. The majority of women diagnosed with **AIDS (acquired immunodeficiency syndrome)** are ethnic minority women. Amaro (1988) first reported that women and children are overrepresented among individuals diagnosed with AIDS. The highest risk factors for women are intravenous drug users and heterosexual contact with an individual at risk for AIDS (Suffet & Lifshitz, 1991; World Health Organization, 1999). Heterosexual contact includes contact with bisexual men or men having unprotected intercourse with multiple partners.

Flora and Thoresen (1988) and Gentry (1993) noted the epidemiological features of AIDS for women: It is related to women's economic and social status. Furthermore, the majority of women who contract HIV infection do so through participation in behaviors that involve intimate contact with HIV-infected bodily fluids—blood, semen, and vaginal secretions. Most pediatric cases of AIDS result from infection acquired from an HIV-positive mother (World Health Organization, 1999).

While the number of individuals infected with HIV continues to become quite large, the number of AIDS deaths started to decline in 1997. New treatments, especially protease inhibitors (Altman, 1997) have contributed to individuals' living longer. We should note, however, that this treatment is expensive and may be out of the reach of many people who are most likely to be at risk for contracting HIV.

The World Health Organization (1999) identified the following factors that make women, especially adolescent girls, susceptible to HIV: lack of sexual knowledge (see Chapter 6), sexual abuse (see Chapter 10), and embarrassment over HIV infection.

The World Health Organization offered recommendations about how to reduce girls' and women's vulnerability to HIV: gender equality awareness, the promotion of HIV technologies, improved health care and health education access, and support services for girls and women with HIV/AIDS. All of these recommendations have been based on empirical research findings related to adolescent girls and boys not using condoms during sexual intercourse.

Research has also indicated that effective communication about sex is not considered appropriate behavior in many cultures, including Latin American cultures (Amaro & Gornemann, 1992). Consequently, women feel unable to assert themselves by suggesting their partners wear condoms (Amaro & Gornemann, 1992). This behavior puts themselves and their partners at risk for sexually transmitted diseases as well as at risk for pregnancy. Amaro and Gornemann (1992) further pointed out that should men suggest they use condoms, women attribute their motives to sex for pleasure, not for love and with the intention of marriage. Thus, condoms may only be viewed as a form of birth control and not for their use in protection against sexually transmitted diseases, including HIV.

Under the aforementioned circumstances, counseling and testing should be more widely used. Jeanne Brooks-Gunn, Cherrie Boyer, and Karen Hein (1988) reported that the majority of parents interviewed about education on AIDS stated that the schools should provide such information. Most schools in the United States have initiated AIDS education, but these programs tend to be very short and have not taken into account differences in the understanding of HIV transmission among elementary, junior high, and high school students. Brooks-Gunn and her colleagues stated:

> It has been proposed that education begin in elementary school, with the focus on the role of blood products in transmitting the disease. In junior high school, sexual transmission would be included in the curriculum. In high school, more information on sexual transmission would be added, including topics such as transmission by same-sex acts as well as heterosexual acts, effectiveness of contraceptive methods, skills training in the use of contraceptives, and decision making in terms of whether to have sexual intercourse and with whom. (p. 961)

Another important aspect to HIV/AIDS education is to include information regarding stereotypes about women, men, sexuality, and lesbian, gay, and bisexual orientations. Many people still believe that HIV/AIDS is a punishment inflicted on homosexuals because of their sexual orientation (Herek & Glunt, 1997). Thus, educational curricula on HIV/AIDS needs to strive to reduce antigay prejudice.

In addition, education for adolescents must deal with their concrete thinking skills and egocentric behavior. Adolescents may also have a "personal fable" (Elkind, 1967) in which they tell themselves they are unique and not vulnerable to pregnancy, HIV, and AIDS.

Although the majority of adolescents are engaging in sexual intercourse (Michael, Gagnon, Laumann, & Kolata, 1994), they are not using contraceptives or practicing safe sex (Lagana, 1999). As we will discuss in Chapter 6, one result of adolescents not using contraception is that one out of every eight women age 15 to 19 (most of them unmarried) becomes pregnant each year in the United States (Hyde & DeLamater, 1999). Adolescents account for one-third of all out-of-wedlock births each year nationwide (Michael et al., 1994). Approximately 30 percent of these pregnancies are terminated by abortion, 50 percent result in live births, and the remainder end in miscarriage (Hyde & DeLamater, 1999). Those adolescents who use condoms typically view their use as a form of birth control only, not for their protection against sexually transmitted diseases. Adolescents' personal fables are often supported by a long latency between HIV transmission and the emergence of AIDS symptoms, a period that may last eight to ten years.

We should note, however, that even when adolescents participate in AIDS education programs, most do not modify their behavior (Brown, Baranowski, Kulig, Stephenson, & Perry, 1996). Brown and colleagues (1996) conducted research with adolescent boys and girls about their attitudes toward HIV and AIDS following Magic Johnson's disclosure that he was HIV positive. Sixty percent of the adolescents in their study reported that Mr. Johnson's announcement had increased their awareness of AIDS. However, a small percentage of the adolescents reported an increase in personal threat from the disease. Brown and colleagues (1996) recommended that AIDS education should include cognitive approaches (e.g., knowledge about sexually transmitted diseases, including HIV), behavioral approaches (e.g., learning how to resist peer pressure for sex), and environmental approaches (e.g., parents talk with adolescents about intimacy in relationships being broader than engaging in sexual activity).

HOW THE MEDICAL ESTABLISHMENT CONSTRUCTS WOMEN

The medical profession has become a powerful influence controlling nearly every facet of the women's health care system (Albino et al., 1990; Theriot, 1993). The career of physician is one of the most prestigious and high-status occupations in our

---

BOX 5.1
RESOURCES ON WOMEN'S HEALTH

Also check websites on eating disorders, women's health, feminist women's health, breast cancer, and drug abuse. These websites include:

www.womenshealth.about
www.fwhc.org
www.twu.ca/eating
www.aabainc.org
www.medscape.com

American Anorexia and Bulimia Association
212–575-6200

American Heart Association National Center
1-800-AHA-USA1

American Cancer Society
1-800-ACS-2345

National Eating Disorders Organization
918-481-4044

National Eating Disorders Centre
416-340-4156

AIDS Prevention Hotline
1-800-541-2437

Women's Cancer Center
1-800-633-6253

Women's Healthcare Services
1-800-882-0488

---

society (Betz, 1993). Women are becoming physicians in increasing numbers; however, the field continues to be heavily populated by men. The control exercised by the medical profession is implicated in the training of medical students and new physicians and in men's and women's attitudes toward women patients (Theriot, 1993). Women's physical complaints are devalued, interpreted as "psychological" or "emotional" in etiology, and dismissed as trivial (Travis, 1993). Women who ask questions of their physician are referred to as "problem patients" because of this questioning. As Albino and colleagues (1990) concluded:

> Efforts of female patients to gain information and to take responsibility for their health are reconstructed by physicians to reflect women as emotionally dependent and hypochondriacal. . . . The maintenance of a male power advantage through witholding

and reconstructing information . . . reflects . . . the white male middle-class monopoly on medical knowledge and practice. The problem for women then is twofold: first, it involves gaining access to health care and then, gaining full benefit from health care (pp. 232–233).

Women who are seeking information about a medical condition, or who are trying to stay well, run a risk of having their experiences trivialized by physicians. Women patients typically do not receive adequate information about their health care. For example, early research by Wallen, Waitzkin, and Stoeckle (1979) found that women patients ask questions as a result of physicians' not giving them complete information. When asked to respond to questions on attitudes and beliefs about their patients, physicians in this study did not perceive women to need or want more information than men about their health care. Physicians may attribute women's questioning to other motives, including emotional ones (Albino et al., 1990). This could explain the other finding from this study—that physicians "talked down" to women patients and they did not use technical language because they believed the women could not understand the scientific and medical terminology.

Verbrugge (1984) found that when women complained of physical symptoms, they were often diagnosed as mentally disturbed. Physicians also devalued women's mental distress; they did not take these complaints as seriously as they did men's. Verbrugge also reported that women receive limited examinations and more prescriptions for medications than do men. The data suggest that physicians view women as emotional, dependent, childlike, unable to separate mental and physical symptoms, and easily excitable in a crisis. These are identical to the results we discussed in Chapter 3, from the study by Inge Broverman and her colleagues (Broverman, Broverman, Clarkson, Rosenkrantz, & Vogel, 1970).

Broverman found that the clinicians in her study had a "double standard" for mental health: Their criteria of mental health for adults applied to adult men but not to adult women. Broverman noted that "the general standard of health is actually applied only to men, while healthy women are perceived as significantly less healthy by adult standards" (p. 5). A similar sentiment is suggested from the literature on women's physical health care.

Broverman and her colleagues found considerable agreement in the way the clinicians described the characteristics of adult men and adults in general (e.g., very direct, very logical, can make decisions easily, never cry), but they differed from the characteristics assigned to adult women (e.g., very excitable in minor crises, more easily influenced, less adventurous, less independent, very illogical, very sneaky).

FEMINIST HEALTH CARE FOR WOMEN

The **feminist health care movement for women** had its origins in (a) the reemergence of the women's liberation movement in this country and (b) the consumer movement (Thomas, 1999). Albino and colleagues (1990) reported:

> [Women] were beginning to lose faith in the medical profession's competence and commitment to safe and effective care. For instance, in the late 1960s and early 1970s DES was still prescribed as a "morning after" contraceptive pill despite the fact that it was found to cause vaginal cancer in women whose mothers took DES during pregnancy. Radical mastectomy was long considered the preferred treatment for breast cancer despite its disfiguring effects and the lack of any proof that it was more effective than less traumatic procedures in preventing recurrence. Modern childbirth practices were designed more for the convenience of the physician than for the health of the mother and the fetus. . . . Women began to question the male monopoly of medical information and practice which rendered them submissive and robbed them of control over their bodies. (p. 242)

Women's reclamation of control over their health is perhaps best illustrated by the experience of many women who were fitted with a Dalkon Shield, a contraceptive device introduced in this country in the early 1970s. The shield became the most popular contraceptive device; approximately 88,000 of them were inserted in U.S. women in one month alone, and 200,000 were sent to women in South Korea. The Dalkon Shield is now referred to as "the Bhopal of the women's health movement, a continuing worldwide problem." The medical tragedies that occurred as a result of this contraceptive device included septic abortion deaths, early hysterectomies, perforations of the uterus, tissue masses, kidney damage, colon damage, and death.

In individual lawsuits and a class action suit, women have sued the A.H. Robins Company for the damages they incurred by being fitted with the shield. It appears that the Dalkon Shield inventor, Dr. Hugh Davis, was aware that the shield was not safe.

The women's health movement in this country rejected the assumption of the male medical profession: that women lose control of their bodies out of ignorance. Consciousness-raising groups (see Chapter 4) and self-help groups were formed throughout the country in order to instruct women about their bodies, reproductive rights, nutrition, and health care. Information was also shared on how to conduct breast and pelvic self-examination (Boston Women's Health Book Collective, 1984). Medical schools have incorporated some teaching modules adopted from the "know your body" courses, including teaching sensitivity in performing a pelvic examination.

One of the goals of the **Boston Women's Health Book Collective,** formed in 1969, is to teach women about their physical and mental health. *The New Our Bodies, Ourselves* and *Ourselves Getting Older* are each updated periodically. More than 1,000 women's health organizations have been formed in the United States since 1969, in addition to alternative women's clinics and self-help groups (Corea, 1977).

A second example of the changes in health care achieved by the women's health movement is the increase in women **midwife deliveries** (Scully, 1980; Travis, 1993). For centuries, women gave birth at home and were attended by lay midwives. Scully (1980) points out, however, that when men midwives (the title given to early obstetricians) wanted to make obstetrics a medical specialty, childbirth was redefined and became a surgical specialty. Midwives attended primarily poor and immigrant women.

The feminist health care movement has provided many women with affordable, safe, and affirming medical services. This movement has made it more likely that women won't have to wait twice as long as men to see an emergency room physician or wait twice as long as men to be given an electrocardiogram (Albino et al., 1990). The feminist health care movement has alerted us to the fact that women receive fewer diagnostic tests and medical procedures for chest pains than men do (Schwartz, Fisher, & Wright, 1997).

We note that these gains for women's health have had a corresponding impact on men's health, especially for men of color, working-class men, and poor men, who are often treated in disrespectful way by physicians (Paludi, Paludi & Doyle, in press).

The work of feminist health care for women will contribute to an enlightened health care system, one that values women and women's bodies. We shall return to this issue in Chapter 6, when we discuss women's reproductive rights and reproductive health.

NEW TERMS

acquired immunodeficiency syndrome (AIDS)

amenorrhea

anorexia nervosa

baseline mammogram

binge-purge syndrome

Body-Self-Relations Questionnaire

Boston Women's Health Book Collective

breast diseases

breast self-examination

bulimia

eating disorders

feminist health care movement for women

fetal alcohol syndrome

fibroadenomas

fibrocystic condition

lanugo

lung cancer

mammograms

midwife deliveries

mood-altering drugs

overweight

substance abuse

CHAPTER REVIEW QUESTIONS

1. Offer some explanations for why adolescent and adult women diet excessively.

2. Summarize the research by Linda Jackson and her colleagues about gender-role orientation and body image.

3. Discuss Laura Brown's research about lesbian women's experiences with eating disorders.

4. Define anorexia nervosa. What is the incidence of this eating disorder among adolescent and adult women?

5. How are bulimia and anorexia similar? Different?

6. Design an educational program for girls in senior high school about substance abuse in women. What issues would you include? Why?

7. Offer suggestions for encouraging women to perform breast self-examinations.

8. Pretend you are asked to give a lecture to your class about women and AIDS. Cite the information you would include in your lecture. What resources would you make available to your classmates?

9. Discuss feminist health care for women. Offer suggestions for making women more aware of choices they have for their health care.

SELECTED READINGS

Gannon, L. (1998). The impact of medical and sexual politics on women's health. *Feminism and Psychology, 8*, 285–302.

Kilbourne, J. (1999). *Deadly persuasion: Why women and girls must fight the addictive power of advertising*. New York: Free Press.

Thomas, J. (1999). "Everything about us is feminist": The significance of ideology in organizational change. *Gender and Society, 13*, 101–119.

LEARNING MORE ABOUT . . .

Suggestions for Term Papers and Independent Studies Related to *Women's Health Issues*

Current legislation on women's health

Controversy surrounding mammography screening for women under 50 years of age

Women in the health care system as providers

Empowerment for women through feminist health care

Psychological effects of mastectomy on women's self-concept

Women physicians: More feminist in their practice?

TAKING ACTION . . .

on *Women's Health Issues*

1. Inquire about the legislation on women's health issues currently pending in your state assembly and state senate. You can obtain this information by contacting the state legislature directly or by contacting your local representative to the senate or assembly.

2. Write your state assemblymember and senator about current legislation concerning women's health. Offer research cited in this chapter to help guide their voting on the legislation.

   In your letter also inquire about the following:

   How long have the bills been under consideration?

   What has held these bills up in committee?

   Do the bills take into account women who are more vulnerable to illness?

   Do the bills provide for curriculum development to teach children and adolescents about women's health?

   What support do the legislators need from their constituents regarding the passage of these bills?

3. Present the information you obtain from your representatives to your class.

4. Consider inviting your representatives to your class to discuss the legislation needed on women's health.

REFERENCES

Albino, J., Tedesco, L., & Shenkle, C. (1990). Images of women: Reflections from the medical care system. In M. Paludi & G. Steuernagel (Eds.), *Foundations for a feminist restructuring of the academic disciplines*. New York: Haworth.

Altman, L. (1997, April 29). Health panel seeks sweeping changes in fertility therapy. *New York Times,* pp. A1,22.

Amaro, H. (1988). Considerations for prevention of HIV infection among Hispanic women. *Psychology of Women Quarterly, 12,* 429–444.

Amaro, H., & Gornemann, I. (1992). HIV/AIDS. Reported in H. Amaro, (1995), Love, sex, and power: Considering women's realities in HIV prevention. *American Psychologist, 50,* 437–447.

Barnes, G., Farrell, M., & Dintcheff, B. (1997). Family socialization effects on alcohol abuse and related problem behaviors among female and male adolescents. In R. Wilsnack & S. Wilsnack (Eds.), *Gender and alcohol*. New Brunswick, NJ: Rutgers Center of Alcohol Studies.

Betz, N. (1993). Women's career development. In F. L. Denmark & M. A. Paludi (Eds.), *The psychology of women: A handbook*. Westport, CT: Greenwood Press.

Boskind-White, M., & White, W. (1986). Bulimarexia: A historical-sociocultural perspective. In K. Brownell & J. Foreyt (Eds.), *Handbook of eating disorders*. New York: Basic Books.

Boston Women's Health Book Collective. (1984). *The new our bodies, ourselves*. New York: Simon & Schuster.

Boston Women's Health Book Collective (1987). *Ourselves growing older*. New York: Simon & Schuster.

Brooks-Gunn, J., Boyer, C. B., & Hein, K. (1988). Preventing HIV infection and AIDS in children and adolescents. *American Psychologist, 43,* 958–964.

Broverman, I., Broverman, D., Clarkson, F., Rosenkrantz, P., & Vogel, S. (1970). Sex-role stereotypes and clinical judgments of mental health. *Journal of Consulting and Clinical Psychology, 34,* 1–7.

Brown, K., Bryant, C., Forthofer, M., Perrin, K., Quinn, G., Wolper, M., & Lindenberger, J. (2000). Florida cars for women social marketing campaign: A case study. *American Journal of Health Behavior, 24,* 44–52.

Brown, L. (1987). Lesbians, weight, and eating: New analyses and perspectives. In *Lesbian psychologies: Explorations and challenges*. Urbana: University of Illinois Press.

Brown, R., Baranowski, M., Kulig, J., Stephenson, H. J., & Perry, B. (1996). Searching for the Magic Johnson effect: AIDS, adolescents, and celebrity disclosure. *Adolescence, 31,* 253–254.

Brownmiller, S. (1984). *Femininity*. New York: Fawcett-Columbine.

Children Now & the Kaiser Family Foundation (1997). *A national survey of children: Reflections of girls in the media—A summary of findings and toplines.* Menlo Park, CA: Author.

Corea, G. (1977). *The hidden malpractice: How American medicine treats women as patients and professionals.* Garden City, NY: Anchor Press.

Corrigan, E., & Butler, S. (1991). Irish alcoholic women in treatment: Early findings. *International Journal of the Addictions, 26,* 281–292.

Crandall, C. (1988). Social contagion in binge eating. *Journal of Personality and Social Psychology, 55,* 588–596.

Davis, C., Claridge, G., & Fox, J. (2000). Not just a pretty face: Physical attractiveness and perfectionism in the risk for eating disorders. *International Journal of Eating Disorders, 27,* 67–73.

Donovan, K., & Tucker, D. (2000). Knowledge about genetic risk for breast cancer and perceptions of genetic testing in a sociodemographically diverse sample. *Journal of Behavioral Medicine, 23,* 15–36.

Dyer, G., & Tiggermann, M. (1996). The effect of school environment on body concerns in adolescent women. *Sex Roles, 34,* 127–138.

Elkind, D. (1967). Egocentrism in adolescence. *Child Development, 38,* 1025–1034.

Ettorre, E. (1997). *Women and alcohol: A private pleasure or a public problem?* London: Women's Press.

Fairburn, C. (1981). A cognitive-behavioral approach to the treatment of bulimia. *Psychological Medicine, 11,* 707–711.

Fallon, P., Katzman, M., & Wooley, S. (Eds.). (1994). *Feminist perspectives on eating disorders.* New York: Guilford Press.

Ferron, C. (1997). Body image in adolescence: Cross-cultural research—Results of the preliminary phase of a quantitative survey. *Adolescence, 32,* 735–744.

Flora, J., & Thoresen, C. E. (1988). Reducing the risk of AIDS in adolescents. *American Psychologist, 43,* 965–970.

Fodor, I. G., & Thal, J. (1984). Weight disorders: Overweight and anorexia. In E. A. Blechman (Ed.), *Behavior modification with women.* New York: Guilford Press.

Freeza, H., Padova, C., Pozzato, G., Terpin, M., Baraona, E., & Lieber, C. (1990). High blood alcohol levels in women: The role of decreased gastric alcohol dehydrogenase activity and first-pass metabolism. *The New England Journal of Medicine, 322,* 95–99.

Fulmore, C. (1999). Applying cognitive-social theory of health protective behavior to breast self-examination. *Dissertation Abstracts International, 60* (3–B), 1300.

Garfinkel, P. E., & Garner, D. M. (1982). *Anorexia nervosa.* New York: Brunnel/Mazel.

Gentry, J. (1993). Women and AIDS. In *Psychology and AIDS exchange.* Washington, DC: American Psychological Association.

George, S. (2000). Barriers to breast cancer screening: An integrative review. *Health Care for Women International, 21,* 53–65.

Gomberg, E. (1993). Women and alcohol: Use and abuse. *Journal of Nervous and Mental Diseases, 181,* 211–219.

Grady, K. (1988). Older women and the practice of breast self-examination. *Psychology of Women Quarterly, 12,* 473–487.

Guidry, J., Fagan, P., & Walker, V. (1998). Cultural sensitivity and readability of breast and prostate printed cancer education materials targeting African Americans. *Journal of the National Medical Association,* 90, 165–169.

Gupta, M. (1995). Concerns about aging and a drive for thinness: A factor in the biopsychosocial model of eating disorders? *International Journal of Eating Disorders, 18,* 351–357.

Halpern, C., Udry, J., Campbell, B., & Suchindran, C. (1999). Effects of body fat on weight concerns, dating, and sexual activity. *Developmental Psychology, 35,* 721–736.

Hanson, M. (1994). Sociocultural and physiological correlates of cigarette smoking in women. *Health Care for Women International, 15,* 549–562.

Haworth-Hoeppner, S. (2000). The critical shapes of body image: The role of culture and family in the production of eating disorders. *Journal of Marriage and the Family, 62,* 212–227.

Helgeson, V., Cohen, S., Schultz, R. & Yasko, J. (2000). Group support interventions for women with breast cancer: Who benefits from what? *Health Psychology, 19,* 197–114.

Henriques, G., Calhoun, L., & Cann, A. (1996). Ethnic differences in women's body satisfaction: An experimental investigation. *Journal of Social Psychology, 136,* 689–697.

Herek, G. M., & Glunt, E. K. (1988). An epidemic of stigma: Public reactions to AIDS. *American Psychologist, 43,* 886–891.

Hinz, L., & Williamson, D. (1987). Bulimia and depression: A review of the affective variant hypothesis. *Psychological Bulletin, 102,* 150–158.

Hyde, J., & DeLamater, J. (1999). *Understanding human sexuality.* New York: McGraw Hill.

Jackson, L. (1992). *Physical appearance and gender.* Albany: State University of New York Press.

Jackson, L., Sullivan, L., & Rostker, R. (1988). Gender, gender role, and body image. *Sex Roles, 19,* 429–443.

Kempa, M., & Thomas, A. (2000). Culturally sensitive assessment and treatment of eating disorders. *Eating Disorders: The Journal of Treatment and Prevention, 8,* 17–30.

Kent, G., Howie, H., Fletcher, M., Newbury, R., & Hosie, K. (2000). The relationship between perceived risk, thought intrusiveness and emotional well-being in women receiving counselling for breast cancer risk in a family history clinic. *British Journal of Health Psychology, 5,* 15–26.

Kilbourne, J. (1999). *Deadly persuasion*. New York: Free Press.

Kline, K., & Mattison, M. (2000). Breast self-examination pamphlets: A content analysis grounded in fear appeal research. *Health Communication, 12,* 1–21.

LaFromboise, T., Choney, S., James, A., & Running Wolf, P. (1995). American Indian women and psychology. In H. Landrine (Ed.), *Bringing cultural diversity to feminist psychology*. Washington, DC: American Psychological Association.

Lagana, L. (1999). Psychosocial correlates of contraceptive practices during late adolescence. *Adolescence, 34,* 463–482.

Lanis, K. & Covell, K. (1995). Images of women in advertisements: Effects on attitudes related to sexual aggression. *Sex Roles,* 639–649.

Lask, B., & Bryant-Waugh, R. (Eds.). (2000). *Anorexia nervosa and related eating disorders in childhood* and *adolescence*. Hove, England: Taylor & Francis.

McCaul, K., & O'Donnell, S. (1998). Cancer prevention and control. *Women's Health: Research on Gender, Behavior, and Policy, 4,* 93–101.

McKinley, N. (1999). Women and objectified body consciousness: Mothers' and daughters' body experience in cultural, developmental, and familial context. *Developmental Psychology, 35,* 760–769.

Media Report to Women (MRTW). (1997, Spring). *Media reinforce some stereotypes, break others*, pp. 1–3.

Michael, R., Gagnon, J., Laumann, E., & Kolata, G. (1994). *Sex in America: A definitive survey*. Boston: Little, Brown.

Paludi, M., Paludi, C., & Doyle, J. (in press). *Sex and gender* (5th ed.). New York: McGraw Hill

Pipher, M. (1994). *Reviving Ophelia*. New York: Ballantine.

Preston, J., Scinto, J., Grady, J., Schulz, A., & Petrillo, M. (2000). *Journal of the American Geriatrics* Society, *48, 1–7.*

Rodin, J., Silberstein, L., & Striegel-Moore, R. (1985). Women and weight: A normative discontent. In T. Sonderegger (Ed.), *Psychology and gender: Nebraska Symposium on Motivation*. Lincoln: University of Nebraska Press.

Rothblum, E. (1992). The stigma of women's weight: Social and economic realities. *Feminism and Psychology, 2,* 61–73.

Schapira, M., McAuliffe, T., & Nattinger, A. (2000). Underutilization of mammography in older breast cancer survivors. *Medical Care, 38,* 281–289.

Schlesier-Stroop, B. (1984). Bulimia: A review of the literature. *Psychological Bulletin, 95,* 247–257.

Schwartz, L., Fisher, E., & Wright, B. (1997). Treatment and health outcomes of women and men in a cohort with coronary heart disease. *Archives of Internal Medicine, 157,* 1545–1552.

Scully, D. (1980). *Men who control women's health: The miseducation of obstetricians-gynecologists.* Boston: Houghton Mifflin.

Silverstein, B., Perdue, L., Wolf, C., & Pizzolo, C. (1988). Binging, purging and estimates of parental attitudes regarding female achievement. *Sex Roles, 19,* 723–733.

Smith, C. (1996). Women and weight. In J. Chrisler, C. Golden, & P. Rozee (Eds.), *Lectures on the psychology of women.* New York: McGraw-Hill.

Snyder, R., & Hasbrouck, L. (1996). Feminist identity, gender traits, and symptoms of disturbed eating among college women. *Psychology of Women Quarterly, 20,* 593–598.

Striegel-Moore, R., Schreiber, G., Lo, A., Crawford, P., Obarzanek, E., & Rodin, J. (2000). Eating disorder symptoms in a cohort of 11-to 16-year-old black and white girls: The NHLBI Growth and Health Study. *International Journal of Eating Disorders, 27,* 49–68.

Striegel-Moore, R., & Smolak, L. (2000). The influence of ethnicity on eating disorders in women. In R. Eisler et al. (Eds.), *Handbook of gender, culture, and health.* Mahwah, NJ: Erlbaum.

Suffet, F., & Lifshitz, M. (1991). Women addicts and the threat of AIDS. *Qualitative Health Research, 1,* 51–79.

Theriot, N. (1993). Women's voices in nineteenth-century medical discourse: A step toward deconstructing science. *Signs, 19,* 1–31.

Thomas, J. (1999). "Everything about is feminist": The significance of ideology in organizational change. *Gender and Society,* 13, 101–119.

Thompson, S., Sargent, R., & Kemper, K. (1996). Black and white adolescent males' perceptions of ideal body size. *Sex Roles, 34,* 391–406.

Travis, C. (1988). *Women and health psychology: Mental health issues.* Hillsdale, NJ: Erlbaum.

Travis, C. (1993). Women and health. In F. L. Denmark & M. A. Paludi (Eds.), *Psychology of women: A handbook of issues and theories.* Westport, CT: Greenwood Press.

Verbrugge, L. (1984). How physicians treat mentally distressed men and women. *Social Science and Medicine, 18,* 1–9

Waldron, I. (1995). Contributions of changing gender differences in behavior and social roles to changing gender differences in mortality. In D. Sabo & D. Gordon (Eds.), *Men's health and illness.* Thousand Oaks, CA: Sage.

Wallen, J., Waitzkin, H., & Stoeckle, J. (1979). Physician stereotypes about female health and illness: A study of patients' sex and the informative process during medical interviews. *Women and Health, 4,* 135–146.

Wiederman, M., & Pryor, T. (2000). Body dissatisfaction, bulimia, and depression among women: The mediating role of drive for thinness. *International Journal of Eating Disorders, 27,* 90–95.

Wilsnack, S., & Wilsnack, R. (1991). Epidemiology of women's drinking. *Journal of Substance Abuse, 3*, 133–157.

Wolf, N. (1991). *The beauty myth*. New York: Viking.

Wooley, S., & Wooley, O. W. (1980). Eating disorders: Obesity and anorexia. In A. Brodsky & R. Hare-Mustin (Eds.), *Women and psychotherapy*. New York: Guilford.

World Health Organization (1999). *AIDS: 5 years since ICPD: Emerging issues and challenges for women, young people, and infants*. Geneva, Switzerland: Author.

SIX

WOMEN'S SEXUALITY, REPRODUCTIVE RIGHTS, AND REPRODUCTIVE HEALTH

IN WOMEN'S VOICES

Reproductive rights are fundamental to women's achievement of a just status in society. Reproductive health care services are essential for the exercise of these rights. Achieving total health for women demands their full participation in defining their health needs and in designing and implementing health policies.

Statement of the Christopher Tietze International Symposium on Women's Health in the Third World, Rio de Janeiro, Brazil, 1988

~

No woman can call herself free who does not own and control her own body. No woman can call herself free until she can choose conscientiously whether she will or will not be a mother.

Margaret Sanger

~

Lesbian existence is both the breaking of a taboo and the rejection of a compulsory way of life.

Adrienne Rich

Chapter Outline

Questions for Reflection

1. How do you define "sexuality"?

2. From whom did you learn about sexuality? At what age did you acquire this information?

3. Why do you believe information about lesbian relationships and bisexual relationships are typically omitted from discussions about women's sexuality between parents and their daughters?

4. What are the phases of women's sexual response cycle?

5. Do you believe your legislators should decide about women's reproductive rights or do you believe it is the woman's choice?

6. Have you heard of the term "reproductive freedom"? What do you believe this term means?

7. What do you believe is the impact of religion on individuals' views about sexuality?

8. How would you discuss sexuality with your daughter? Would you include the following topics in your discussion: birth control, sexually transmitted diseases, lesbian sexuality, bisexuality, abortion, responsibility, emotional aspects of sexuality?

INTRODUCTION: WOMEN'S BODILY INTEGRITY

In the late 1990s HBO aired the first of a series of movies entitled "If These Walls Could Talk." These programs examine how the laws and attitudes about women's reproductive rights have, on the one hand, changed over the course of thirty years but, at the same time, have remained much the same. The first program, "If These Walls Could Talk," is a trilogy of stories of women in three different time periods (in the 1950s, 1970s, and 1990s) in which they have to face the decision about what to do with an unplanned and unwanted pregnancy. The program highlights the different choices different women make, in the midst of different political climates, limited financial means, being recently widowed, judgmental family members, and pro-life demonstrations outside abortion clinics.

The programs have prompted further discussion of women's reproductive freedom and reproductive rights. **Reproductive freedom** means being able to choose whether or when to have children. Reproductive freedom also means that all women's choices should be respected and supported. As Gloria Steinem (1989) commented:

> . . . reproductive issues are part of a convergence of concerns, nationally and globally, that may lead to a new and all-encompassing human right called bodily integrity. There are many elements leading to this need: the abuse of organ transplant already beginning between rich countries with recipients and poor countries with donors; blood and urine tests that are required without probable cause or individual suspicion; proposals for mass AIDS testing that amounts to a suspicionless search of the human body; mind-altering drugs that are used for purposes of brainwashing or social control; children and old people who are drugged for easier handling by schools and institutions; the efforts to outlaw forced sterilization in Asia, female genital mutilation in Africa, and other reproductive abuses: all these and more are leading toward a shared and growing belief "the power of a government, any government, has to stop at our skins. Our bodies cannot be invaded. They are our castles to rule." (p. 41)

Bodily integrity reflects women's experiences as childbearers and nurturers who have to maintain control over the conditions of their reproduction in order to do it well. As Rosalind Petchesky (1990) commented, bodily integrity also "resonates with religious and cosmological traditions that value women's bodies as the source of life and nourishment . . . as an integral part of the self, not separate from (or below) the soul or spirit" (p. 3).

Since the mid-1980s, feminist advocates, women's health activists, and women's grassroots organizations have collaborated on developing an expansive conception of reproductive rights to include the health, well-being, and empowerment of women. Sally Mugabe of Zimbabwe addressed the United Nations Decade Conference in Nairobi and declared, "Women must control their own fertility, which forms the basis for enjoying all other rights. First and foremost, our bodies belong to us." This women-centered focus for women's reproductive rights issues includes the following topics (Petchesky, 1990):

Explicitness about sexuality: Women have the right to lead self-determined sexual lives.

Emphasis on health: An emphasis on reducing women's morbidity and mortality related to sex and reproduction, and maximizing conditions that make authentic choice possible.

In this chapter, I will discuss these issues in detail, focusing on broad economic, cultural, and social changes that are needed if "choice" is to be meaningful for women. Throughout my discussion, I will note how the masculine bias in research methodology and conceptualization of sex research has resulted in incorrectly describing women's sexuality as well as pathologizing. An underlying theme of this chapter is that sexuality is a social construct of male power.

(Courtesy of National Organization for Women)

EXPLICITNESS ABOUT SEXUALITY

According to Petchesky (1990):

> . . . one of the major foundations of feminist thinking about reproductive rights . . . is the belief that women as much as men have the right to lead self-determined sexual lives, free of the fear of pregnancy, cultural stigma, or diseases. This includes the right to live as lesbians or outside the domain of patriarchal marriage and family, as well as the right to be free from sexual harassment, abuse, or violence. Indeed, self-determination and pleasure in sexuality is one of the primary meanings of the idea of "control over one's body" as well as a principal reason for the need for access to safe abortion and birth control. (p. 4)

In this section, I will discuss women's physiological and psychological sexual responses. Let's begin with the following quiz. Try answering these true-false questions:

A woman or teenage girl can get pregnant during her menstrual flow (her "period").

Unless they are having sex, women do not need to have regular gynecological examinations.

It is usually difficult to tell whether people are or are not homosexual just by their appearance or gestures.

A woman or teenage girl can get pregnant even if the man withdraws his penis before he ejaculates.

In 1990, Dr. Judith Reinisch published the *Kinsey Institute New Report on Sex*. In this book, Reinisch reported the results of the Kinsey test of basic sexual knowledge that was conducted in 1989. The questions you just read are some of the items from this survey. I invite you to answer the other questions that are presented in Box 6.1.

The Kinsey test was administered to 1,034 women and 940 men in four regions of the United States: Northeast, Midwest, South, and West. Individuals ranged in age from 18 to 60 years, were predominantly Protestant or Catholic, and were either single, separated/divorced, widowed, or married. The majority of respondents are white, but African American and Hispanic women and men also participated in this survey. Reinisch (1990) concluded that, "Unfortunately, Americans failed the test. . . . This poll . . . shows that Americans either don't have the facts or are misinformed about a range of sexual topics, including AIDS, contraception, homosexuality, erection problems, infidelity, and menopause" (p. 1).

The Kinsey survey also asked respondents to indicate their sources for information about sex when they were growing up as well as currently. Women reported asking their mothers about sex and were seven times as likely to ask their mothers than their fathers. More than twice as many men as women reported relying on magazines for information about sex. And women were less likely than men to ask their friends about sex when they were growing up.

When asked about the sources they use as adults, women still indicated that they asked their mothers. Other sources for information as adults included a nurse or physician, book, friend, mate, health care center or family-planning clinic, and counselor/therapist. These sources of sex information were related to whether women (and men) correctly answered the items on the Kinsey survey. The majority of women (and men) who passed the test reported getting their information from sex education classes, books, health centers, and family-planning clinics. Other sources related to correctly or incorrectly answering the survey items were friends and magazines, suggesting that talking about sexuality and actively seeking information about sexuality are related to being accurate in one's understanding about

BOX 6.1
KINSEY INSTITUTE SEX KNOWLEDGE TEST

1. Nowadays, what do you think is the age at which the average or typical American first has sexual intercourse?
   - a. 11 or younger
   - b. 12
   - c. 13
   - d. 14
   - e. 15
   - f. 16
   - g. 17
   - h. 18
   - i. 19
   - j. 20
   - k. 21 or older
   - l. Don't know

2. Out of every ten married American men, how many would you estimate had had an extramarital affair—that is, have been sexually unfaithful to their wives?
   - a. Less than one out of ten
   - b. One out of ten (10%)
   - c. Two out of ten (20%)
   - d. Three out of ten (30%)
   - e. Four out of ten (40%)
   - f. Five out of ten (50%)
   - g. Six out of ten (60%)
   - h. Seven out of ten (70%)
   - i. Eight out of ten (80%)
   - j. Nine out of ten (90%)
   - k. More than nine out of ten
   - l. Don't know

3. Out of every ten American women, how many would you estimate have had anal (rectal) intercourse?
   - a. Less than one out of ten
   - b. One out of ten (10%)
   - c. Two out of ten (20%)
   - d. Three out of ten (30%)
   - e. Four out of ten (40%)
   - f. Five out of ten (50%)
   - g. Six out of ten (60%)
   - h. Seven out of ten (70%)
   - i. Eight out of ten (80%)
   - j. Nine out of ten (90%)
   - k. More than nine out of ten
   - l. Don't know

4. A person can get AIDS by having anal (rectal) intercourse even if neither partner is infected with the AIDS virus.
   True   False   Don't know

5. Petroleum jelly, Vaseline Intensive Care, baby oil, and Nivea are not good lubricants to use with a condom or diaphragm.
   True   False   Don't know

6. More than one out of four (25 percent) of American men have had a sexual experiment with another male during either their teens or adult years.
   True   False   Don't know

7. It is usually difficult to tell whether people are or are not homosexual just by their appearance or gestures.
   True   False   Don't know

(continued)

8. A woman or teenage girl can get pregnant during her menstrual flow (her "period").
   True   False   Don't know

9. A woman or teenage girl can get pregnant even if the man withdraws his penis before he ejaculates (before he "comes").
   True   False   Don't know

10. Unless they are having sex, women do not need to have regular gynecological examinations.
    True   False   Don't know

11. Teenage boys should examine their testicles ("balls") regularly just as women self-examine their breasts for lumps.
    True   False   Don't know

12. Problems with erection are most often started by a physical problem.
    True   False   Don't know

13. Almost all erection problems can be successfully treated.
    True   False   Don't know

14. Menopause, or change of life as it is often called, does not cause most women to lose interest in having sex.
    True   False   Don't know

15. Out of every ten American women, how many would you estimate have masturbated either as children or after they were grown up?
    a. Less than one out of ten
    b. One out of ten (10%)
    c. Two out of ten (20%)
    d. Three out of ten (30%)
    e. Four out of ten (40%)
    f. Five out of ten (50%)
    g. Six out of ten (60%)
    h. Seven out of ten (70%)
    i. Eight out of ten (80%)
    j. Nine out of ten (90%)
    k. More than nine out of ten
    l. Don't know

16. What do you think is the length of the average man's erect penis?
    a. 2 inches
    b. 3 inches
    c. 4 inches
    d. 5 inches
    e. 6 inches
    f. 7 inches
    g. 8 inches
    h. 9 inches
    i. 10 inches
    j. 11 inches
    k. 12 inches
    l. Don't know

17. Most women prefer a sexual partner with a larger-than-average penis.
    True   False   Don't know

Scoring the Test

Each question is worth one point. The total possible number of points you can get is
17. Score each item and then add up your total number of points. When a range of possi-

ble answers is correct, according to currently available research data, all respondents choosing one of the answers in the correct range are given a point.

Correct Answer(s)

Detailed research-based explanations of the correct answers can be found in THE KINSEY INSTITUTE NEW REPORT ON SEX, St. Martin's Press Paperbacks Edition, March 1994.

1. f,g	5. True	9. True	12. True	15. g,h,i
2. d,e	6. True	10. False	13. True	16. d,e,f
3. d,e	7. True	11. True	14. True	17. False
4. False	8. True			

If you get this number of points	You receive this grade
16–17	A
14–15	B
12–13	C
10–11	D
1–9	F

sex. However, the sources of sex information available to these individuals were inadequate, given the results of the Kinsey survey.

Reinisch (1990) pointed out that women tended to correctly answer questions about women's health care and contraception; men tended to know the answers to questions relating to penis size, treatment of erection problems, and actual sex behavior (specifically, masturbation, anal intercourse, and extramarital sex). The information women and men are seeking from sources is thus related to their **divergent meanings of sexuality.** The fact that sexuality is related to gender-role development is further illustrated by the results of a study by Susan Hendrick and her colleagues (Hendrick, Hendrick, Slapion-Foote, & Foote, 1985). In this study, college women expressed less support than college men for sexual permissiveness and more support for sexual responsibility. Philip Blumstein and Pepper Schwartz (1983) also reported, from their study of 12,000 U.S. couples, that "men and women represent two very distinct modes of behavior" (p. 302) and that "lesbians are more like heterosexual women than either is like gay or heterosexual men" (p. 303).

Thus, gender-role socialization shapes women's and men's sexual experiences and sexual knowledge (Reid & Bing, 2000). Feminist theories of sexuality place sexuality within a theory of gender inequality (the hierarchy of men over women). In the next section, I will discuss how the social context in which sexual behavior and sexual attitudes are learned impacts women's attitudes toward sexuality.

WOMEN AND SEXUALITY: INTERFACE OF ETHNICITY AND GENDER-ROLE SOCIALIZATION

What does sexuality mean to girls and women? Adolescent girls are typically socialized to believe that sexual activity is a means to attract and keep a mate (i.e., boy) and that girls should restrain and temper boys' sexual impulses and engage in sexual behavior only to the extent necessary to satisfy their dates' needs (Reid & Bing, 2000). Their own needs are seldom considered.

As Zellman and Goodchilds (1983) suggested: "having sex," among college students, was regarded "as a male goal and avoiding sex as a female goal." College women report using strategies more to avoid sex; college men use strategies to have sex. Women report themselves to be less comfortable with initiating sex and more comfortable refusing it.

Engaging in sexual behavior confers high status and signifies adulthood for adolescent boys. For adolescent girls, sexual relations lower their status, decrease their "respectability," and connote them as being "bad." This distinction is referred to as the **double standard of sexuality.** Lillian Rubin's (1976) words of more than thirty years ago are still true today:

> . . . the media [tell] us that the double standard of sexual morality is dead . . . women don't believe it. They know from experience that it is alive and well, that it exists side by side with the new ideology that heralds their sexual liberation. They know all about who are the "bad girls" in school, in the neighborhood; who are the "good girls." Everybody knows! . . . The definitions of "good girl" and "bad girl" may vary somewhat according to class, but the fundamental ideas those words encompass are not yet gone either from our culture or our consciousness at any class level. (p. 136)

For many adolescents, sexuality is a socially scripted activity (Travis, Meginnis, & Bardari, 2000). The expression of sexuality is governed less by biological drives per se than by the expectations and social significance associated with certain patterns of sexual activity. This scripting is further governed by adolescents' and adults' ethnic background (Reid & Bing, 2000). For example, discussing sex is not appropriate behavior, especially for women, in many Latin American communities (Unger & Molina, 2000). Typically, women and men do not share information about past or current sexual partners or practices. This is especially true with regard to the use of birth control methods and the prevention of sexually transmitted diseases. Worth and Rodriquez (1987) suggested that traditional beliefs about gender roles continue to have a major influence on how women and men interact as well as on their attitudes about sex and gender. Their observations of the interplay between *marianismo* and *machismo* in Latin American communities suggested that marianismo demands that women defer to men:

> Attractiveness is seen as being synonymous with sexual inexperience or purity. The males are seen as the seducers of the inexperienced (sexually uneducated) women. A woman prepared for sex (e.g., carrying condoms) is perceived to be experienced, loose, and therefore unattractive. (p. 6)

Consequently, women may feel unable to assert themselves by suggesting that their partners wear condoms. As a result, they and their partners are at risk for sexually transmitted diseases. Furthermore, if men suggest they use condoms, women may perceive men as wanting sex for pleasure—not for love and with the intention of marriage (Reid & Bing, 2000).

Teresa LaFromboise and her colleagues (LaFromboise, Choney, James, & Running Wolf, 1995) noted that adolescent Native American girls are a vulnerable population: Those who are sexually active use contraception at one-half the rate of their white European American peers. Consequently, the pregnancy rate among Native American adolescent girls is higher than it is for white adolescents. Furthermore, the U.S. Congress (1990) reported that Native American girls are six times more likely to be sexually abused than are Native American boys (see Chapter 10).

WHAT IS SEXUALITY?

Sexuality includes a wide range of feelings, preferences, behaviors, and values. Sexuality is an integral part of women's (and men's) identity; it interacts with all aspects of the self and is part of the way women (and men) define who they are (Travis et al., 2000). Sexuality constantly develops; it does not end in adolescence. It continues throughout the life cycle in interaction with psychological, social, religious, cultural, and biological influences. For women, culture has shaped and limited their experiences with sexuality (Reid & Bing, 2000). Women who are older, disabled, or overweight are frequently seen as having no "right" to be sexual because they do not conform to a masculine standard of female beauty. And, as a result of cultural stereotypes, ethnic minority women are viewed as being more sexually active and responsive than they choose to be (DeFour, 1996; Root, 1995).

Perhaps advice columnist Ann Landers is accurate when she tells her readers that the most important sex organ is the *brain.*

Let's now discuss women's physiological sexual responses.

PHYSIOLOGY OF WOMEN'S SEXUAL RESPONSES

In Chapter 3, I discussed women's internal and external genitalia and reproductive cycles. In this section, I will discuss the physiology of women's sexual responses. William Masters and Virginia Johnson (1966) outlined women's sexual response cycle as having four phases: excitation, plateau, orgasm, and resolution. Reactions of women's sex organs, and other bodily reactions, during each of these phases are summarized in Figure 6.1. The timing of these phases is a generalization based on observations of a large sample; thus, individual variations from these results can be expected (Andersen & Cyranowski, 1995; Tiefer, 1995). For example, a woman may return from near orgasm to plateau several times in a cycle. Cycles may last from a few minutes to several hours. The four phases are not necessarily discrete; plateau, for example, is a direct extension of excitement. These four phases of physiological responses occur in women through masturbation or with a woman or man partner.

In the **excitement phase,** physical changes accompany women's psychological arousal. The nervous system sends messages to certain brain centers, causing measurable changes in women's bodies. Blood pressure rises, and breathing and heart rates are modified. There is increased skin sensitivity and altered muscle tension as a result of blood rushing to the genitals. Women's identification of these physiological changes as sexual arousal contributes to their arousal process.

Vaginal lubrication begins as the level of arousal increases. This lubrication enters the vaginal walls because of the vasocongestion that develops in the pelvic area. The congestion, an accumulation of blood and fluids, pushes fluids to the tissues and results in the lubrication of the vagina. In addition, the inner two-thirds of the vagina expands, the labia majora open, the labia minora enlarge, and the clitoris swells. Women's nipples also become erect (as a consequence of **myotonia,** the contraction of fibers in various muscles).

In the **plateau phase,** women/s arousal becomes more intensified, and sexual and muscular tension increases. Women's breathing rate, heart rate, and blood pressure increase. A **sex flush** appears on the skin covering the chest, neck, or other areas of the body. The outer one-third of the vagina swells and narrows the opening. The inner two-thirds of the vagina balloons up, lifting the cervix and uterus away from the end of the vagina. The labia minora may become two or three times thicker

---

BOX 6.2
RESOURCES CONCERNING WOMEN'S REPRODUCTIVE RIGHTS AND REPRODUCTIVE HEALTH

American Association of Sex Educators, Counselors, and Therapists
11 Dupont Circle
Washington, DC 20036

Association of Reproductive Health Professionals
2401 Penn Avenue, NW
Washington, DC 20037

Information Service of the Kinsey Institute for Sex Research
Indiana University
Bloomington, IN 47401

National Gay Task Force
80 Fifth Avenue
New York, NY 10011

Sex Information and Education Council of the United States
84 Fifth Avenue
New York, NY 10011

United States Department of Health and Human Services
2101 East Jefferson Street
Rockville, MD 20852

Websites

www.choice.org/resources.html
www.feminist.com
www.prochoice.org
www.ssc.wisc.edu/sss
www.sexuality.org
www.nih.gov/nia/health/pubpub/sexuality.htm
www.sexhealth.org/infocenter/GuideBS/GuideBS.htm

FIGURE 6.1   *The four phases of the female sexual response cycle.*

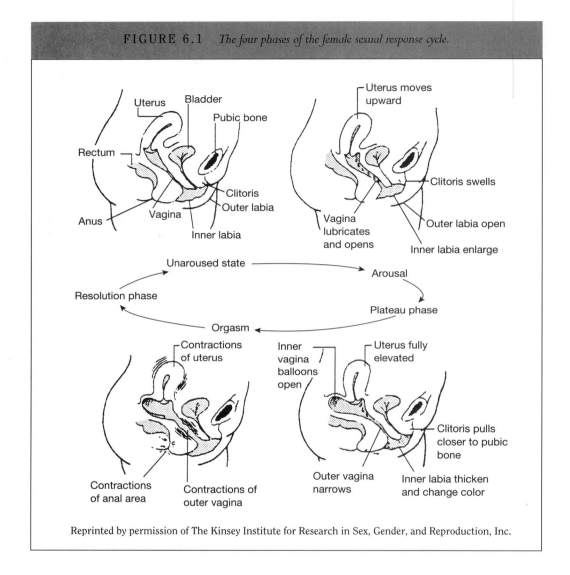

Reprinted by permission of The Kinsey Institute for Research in Sex, Gender, and Reproduction, Inc.

than when not sexually aroused and may evidence a more vibrant or darker color. The clitoris pulls closer to the pubic bone and may be covered by the enlarged labia. And, the areola surrounding women's nipples may swell; the breasts may increase in size.

An **orgasm** (or **climax**) is a neuromuscular discharge that occurs with appropriate stimulation and buildup of pelvic vasocongestion. The **orgasmic phase** is characterized by a sequence of rhythmic contractions of the **orgasmic platform,** the congested walls in which the rhythmic contractions of the orgasm are most manifest.

Unlike the other phases of women's sexual responsiveness, the orgasm lasts only a few seconds. Involuntary vocal sounds and changes in facial expression may occur. The intensity of the orgasm varies from woman to woman and from one time to another for the same woman. For example, the muscular contractions may range from a slight throbbing in women's genitals to involuntary rigidity of the entire body. Orgasm in women consists of three to ten muscular contractions (less than one second apart) of the outer one-third of the vagina, uterus, and anus. Pleasurable sensations may also occur throughout the genital and pelvic areas, including the clitoris.

In **women's resolution phase,** blood leaves the genital area and organs gradually return to their original positions, color, and size. The clitoris emerges from its retracted position. The orgasmic platform also subsides. The "sex flush" disappears, breathing and heart rate slow, and blood pressure returns to the normal level. This phase of women's sexual response is the time it takes for their bodies to return to their **unaroused states.** However, if women's sexual interest continues after orgasm and they are stimulated, women may reenter the **orgasmic plateau** phase and have other orgasms, referred to as **multiple orgasms.** Vasocongestion underlies women's capacities for experiencing orgasms; as long as vasocongestion exists, women may experience multiple orgasms. However, the congestion may be a discomfort after prolonged stimulation if a woman does not have an orgasm. As Reinisch (1990) concluded: "[Just] because theoretical capacity for multiple orgasms exists does not mean that trying to have them should be a goal or a measure of 'good sex' for either the woman or her partner. In fact, many women find continued stimulation of the genitals after one orgasm uncomfortable" (p. 84).

These sexual responses described by Masters and Johnson are not to be used as a checklist against which women should measure their sexual performance or the performance of their partner.

There are factors that relate to changes in women's physiological responses to sex (Collins, 1999; Sipski, Alexander, & Rosen, 1999). I will briefly discuss the climacteric and women's health concerns, especially the impact of a hysterectomy on women's physiological responses.

SEXUALITY AND WOMEN AT MIDLIFE AND IN OLDER ADULTHOOD

With declining estrogen levels and other normative effects of aging, including menopause (see Chapter 3), some changes have been observed (Gannon, 1999; Mansfield & Koch, 1998) in women's physiological responses to sex. Sexual arousal may be slower for women in their 50s and beyond. There tends to be less engorgement of the clitoris and labia, and the vagina is less elastic, especially for women who have not been sexually active (Hillman, 2000; Pangman & Seguire, 2000). Midlife women's orgasmic responses, however, are not impaired. The intensity of muscle spasm and the number of orgasmic contractions may decrease (Hyde & DeLamater, 1999). Research by Patricia Morokoff and her colleagues (Myers & Morokoff, 1986) suggests little or no changes in women's subjective sexual arousal. Their psychological experiences of sexual pleasure are not correlated with physiological indexes of arousal.

Sandra Risa Leiblum and her colleagues (Leiblum, Bachmann, Kemmann, Colburn, & Swartzman, 1983) found that perimenopausal women do not refrain from sexual intercourse even when **dyspareunia** (pain with intercourse) exists:

> It is likely that as women feel more "entitled" to say "no" to sex when they do not want to engage in it or to negotiate changes in the sexual script that will enhance their comfort and satisfaction when they do want sexual exchange, fewer women will be willing to endure unpleasant or painful coitus. (p. 498)

In addition to the physiological changes accompanying midlife for women, a number of social factors contribute to their not engaging in sexual activity with their partner, especially if their partner is a man (Mansfield & Koch, 1998). Middle-age heterosexual women are more subject than are lesbian women to their mate's attraction to and interest in younger women, an issue captured by Hollywood in the 1996 release of "The First Wives Club." Women at midlife and beyond are reminders to their male peers that they, too, are aging and growing "old."

Cole and Rothblum (1990) asked midlife lesbian women in their sample to complete the following sentence: "Based on my experience, sex at menopause is . . ." Thirty-one women (76%) reported that they did not have a sex problem. Problems mentioned by ten women in the sample included less interest in initiating sex, taking longer to reach orgasm, and difficulty with vaginal lubrication. Cole and Rothblum reported, however, that these "problems" were qualified by statements such as "This isn't really a problem; it's just a difference since menopause" (p. 512). Cole and Rothblum concluded:

> . . . studies of heterosexual women suggest concern with sexual functioning, arousal time, vaginal dryness, loss of clitoral sensitivity, and so on. There is worry, for many, about deteriorating sexuality and fears about disappointing one's partner. In contrast, and for the most part, the responses to our questionnaire had a celebratory quality. And perhaps most important, sex was invariably discussed within the context of a relationship: relationships, not functioning, were firmly emphasized. (p. 512)

Cole and Rothblum's work reminds us that there is a virtual assumption that all of the women respondents in research on sexuality are heterosexual. There is a need for women, as consumers of psychological research, to interpret findings with caution.

WOMEN'S HEALTH CONCERNS AND SEXUALITY

Research has suggested that there can be an indirect or a direct association between a medical condition or disease and women's sexual functioning (Pangman & Seguire, 2000; Sawyer & Roberts, 1999). Such diseases include spinal cord injury (Collins, 1999; Sipski et al., 1999), cardiovascular problems (Butler & Lewis, 1982; Gannon, 1999), and arthritis and related diseases involving inflammation and pain in the joints and connective tissues (e.g., multiple sclerosis, lupus) (Gannon, 1999). These conditions are common in women (young adult women as well as older women). Stiffness and pain in the hip joints are frequent causes of difficulty during sexual activity. Medications used to treat arthritis (especially corticosteroids) may reduce women's desire to have sex. Sex counseling of women with arthritis suggests techniques that may improve sexual functioning, including mild exercise, using positions for sexual activity that put minimal stress on the hips and other joints, taking warm baths, and using pillows to support weight and to cushion painful joints (Hyde & DeLamater, 1999).

Sexual Activity Following a Hysterectomy

Women who have had **hysterectomies** (surgical removal of the uterus and/or cervix) may experience difficulty in sexual activity (Leiblum, 1990; Williams & Clark, 2000). Many woman experience orgasms primarily when there is stimulation against the cervix and uterus, causing uterine contractions and increased stimulation of the peritoneum (abdominal lining). Without the cervix or uterus, there may be less of this sensation (Hyde & DeLamater, 1999). If women's ovaries are removed (**oophorectomy**), ovarian androgens may be greatly reduced and, consequently, women's sexual response may be lowered. When oophorectomy does not accompany a hysterectomy, the hormonal change may occur because the surgery interferes with the blood supply (Lewis, Groft, Herman, McKeown, & Wilcox, 2000). Vaginal lubrication lessens after oophorectomy, but postoperative hormone replacement will maintain vaginal lubrication. Androgenic stimulation may also restore women's sexual responsiveness (Hyde & DeLamater, 1999).

Some psychological factors may affect women's sexual functioning following a hysterectomy (Mingo, Herman, & Jasperse, 2000). For example, one symbol of femininity, for many women, is the uterus and the ability to have children. Removal of the uterus signifies loss of fertility. Thus, women whose identity as a childbearer has changed may have a lowered self-concept and self-image following a hysterectomy (Williams & Clark, 2000).

On the other hand, many women report improvement in their sexual activity following a hysterectomy (Galavotti & Richter, 2000), especially if the surgery helped to reduce heavy bleeding or to relieve a painful condition such as **endometriosis** (in which the endometrial tissue is found growing on the ovaries or fallopian tubes, or in other parts of the pelvis) (Hyde & DeLamater, 1999).

LESBIAN SEXUALITY: ATTITUDES, PREJUDICES, MYTHS, AND REALITIES REVISITED

I have discussed the myths and stereotypes surrounding women's sexuality, especially for women who have medical conditions, are middle-aged and older, and/or have had hysterectomies. Lesbian women have had strong negative attitudes and prejudices prevail against them as well (Rothblum, 1994). Hostility toward lesbian women (and gay men) is termed **anti-gay prejudice.** Homophobia is expressed in several ways, including jokes about homosexuality, derogatory comments and labels for lesbian women, and sexual harassment and other forms of hate crimes (Cogan, 1996; Mohr & Sedlacek, 2000; Williamson, 2000). Many lesbians have been fired from their jobs when their sexual orientation was revealed. Many have been denied bank loans, child custody, housing, and medical care because of their sexual orientation. Consequently, many lesbians do not disclose their sexual orientation (Rothblum & Bond, 1996). The negative feelings toward lesbians are based on stereotypes of lesbian lifestyles and homosexuality in general (Cogan, 1996; Rothblum & Bond, 1996). In women's own voices:

> Being a lesbian for me is about the joy and wonder of loving women. It means being woman identified, making women my priority. It is a way of life, so much more than a matter of who I sleep with. Sometimes when I talk about being a lesbian, heterosexual friends say they hear me criticizing their choice to be with men. That's not true. For me, part of what's essential in my being a lesbian is caring for other women, and this includes women who have made choices other than mine.
>
> Boston Women's Health Book Collective, 1984, p. 141

We're taught that we're heterosexual. . . . The movies you see, the books you read: all are about how this "girl" falls in love with this "young man." That's the whole direction in my case, that if someone had said both [genders] are possibilities [as sexual partners] a long time ago, I probably would have said, "Oh, both are possibilities." And it really would have been "You're a person and therefore I can be with you." . . . If . . . somewhere I had read one book that said this is a possibility, it would have been a possibility.

I guess that if the choice were absolute, I would choose living among lesbians. . . . I would be extremely unhappy if all my Latin culture were taken out of my lesbian life. I had a hard time with all the questions that made me choose between Cuban and lesbian, or at least, made me feel as if I had to choose. It made it real clear to me that I identify myself as a lesbian more intensely than as Cuban/Latin. But it is a very painful question because I feel that I am both, and I don't want to have to choose. Clearly, straight people don't even get asked this question and it is unfair that we have to. . . .

Boston Lesbian Psychologies Collective, 1987, pp. 47, 58

Adrienne Rich (1980) asked us to view lesbianism as a continuum or range of woman-identified behaviors and attitudes that enhance power and include supporting, sharing, and bonding among women and resistance to marriage. **Lesbian communities** or networks have been established to provide this mutual support identified by Rich. These communities also assist women in maintaining high levels of political consciousness. The communities may function in many of the same ways that families do for heterosexual women (Perlman, 1987). According to Susan Krieger (1982),

[Lesbian communities enhance] sense of self . . . [and] provide a haven or home in a hostile or distrusting outside world. They lend support for what is frequently a stigmatized life style choice. (p. 91)

Rich's conceptualization of lesbianism does not necessarily include sexual relations between women. Ann Ferguson (1981) has pointed out that omitting this from the definition of lesbianism "unsexes lesbianism" and makes it agreeable to individuals by understating an important difference between lesbian and heterosexual women. Ferguson offered the following definition:

A lesbian is a woman who has sexual and erotic emotional ties primarily with women or who sees herself as centrally involved with a community of self identified lesbians whose sexual and erotic emotional ties are primarily with women and who is herself a self identified lesbian. (p. 166)

Women's recognition and acceptance of themselves as lesbians is a developmental process that may occur at any stage or age of their lives. The term **coming out** (Coleman, 1982) is used to refer to this process of accepting and affirming a lesbian identity and choosing how open one wants to be about one's sexual orientation. The coming-out process may include telling friends and/or family members, participating in a gay rights march, or disclosing one's sexual orientation to coworkers. Coming out is a choice for women. Among the several factors that influence the coming-out process are: ethnicity (Espin, 1987), religion, birth order, being physically challenged, and age (Zitter, 1987). Oliva Espin (1987) has discussed how Latina lesbians have to embrace three stigmatized identities: woman, lesbian, and ethnic minority. A Latina lesbian very often must choose between leading a "double life" within her culture or ending the possibility of serving the community.

Cass (1979) identified the following six stages in the identity development of a lesbian and gay man: Identity confusion, identity comparison, identity tolerance, identity acceptance, identity pride, and identity synthesis. Let's define each of these stages in the identity process.

Identity confusion: Individuals most likely assumed a heterosexual identity because heterosexuality is perceived as normative in society. As these individuals become attracted to others of the same sex they begin to ask themselves questions concerning their sexual identity, for example, "Who am I?"

Identity comparison: As individuals begin questioning their sexual identity they may indicate to themselves that they are gay or lesbian.

Identity tolerance: During this stage individuals are telling themselves they are gay or lesbian. It is at this stage in their identity development that they seek out other lesbians or gay men to get affirmation for their identity.

Identity acceptance: Individuals at this stage in their identity development can state they are gay or lesbian and accept this identity rather than only tolerate it.

Identity pride: A strong identification with gay or lesbian communities occurs during this stage. In addition, there is increased coming out with friends and family.

Identity synthesis: During this stage, individuals no longer avoid heterosexuals but transcend labels, recognizing that there are some heterosexuals that are supportive of their sexual orientation just as there are lesbians and gays who are supportive of it.

There is no "right" way to be a lesbian and no one way to be sexual as a lesbian. From lesbians' accounts of their experiences and feelings, and from the perspectives shared by Rich, Ferguson, and Krieger, we may describe lesbianism as a lifestyle choice that is associated with women's sense of personal identity. Lesbianism is a product of multiple influences; it is not explained by one single cause (either biology or culture). Carla Golden (1987) stated:

> . . . our being born female does not mean that we automatically and naturally prefer certain roles and activities. We have recognized that the category woman has been socially constructed, and that societal definitions notwithstanding, women are a diverse group with interests, attitudes, and identities that do not always conform to what is traditionally considered feminine. . . . Just as we have protested the constricting social definition of what a real woman is, precisely because it has served to oppress women and to limit the expression of our diverse potentials, so too must we be careful in our social construction of sexuality not to construct categories that are so rigid and inflexible that women's self definitions put them at odds with the social definitions. To do so only limits the expression of the diversities and variabilities in women's sexual identities. (p. 33)

EMPHASIS ON HEALTH

Research has indicated that a half million women die each year in pregnancy and birth; the vast majority of these deaths occur in developing countries (Travis, 1993). Stein and Maine (1986) reported that, in the United States, about 2 percent of all deaths are associated with pregnancy and childbirth. In Indonesia and Egypt, however, the rate is close to 20 percent. Maternal mortality rates are estimated at 22 per 10,000 births in Ecuador, 49.6 per 10,000 in Paraguay, 48 per 10,000 in Bolivia, and 31.4 per 10,000 in Peru (Browning, 1990). Incidence rates are compounded by high fertility. In Africa, for example, women have an average of 8 to 10 pregnancies that result in 6 births.

Precipitating causes of maternal death include chronic health problems (e.g., hepatitis), poor health due to infectious and parasitic diseases, inadequate sanitation, and limited access to health care (Kim, Kols, Mwarogo, & Awasum, 2000; Russell, Sobo, & Thompson, 2000). Ferguson (1981) also suggested that maternal death is explained by young age at marriage intercourse, as well as the cumulative effects of frequent pregnancy, malnutrition, and anemia (Russell et al., 2000).

The heavy burden of agricultural work is a major factor in women's protein and energy requirements (Greenwood, 1985). Women agricultural workers are often exposed to organochlorines and organophosphorus products during pregnancy (Travis, 1993). Women are also more likely to be at risk for schistosomiasis (a waterborne parasitic infection-producing disease in organ systems, particularly the intestines and liver) and other parasitic infections because of their work in watering and caring for livestock in rivers and water impoundments, collecting home drinking water, maintaining irrigation systems, and washing laundry. These activities involve prolonged exposure. According to Vicki Browning (1990), the tragic reality of maternal morbidity and mortality in Third World countries reflects the particular forms of subordination women in those countries suffer.

Dazon Dixon (1990) and Vernice Miller (1990) have pointed out that if we disaggregate the population of poor, black, native, and immigrant women living in inner-city and rural areas of the United States, Europe, and Canada, maternal mortality rates are often as high as those in the Third World. Poverty and poor health are related. Dixon argued that while there is a need for good prenatal care, it must be acknowledged that women have a right to "wellness" and the first is not likely to be achieved without the second.

Governmental support for family planning, access to contraception, and access to abortion are related to maternal mortality (Russell et al., 2000). Relatively strong support is available for family planning in India, Thailand, China, Mexico, and Indonesia, and moderate support is available in African countries (e.g., Kaler, 2000; Kanaaneh, 2000; Stark, 2000). Several countries, however, provide no support or have prohibitions on family planning: Niger, Libya, Saudi Arabia, Romania, and Argentina (Travis, 1993).

Marge Berer (1990) of the Women's Global Network for Reproductive Rights argues for the construction of a population policy that feminists should advocate. A major part of this plan would realize that "when women are pregnant, their lives and health are at risk . . . if they are not in good health and do not have access to good services for pregnancy, childbirth and abortion." A feminist population policy would work toward alleviating women's poverty as an essential component. We need to address the fact of the earth's diminishing capacity for population growth and develop a population policy compatible with women's needs (Petchesky, 1990).

ABORTION

On January 22, 1973, in the landmark decision *Roe v. Wade,* the U.S. Supreme Court found that a statute that made criminal all abortions except those to save the life of the mother violated the constitutional right to privacy. In *Roe v. Wade,* the right to privacy was found "broad enough to encompass a woman's decision whether or not to terminate her pregnancy." The Court held that, through the end

Nashville NOW members braved the winter weather for a vigil to commemorate Roe v. Wade. Their memorial reads: "In memory of the courageous women who died from illegal, unsafe abortions because they had no choice."(From National Organization for Women newsletter, Spring 2000.)

of the first trimester of pregnancy, only a pregnant woman and her physician have the legal right to make the decision about an abortion. The Court also ruled that states may impose certain regulations in the second trimester in order to protect women's health and may take steps to protect fetal life in the final trimester. The vote was 7 to 2.

On this same date, in *Roe v. Bolton,* the Supreme Court removed restrictions on places that could be used to perform abortions, a ruling that gave rise to abortion clinics. These two decisions decriminalized abortion, made federal Medicaid funding available for abortions, and made safer abortions possible. Some women's groups set up public referral services; others organized women-controlled nonprofit abortion clinics.

On July 3, 1989, in *Webster v. Reproductive Health Services,* the Supreme Court ruled that states could limit a woman's right to abortion but stopped short of reversing its 1973 decision legalizing abortion. *The vote was 5 to 4.* On June 25, 1990, in *Hodgson v. Minnesota,* the Supreme Court ruled that a state could require that a pregnant adolescent girl inform both her parents before having an abortion, so long as the law provides the alternative of a judicial hearing. The vote was 5 to 4.

Policies on abortion in other countries vary widely. In Japan and Russia abortion is legal and widely practiced. The same is true in South America, Japan, and parts of eastern and central Europe. In Africa and Asia, abortion is limited because of the scarcity of medical facilities (Georges, 1996; Henshaw, 1990). There are several **abortion** procedures that are available; they are selected on the basis of how far the pregnancy has progressed (Hyde & DeLamater, 1999). These methods include: vacuum aspiration, saline-induced abortion, prostaglandin abortion, hysterotomy, and RU-486.

The **vacuum aspiration** procedure is performed during the first trimester of the pregnancy (up to 14 weeks' gestation) and involves suctioning out the contents of the uterus (Hatcher et al., 1998). This procedure is also referred to as vacuum suction or vacuum curettage. The **saline-induced abortion** is performed in the late second trimester, usually from 13 to 16 weeks' gestation. Labor is induced by having a saline solution injected into the amniotic sac (Hyde & DeLamater, 1999).

A variation on the saline-induced abortion is referred to as the **prostaglandin abortion.** Prostaglandins are hormone-like substances that cause contractions. Prostaglandins are injected into the amniotic sac, intravenously, or via a vaginal suppository (Hyde & DeLamater, 1999). Prostaglandin abortions are usually performed late in the second trimester.

A **hysterotomy** is a surgical abortion procedure. It is performed in the second trimester, usually from 16 to 24 weeks. This procedure is essentially a cesarean section from which the fetus is removed.

RU-486, referred to as the "abortion pill" (Couzinet, 1986) is mifepristone. It induces an early abortion. The drug has an antiprogesterone effect that causes the woman's endometrium of the uterus to be sloughed off (Spitz et al., 1998).

Attitudes of Women Who Have Had Abortions

The majority of women who have abortions do not experience negative psychological responses to the abortion (Adler et al., 1992; Major & Gramzow, 1999). Some research does indicate that some women may experience negative reactions to the abortion, including depressed mood, anxiety, and guilt. Travis (1993) noted, however, that the data on the proportion of women susceptible to negative reactions concerning the abortion may be biased by the fact that their health care providers expect women to have negative reactions and, consequently, may subtly impose demand characteristics on women. Major and Gramzow (1999) reported that women who felt stigmatized by abortion were significantly more likely to conceal the abortion from friends and family.

MEET MARGARET SANGER

Margaret Higgins Sanger started writing a newspaper column in 1912 entitled "What Every Girl Should Know." In 1914 her article on venereal disease was censored since it was believed to be "obscene." Sanger then began publishing "The Woman Rebel," a monthly feminist paper. She was soon charged with violating postal obscenity laws because she advocated birth control.

In order to avoid going to jail, Sanger went to England. Her husband, William Sanger, was jailed in 1915 for distributing a pamphlet entitled "Family Limitation" that provided information on birth control methods. Charges against Margaret Sanger were dropped when her 5-year-old daughter died.

She began a nationwide tour to promote contraception. In 1916 she opened a clinic in New York. In her clinic she distributed diaphragms. Consequently, she was arrested, convicted, and served jail time.

The New York State Legislature eventually amended state law to permit physicians to prescribe birth control devices for medical reasons.

In 1923 Sanger started the first legal family planning clinic in the United States. In 1952 she helped establish the International Planned Parenthood Federation.

The United States Supreme Court gave private citizens the right to obtain and use birth control in 1965. This occurred one year prior to Margaret Sanger's death.

Nonjudgmental counseling has been reported to be helpful for women who decide to have an abortion. Brenda Major and her colleagues (Major, Mueller, & Hildebrandt, 1985) found that women's attitudes prior to the abortion are good predictors of reactions to this experience. Women who favor abortion generally report continued favorable opinions and a sense of relief. Research with ethnic minority women also suggests that the women are satisfied with their decision to terminate the pregnancy and do not experience severe negative reactions (Eisen & Zellman, 1984). An additional predictor of positive coping with abortion is strong social support from friends, partner, family, and/or other social groups. Post-abortion support groups are helpful for women who benefit from talking about the experience (Lodl, McGettigan, & Bucy, 1984).

For adolescent women who need to decide whether to have an abortion, this may be the first major decision they have to make in their lives (Adler, Smith, & Tschann, 1998). Many adolescent women who conceived knew about birth control and chose not to use it. Why? In the United States, adolescent women are placed in a double bind when it comes to sex and sexuality (Travis et al., 2000). They are encouraged by the media, peers, and family members to be sexy. Yet they are also given the clear message to *not* be sexual. Using contraception is a clear signal: One is sexually active. Adolescent women may not be able to face their family with this marker of their adult status. When they fail to use contraception, being "swept off their feet" in passionate romance may be one way to not take total responsibility for their actions in a society that condemns women's sexuality (Kilbourne, 1999). Consequently, adolescent women may not use birth control because of its social meaning, a meaning not created by women (Amaro, 1995; Reid & Bing, 2000).

Katharina Ungruh's (1990) research on the attitudes of women in Ireland who have had abortions in England and Bolks and colleagues' (Bolks, Evans, Pollnard, & Wrinkle, 2000) research with Mexican Americans, Puerto Ricans, and Cubans suggest the strong element of silence that surrounds the issue of abortion. Ungruh found that women's main fear governing their attitudes is the fear of "getting caught," not having sex or the abortion itself. The consequences are frightening for women in Ireland. One woman told Ungruh that a neighbor of hers became pregnant and was placed in a mental hospital. The baby was adopted, but the woman was left in the mental hospital. Ungruh also reported that women's decision to have abortions was based on not wanting to hurt their parents; "I couldn't have told them" is a common response.

Johnson, Gotthaffer, and Lauffer (1999) investigated the sexual and reproductive health content of Latino and African American magazines published between 1995 and 1998. The topic of abortion was present in less than 10 percent of the articles in these magazines. The coverage of sexually transmitted diseases, including HIV, and contraception were also rarely covered in the magazines. The authors noted that since sexually transmitted diseases are epidemic in Latino and African American communities and that the pregnancy rate is approximately doubled that of white women, the magazines did a disservice to their women readers.

We may view abortion, sexuality, and reproduction as inseparable from one another and from gender-role socialization. Catherine MacKinnon (1989) stated:

> [It] becomes clear why the struggle for reproductive freedom has never included a woman's right to refuse sex. In the concept of sexual liberation which has undergirded the politics of choice, sexual equality has been a struggle for women to have sex with men on the same term as men: "without consequences." Meaning, no children. . . . The abortion right is situated within a very different problematic: the social and political inequality of the sexes. (pp. 188–189)

The initial socially acceptable justification for birth control and abortion in the United States was based on concerns for overpopulation and limited resources

(Travis, 1993). When birth control and abortion were advocated as elements in a woman's right to self-determination, extensive legal and political forces were established to cease this movement (Petchesky, 1990).

Incidence of Abortion in the United States

Travis (1993) reported that utilization of abortion differs by race. Abortion ratios for white women are below those for women of color. Travis noted:

> . . . this difference reflects the effects of a number of diverse variables, including limited access to counseling, health care and family planning services, as well as styles of female-male relationships. Additionally, the lower socioeconomic standing of most minorities may mean an unplanned pregnancy has less impact on career, job aspirations, or income. (pp. 292–293)

One important health effect of legal abortion in the United States is a decline in abortion-related deaths (Hyde & DeLamater, 1999). According to Travis, "[Legal] abortion has a significant impact on life and death for women. The relative risk of death from early abortions (gestation under nine weeks) is minimal, and is currently estimated at one maternal death per 500,000" (p. 293).

However, research with women in other countries suggests that mortality rates are higher. For example, 75 percent of the maternal deaths in developing countries are caused by one of five obstetric complications: hemorrhage, obstructed labor, infection, eclampsia, and abortion (Browning, 1990; Das Gupta, 1995).

EDUCATING ABOUT REPRODUCTIVE RIGHTS AND REPRODUCTIVE FREEDOM

Abortion, adoption, and motherhood have problems associated with them (Travis et al., 2000). The least amount of psychological problems result from preventing unwanted pregnancies to begin with (Lammers, Ireland, Resnick, & Blum, 2000). Education about contraception will assist women in not having to make an intolerable choice among adoption, abortion, or motherhood (Peremans, Hermann, Avonts, Van-Royen, & Denekens, 2000; Poppen & Reisen, 1999). It is true that women want to control reproduction. Yet, is it essential that *only* women must take responsibility and risk every time they have intercourse, until they reach menopause? (Hyde & DeLamater, 1999).

We can educate adolescent *women and men* about birth control and sexuality (Becker & Barth, 2000; Belicose, 1999; Kirby, 2000). We can replace the myths with facts. It is important to discuss the meaning of sexuality in our lives (Coleman & Ingham, 1999). We also need to inform women about the effectiveness, side effects, and disadvantages of birth control methods (Hyde & DeLamater, 1999). And, finally, we need to provide role models for adolescent women and men: Women and men in movies, television programs, magazines, and books rarely discuss contraception. This contributes to the belief that sex is spontaneous and "natural," and contraception is not (Kvalem, Sundet, Rivo, & Eilertsen, 1996).

TO THE FUTURE

At the Fourth International Interdisciplinary Congress on Women, held in New York City in June 1990, activists and scholars in women's reproductive rights called for the following issues to be addressed in the near future (Petchesky, 1990):

1. Developing an expanded definition of reproductive rights, one that takes into account the specificities of women's conditions by class, race, age, ethnicity, region, country and locale; and that links technologies and services to economic and social needs.

2. Investigating the relation between poor women's attitudes and concerns about their children—particularly their children's health, nutrition, and care—and their ability to attend to their own reproductive health.

3. Increasing our understanding of the links between the spread of the AIDS virus among women and children in all countries and its effects on reproductive health needs and practices.

4. Generating more data about the relation between malnutrition and women's reproductive health.

5. Investigating and monitoring more diligently the continued patterns of abuse and neglect in family planning services and their specific forms in different countries; developing a "human rights" framework to critique and confront these abuses.

6. Generating data [perhaps in conjunction with Amnesty International] about where and how many women and medical practitioners are being jailed or persecuted for illegal abortions.

7. Developing a rigorous analysis of the connections between international population policies and international economic and environmental policies (those of governments, donor and lending agencies), and a feminist critique. (pp. 37–38)

NEW TERMS

abortion	multiple orgasms
anti-gay prejudice	myotonia
climax	oophorectomy
coming out	orgasm
divergent meanings of sexuality	orgasmic phase
double standard of sexuality	orgasmic plateau
dyspareunia	orgasmic platform
endometriosis	plateau phase
excitement phase	prostaglandin abortion
hysterectomy	reproductive freedom
hysterotomy	resolution phase
identity acceptance	RU-486
identity comparison	saline-induced abortion
identity confusion	sex flush
identity pride	unaroused states
identity synthesis	vacuum aspiration
identity tolerance	vaginal lubrication
lesbian communities	

CHAPTER REVIEW QUESTIONS

1. Offer some explanations for the failure of U.S. women and men to be adequately informed about sexuality.

2. Give some examples of ways in which gender-role socialization shapes girls' and women's sexual experiences and sexual knowledge.

3. How do you define human sexuality? Why do you include the issues you do in this definition? Why do you omit some issues?

4. Discuss the four stages of women's sexual response.

5. Offer some suggestions for educating middle-aged and older women about the relationships between menopause and sexuality.

6. Why is information about lesbian relationships typically omitted from discussions of women's sexuality?

7. How have feminist researchers changed the androcentric nature of the study of sexuality?

8. Discuss some cross-cultural research on the practice and perceptions of abortion.

9. Do you think radio and television talk shows (with phone-ins) dealing with sexuality (e.g., Dr. Ruth Westheimer, Ask Dr. Drew) are helpful? Why or why not?

10. Offer some suggestions for empowering women in terms of their reproductive rights.

SELECTED READINGS

Amaro, H. (1995). Love, sex, and power: Considering women's realities in HIV prevention. *American Psychologist, 50,* 437–447.

Hyde, J., & DeLamater, J. (1999). *Understanding human sexuality.* New York: McGraw Hill.

Travis, C., Meginnis, K., & Bardari, K. (2000). Beauty, sexuality, and identity: The social control of women. In C. Travis & J. White (Eds.), *Sexuality, society, and feminism* (pp. 237–272). Washington, DC: American Psychological Association.

LEARNING MORE ABOUT . . .

Suggestions for Term Papers and Independent Studies Related to *Women's Sexuality, Reproductive Rights, and Reproductive Health*

The double bind posed for adolescent girls: Be sexy but not sexual

Stereotypes about women's sexuality

Discussing information about sexually transmitted diseases with adolescent girls

How feminist researchers have changed the androcentric nature of the study of sexuality

How the media perpetuate stereotypes about women's sexuality

Ways to empower women to use breast self-examinations

TAKING ACTION . . .

on *Women's Sexuality, Reproductive Rights, and Reproductive Health*

1. Ask friends and family to state their beliefs about women's reproductive rights. How do they feel about teaching girls and women about sexuality? About premarital sex? About contraception? About abortion?

   a. Note religious themes in these individuals' responses.

   b. Share with these individuals the research and theories from this chapter and from your class lecture/discussion.

    c. How do they respond?

    d. How do you interpret their responses?

2. a. Locate educational programs/support groups for women's reproductive health care concerns that are present in your campus community.

    b. Obtain a brochure/pamphlet from at least one of the programs you locate.

    c. Bring the educational material to your class. Set up a "Women's Health/ Health Care" display in your class and have your classmates and professor browse through the material during the class period.

    d. Put the material on display in the Psychology Department Office or Women's Center. Also have the information summarized in the college's newspaper.

3. a. View two or three comedy programs and/or variety shows.

    b. Record the number of anti-lesbian jokes and remarks delivered in the programs.

    c. Analyze the comments in terms of stereotypes of lesbians.

    d. How would you feel if you were a lesbian and heard these comments?

    e. Discuss the research on lesbian women's relationships and expressions of homophobia with your friends and family.

REFERENCES

Adler, N., David, H., Major, B., Roth, S., Russo, N. F., & Wyatt, G. (1992). Psychological factors in abortion: A review. *American Psychologist, 47,* 1194–1204.

Adler, N., Smith, L., & Tschann, J. (1998). Abortion among adolescents. In L. Beckman et al. (Eds.), *The new civil war: The psychology, culture, and politics of abortion.* Washington, DC: American Psychological Association.

Amaro, H. (1995). Love, sex, and power: Considering women's realities in HIV prevention. *American Psychologist, 50,* 437–447.

Andersen, B., & Cyranowski, J. (1995). Women's sexuality: Behaviors, responses, and individual differences. *Journal of Consulting and Clinical Psychology, 63,* 891–906.

Becker, M., & Barth, R. (2000). Power through choices: The development of a sexuality education curriculum for youths in out-of-home care. *Child Welfare, 79,* 269–282.

Belicose, R. (1999). The influence of cognitive development and reference groups on teen contraceptive use. *Dissertation Abstracts International, 59* (8–A), 3205.

Berer, M. (1990, June). *International population and family planning from a feminist perspective.* Paper presented at the Fourth International Interdisciplinary Congress on Women, New York.

Blumstein, P., & Schwartz, P. (1983). *American couples: Money, work, and sex.* New York: Morrow.

Bolks, S., Evans, D., Pollnard, J., & Wrinkle, R. (2000). Core beliefs and abortion attitudes: A look at Latinos. *Social Science Quarterly, 81,* 253–260.

Boston Lesbian Psychologies Collective. (Eds.). (1987). *Lesbian psychologies: Explorations and challenges.* Urbana: University of Illinois Press.

Boston Women's Health Book Collective. (1984). *The new our bodies, ourselves.* New York: Simon & Schuster.

Browning, V. (1990, June). *Maternal mortality.* Paper presented at the International Interdisciplinary Congress on Women, New York.

Butler, R., & Lewis, M. (1982). *Aging and mental health.* St. Louis: Mosby.

Cass, V. (1979). Homosexual identity formation: A theoretical model. *Journal of Homosexuality, 4,* 219–235.

Cogan, J. (1996). The prevention of anti-lesbian/gay hate crimes through social change and empowerment. In E. Rothblum & L. Bond (Eds.), *Preventing heterosexism and homophobia.* Thousand Oaks, CA: Sage.

Cole, E. & Rothblum, E. (1990). Commentary on "Sexuality and the midlife woman." *Psychology of Women Quarterly, 14,* 509–512.

Coleman, E. (1982). Developmental stages of the coming-out process. In W. Paul, et al., (Eds.), *Homosexuality: Social, psychological, and biological issues.* Beverly Hills, CA: Sage.

Coleman, L., & Ingham, R. (1999). Exploring young peoples' difficulties in talking about contraception: How can we encourage more discussion between partners? *Health Education Research, 14,* 741–750.

Collins, C. (1999). Reproductive technologies for women with physical disabilities. *Sexuality and Disability, 17,* 299–307.

Couzinet, B. (1986). Termination of early pregnancy by the progesterone antagonist RU486. *New England Journal of Medicine, 315,* 1565–1569.

Das Gupta, M. (1995). Life course perspectives on women's autonomy and health outcomes. *American Anthropologist, 97,* 481–491.

DeFour, D. C. (1996). The interface of racism and sexism in sexual harassment. In M. A. Paludi (Ed.), *Sexual harassment on college campuses: Abusing the ivory power.* Albany: State University of New York Press.

Dixon, D. (1990, June). *Women of color and reproductive rights in the United States.* Paper presented at the Fourth International Interdisciplinary Congress on Women, New York.

Eisen, M., & Zellman, G. L. (1984). Factors predicting pregnancy resolution decision satisfaction of unmarried adolescents. *Journal of Genetic Psychology, 145,* 231–239.

Espin, O. (1987). Issues of identity in the psychology of Latina lesbians. In Boston Lesbians Psychologies Collective (Eds.), *Lesbian psychologies.* Urbana: University of Illinois Press.

Ferguson, A. (1981). Patriarchy, sexual identity, and the sexual revolution. *Signs, 7,* 158–172.

Galavotti, C., & Richter, D. (2000). Talking about hysterectomy: The experiences of women from four cultural groups. *Journal of Women's Health and Gender Based Medicine, 9,* S-63–S-67.

Gannon, L. (1999). *Women and aging: Transcending the myths.* New York: Routledge.

Georges, E. (1996). Abortion policy and practice in Greece. *Social Science and Medicine, 42,* 509–519.

Golden, C. (1987). Diversity and variability in women's sexual identities. In Boston Lesbian Psychologies Collective (Eds.), *Lesbian psychologies.* Urbana: University of Illinois Press.

Greenwood, M. (1985). Methylmercury poisoning in Iraq. An epidemiological study of the 1971–1972 outbreak. *Journal of Applied Toxicology, 5,* 148–159.

Hendrick, S., Hendrick, C., Slapion-Foote, M., & Foote, F. (1985). Gender differences in sexual attitudes. *Journal of Personality and Social Psychology, 48,* 1630–1642.

Henshaw, S. (1990). Induced abortion: A world review, 1990. *Family Planning Perspectives, 22,* 76–89.

Hillman, J. (2000). *Clinical perspectives on elderly sexuality.* New York: Plenum.

Hyde, J. S., & DeLamater, J. (1999). *Understanding human sexuality.* New York: McGraw Hill.

Johnson, M., Gotthoffer, A., & Lauffer, K. (1999). The sexual and reproductive health content of African American and Latino magazines. *Howard Journal of Communications, 10,* 169–187.

Kaler, A. (2000). "Who has told you to do this thing?" Toward a feminist interpretation of contraceptive diffusion in Rhodesia, 1970–1980. *Signs, 25,* 677–708.

Kanaaneh, R. (2000). New reproductive rights and wrongs in the Galilee. In A. Russell et al. (Eds.), *Contraception across cultures: Technologies, choices, constraints.* New York: Berg.

Kilbourne, J. (1999). *Deadly persuasion.* New York: Free Press.

Kim, Y., Kols, A., Mwarogo, P., & Awasum, D. (2000). Differences in counseling men and women: Family planning in Kenya. *Patient Education and Counseling, 39,* 37–47.

Kirby, D. (2000). School-based interventions to prevent unprotected sex and HIV among adolescents. In J. Peterson et al. (Eds.), *Handbook of HIV prevention.* New York: Plenum.

Krieger, S. (1982). Lesbian identity and community: Recent social science literature. *Signs, 8,* 91–108.

Kvalem, I., Sundet, J., Rivo, K., & Eilertsen, D. (1996). The effect of sex education on adolescents' use of condoms: Applying the Solomon four-group design. *Health Education Quarterly, 23,* 34–47.

LaFromboise, T., Choney, S., James, A., & Running Wolf, P. (1995). American Indian women and psychology. In H. Landrine (Ed.), *Bringing cultural diversity to feminist psychology.* Washington, DC: American Psychological Association.

Lammers, C., Ireland, M., Resnick, M., & Blum, R. (2000). Influences on adolescents' decision to postpone onset of sexual intercourse: A survival analysis of virginity among youths aged 13 to 18 years. *Journal of Adolescent Health, 26,* 42–48.

Leiblum, S. R. (1990). Sexuality and the midlife woman. *Psychology of Women Quarterly, 14,* 495–508.

Leiblum, S., Bachmann, G., Kemmann, E., Colburn, D., & Swartzman, L. (1983). Vaginal atrophy in the postmenopausal woman: The importance of sexual activity and hormones. *Journal of the American Medical Association, 249,* 2195–2198.

Lewis, C., Groff, J., Herman, C., McKeown, R., & Wilcox, L. (2000). Overview of women's decision making regarding elective hysterectomy, oophorectomy, and hormone replacement therapy. *Journal of Women's Health and Gender Based Medicine,* S-5–S-14.

Lodl, K., McGettigan, M., & Bucy, J. (1984). Women's responses to abortion: Implications for post-abortion support groups. *Journal of Social Work and Human Sexuality,* 119–132.

MacKinnon, C. (1989). *Toward a feminist theory of the state.* Cambridge, MA: Harvard University Press.

Major, B., & Gramzow, R. (1999). Abortion as stigma: Cognitive and emotional implications of concealment. *Journal of Personality and Social Psychology, 77,* 735–745.

Major, B., Mueller, P., & Hildebrandt, K. (1985). Attributions, expectations, and coping with abortion. *Journal of Personality and Social Psychology, 48,* 585–599.

Mansfield, P., & Koch, P. (1998). Qualities midlife women desire in their sexual relationships and their changing sexual response. *Psychology of Women Quarterly, 22,* 285–303.

Masters, W., & Johnson, V. (1966). *Human sexual response.* Boston: Little, Brown.

Miller, V. (1990, June). *Women's reproductive rights in eight national settings.* Paper presented at the Fourth International Interdisciplinary Congress on Women, New York.

Mingo, C., Herman, C., & Jasperse, M. (2000). Women's stories: Ethnic variations in women's attitudes and experiences of menopause, hysterectomy, and hormone replacement therapy. *Journal of Women's Health and Gender Based Medicine, 9,* S-27–S-38.

Mohr, J., & Sedlacek, W. (2000). Perceived barriers to friendship with lesbians and gay men among university students. *Journal of College Student Development, 41,* 70–80.

Myers, L., & Morokoff, P. (1986). Psychological and subjective sexual arousal in pre- and post-menopausal women and post-menopausal women taking replacement therapy. *Psychophysiology, 23,* 283–292.

Pangman, V., & Seguire, M. (2000). Sexuality and the chronically ill older adult: A social justice issue. *Sexuality and Disability, 18,* 49–59.

Peremans, L., Hermann, I., Avonts, D., Van-Royen, P., & Denekens, J. (2000). Contraceptive knowledge and expectations by adolescents: An explanation by focus groups. *Patient Education and Counseling, 40,* 133–141.

Perlman, S. (1987). The saga of continuing clash in the lesbian community, or will an army of ex-lovers fail? In Boston Lesbian Psychologies Collective (Eds.), *Lesbian psychologies.* Urbana: University of Illinois Press.

Petchesky, R. (1990, June). *Global feminist perspectives on reproductive rights and repro- ductive health.* A report on the Special Sessions held at the Fourth International Interdis- ciplinary Congress on Women, New York.

Poppen, P., & Reisen, C. (1999). Women's use of dual methods of sexual self-protection. *Women and Health, 30,* 53–66.

Reid, P. T., & Bing, V. (2000). Sexual roles of girls and women: An ethnocultural lifespan per- spective. In C. Travis et al. (Eds.), *Sexuality, society, and feminism.* Washington, DC: American Psychological Association.

Reinisch, J. (1990). *The Kinsey Institute new report on sex: What you must know to be sex- ually literate.* New York: St. Martin's Press.

Rich, A. (1980). Compulsory heterosexuality and lesbian existence. *Signs, 5,* 631–660.

Root, M. (1995). Psychology of Asian American women. In H. Landrine (Ed.), *Bringing cul- tural diversity to feminist psychology.* Washington, DC: American Psychological Associa- tion.

Rothblum, E. (1994). Transforming lesbian sexuality. *Psychology of Women Quarterly, 18,* 627–641.

Rubin, L. (1976). *Intimate strangers: Men and women together.* New York: Harper & Row.

Russell, A., Sobo, E., & Thompson, M. (Eds.). (2000). *Contraception across cultures: tech- nologies, choices, constraints.* New York: Berg.

Sawyer, S., & Roberts, S. (1999). Sexual and reproductive health in young people with spina bifida. *Developmental Medicine and Child Neurology, 41,* 671–675.

Sipski, M., Alexander, C., & Rosen, R. (1999). Sexual response in women with spinal cord in- juries: Implications for our understanding of the abled bodied. *Journal of Sex and Marital Therapy, 25,* 11–22.

Spitz, I., et al. (1998). Early pregnancy termination with mifepristone and misoprostol in the United States. *New England Journal of Medicine, 338,* 1241–1247.

Stark, N. (2000). My body, my problem: Contraceptive decision making among rural Bangladeshi women. In A. Russell et al. (Eds.), *Contraception across cultures: Technolo- gies, choices, constraints.* New York: Berg.

Stein, A., & Maine, D. (1986). The health of women. *International Journal of Epidemiology, 15,* 303–305.

Steinem, G. (1989). A basic human right. *MS., xviii,* 39–41.

Tiefer, L. (1995). *Sex is not a natural act, and other essays.* Boulder, CO: Westview.

Travis, C. (1993). Women and health. In F. L. Denmark & M. A. Paludi (Eds.), *Psychology of women: A handbook of issues and theories.* Westport, CT: Greenwood.

Travis, C., Meginnis, K., & Bardari, K. (2000). Beauty, sexuality, and identity: The social control of women. In C. Travis, et al. (Eds.), *Sexuality, society, and feminism.* Washington, DC: American Psychological Association.

Ungruh, K. (1990, June). *Abortion in the Republic of Ireland.* Paper presented at the Fourth International Interdisciplinary Congress on Women, New York.

Unger, J., & Molina, G. (2000). Acculturation and attitudes about contraceptive use among Latina women. *Health Care for Women International, 21,* 235–249.

United States Congress. (1990). *Indian adolescent mental health* (Tech. Rep. No. OTA = H = 446). Washington, DC: U.S. Government Printing Office.

Williams, R., & Clark, A. (2000). A qualitative study of women's hysterectomy experience. *Journal of Women's Health and Gender Based Medicine, 9,* S-15–S-25.

Williamson, I. (2000). Internalized homophobia and health issues affecting lesbians and gay men. *Health Education Research, 15,* 97–107.

Worth, D., & Rodriguez, R. (1987, January-February). Latina women and AIDS. *SIECUS Report,* pp. 5–7.

Zellman, G., & Goodchilds, J. (1983). Becoming sexual in adolescence. In E. Allgeier & N. McCormick (Eds.), *Changing boundaries: Gender roles and sexual behavior.* Palo Alto, CA: Mayfield.

Zitter, S. (1987). Coming out to mom: Theoretical aspects of the mother-daughter process. In Boston Lesbian Psychologies Collective (Eds.), *Lesbian psychologies.* Urbana: University of Illinois Press.

SEVEN

VERBAL AND NONVERBAL COMMUNICATIONS BY AND ABOUT WOMEN

IN WOMEN'S VOICES

The feminist thinker who wishes to tackle the puzzles of power and take up the questions of meaning must consider the nature of language itself.

Jean B. Elshtain

~

I challenge the assumption that talking in an indirect way reveals powerlessness, lack of self-confidence, or anything else about the character of the speaker.

Deborah Tannen

~

Now we have the dreams and tools to move beyond words and history, beyond the possible to the imagined, and into a life both ancient and new, where we will look back to see our present dreams trailing behind us as markers of where we have been.

Gloria Steinem

~

Many American Indian women maintain an intense respect for the power of the spoken word. They are taught that words can be used to think, talk to oneself, inform, and move or reconcile with others. Words also can be used to insult, frighten, threaten, or conceal. Great care should be taken in the selection of words, and a clear understanding of the purpose for which they are used must be established.

Teresa LaFromboise, Sandra Bennett Choney, Amy James, and Paulette Running Wolf

Chapter Outline

Questions for Reflection

1. Do you smile even though you aren't happy? Why do you think you do this?

2. Do you rely on nonverbal cues when talking with your friends? For example, do you rely on smiling? Eye contact? Body posture? Physical distance?

3. Do you gesture when you speak?

4. Have you noticed that your speech often contains the following: "well, y'know," "kinda," "sorta," "I guess"?

5. How do you feel when there is silence in a conversation? Do you want to hurry up and start talking to end the silence? Or are you comfortable with silence?

6. Which is more important to you: verbal communication or nonverbal communication? Upon which do you rely most?

7. What images do magazine advertisements portray about women? About women of color?

8. How do you believe women are treated in the English language?

INTRODUCTION: PATTERNS OF COMMUNICATION— REFLECTIONS OF POWER AND STATUS

For the next few minutes, look at the following words:

clergymen

househusband

busboy

manpower

metermaid   repairman

coed   laundress

For each word, jot down the first three things you think of.

When asked to do this exercise, one student wrote down these terms alongside the word *househusband:*

out of work

unhappy

unfocused

Do you think these three responses would have been the same if I had asked the students to respond to the word *housewife?* Why do you think this student believes a househusband is out of work—is child care a secondary priority for men? Are women who are housewives not considered to be "working"?

Do you believe nonsexist alternatives to these words would be better? For example, clergy rather than clergymen, college student instead of coed?

In my courses on the psychology of women and the psychology of gender, I frequently ask students to complete an exercise in which they are asked to do the following:

1. Read a newspaper or magazine article and discuss the direct and indirect messages about women and men.

2. Reverse the pronouns and reread the article with the modifications.

3. Compare and contrast the messages about women and men before and after the modifications.

Students have reported being surprised at the differences in meaning and symbolism in popularly written articles. Most students have reported that their "modified" article "doesn't make sense" or "sounds silly," as have students in research by Parks and Roberton (1998).

Here is an example of a "modified" statement:

I enjoy working in my herb garden by day. I also typically bathe in herb sachets (made from my garden) by night, while my wife makes one of her gourmet dinners.

Does this statement sound odd to you? Why? This is the same sentence before the modifications:

I enjoy working in my herb garden by day. I also typically bathe in herb sachets (made from my garden) by night, while my husband makes one of his gourmet dinners.

Do you now believe this sentence "makes sense"? Why? Does it fit with your gender schemas? Do you believe women talk differently than men? Let's discuss some of the ways women communicate **verbally** and **nonverbally** and how these communication styles reflect relative powerlessness in certain situations. Our other topics will be how women's communication styles reflect warmth, encouragement, and support, and how the English language and different media picture women as invisible and not noteworthy.

Women's Verbal Communication Styles

Here is a question for you: Do you believe women and men talk differently? If you are like most people who are asked this question, you replied "Yes." Here's another question: Do you believe there are gender differences in speech acquisition? The answer to this question appears to be "Yes." Research suggests gender differences are common in children's development of language: girls appear to have more of an advantage in vocabulary acquisition during the preschool years (Bee, Mitchell, Barnard, Eyres, & Hammond, 1984; Kojima, 1999). In addition, there is a positive correlation between preschoolers' language development and their socioeconomic status (Hart & Risley, 1995). Preschoolers who live in poverty tend to hear a smaller quantity and variety of language from their caregivers than do preschoolers who live in more affluent homes. Hart and Risley (1995) found that by the age of 4, preschoolers in families that received welfare assistance were likely to have been exposed to approximately 13 million fewer words than those preschoolers in families considered professional. Preschoolers in families who received welfare assistance were also apt to hear prohibitions, that is, the word "NO" twice as frequently as those in families classified as professional. Later in childhood, preschoolers who live in poverty perform more poorly on measures of intelligence than their peers of affluence (Paludi, 2001).

In addition, race influences on preschoolers' language development have been noted (Roberts, Burchinal, & Durham, 1999). For example, Roberts and colleagues (1999) reported that African American preschoolers who lived in responsive and stimulating homes had larger vocabularies, used more irregular nouns and verbs, used longer utterances, and had more rapid rates of language acquisition than preschoolers from less responsive and stimulating homes. Roberts and colleagues also noted gender comparisons: Girls used longer utterances and more irregular forms than boys. Girls also had larger vocabularies than boys.

Several researchers have argued that speech patterns as well as topics can be divided into "feminine" and "masculine" speech (Carli & Bukato, 2000; Tannen, 1999; 2000). For example, Robin Lakoff (1975) argued that women experience discrimination in language in the following ways: (1) by being taught a form of language that is relatively weaker when compared to the language taught to men (i.e., containing tag questions and qualifiers, to be discussed below), and (2) from the sexism in the structure of language (e.g., nonparallel terms such as master/mistress). According to Lakoff:

> The data on which I am basing my claims have been gathered mainly by introspection: I have examined my own speech and that of my acquaintances and have used my own intuitions in analyzing it. I have also made use of the media . . . is the educated, white, middle-class group that the writer of the book identifies with less worthy of study than any other? (pp. 4–5)

Researchers who study language patterns have noted that, in general, feminine speech appears indirect and powerless, while masculine speech seems direct and powerful (Tannen, 2000). Linda Carli (1999) reported that women generally have more difficulty than men in exerting influence, especially when they convey competence and authority. Carli interpreted this finding as indicating that gender differences in influence are mediated by gender differences in power. Robin Lakoff (1975) noted that women's speech patterns contain significantly more tag questions, qualifiers, and longer request phrases, all of which convey a sense of powerlessness in their conversations with others, and empirical studies have confirmed Lakoff's intuitive analysis in comparing women's and men's speech patterns (e.g., Crosby, 1982; Kemper, 1984). An individual who uses "feminine" speech patterns is perceived by others as less competent and less convincing than one who does not use such speech patterns, regardless of whether the speaker is a woman or a man (Tannen, 2000).

Girls and women are likely to use tag questions, qualifiers, longer requests, and fillers in their speech. A **tag question** is partly a statement and partly a question. Let's say you hear a classmate say, "'All My Children' is a fantastic soap opera, isn't it?" Here we have a statement, "'All My Children' is a fantastic soap opera," and a tag question, "isn't it?" What do tag questions connote? Tag questions have been interpreted as meaning weakness, passivity, and doubt. In some situations—business meetings, debate team competitions, college and graduate school classrooms—tag questions may be viewed as illustrating that the speakers are unsure of their opinions and cannot stand up for their own ideas in the face of rejection.

Another interpretation is that tag questions encourage conversation and imply politeness: One person is asking another person's opinion on a topic. Thus, tag questions are perceived to connote warmth and sensitivity (Carli, 1990; Carli & Bukato, 2000).

Robin Lakoff (1973) suggested that women are more likely to use tag questions when discussing their personal feelings. Thus, women's greater tentativeness in expressing their strong beliefs may partially result from the power difference between women and men.

A **qualifier** is a word or phrase that softens a statement. If you said, "This class is exciting!" you would be putting forth your idea in a very direct way. If you instead said, "Well, ah, I think this psychology course is exciting," or "I know I may be wrong about it, but I think this psychology course is exciting," you would not be so direct. Women tend to use qualifiers in their speech (Carli, 1999; Wood, 1994), which suggests that they are tentative and uncertain about the topic and/or their opinions. Qualifiers may also reflect women's awareness of others' negative attitudes and responses toward women who are assertive and direct.

In addition to tag questions and qualifiers, many women tend to use **long requests** in their speech (Carli, 1999), for example, words like "Please," or phrases such as "I'd appreciate it if . . ." Women also use **fillers**—"you know," "ah," "uhm," "let me see," "well," and "oh." Women use fewer fillers in female-female conversations than in female-male conversations, however—a finding that suggests women are more comfortable in conversing with other women than with men. Why? Perhaps women believe they won't be evaluated negatively for their styles of communication.

Women are often perceived as spending more time talking than men. However, this perception is not supported by empirical data of *total talking time* (Kollock, Blumstein, & Schwartz, 1985; Swacker, 1975; Zimmerman & West, 1975). The research suggests just the opposite: in terms of total talking time, men talk more than women (Kollock et al., 1985). Talking time can be interpreted as illustrating power or dominance. When women have greater power in a dyad, they tend to talk more than men (Kollock et al., 1985).

What can we conclude about women's verbal communication styles? Women and men typically use certain features of language differently, but they are similar in their use of grammar and vocabulary. Thus, there are more similarities than differences in their verbal communication styles.

Deborah Tannen (1994) argued that ways of talking must not be taken as obvious evidence of some intrapsychic states such as lack of self-confidence or insecurity. On the contrary, according to Tannen:

> [C]onsidering the many influences on conversational style, individuals have a wide range of ways of getting things done and expressing their emotional states. Personality characteristics such as insecurity cannot be linked to ways of speaking in an automatic, self-evident way. (p. 86)

Research on verbal communication of women of color suggest several challenges to the research just reviewed (Henley, 1995). Henley (1995) has argued that research on gender and language is founded on the belief of white, upper-middle-class women's and men's experiences. Thus, she believes that language is influenced by the social context. Nichols (1983) reported that African American women use innovative speech, thus not supporting Lakoff's claim of universal female linguistic conservatism. Henley (1995) interpreted Nichols' results as evidence that Lakoff's hypotheses were based on the division of labor within the white middle class and thus cannot be generalized to other ethnic groups and races.

Native American women are socialized to believe that words are to be respected because words can be used to inform, reconcile with a loved one, threaten, or conceal (LaFromboise, Choney, James, & Running Wolf, 1995). Latinas value *respeto* (respect), which refers to valuing hierarchies that exist because of age, sex, class, and race. Because of *respeto,* Latinas exhibit a subordinate attitude in their communicating (Ginorio, Gutierrez, Cauce, & Acosta, 1995).

Silencing Women

In general, women are not expected to make substantive verbal contributions in a mixed setting (Beaumont et al., 1998; Libra, 1987; Welte, 1998). In addition, girls' and women's silence is linked to attractiveness. Consider the following lyrics from a song in the movie, "The Little Mermaid":

You'll have to have your looks, your pretty face
And don't underestimate the importance of body language
The men up there don't like a lot of blabber
They think a girl who gossips is a bore
Yes on land it's much preferred for ladies not to say a word
And after all, dear, what is idle prattle for?
Come on, they're not all that impressed with conversation—
True gentlemen avoid it when they can—
But they dote and swoon and fawn on a lady who's withdrawn
It's she who holds her tongue who gets her man.

Research suggests that women are silenced intellectually and creatively (Welte, 1998; see Chapter 9). For example, Hall and Sandler (1982) reported that women college students frequently reported they were silenced in their classes:

> I have witnessed female students in two lower division courses treated as ornaments—as if they lacked any semblance of intellectual capacity—both occasions by male instructors. (p. 6)

> In classes, I have experienced myself as a person to be taken lightly. In one seminar, I was never allowed to finish a sentence. There seemed to be a tacit understanding that I never had anything to say. (p. 7)

> She (a black female medical student) cited a small group learning situation in which the instructor never looked at her and responded only to the other people on either side of her. (p. 12)

Koch (1999) reported that women political candidates are silenced as well. In this research, women candidates were perceived to be able to deal with social issues and be leaders; however, they suffered a disadvantage with regard to their perceived competence.

As another example of **silencing,** let's consider children's story books. In these books girls and boys receive confirmation of social assumptions that girls should be silenced; that they do not take risks, accomplish exciting feats, or leave the security of their homes and the protection of men (Tepper & Cassidy, 1999). Tepper and Cassidy (1999) content analyzed children's picture books. They found that males had higher representation in book titles, pictures, and central role of characters. Similar findings were obtained by Evans and Davies (2000). These researchers examined textbooks used by first, third, and fifth graders. They concluded that despite nonsexist guidelines offered by textbook publishers, boys and men were still primarily portrayed in stereotypical activities and personality characteristics, including aggressiveness, argumentativeness, and competitiveness. Furthermore, the absence of girls and women in literature conveys a message that they are not even important enough to be represented (Paludi, Paludi, & Doyle, in press), as we will discuss later in this chapter.

Lakoff (1973) represented this silencing on the front cover of her book on which she depicts a woman with a bandage over her mouth. As we will discuss in Chapter 10, women who have been sexually victimized have been silenced by law enforcement personnel, physicians, family, friends, and the legal system (Nugent, 1994; Paludi, 1999).

MEET DR. NANCY HENLEY

Dr. Nancy Henley is Professor of Psychology at the University of California, Los Angeles. A former Director of Women's Studies at UCLA and the Editor of Psychology of Women Quarterly (1980–1986), Dr. Henley is the recipient of the Distinguished Publication Award for her book: *Body Politics: Power, Sex, and Nonverbal Communication* (1977).

Question: How would you describe your research on women's nonverbal communication styles?

Dr. Henley's response: My major themes have been that nonverbal dominance and submission gestures provide a micropolitical structure that supports the macropolitical one: that power gestures are made more often by males than by females (generally unwittingly) and that a major distinction between an interpretation of power and one of intimacy for power gestures often lies in the degree of mutuality of the gesture (i.e., to what extent gesturer and gestured-to are free to make the same gesture to the other).

In the realm of language I have also been interested in power and gender, specifically in pursuing the various consequences of the fact that male-biased language (especially the "generic masculine" usage) biases readers' and hearers' comprehension, making them think of males to a greater extent than of females.

Women's Nonverbal Communication Styles

The next time you are at the dining service, observe three or four mixed-sex pairs. Specifically, record the following:

1. How often the women touch the men.

2. How often the men touch the women.

3. Whether one individual of each pair moves toward and/or away from the other person.

4. The parts of the body that are touched by individuals.

As you read this section, compare your results to previously published research, summarized below.

We saw in the last section that women and men differ in their verbal communication patterns. It should not come as a surprise, therefore, to find that men and women also differ in some of their nonverbal communication patterns as well (Hall,

Carter, & Horgan, 2000). Women are better able than men to express their emotions or feelings verbally and nonverbally. And women often express or send nonverbal messages as well as receive and decipher others' nonverbal messages (Hall et al., 2000; Mayo & Henley, 1981). **Encoding** describes the ability to communicate nonverbally; **decoding** describes the ability to evaluate or judge others' nonverbal messages (Hall et al., 2000).

Most girls and women are encouraged by parents, teachers, and their peers to be emotionally expressive, both verbally and nonverbally. Marianne LaFrance and her colleagues (e.g., LaFrance & Carmen, 1980) have found that differential parental treatment affects girls' (and boys') nonverbal ability. The way individuals socialize girls and women influences their skill in nonverbal ways of relating. Pamela Reid and I (1993) reported that parental responses vary, based on both ethnicity and social class (also see Fernandez, Carrera, Sanchez, Paez, & Candia, 2000). For example, compared to parents of white girls, parents of African American preschool girls typically expect the girls to be more mature and responsible. Anecdotal data from other ethnic groups suggest that Hispanic American and Asian American parents have even higher expectations that their daughters will be submissive and dependent (Root, 1995).

Nonverbal and verbal communication styles may symbolize the unequal balance of power between women and men, or what psychologist Rhoda Unger (1979) has referred to as "the politics of gender." As Judith Worell (1990) pointed out:

> In most cultures, the asymmetry of power relationships favors the higher status male, who retains the potential for social control and influence. . . . The translation of this view into human transactions has demonstrated that what have been regarded as sex differences are frequently examples of status and power differences . . . wherein male power legitimizes social initiative and dominance, while female powerlessness precipitates defensive, submissive, and ingratiating behavior. (pp. 205–206)

We can extend this "politics of gender" concept to include the unequal balance of power due to racial, ethnic, and class distinctions.

In conversations between women and men, women spend considerable time looking at the other individual—that is, they make **social eye contact** (Hall et al., 2000). The use of eye contact may indicate a woman's expression of affection or her interest in developing a more intimate relationship with the other person. Wayne Podrouzek and David Furrow (1988) found this result in girls as young as 2 and 4 years of age. Althea Smith (1983) documented racial distinctions in eye contact. She found that African American women have less eye contact than white women do.

Another form of eye contact is staring. For many women, staring implies aggression. Most women tend to look away when they notice someone (typically, a man) staring at them. Women's avoidance of staring is related to the belief that staring is often an aggressive or sexual nonverbal message (see Chapter 10).

Women tend to take less **personal space** around their bodies than men do. Women are also assigned to smaller spaces, such as smaller offices or shared offices (Hall et al., 2000; Jacobson, 1999). From this specific nonverbal message, individuals infer that men are more dominant and have a higher status than women; a person who controls more physical space is more powerful and more dominant and has a higher status than a person who controls less space. Meta-analytic studies (e.g., Hall, 1984) suggest that these gender differences are moderately large.

With respect to **body position,** women tend to sit in a less relaxed way than men. Women display a more restricted body posture than men, who seem to have a wider range of possible body positions. Girls and adult women are encouraged to sit in "ladylike" ways (i.e., with their legs close together or crossed at the ankles, and their hands placed on their lap). Women are less likely to sit with the ankle of one leg over the knee of the other leg, or with their legs apart (Hall et al., 2000).

In addition, women are likely to *smile* more than men (Hall et al., 2000). Meta-analytic studies suggest that this gender difference is moderately large (Hall, 1984). What does smiling mean? Take a look at your high school yearbook. Are the women smiling more than the men? What about you? Are you smiling? If so, why? Were you happy that your photo was being taken? Did you hear a joke? Do you think you look better when you are smiling? Were you trying to appease someone? Or, do you think smiling is just the appropriate thing to do? Research conducted by Deutsch, LeBaron, and Fryer (1987) suggests that women who are not smiling in photographs are rated as less happy and less relaxed in comparison with women who are pictured smiling. Individuals react negatively when women do not smile. Research suggests that women's smiles do not necessarily mean happiness or other positive feelings. In fact, smiling may be associated with negative feelings but women believe they should smile because of gender role expectations (Halberstadt & Saitta, 1987).

Touching another person is considered to be one of the most powerful means of suggesting status or power in a dyad. In general, men, or those with more power and dominance in most situations (e.g., a business meeting), are more apt to touch a woman, but the touching is not reciprocal. Touching may also have an affectional or sexual connotation (Hall et al., 2000; Pearson, 1985). If a woman touches a man's arm or shoulder, he frequently interprets this as being sexual. However, women don't always make the same interpretation. Touching may be interpreted as a friendly gesture or as an abuse of power (see Chapter 10).

Valuing Women's Communication Styles

We have seen that research suggests that girls and women often use tag questions, qualifiers, longer requests, and fillers in their speech. Some researchers and instructors have argued that women should avoid these communication styles and, instead, adopt a "masculine" style in order to achieve more prominence and credibility. Gloria Steinem (1986), however, believes this criticism of women's speech patterns may be a way of dismissing women without dealing with the *content* of what women are saying. Furthermore, when women have adopted a "masculine" style, they have been perceived as "aggressive"; thus, their views, and women in general, may be rejected outright (Hall & Sandler, 1982).

Rather than asking women to conform to men's styles of communicating, I ask that "women's speech" and "nonverbal styles" be considered valuable. Tag questions, fillers, qualifiers, smiling, eye contact, and close body position reflect a more cooperative, less competitive atmosphere in business settings as well as in friendships. They encourage further conversation; women's spoken language and nonverbal gestures are supportive, polite, and expressive (Wood, 1994). We do need to stress the importance of women (and men) being direct with their partners with respect to using contraception and for engaging in safe sex, as we discussed in the last chapter (see Coleman & Ingham, 1999; Hickman & Muehlenhard, 1999). Hickman and Muehlenhard (1999) examined the ways in which women and men communicate sexual content. They reported that women and men attach different meanings to the same signal. Men reported signalling sexual consent using more indirect nonverbal signals than women and making indirect statements about intoxication. Women reported using indirect verbal signals more frequently than men. Unfortunately, both women and men reported most often showing their sexual consent by making no response. Considering the implications of not using contraception and not practicing safe sex, it is imperative to assist adolescents and adults with effective and direct communication skills.

Let's now discuss how the English language itself has been discriminatory against women. This discussion will be extended to media depictions of women.

PORTRAYAL OF WOMEN IN THE ENGLISH LANGUAGE

Sexist ideology is perpetuated and reinforced through the content of a language. **Linguistic sexism** in the English language takes one of three distinct forms: (1) It

ignores women, (2) it **defines women,** and (3) it **deprecates women.** Let's discuss each of these forms of linguistic sexism.

Ignoring Women

Girls and women, although they make up almost 52 percent of the human race, are systematically omitted in daily speech. For example, when individuals talk about the "species as a whole," they typically do not talk about "woman" or "womankind." They speak of "man" or "mankind." Because girls and women are the majority, it would be logical to use "womankind" rather than "mankind" as a generic word meaning the human race. Many individuals use "he" in a generic way, including girls and women as well as boys and men in its definition.

Research on linguistic sexism has suggested that when **generic pronouns** (e.g., his, him, he) are used in printed or spoken forms, listeners or readers typically conjure up a picture of a man, not an image of both a woman and a man. For example, when students were asked to select potential illustrations for a textbook, they were more likely to select all-male photos when the chapter titles were "Industrial Man," or "Social Man," rather than "Industrial Life," or "Society" (Schneider & Hacker, 1973). In addition, students who saw the generic masculine version rated a career in psychology as "less attractive" for women than did students who saw sex-neutral versions.

Roberta Hall and Bernice Sandler (1982) suggested that a learning environment that ignores women contributes to a **"chilly classroom climate"** for women students (also see Chapter 9):

A chilly classroom climate puts women students at a significant educational disadvantage. Overtly disparaging remarks about women, as well as more subtle differential behaviors, can have a critical and lasting effect. When they occur frequently—especially when they involve "gatekeepers" who act as advisors, or serve as chairs of departments—such behaviors can have a profound negative impact on women's academic and career development by . . . discouraging classroom participation, causing students to drop or avoid certain subspecialties within majors, and in some instances to leave a given institution, dampening career aspirations, undermining confidence. Instead of sharpening their intellectual abilities, women may begin to believe and act as though . . . their presence in a given class, department, program or institution is at best peripheral, or at worst an unwelcome intrusion; their capacity for full intellectual development and professional success is limited; their academic and career goals are not matters for serious attention or concern. (p. 3)

Hall and Sandler reported that certain groups of women students are more likely to receive the "chilly" treatment in the classroom: women in traditionally male-populated majors, ethnic minority women, and reentry women students (because of their age and part-time status).

Doyle and Paludi (1998) pointed out that languages that make no distinction between female and male in a third-person pronoun (e.g., Aztec, Chinese, Finnish, Hungarian) do not have this problem of describing an unspecified referent.

Defining Women

A woman is frequently identified by her relationship to a father, brother, husband, or son. Many biographies of women psychologists (see Chapter 1) have discussed women, first, in terms of their relationships to men, and, second, in terms of the contributions they have made to psychology. For example, Anna Freud is frequently described as being "Sigmund Freud's daughter" before it is stated that she was a psychoanalyst and scholar in her own right. Carolyn Wood Sherif, Margaret Harlow, and Janet Taylor Spence are defined as the "wives" of Muzafer, Harry, and Kenneth, respectively, before they are defined as researchers and academicians.

Margaret Intons-Peterson and Jill Crawford (1985) found that, among faculty and students, surnames convey an important sense of identity to women, just as they do to men. Decisions about marital surname choice are influenced by societal beliefs, even when these beliefs have no legal basis. Men, more than women—and married men, more than single men—thought that children should take their fathers' surnames. Women were more willing than men to consider nontraditional surname styles.

What does a change in name signify? If a name is part of one's identity, then changing one's name implies (or even requires) that the person changes or loses some aspect or degree of her or his identity. By taking her husband's name, a married woman, to a large extent, changes her self-identity as well as her social status to include, in the words of sociologist Talcott Parsons, "the woman's fundamental status as that of her husband's wife, the mother of his children." She now becomes, to many people's way of thinking, "Mrs. James Smith," dropping even her given first name in the process.

This discussion about defining women in relation to the men in their lives may seem to some individuals as the making of a mountain out of a mole hill. These same individuals would probably say, when asked if changing a groom's name to that of the bride would be an acceptable practice, that this would be somehow different. This change would indicate that the man was no longer considered the first in the relationship, the one whose name the couple takes as their identity. But isn't that what happens to most married women? They become subsumed under their husbands, and their name change signifies as much (Dion & Cota, 1991). Furthermore, women who choose to use "Miss" or "Mrs." are perceived as lower in instrumental characteristics, such as competence and leadership. They are also perceived to be stronger in expressive traits and are judged more likable than a woman who chooses to use "Ms." (Dion & Cota, 1991), perhaps reflecting individuals' misunderstanding of feminists and feminism (see Chapter 1).

An individual's name is part of her or his identity. And tradition in our culture holds that a woman's identity must be submerged into that of her husband. In Spanish-speaking countries, a woman retains her own name after marriage, adding her husband's surname after her own (Townsend, 1961).

Deprecating Women

In my classes, I frequently facilitate the following experiential exercise (adapted from Paludi, 1996). Try this exercise with your friends!

- On a sheet of paper, put a grid that is first divided in half. Label one half "Girls/Women" and the other half "Boys/Men." Then, divide each half into four columns titled "Plant," "Animal," "Food," and "Other."

- Ask your friends (you can participate too!) to brainstorm names and phrases in each category that are used to refer to girls/women and boys/men. Examples for girls/women might include:

Plant	**Animal**	**Food**	**Other**
Rose	Fox	Cupcake	Baby
	Chick	Sweetcakes	

- Label each word generated as positive, negative, or neutral.

- Count the number of words labeled as positive, negative, or neutral for girls/women and boys/men. Indicate which sex has the more positive names or phrases.

- Discuss the importance of avoiding the use of terms that connote girls/women as something to be consumed or to be *infantilized*. Infantilizing women (referring to them as *baby, babe, chick*) connotes immaturity and irresponsibility.

When we examine some parallel terms, we still find a deprecation of women. For example, mister-mistress or bachelor-spinster. When we note the words indicative of sexual promiscuity, we find that well over 200 such words describe a sexually active woman (e.g., prostitute, harlot, courtesan, concubine, tramp, etc.), but we find just over 20 words to describe lustful men (satyr, dirty old man, etc.) (Stanley, 1977). Lerner (1976) suggested that the linguistic choice of lady, woman, or girl is indicative of an unconscious attitude toward women: "Lady" implies propriety and "girl" implies immaturity. With time, the term *female* has taken on negative connotations and may be used in a pejorative sense. **Pejoration** is assumed to occur because of prejudice; words applied to women take on negative connotations because of the devaluing of women in general (Lerner, 1976).

Euphemisms such as "girl" or "gal" for an adult woman have been found to cause people to look unfavorably at the woman being described (Lipton & Hershaft, 1984). A promale evaluation bias is also present when men and women are asked to evaluate an unsigned academic article or one that has initials or a sexually ambiguous name identifying the author (Paludi & Strayer, 1985; Unger & Saundra, 1993).

Discrimination in the form of evaluation bias is more pronounced when the woman is a member of an ethnic minority group (Romero & Garza, 1986). Darlene DeFour (1996) and Maria Root (1995) noted that, because of myths and stereotypes that portray women of color as sexually active, erotic, and exotic, these women are subjected to harassing comments because of their sex and their ethnicity (see Chapter 10). Irving Allen (1984) studied terms that refer specifically to women of different ethnic groups and concluded that derogatory names for these women display the strains of traditional masculine gender roles and aggression. The words stereotype physical differences among women (e.g., hair texture; shape of eyes) and also make derogatory sexual allusions, using animal and food metaphors (e.g., fortune cookie, hot chocolate, hot tamale).

Language is one of the most powerful features of any culture. The English language has a strong undercurrent of linguistic sexism, exemplified in the words by which women are ignored, defined, and deprecated. Some individuals may regard linguistic sexism as unimportant. However, our language reflects our thought processes. When we use "man," "he," and "mankind," we may be communicating a belief that men are the norm and women are a deviation from the norm. Thus, we need to work at altering our thought processes in order to express equal status for women and men. Once our thought processes change, our language will also change.

In 1848 in Seneca Falls, New York, nineteenth century U.S. feminists wrote the "Declaration of Sentiments" in which they made clear how they understood that the generic "man" of the Declaration of Independence obscured the rights of women:

We hold these truths to be self-evident: that all men and women are created equal. . . . The history of mankind is a history of repeated injuries and usurpations on the part of man toward woman, having in direct object the establishment of an absolute tyranny over her. . . . He has endeavored, in every way he could, to destroy her confidence in her own powers, to lessen her self-respect, and to make her willing to lead a dependent and abject life.

Hyde (1984) created a gender-neutral, fictitious occupation *wudgemaker* but left the pronouns blank in the following description:

Few people have heard of a job in factories, being a wudgemaker. Wudges are made of plastic, oddly shaped, and are an important part of video games. The wudgemaker works from a plan or pattern posted at eye level as ____ puts together the pieces at a table while ____ is sitting down. Eleven plastic pieces must be snapped together. Some of the pieces are tiny, so that ____ must have good coordination in ____ fingers. Once all eleven pieces are put together, ____ must test out the wudge to make sure that all of the moving pieces move properly. The wudgemaker is well paid, and must be a high school graduate, but ____ does not have to have gone to college to get the job.

In Hyde's research with children, one-third of the group received this description with "he" or "his" in all the blanks; one-third received the description with "they" or "their," and one-third received the version with "she" or "her" in all the blanks. Hyde instructed the children to rate how well a woman would do the wudgemaker job, using a three-point scale: 3: very well; 2: just okay; and 1: not very well. Hyde also asked the children how well they believed a man could do this job of making wudges.

Hyde's findings suggest that pronoun choice has an effect on the concepts children form. The children did not seem to be influenced by which pronoun they were given when it came to rating men's performance as a wudgemaker. However, the pronoun did have an effect on how the woman was rated as a wudgemaker. Children who had the job description with "he" thought that women were significantly less competent at the job. Children who heard the other two pronouns did not make that judgment. Hyde's research thus suggests that language (in the form of pronoun usage) effects children's concepts of occupations.

Children in kindergarten through fifth grade as well as college students give male-biased responses to story cues that contain the pronoun "he." Hyde's (1984) research provided children with the following cue: *When a kid goes to school, ____ often feels excited on the first day.* When the pronoun in the cue was *he,* 12 percent of the stories students went on to write were about girls, as compared to 18 percent when the pronoun was *they,* and 42 percent when the pronoun was *he or she.* What does Hyde's research suggest? One answer to this question is that children think of boys when a masculine pronoun is provided to them. Her research also found that fewer than half of the children believe that the pronoun *he* could be used as a generic term referring to individuals in general.

Casey Miller and Kate Swift (1988), in their book *The Handbook of Non-Sexist Writing,* offer a thesaurus for eliminating generic masculine terms from the English language. For example:

Want to Avoid?	**Try:**
Businessman	**Businessperson**
Career Girl	**Businesswoman**
Coed	**Student**
Man-made	**Handmade, Synthetic**
Seamstress	**Tailor**
Waiter, Waitress	**Server**
Housewife, Househusband	**Homemaker**
Chairman, Chairwoman	**Chair, Head, Leader, Moderator, Coordinator**

COMMUNICATING ABOUT WOMEN IN THE MEDIA

As I discussed in Chapter 5, I frequently ask participants in the psychology of women course to read the advertisements addressed to women in the back pages of magazines such as *Cosmopolitan, Vogue, Bazaar, Woman, Leers, Essence, Seventeen,* and *Mademoiselle.* I also invite them to bring to class the advertisements they read. One semester, the class compiled the following ad headlines:

Liposuction: The Answer to Your Dreams?
Sexier, More Beautiful Breasts
Permanent Hair Removal
Longer, Thicker Hair in 7 Days!
I Went from a Size 16 to Size 4 Without Dieting!
Lose Up to 30 lbs in 30 Day—Act Now to Change Your Life
The Way a Woman Wants to Feel—A Razor to Make You Feel the Way You Want—
    Beautiful, Confident
Do Ugly Scars Embarrass You?

Stop Sweat for 6 Weeks
Lose 15 lbs in 28 Days with the Fat Attack Plan
Why I Had Cosmetic Surgery 7 Times
Train to Be a Model or Just Look Like One

We found advertisements for weight loss, bust enlargement, hair beautifiers, hair straighteners, elegant lingerie, soft skin, head-to-toe makeovers, cosmetic surgery, cosmetic dentistry, hairless skin, light skin, makeup, and long nails. We also looked at the ways in which girls and women were portrayed in magazine advertisements. We found them sitting next to men who were standing; sitting next to children playing; sitting next to a flower garden, sitting in a vegetable garden, sitting with other women (gossiping about a woman or flirting with a man at an adjacent table), and sitting alone (overweight women advertising queen-size pantyhose). Two magazines do portray women who are overweight and portrayed them smiling, with men, and in careers: *MODE* and *BBW.*

We then compared our findings with those obtained by Helen Franzwa (1975). She looked at the ways in which women were portrayed in the fiction of women's magazines, including *Ladies' Home Journal, McCalls,* and *Good Housekeeping.* In these magazines, from 1940 to 1970, several images were stressed:

Marriage is inevitable for every normal female.
To catch a man, you must be less competent than he, passive, and virtuous.
Married women do not work.
Being a housewife-mother is the best career of all.
To solve your problems, have another child.
The childless woman has wasted her life.

We recognized many indirect messages in our magazine advertisements: Women are to be soft, thin, smooth-shaven, flawless, nurturant to children and to men, mothers, and wives, in competition with other women. The advertisements also suggested the desirability of the women's being rich and white. In these advertisements, there was a remarkable absence of ethnic minority women (except in the ads for hair straighteners), older women, and physically challenged women. Thus, advertisements make the sexist, racist, agist, and classist messages explicit (also see Kilbourne, 1999). Susan Wooley and Wayne Wooley (1979) and Darlene DeFour (1996) observed this to be true with television as well. How many women on popular television and in magazines are even a few pounds overweight? Are ethnic mi-

FIGURE 7.1   *Sample advertisements from women's magazines.*

nority women represented? Are older women portrayed accurately? Are disabled women? Are lesbians?

As we discussed in Chapter 5, girls and women are aware of stereotypes in women's magazines and on television (Berel & Irving, 1998; Harrison, 1998; Reed, 1999; Thompson & Heinberg, 1999). They formulate ideas about their roles in society from the media content, and they feel inadequate when they compare themselves with media portrayals of femininity. They feel dissatisfied with their bodies, hair, teeth, weight, breast size, and height (Fodor & Thal, 1984). Adolescent girls perceive the normative physical developmental changes accompanying pubescence—especially the redistribution of weight—as their gaining weight and needing to diet (Pipher, 1994).

All cultures have distinct behavioral expectations for girls and women. These expectations constitute the prescribed gender roles, depending on the girls' and women's age and their stage of physical and cognitive development. Research has indicated that children as young as 3 years of age are aware of stereotypes about femininity and masculinity (Reis & Wright, 1982).

PARENTS AS SOCIALIZERS

As we discussed in Chapter 3, parents are important **socialization agents** for children and adolescents. Parents interact and talk a great deal with their daughters. Infant girls are usually seen as more fragile by mothers and fathers alike (Grieshaber, 1998; Paludi et al., in press). Parents encourage sex-appropriate activities by providing girls with sex-typed toys and clothing. Girls are given dolls, doll houses, and miniature household appliances. Parents engage in "rescuing" behavior with girls—assisting and accompanying them more often than is necessary. Parents' willingness to constantly "help" girls supports high levels of dependency in girls.

In addition, parents shape girls' gender-role development through the kinds of chores they assign them around the house. Lynn White and David Brinnerhoff (1981) collaborated on a statewide study of 669 girls and boys in Nebraska who were between the ages of 2 and 17 years. They reported that girls did "women's work": cleaning the house, doing the dishes, cooking, and babysitting for younger siblings. Boys did "men's work": mowing lawns, shoveling snow, taking out the garbage, and other general yardwork chores. These findings have been replicated in families with heterosexual mothers but not in those with lesbian mothers (Hill, 1988).

Daughters of employed mothers also perceive women's role as involving freedom of choice and satisfaction. They perceive a smaller difference between women and men in terms of warmth and expressiveness than do children of unemployed mothers (see Chapter 9).

Most researchers have focused on white, middle-class families, however. Reid, Haritos, Kelly, and Holland (1995) and Reid and Paludi (1993) suggested that socialization of feminine gender-role behavior does vary with social class and that this socialization impacts girls' achievement motivation and achievement behavior.

CHILDREN'S BOOKS

Authors of recent children's books have tried to improve the representation of female characters (Doyle & Paludi, 1998). Although the sex ratio in the books has improved, *girls and women outnumber boys and men in the real world*—a fact apparently forgotten by most authors of children's literature. Readers and textbooks predominantly portray white characters. African American girls and white girls are seldom depicted in the same story. An absence of female models conveys a message that women are not important enough to be represented. This impression may be especially communicated to ethnic minority girls (Reid & Paludi, 1993). Rarely are ethnic minority characters depicted in a significant way in readers and textbooks.

TELEVISION

Television commercials depict girls and women in the "helping" role, waiting on others and living out their lives in service to others, never really taking charge of their own lives (Lovdal, 1989). This view perpetuates traditional views of women in society. Bretl and Cantor (1988) reported that although women and men now appear equally often in prime-time commercials, women are still more likely to be seen in domestic situations (e.g., advertising cleaning products). Some television sponsors have introduced counterstereotypic presentations of women. Depicting women in a variety of activities has a positive impact on women in the TV audience, in terms of building their confidence as self-determining and achievement-oriented individuals (Geis, Brown, Jennings, & Porter, 1984).

Too many television programs still portray girls and women in very narrow and traditional roles, typically with no definable occupation or means of support. If employed, a majority of the women have occupations associated with traditional "women's work" (e.g., nurse and household worker). Women are also portrayed as being dependent on men. And when the women and men are in the same occupation, they perform gender-role-related behavior.

Ethnic minority women on television are stereotyped relative to white characters and ethnic minority male characters. In all-white families on television, men are more dominant than women (Doyle & Paludi, 1998). However, in all-African American families, women are more dominant. African American women are portrayed as more aggressive than white women. African American women are typically shown within the family, reinforcing myths about African American matriarchy. Representation of physically challenged women and lesbian women on television is virtually nonexistent. By the omission of such characters, the message conveyed to the viewer is that these women are not even important enough to be visible. Root (1995) noted that stereotypes about Asian women relate to their exoticness (the "geisha girl" in television and movies), and/or their innocence and fragility ("China doll") (Goodwin, 1996).

Carol Nagy Jacklin (1989) commented:

> Gender roles and the division of labor may play a strong role in causing gender differences. If interacting with infants and children brings forth nurturance in the caregivers, and there is considerable evidence that it does, then we need to rethink who does the child care in our society. Currently women and girls do most of this care while men and boys may even be discouraged from doing it. Why should nurturance be encouraged in only one sex? Nurturing may be an antidote for violence. (p. 132)

CHANGING CHILDREN'S AND ADULTS' GENDER SCHEMAS

Gender schema theory (Bem, 1981) proposes that children's gender-role acquisition derives from gender-schematic processing as well as a generalized readiness on the part of children to encode information from a variety of socializing agents. Gender-schematic processing is derived from the sex-differentiated practices of the culture in which children are being socialized. By observing the distinctions between women and men, girls (and boys) learn the specific content of femininity and masculinity. Girls in this culture observe that women and girls are described as "nice" and "kind," and men and boys are described as "strong" and "brave." Girls quickly learn that this culture values certain characteristics over others. "Strong" is more valuable than "kind"; "brave" is more prestigious than "nice." Matching their behaviors against the developing gender schema results in girls' evaluation of their adequacy as a person.

In adolescence, this "matching" process may be anxiety-producing for girls. Adolescents gain insight into their own behavior as well as the behaviors of their families, friends, and teachers. Many have a heightened ability for abstract, hypothetical reasoning. One consequence of adolescents' ability to take a variety of perspectives, while remaining preoccupied with their own, is the development of egocentrism. They assume that other people are as interested in them and as fascinated by them and by their behavior as they are themselves. They have a difficult time in distinguishing between their personal concerns and the opinions of others. Many adolescent girls thus conclude that other people are as accepting, or as rejecting and critical, as they are of themselves. They may worry about having their inadequacies discovered by their peers. These behaviors are characterized by David Elkind (1967) as having an **imaginary audience.** In this phenomenon, adolescents feel they are the focus of attention; it is imaginary, however, in that other people are actually not that concerned with the adolescent's thoughts.

The concept of the imaginary audience can explain why adolescent girls are self-conscious about their clothing and body image, spend hours viewing themselves in front of mirrors, and feel painfully on display. Absorbed with their own feelings, adolescents believe their emotions are unique. Their belief in their uniqueness is expressed in a subjective story they tell themselves about their "special qualities." This subjective story is referred to by Elkind (1967) as the **personal fable.** Evidence of this personal fable is present in the diaries adolescents keep. The personal fable is frequently translated into a conviction that they are not subject to the dangers suffered by others. Consequently, adolescent girls may avoid using seat belts, drive too fast, binge and then purge, or dispense with using contraceptives—all because they are convinced that "nothing bad will happen to me; I'm special" (see Chapter 6).

Adolescent egocentrism disappears when girls have the role-taking opportunities that will help to replace the imaginary audience with a real one, and the subjective fable with an objective story. Such role-taking experiences might include part-time employment during high school, participating on a debate team, and dating. Elkind (1967) hypothesized that egocentrism should decline by the time adolescents are 16 or 17 years old. Adolescent girls, however, may not be given such role-taking opportunities because of stereotypic beliefs about the girls becoming argumentative, independent, and assertive. The media and the girls' parents may reinforce personal fables and imaginary audiences for adolescent girls through their romanticizing thinness, facial "makeovers," and fairy tale relationships. This culture reinforces for adolescent girls (and adult women) a focus on popularity and attractiveness—characteristics over which girls and women have limited control. Consequently, adolescent girls may seriously harm themselves in their struggle to "fit in" with this masculine-biased definition of feminine beauty.

Gender schema theory assumes that since gender-role typing is learned, it can also be modified; therefore, stereotypes can be eliminated if children engage in one or more of the following (Papalia & Olds, 1990):

- Discard all schemata, distinguishing the sexes only by anatomical and reproductive differences. (Young children usually fail to do this, basing their decision about a person's sex on other external signals like clothing or hairstyle.)

- Learn the individual-differences schema, that there is great variation within groups. For example, some girls do not like to play baseball, but others do—and that some boys do not.

- Learn the cultural-relativism schema, the understanding that people in different cultures and at different historical times hold different beliefs about what is appropriate for males and females.

- Learn the sexism schema, the conviction that gender-stereotyped roles are not only different but wrong, no matter how common they are. (p. 363)

In Chapter 8 we will continue this discussion about changing gender schemas as we address ways in which the establishment and continuation of romantic relationships are affected by gender-role stereotypes.

NEW TERMS

body position	long requests
chilly classroom climate	nonverbal communication
decoding	pejoration
encoding	personal fable
English language defining women	personal space
English language deprecating women	qualifiers
English language ignoring women	silencing women
fillers	social eye contact
gender schema theory	socialization agent
generic pronouns	tag question
imaginary audience	verbal communication
linguistic sexism	

CHAPTER REVIEW QUESTIONS

1. Discuss the ways that nonverbal and verbal communication styles symbolize the unequal balance of power between women and men.

2. Summarize the research on women's nonverbal styles of communication.

3. Discuss women's communication styles. Explain how these communication patterns encourage conversation and value others' participation in conversations.

4. Discuss how and why women and men using identical linguistic features are perceived differently.

5. Offer illustrations of linguistic sexism. Cite some corrections to the biases against women in the English language.

6. Summarize the research on parents as important socializing agents in girls' acquisition of a gender-role identity.

7. Have authors of recent children's books tried to improve the representation of female characters in their children's stories?

8. What is gender schema theory? How can we help modify girls' gender schema of femininity in our culture?

SELECTED READINGS

Henley, N. (1995). Ethnicity and gender issues in language. In H. Landrine (Ed.), *Bringing cultural diversity to feminist psychology*. Washington, DC: American Psychological Association.

Parks, J., & Roberton, M. A. (1998). Contemporary arguments against nonsexist language. *Sex Roles, 39*, 445–461.

Tannen, D. (1999). *The power of talk: Who gets heard and why*. Boston: McGraw-Hill.

LEARNING MORE ABOUT . . .

Suggestions for Term Papers and Independent Studies Related to *Communications By and About Women*

Positive implications of the use of tag questions

Cultural issues involved in verbal and nonverbal communication patterns

Nonverbal gestures of power in the workforce for women

Gender-role stereotyping in comic strips

Gender displays in photographs

TAKING ACTION . . .

on *Communications By and About Women*

1. Read the advertisements in magazines such as *Self, Allure, Cosmopolitan, Glamour, Essence,* and *Vogue.*

   a. Note the direct and indirect messages given by these advertisements with respect to women's physiques, hair, weight, skin, teeth, and breasts.

   b. You may want to read advertisements in these magazines during the month of February, during which National Eating Disorders Month is celebrated.

   c. Write a letter to the editor in chief of the magazines indicating the seriousness of their advertisements for adolescent and young adult women in terms of self-concept, identity development, and eating disorders. Cite statistics, research findings, and references to the research you cite.

   d. Also write a letter to editors in chief when the magazines have portrayed women realistically and not according to gender role stereotypes. Thank them for treating women with respect and dignity.

2. Watch some rock music videos. Then answer the following questions for each video you watched:

   a. Is there an antiwoman trend in the video?

   b. Do you believe the music videos are sexist? Explain.

   c. Are the videos violent? Explain.

   d. What attitudes toward women and men do you believe are held by the director and writer of the videos?

   Write a letter to a television station that airs these videos. In this letter, discuss the research on the impact that violent and sexist videos can have on children's and adolescents' self-concept, gender-role identity, attitudes toward women, and ways to resolve conflict.

REFERENCES

Allen, I. (1984). Male sex roles and epithets for ethnic women in American slang. *Sex Roles, 11,* 43–50.

Beaumont, S., et al. (1998). Interruptions in adolescent girls' conversations: Comparing mothers and friends. *Journal of Adolescent Research, 13,* 272–292.

Bee, H., Mitchell, S., Barnard, K., Eyres, S., & Hammond, M. (1984). Predicting intellectual outomes: Sex differences in response to early environmental stimulation. *Sex Roles, 10,* 783–803.

Bem, S. L. (1981). Gender schema theory: A cognitive account of sex typing. *Psychological Review, 88,* 354–364.

Berel, S., & Irving, L. (1998). Media and disturbed eating: An analysis of media influence and implications for prevention. *Journal of Primary Prevention, 18,* 415–430.

Bretl, D. J., & Cantor, J. (1988). The portrayal of men and women in U.S. television commercials: A recent content analysis and trends over 15 years. *Sex Roles, 18,* 595–609.

Carli, L. (1990). Gender, language, and influence. *Journal of Personality and Social Psychology, 59,* 941–951.

Carli, L. (1999). Gender, interpersonal power, and social influence. *Journal of Social Issues, 55,* 81–99.

Carli, L., & Bukato, D. (2000). Gender, communication, and social influence: A developmental perspective. In T. Eckes et al. (Eds.), *The developmental social psychology of gender.* Mahwah, NJ: Erlbaum.

Coleman, L., & Ingham, R. (1999). Exploring young people's difficulties in talking about contraception: How can we encourage more discussion between partners? *Health Education Research, 14,* 741–750.

Crosby, F. (1982). *Relative deprivation and working women.* New York: Oxford University Press.

DeFour, D. C. (1996). The interface of racism and sexism in sexual harassment. In M. A. Paludi (Ed.), *Sexual harassment on college campuses: Abusing the ivory power.* Albany: State University of New York Press.

Deutsch, F., LeBaron, D., & Fryer, M. (1987). What is in a smile? *Psychology of Women Quarterly, 11,* 341–352.

Dion, K., & Cota, A. (1991). The Ms. Stereotype: Its domian and the role of explicitness in title preference. *Psychology of Women Quarterly, 15,* 403–410.

Doyle, J., & Paludi, M. (1998). *Sex and gender: The human experience* (4th ed.). New York: McGraw Hill.

Elkind, D. (1967). Egocentrism in adolescence. *Child Development, 38,* 1025–1034.

Evans, L., & Davies, K. (2000). No sissy boys here: A content analysis of the representation of masculinity in elementary school reading textbooks. *Sex Roles, 42,* 255–270.

Fernandez, I., Carrera, P., Sanchez, F., Paez, D., & Candia, L. (2000). Differences between cultures in emotional verbal and nonverbal reactions. *Psicotherm, 12,* 83–92.

Fodor, I., & Thal, J. (1984). Weight disorders: Overweight and anorexia. In E. Blechman (Ed.), *Behavior modification with women.* New York: Guilford Press.

Franzwa, H. (1975). Female roles in women's magazine fiction, 1940–1970. In R. Unger & F. L. Denmark (Eds.), *Woman.* New York: Psychological Dimensions.

Geis, F., Brown, V., Jennings (Walstedt), J., & Porter, N. (1984). TV commercials as achievement scripts for women. *Sex Roles, 10,* 513–525.

Ginorio, A., Gutierrez, L., Cauce, A., & Acosta, M. (1995). Psychological issues for Latinas. In H. Landrine (Ed.), *Bringing cultural diversity to feminist psychology.* Washington, DC: American Psychological Association.

Goodwin, B. (1996). The impact of popular culture on images of African American women. In J. Chrisler, C. Golden, & P. Rozee (Eds.), *Lectures on the psychology of women.* New York: McGraw Hill.

Grieshaber, S. (1998). Constructing the gendered infant. In N. Yelland et al. (Eds.), *Gender in early childhood.* New York: Routledge.

Halberstadt, A., & Saitta, M. (1987). Gender, nonverbal behavior, and perceived dominance: A test of the theory. *Journal of Personality and Social Psychology, 53,* 257–272.

Hall, J. (1984). *Nonverbal sex differences.* Baltimore: Johns Hopkins University Press.

Hall, J., Carter, J., & Horgan, T. (2000). Gender differences in nonverbal communication of emotion. In A. Fischer et al. (Eds.), *Gender and emotion: Social psychological perspectives.* New York: Cambridge University Press.

Hall, R., & Sandler, B. (1982). *The classroom climate: A chilly one for women.* Washington, DC: Project on the Status and Education of Women.

Harrison, K. (1998). The role of self-discrepancies in the relationship between media exposure and eating disorders. *Dissertation Abstracts International, 59* (3-A), 0648.

Hart, B., & Risley, T. (1995). *Meaningful differences in the everyday experience of young American children.* Baltimore: Brookes.

Henley, N. (1995). Ethnicity and gender issues in language. In H. Landrine (Ed.), *Bringing cultural diversity to feminist psychology: Theory, research, and practice.* Washington, DC: American Psychological Association.

Hickman, S., & Muehlenhard, C. (1999). "By the semi-mystical appearance of a condom": How young women and men communicate sexual consent in heterosexual situations. *Journal of Sex Research, 36,* 258–272.

Hill, M. (1988). Child rearing attitudes of black lesbian mothers. In Boston Lesbian Psychologies Collective (Ed.), *Lesbian psychologies: Explorations and challenges.* Urbana: University of Illinois Press.

Hyde, J. S. (1984). Children's understanding of sexist language. *Developmental Psychology, 20,* 697–706.

Intons-Peterson, M., & Crawford, J. (1985). The meanings of marital surnames. *Sex Roles, 12,* 1163–1171.

Jacklin, C. N. (1989). Female and male: Issues of gender. *American Psychologist, 44,* 127–133.

Jacobson, R. (1999). Personal space within two interaction conditions as a function of confederate age and gender differences. *Dissertation Abstracts International, 59* (7-B), 3743.

Kemper, S. (1984). When to speak like a lady. *Sex Roles, 10,* 435–443.

Kilbourne, J. (1999). *Deadly persuasion.* New York: Free Press.

Koch, J. (1999). Candidate gender and assessments of Senate candidates. *Social Science Quarterly, 80,* 84–96.

Kojima, Y. (1999). Mothers' adjustment to the birth of a second child: A longituindal study on use of verbal and nonverbal behaviors toward two children. *Psychological Reports, 84,* 141–144.

Kollock, P., Blumstein, P., & Schwartz, P. (1985). Sex and power in interaction: Conversational privileges and duties. *American Sociological Review, 50,* 34–46.

LaFrance, M., & Carmen, B. (1980). The nonverbal display of psychological androgyny. *Journal of Personality and Social Psychology, 38,* 36–49.

LaFromboise, T., Choney, S., James, A., & Running Wolf, P. (1995). American Indian women and psychology. In H. Landrine (Ed.), *Bringing cultural diversity to feminist psychology.* Washington, DC: American Psychological Association.

Lakoff, R. (1973). Language and women's place. *Language in Society, 2,* 45–79.

Lakoff, R. (1975). *Language and women's place.* New York: Harper & Row.

Lerner, H. (1976). Girls, ladies, or women? The unconscious dynamic of language choice. *Comprehensive Psychiatry, 17,* 295–299.

Libra, T. S. (1987). The cultural significance of silence in Japanese communication. *Multilingua, 6,* 343–357.

Lipton, J., & Hershaft, A. (1984). "Girl," "woman," "guy," "man": The effects of sexist labeling. *Sex Roles, 10,* 183–194.

Lovdal, L. (1989). Sex messages in television commercials: An update. *Sex Roles, 21,* 715–724.

Mayo, C., & Henley, N. (Eds.). (1981). *Gender and nonverbal behavior.* New York: Springer-Verlag.

Miller, C., & Swift, K. (1988). *Words and women.* New York: HarperCollins.

Nichols, P. (1983). Linguistic options and choices for black women in the rural south. In B. Thorne, C. Kramarae, & N. Henley (Eds.), *Language, gender and society.* Rowley, MA: Newbury House.

Nugent, C. (1994). Blaming the victims: Silencing women sexually exploited by psychotherapists. *Journal of Mind and Behavior, 15,* 113–138.

Paludi, M. A. (1996). *Exploring/teaching the psychology of women: A resource manual* (2nd ed.). Albany: State University of New York Press.

Paludi, M. (Ed.). (1999). *The psychology of sexual victimization: A handbook.* Westport, CT: Greenwood.

Paludi, M. (Ed.). (2001). *Human development in multicultural contexts: A book of readings.* Upper Saddle River, NJ: Prentice Hall.

Paludi, M., Paludi, C., & Doyle, J. (in press). *Sex and gender.* (5th ed.). New York: McGraw Hill.

Paludi, M. A., & Strayer, L. (1985). What's in an author's name? Differential evaluations of performance as a function of author's name. *Sex Roles, 12,* 353–361.

Papalia, S., & Olds, S. W. (1990). *A child's world: Infancy through adolescence.* New York: McGraw-Hill.

Parks, J., & Roberton, M. (1998). Contemporary arguments against nonsexist language: Blaubergs (1980) revisited. *Sex Roles, 39,* 445–461.

Pearson, J. (1985). *Gender and communication.* Dubuque, IA: Brown.

Pipher, M. (1994). *Reviving Ophelia.* New York: Ballantine Books.

Podrouzek, W., & Furrow, D. (1988). Preschoolers' use of eye contact while speaking: The influence of sex, age, and conversational pattern. *Psycholinguistic Research, 17,* 89–98.

Reed, R. (1999). Image and attitude: The impact of media images on the self-esteem, body image and sexual attitudes of college students. *Dissertation Abstracts International, 59* (8-B), 4542.

Reid, P. T., Haritos, C., Kelly, E., & Holland, N. (1995). Socialization of girls: Issues of ethnicity in gender development. In H. Landrine (Ed.), *Bringing cultural diversity to feminist psychology.* Washington: American Psychological Association.

Reid, P. T., & Paludi, M. A. (1993). Psychology of women: Conception to adolescence. In F. L. Denmark & M. A. Paludi (Eds.), *Psychology of women: A handbook of issues and theories.* Westport, CT: Greenwood Press.

Reis, H., & Wright, S. (1982). Knowledge of sex role stereotypes in children aged 3 to 5. *Sex Roles, 8,* 1049–1056.

Roberts, J., Burchinal, M., & Durham, M. (1999). Parents' reports of vocabulary and grammatical development of African-American preschoolers. *Child Development, 70,* 92–106.

Romero, G., & Garza, R. (1986). Attributions for the occupational success/failure of ethnic minority and nonminority women. *Sex Roles, 14,* 445–452.

Root, M. (1995). The psychology of Asian American women. In H. Landrine (Ed.), *Bringing cultural diversity to feminist psychology.* Washington, DC: American Psychological Association.

Schneider, J., & Hacker, S. (1973). Sex role imagery and the use of the generic "man" in introductory texts. *American Sociologist, 8,* 12–18.

Smith, A. (1983). Nonverbal communication among black female dyads: An assessment of intimacy, gender, and race. *Journal of Social Issues, 39,* 55–67.

Stanley, J. (1977). Paradigmatic woman: The prostitute. In D. Shores (Ed.), *Papers in language variation.* Birmingham: University of Alabama Press.

Steinem, G. (1986). Men and women talking. In G. Steinem, *Outrageous acts and everyday rebellions.* New York: Holt.

Swacker, M. (1975). The sex of the speaker as a sociolinguistic variable. In B. Thorne & N. Henley (Eds.), *Language and sex.* Rowley, MA: Newbury House.

Tannen, D. (1994). *Talking from 9 to 5: Women and men in the workplace. Language, sex, and power.* New York: Avon Books.

Tannen, D. (1999). The power of talk: Who gets heard and why. In R. Lewicki et al. (Eds.), *Negotiation: Readings, exercises, and cases.* Boston: McGraw Hill.

Tannen, D. (2000). Framing and reframing. In R. Lewicki et al. (Eds.), *Negotiation: Readings, exercises, and cases.* Boston: McGraw Hill.

Tepper, C., & Cassidy, K. (1999). Gender differences in emotional language in children's picture books. *Sex Roles, 40,* 265–280.

Thompson, J., & Heinberg, L. (1999). The media's influence on body image disturbance and eating disorders: We've reviled them, now can we rehabilitate them. *Journal of Social Issues, 55,* 339–353.

Townsend, E. (1961). Names and titles. *Latin American Courtesy.* Summer Institute of Linguistics.

Unger, R. (1979). *Female and male: Psychological perspectives.* New York: Harper & Row.

Unger, R., & Saundra. (1993). Stereotypes about women. In F. L. Denmark & M. A. Paludi (Eds.), *Psychology of women: A handbook of issues and theories.* Westport, CT: Greenwood Press.

Welte, S. (1998). Good students, good daughters: Girls and women struggling with voice and silence to meet social and cultural expectations. *Dissertation Abstracts International, 58* (9-A), 3421.

White, L., & Brinnerhoff, D. (1981). The sexual division of labor: Evidence from childhood. *Social Forces, 60,* 170–181.

Wood, J. (1994). *Gendered lives: Communication, gender, and culture.* Belmont, CA: Wadsworth.

Wooley, S., & Wooley, O. (1979). Obesity and women: II. A neglected feminist topic. *Women's Studies International Quarterly, 2,* 81–92.

Worell, J. (1990). Women: The psychological perspective. In M. A. Paludi & G. Steuernagel (Eds.), *Foundations for a feminist restructuring of the academic disciplines.* New York: Haworth.

Zimmerman, D., & West, C. (1975). Sex roles, interruptions, and silences in conversations. In B. Thorne & N. Henley (Eds.), *Language and sex.* Rowley, MA: Newbury House.

EIGHT

WOMEN AND INTIMATE RELATIONSHIPS

IN WOMEN'S VOICES

I have always felt that "love," perhaps because it is considered to be the center, if not the totality of a woman's life, is a risky business, and one to which feminists should address much energy and ingenuity. . . . It is in the emotional dynamics of love relationships, and in the psychological assumptions, that stereotypes about women that remain most deeply embedded. And also, women have been defined by society for a very long time in terms of "love," i.e., told that they must raise a family, be loved by a man, married, or face being an "outcast."

Naomi Weisstein

~

What is the meaning of love after all? Feeling a deep connection to another person, to friends or family, letting one's soul feel alive—or, when we are alone, those moments when everything seems real and our awareness of the beauty of life is heightened—or the memories we have of long-ago times we spent with those we loved and love still—aren't these moments the times we feel most ourselves? Is this love?

Shere Hite

Chapter Outline

Questions for Reflection

1. What qualities do you look for in a friend? Are these qualities the same for your female and male friends? Or, do you look for different qualities in a female and male friend?

2. Do you have friends of different races than yourself?

3. Do you have friends who are physically challenged, that is, have a physical disability?

4. Do you have friends who have a different sexual orientation than yourself?

5. Do you see yourself establishing a long-term committed relationship with another individual?

6. What were you told as a child about friendships in terms of trust, commitment, duration, resolving conflicts, and so on?

7. Do you watch the television program, "Friends"? Do you believe this program accurately portrays same-sex and other-sex friendships? Why or why not?

8. Do you believe it's possible for men and women to be friends? Why or why not?

INTRODUCTION

For the next few minutes, list the names of your "best" women friends on a sheet of paper. For each woman friend you listed, jot down answers to the following characteristics about her:

Her age

Personality characteristics she admires

Her race
Physical attributes she likes

Analyze your responses according to any themes, for example, are the women friends all of the same race as you? Are they relatively thin? Are they majoring in female-populated college majors?

Now repeat this exercise for men best friends you have. For each man friend you listed, write down answers to each of the following characteristics next to his name:

His age
Personality characteristics he admires
His race
Physical attributes he likes

Have you noticed any similarities in your two lists? Do you use the same characteristics in both female and male friends? Have you noticed any differences in your two lists? If so, to what do you attribute the differences? As you compare your lists, do you believe women and men can be friends? Are friendships between women and men similar to female-female friendships? To male-male friendships?

If you have seen the movie, "When Harry Met Sally," you'll know that this issue was debated throughout the film. Sally (played by Meg Ryan) exclaimed that friendship is not only possible but definitely likely between women and men. Harry (played by Billy Crystal) disagreed with Sally's analysis. Harry suggested that men can never be friends with women to whom they are sexually attracted. What is your opinion? Do you agree with Harry or with Sally? Do you believe women and men can be friends when one or both are in a romantic relationship? When one or both are married?

Suzanna Rose's (1995, 1997) research on friendship indicated that women do not list sexual attraction as motivating them to be friends with men. They reported, however, that sexual attraction is the primary motivating factor of men pursuing friendships with women. Men confirmed women's beliefs in this research: Being sexually attracted to women was what prompted them to pursue a friendship.

Perhaps women and men differ in the ways they define "friendship." What is your definition of the word "friendship"? Do you include the following behaviors in your definition: Talking every day? Seeing each other regularly? Spending quality time together? Sharing thoughts, hopes, dreams, fears? Helping each other through rough times? Being a good listener? Can a friendship become a romantic relationship? How do women handle the break-up of a friendship and romantic relationship?

These are the issues we will address in this chapter on women and intimate relationships. Let's begin with an overview of girls' and women's friendships across the life cycle.

FRIENDSHIPS FOR GIRLS AND WOMEN ACROSS THE LIFE CYCLE

Preschool Period

An important aspect of preschoolers' (children 3 to 5 years of age) social development is the development of friendships with peers (Vaughn et al., 2000). Preschoolers begin to participate in fewer solitary activities and become more involved in playing with peers. Their gains in language make communication with peers possible; they thus talk about what they are doing in their play (Lim, 1998; Weissman, 1999). Play provides opportunities for preschoolers to interact with children of the same age and from different backgrounds (e.g., preschoolers who do or do not have siblings, two parents, grandparents). Interactions with children who are from different types of families contribute to children asking question about themselves, including why they don't have two parents or grandparents (Roopnarine, Johnson, & Hooper, 1994).

Middle Childhood

During middle childhood (children 6 to 10), children become considerably more sensitive to the importance of their peer group (Van-Aken, 1999). Their friendships influences their development in a variety of ways, including support to allow children to respond more effectively to stress. Thus, friends teach each other how to manage their emotions (Bukowski, Newcomb, & Hartup, 1999). In addition, children during this stage of the life cycle focus on intimacy and loyalty in their friendships (Bukowski et al., 1999). Friendships also display status hierarchies during middle childhood: High status in a peer group leads to a greater number of friendships (Hartup, 1998).

During middle childhood, children's closest friends are other children of the same sex and race as they are (Benenson, Apostoleris, & Pamass, 1998; Hartup, 1998). Same-sex segregation may be a function of the types of activities in which children engage. For example, girls typically get assigned to activities that boys do not and vice versa. Segregation in play and in performing chores at home and at school leads to sex segregation in friendships (DeFosier & Kupersmidt, 1999).

Girls' friendships involve one or two close relationships, equal status among friends, and reliance on cooperation with the avoidance of confrontation (Collins & Miller, 1994; Van-Aken, 1999). This friendship pattern is in contrast to boy's friendships, which are characterized by groups of more than two and status hierarchies. Furthermore, girls typically report greater satisfaction in their friendships than do boys, thus supporting mutual dependence in girls' friendships (DeFosier & Kupersmidt, 1999).

Adolescence

Similar to girls in middle childhood, girls in adolescence prefer to have a **clique**— a few close friendships (typically all girls)—rather than many less intimate friendships (McNelles & Connolly, 1999; Roy, Benenson, & Lilly, 2000). Adolescent girls seek out other girls in whom they confide the intimate details of their life and from whom they can obtain emotional support (Kuttler, LaGreca, & Prinstein, 1999). Adolescent girls also have a capacity for intimacy in their relationships. They express this intimacy verbally, for example, through discussing intimate issues such as career paths, love interests, and concerns about appearance (Kuttler et al., 1999). They express intimacy nonverbally through maintaining eye contact, a relaxed body posture, and touch (e.g., holding someone who is crying; patting someone on the arm or hand when they are in need of comfort) (Podrouzek & Furrow, 1998; see Chapter 7).

Adolescent girls report feeling more comfortable in friendships with girls than with boys (Cheng & Chan, 1999). Hartup and Stevens (1999) found that adolescent boys also feel more comfortable interacting with girls since girls encourage intimacy and comfortableness in conversations. Boys may feel more like disclosing their feelings with girls rather than with other boys. In their friendships with girls, boys are reinforced for disclosing their feelings, something for which they are punished when with other boys. Self-disclosure is not perceived to be a "masculine" trait; it is seen as "feminine" (Paludi, Paludi, & Doyle, in press; Tannen, 1995).

Adulthood

Three friendships styles have been documented in the literature for adulthood: independent, discriminative, and gregarious (Cavanaugh, 1998; Matthews, 1986). The *independent* friendship style is characteristic of individuals who do not regard anyone as a best friend. Independent adults emphasize their own self-sufficiency and maintain a distance from others. Adults who are characterized as discriminative typically have a small number of friends to whom they feel close. *Discriminative* adults make a distinction among their friends, for example, those friends who are close, those who are trusted, those who are long-term friends, and so on. The *gregarious* friendship style is common among adults who feel close to a large number of people. They have many close friends. Furthermore, they are optimistic about making new friends throughout their lives.

Filed (1999) reported that women's involvement with friends and the intimacy of their friendships remained the same throughout adulthood while men declined in the number of new friends, in their wanting close friendships, and in the less intimate nature of their interactions with friends. Women, especially women in adulthood, are concerned about the loss of their friends through relocation, divorce, or death (Stevens & van Tilburg, 2000).

Similar to Filed's (1999) results, Antonucci and Akiymaya (1987) reported that older women consistently have large, social support networks, that is, a variety of individuals who serve very different functions. Furthermore, women report both asking for and receiving strong support from their friendship network during personally stressful events. When women have a network of friends (e.g., are gregarious in their friendship style), they report high levels of satisfaction and happiness. For women who are single, friends are considered "family" (Etaugh, 1993). Widowed women rely on friendships as well; friendships represent an important social system (Luria & Meade, 1984). Etaugh (1993) found that widowed women who reported loneliness were those who had few social networks or supports. McGloshen and O'Bryant (1988) found that following the death of their husbands, women have a relatively easier time making and sustaining friendships than do men following the death of their wives—most likely a result of women's experiences with and enjoyment of initiating social contacts. Similar results were reported by Filed (1999) and Stevens and van Tilburg (2000).

As this overview suggests, friendships are very important to girls and women across the life span (Kuttler et al., 1999; Rose, 1995; Rose & Roades, 1987; Roy et al., 2000; Stevens & van Tilberg, 2000). Some researchers have reported that, to some women, the end of a friendship is a more painful experience than the end of a romantic relationship. Shere Hite (1989), in her study of several thousand women's experiences with friendships and romantic relationships, found that women rated their friendships with other women "as some of the happiest, most fulfilling parts of their lives" (p. 457). Eighty-seven percent of married women in Hite's research reported having their deepest emotional relationship with a woman friend; 95 percent of single women reported similar experiences.

Women report that women friends should be sensitive, supportive, trustworthy, and honest. Women want to get together with friends "just to talk," not necessarily to engage in specific activities. Caldwell and Peplau (1982) commented that women's greater interest in talking suggests greater emotional sharing within women-women friendships. Similar findings were reported by Schultz (1991) and Roy and colleagues (2000).

Sidney Jourard (1964) used the term **"self-disclosure"** to describe the sharing of personal or intimate information about oneself with others. Women disclose a great deal of information about themselves to their women friends, and they like their friends to self-disclose to them (see Chapter 7).

WOMEN'S FRIENDSHIPS WITH MEN

Recall I asked you a question at the beginning of this chapter: Do you believe women and men can be friends? How can we account for the finding that women and men differ in their views about sexual attraction and friendship? Perhaps men misinterpret women's friendship overtures, labeling them instead as "sexual interest." Women and men may be interpreting each other's behavior in terms of their own perspective. Instead, women and men need to label and interpret their communication in light of traditional gender-role socialization experiences (see Chapter 7).

Women like men friends to self-disclose to them in the way their women friends do. However, men typically are uncomfortable when asked to self-disclose and when another individual discloses too much. For many men, especially men who are traditional in their views on women and gender roles, self-disclosure is interpreted as a sign of weakness (Gray, 1996). Consequently, men may shun any sign of weakness for fear of appearing less powerful, that is, "feminine" (Felmlee, 1994; Paludi et al., in press; Chapter 7).

Sexual segregation of activities limits women's and men's opportunities for becoming friends (Benenson et al., 1998). Women have reported that their friendships with men have been less rewarding, less intimate, and less accepting than their friendships with women (Basow, 1986). Susan Basow noted that, in most women-men relationships, men tend to disclose their strengths, and women reveal their weaknesses. She believes that these friendships do not match the relative spontaneity of same-sex friendships because of gender-role expectations.

WOMEN AND ROMANTIC RELATIONSHIPS

Have you had an opportunity to read the Personals section in your local newspaper or on-line? What qualities do men typically look for in a romantic partner? What qualities do women seek in a romantic partner? In 1984 Kay Deaux and Randel

Hanna reviewed 800 personal advertisements from four newspapers circulated on the east and west coasts: *The Village Voice, National Single Register, The Wishing Well,* and *Advocate.* Lesbian, gay, and male-female heterosexual advertisements were included in this research. Deaux and Hanna coded each advertisement for present/absent words and terms in each of the following categories:

Attractiveness (good looking, cute, muscular, handsome, beautiful)
Sexuality (passionate, lustful, erotic, potent, butch, stacked)
Physical characteristics (weight, height, hair color, bearded, eye color)
Financial security (affluent, financially secure, well established)
Sincerity (dependable, loyal, trustworthy, honest)
Personality traits (intelligent, sense of humor, spiritual, caring, sensible, mature)
Hobbies/interests (likes to cook, art lover, athletic)
Occupation (career woman, lawyer, executive)
Demographic variables (race/ethnicity, marital status, age)
Interest in marriage (marriage-minded)
Interest in permanent relationship (long-term relationship, lasting relationship)
Request for photograph
Request for telephone number

Deaux and Hanna reported that women in general were interested in the psychological aspects of a potential relationship; men in general were concerned with objective and physical characteristics. Heterosexual women were concerned with financial security, specific occupational information, and sincerity. Lesbian women placed less emphasis on physical characteristics and offered more information about their interests, hobbies, and their own sincerity. Women are thus less likely to report that they want an attractive partner.

Erich Goode (1996) reviewed the responses to fictional advertisements that were placed in four personal columns. The advertisements, seeking "a beautiful waitress," "an average looking female lawyer," "a handsome cabdriver," and an "average looking male lawyer," were designed to determine the relative importance of physical attractiveness and financial/occupational success in attracting dating partners. The advertisement for a "beautiful waitress" received 668 responses; the ad describing the "average looking female lawyer" received 240 responses; the ad describing an "average looking male lawyer" received 64 responses; and 15 individuals responded to the ad for "a handsome cabdriver." What do Goode's results suggest? Men were more influenced by physical attraction than by success; women, on the other hand, were more influenced by occupational success than by physical attraction. Furthermore, Goode's findings suggest that within romantic relationships, gender-role stereotypes are being played out by women and men in the establishment stage of the relationship and in the continuation of the relationship.

The emphasis on physical attractiveness in the advertisements that appeal to heterosexual men can be damaging to women (Kilbourne, 1999). Many women, especially those with chronic illness or disability, cannot match this male-defined view of attractiveness (Paludi et al., in press; see Chapter 7). Women are evaluated in terms of their physical attractiveness; men are not (Diamond, Savin-Williams, Ritch, & Dube, 1999). In fact, adolescent women who believe they are attractive report more positive self-concepts than adolescent women who consider themselves unattractive (Diamond et al., 1999). Self-concept is unrelated to perceived attractiveness in adolescent men. Some adolescent women admit that they will "play dumb" or pretend to be inferior to their dates (Betz, 1993). Women are likely to hide their intellectual talents, not their athletic or artistic abilities (Betz, 1993).

In romantic relationships, women bring a quality of intimacy that is similar to their contribution to their friendships with women and men (Diamond et al., 1999). This intimacy is often discouraged, however, as a result of the gender-role stereotypes that emphasize "attracting" a mate (the goal) for women and "sexual achievement" (the goal) for men (Diamond et al., 1999; Hyde & DeLamater, 1999). Intimacy in romantic relationships may also be discouraged because of the ritualized, unequal nature of the majority of dating situations: Men initiate; women accept or refuse men's requests. Women who initiate dates are evaluated negatively; they are seen as "pushy," "aggressive," and "overly sexual" (Green & Sandos, 1983).

Many women and men have been socialized to believe that a woman's love for a man is equated with a woman's submission to the man (see Chapter 4). This aspect of romantic relationships causes considerable role strain for women, who report being pressured to be active and passive simultaneously. As Simone de Beauvoir (1949/1961) wrote:

> Shut up in the sphere of the relative, destined to the male from childhood, habituated to seeing in him a superb being whom she cannot possibly equal, the woman . . . will dream . . . of amalgamating herself with the sovereign. . . . She chooses to desire her enslavement so ardently that it will seem to her the expression of her liberty. . . . Love becomes for her a religion. (p. 604)

As a consequence of the gender-role related characteristics that are played out in romantic relationships, Lillian Rubin (1976) referred to women and men in such ro-

MEET DR. LETITIA ANNE PEPLAU

Dr. Letitia Anne Peplau has studied the complex ways in which gender and changing roles for women and men affect their personal relationships.

Question: Can you describe your research program on women's friendships?

Dr. Peplau's response: Our research shows that men and women share fundamentally similar human needs for intimacy and support from their close relationships. Society exaggerates gender differences by teaching people that women and men should have different interests and skills and should play distinctive roles in dating and marriage, based on their sex. Even though more than half of American women hold paying jobs, many elements of traditional gender roles persist today. These traditional beliefs can put women at a power disadvantage in male-female relationships and are one reason why women with full-time paid jobs continue to perform most of the housework and child care at home. Our research is comparing the close relationships of feminists and traditionalists, seeking to understand how individual differences in sex-role attitudes affect male-female relations.

mantic relationships as "intimate strangers." Rubin's sentiment also refers to the unequal power in many romantic relationships, an issue we will now address.

WOMEN, MEN, ROMANTIC RELATIONSHIPS, AND POWER

Letitia Anne Peplau and her colleagues (Peplau, Rubin, & Hill, 1977) asked more than 200 dating couples the following question. I invite you to answer the question for yourself too!

"Who has more to say in your relationship?"

For example, who has the last word about which restaurant to go to? Who decides which movie to see? Who decides to whether to have sexual intercourse?

All of these issues are ways that power can be expressed in intimate relationships. Approximately half of the couples in Peplau and colleagues' study reported an **egalitarian relationship,** in which power is shared fairly equally between the partners. The other participants in this research reported that the man had the final say in the relationship.

Diane Felmlee (1994) asked 413 heterosexual dating undergraduates about female-male power imbalance in romantic dyads. Fewer than half of the research participants perceived their relationship to be equal in the distribution of power. Men were more than twice as likely as women to be viewed as the partner having more power in the relationship. Most women and men reported that the male partner made more of the decisions, was less emotionally invested in the relationship, and in general was "getting a better deal."

Peplau and colleagues (1977) classified married individuals in terms of egalitarian marriages, **traditional** marriages, or **modern** marriages. Egalitarian marriages involve, as indicated above, both partners' sharing power equally; traditional gender roles are absent. Gray-Little and Burks (1983) defined two types of egalitarian marriages: syncratic and autonomic. The **syncratic** relationship describes a marital pattern in which wife and husband wield power and make decisions jointly in all areas (e.g., child care, vacations, money to buy food). The **autonomic** pattern refers to an egalitarian relationship in which wife and husband each exercise power over separate areas.

In a traditional marriage, the husband is more dominant than the wife; both partners maintain traditional gender roles. In traditional marriages, wives make decisions about housework and child care. Husbands have the ultimate authority in family decisions (Gray-Little & Burks, 1983). In a modern marriage, husbands are less dominant; traditional gender roles are somewhat modified. Wives' employment is tolerated in this type of marriage; however, it is perceived as secondary to husbands' employment. If the couple's child is ill, for example, the husband makes it clear that the wife will miss work to care for the child (Peplau et al., 1977).

In traditional and modern marriages, money is correlated with power. Men have higher incomes, on average, than women; thus, they believe they should have relatively more power in the family (see Chapter 9). Gray-Little and Burks (1983) found that, in marriages in which the wife had most of the power, greater dissatisfaction was expressed than in egalitarian relationships or traditional marriages. Similar results were obtained from dating couples by Felmlee (1994). One explanation for this finding is that wife-dominant marriages are at odds with cultural norms (Paludi et al., in press). Couples in traditional or egalitarian marriages would sense that their marital arrangement is accepted and approved by society. Consequently, they would feel more positive about their relationship and would report greater satisfaction with it. In a wife-dominated marriage, there is still lack of cultural approval; the mate may feel less satisfied being in a relationship that others view as a departure from the norm. The couple may thus report dissatisfaction in their marital relationship (Felmlee, 1994).

Felmlee (1994) interviewed approximately 400 heterosexual dating undergraduate students about male-female power in romantic relationships. Felmlee found that fewer than half of the student perceived their relationship to be equal in terms of the distribution of power. Men were more than twice as likely as women to be viewed as the partner having the more power in the relationship. The majority of women and men reported that the man made more of the decisions in the relationship as well as being less emotionally invested in the relationship.

Guilbert, Vace, and Pasley (2000) relied on longitudinal survey data from 469 women and 294 men in their study of the pattern among gender-role beliefs, negativity, distancing, and marital instability. Results from this study indicated that women who held more egalitarian than traditional gender-role beliefs reported higher levels of marital instability than did women who held gender-role beliefs considered more traditional. Women who were egalitarian also reported higher levels of negativity and greater distancing than women who were traditional. Guilbert and colleagues also found that men who reported more distancing also reported more marital instability.

LESBIAN ROMANTIC RELATIONSHIPS

Do you believe gender-role stereotypes and expressions of power are central to lesbian relationships as they are in heterosexual relationships? Deaux and Hanna (1984) found:

> [The] heterosexual context seems to place far greater stress on the surface appearance that can be brought to a relationship. The differences between heterosexual and homosexual women also appear to be stronger in what one offers to a relationship than in what one seeks. We might suggest that the heterosexual relationship sets up certain expectations for women, and the woman who chooses a different (homosexual) type of relationship is free to define herself in different ways, responding to a lessened (or at least a different) set of role demands. (p. 374)

Other research also suggests that lesbian relationships rely less on gender-role stereotypic behavior than do heterosexual relationships. For example, Caldwell and Peplau (1984) studied lesbians who were in a romantic/sexual relationship. Ninety-seven percent of the women in this study (77 in all participated) believed that both partners should have equal power in a relationship. Sixty-one percent reported that they were enjoying an equal-power relationship. Similar results were reported by Garnets (1996). Lesbians value equality; the majority of lesbian relationships are characterized as being equal in power (Garnets, 1996).

There are, of course, some similarities that exist between lesbian relationships and heterosexual relationships (Garnets, 1996). For example, conflicts may occur because of financial pressures, or the amount of time one of the partners spends doing work. Work that intrudes into the relationship may be challenged (Kurdek, 1999; Caldwell & Peplau, 1984). As Garnets (1996) concluded:

> Lesbians neither adhere rigidly to traditional gender-roles nor consistently engage in cross-gender behavior. Frequently, lesbians adopt a nontraditional identity that includes nontraditional gender role norms. Lesbians may be more androgynous than heterosexual women. Comparative studies of heterosexual women and lesbian women found lesbians to be more autonomous, spontaneous, assertive, sensitive to their own needs and fears, unconventional, self-confident, and inner-directed. (p. 146)

In addition, the adjustment and mental health of children in lesbian families are no different from those of children raised in heterosexual families (Golombok & Tasker, 1996). Children raised by lesbians also do as well as children raised in heterosexual families in terms of social skills and popularity with a peer group (Golombok & Tasker, 1996; Recer, 1997). Lesbians and gay men and their children face homophobia from several sources, including employers, schools, and religious groups as well as from some family and friends (Herek & Berrill, 1992).

Adrienne Rich (1980) argued that women experience **"compulsory" heterosexuality** and suggests that it "needs to be recognized and studied as a political institution" (p. 637). Rich further suggests that lesbian relationships can be viewed along a continuum of woman-identified behaviors that empower women, such as sharing, supporting, and bonding among women. Many lesbian communities have been established in which women work on maintaining a high level of political consciousness, intimacy, and shared values. Susan Krieger (1982) commented that lesbian networks or communities:

> . . . provide a haven or home in a hostile or distrusting outside world. They lend support for what is frequently a stigmatized lifestyle choice. They command recognition of a distinctively lesbian sensibility-a sensibility that is unusual because of the value it places on intimacy between women. (p. 91)

Garnets (1996) further pointed out that changing gender roles for all women may make it possible for lesbians to be viewed as "real" women. Lesbians work toward a redefinition of power and relationships.

INTIMACY REDEFINED: CHOOSING
TO REMAIN SINGLE

Would you choose to remain single throughout your life span? Why or why not?

Research supports the following factors contributing to women's remaining single: career goals; social conditions; and family background. Let's briefly discuss the findings in each of these areas. Many single women have reported that they believe remaining single will assist them in establishing their careers (Betz, 1993). In fact, research has suggested that women who remain single tend to have higher levels of education, occupational status, and earnings than women who were married while in or after completing their graduate training. Single, middle-aged women view themselves as more independent and assertive than married women, and they place greater value on achievement and personal growth (Etaugh, 1993).

Social circumstances have an impact on women's decision to remain single (Chasteen, 1994). For example, economic depressions and wars result in lower marriage rates and later age at marriage. Furthermore, the sex ratio (number of males per 100 females) varies from decade to decade.

In addition, being raised in a home where there was marital discord, separation, and/or divorce may make individuals hesitant to marry (Etaugh, 1993). Some women may prefer **singlehood** because they value the lifestyle choice and the opportunities they might not be able to pursue if married (Etaugh, 1993).

Thus, for a variety of reasons, women may remain single throughout the life span. Being single does not necessarily mean that women live alone or are lonely, however. Some single women remain with siblings and/or parent(s). Other single women live alone or share homes or apartments with friends. A single woman may cohabit with a man or with a woman. Thus, single women fulfill some of their intimacy needs by living with friends or parents or by cohabiting. By establishing a number of relationships, single women create their own family. A support group of nonkin is referred to as a **network family:** individuals who are available to support one another in the same way as a family related by marriage or blood.

Barbara Levy Simon (1987) noted the importance of friendships for single women. Women in her study tended to develop the friendship bonds in their 30s.

They typically became friends with other women who had also decided to remain single throughout their life span. Some decided to raise children.

Negative stereotypes about single women persist (Chasteen, 1994). Claire Etaugh and her colleagues (Etaugh & Malstrom, 1981; Etaugh & Petroski, 1985; Etaugh & Stern, 1984), for example, reported that middle-aged single women are judged to be less sociable, less likable, less well-adjusted, and less attractive than middle-aged married women. It is typically assumed that remaining single is not due to women's choice but, rather, to their not "being asked" by men. These social judgments about single women may stem from the implied threat to masculine dominance—especially the fact that women are able to take care of themselves (Etaugh, 1993)—which contradicts many individuals' expectations about "femininity."

These social judgments may decrease single women's self-esteem and self-concept. In patriarchal, heterosexual cultures, women receive a message that only through the love of men will they achieve intimacy, completeness, and "adulthood" status. As Shulamith Firestone (1971) noted, a woman's "whole identity hangs in the balance of her love life. She is allowed to love herself only if a man finds her worthy of love" (p. 132). Women need to be valued for themselves, not for their relationships with or without men.

LOVE, CARING, AND INTIMACY: A NEW VIEW OF WOMEN'S DEVELOPMENT

Lillian Rubin (1976) described intimacy as love: the "reciprocal expression of feeling and thought, not out of fear of dependent need, but out of a wish to know another's inner life and to be able to share one's own" (p. 90). Cancian (1986) reported that love is defined to include honesty and open communication. Other qualities offered were caring, support, tolerance, and understanding.

Carol Gilligan (1982) has commented, however, that these aspects of love have been devalued, which in turn has led to the devaluation of women. Most psychological theories of personality development (e.g., Erikson and Freud; see Chapter 4) have stressed that a "healthy" person matures from a dependent child to an autonomous, independent adult. Gilligan responded that "development itself comes to be identified with separation, and attachments appear to be developmental impediments" (pp. 12–13). Women's focus on intimacy and love, therefore, is frequently judged to be developmentally immature and not individuated, as the research by Inge Broverman and her colleagues (Broverman, Broverman, Clarkson, Rosenkrantz, & Vogel, 1970) suggested (see Chapter 4).

Jean Baker Miller (1984) suggested a **"self-in-relation" theory,** which posits that early socialization experiences account for women's communication styles and skills in intimacy. She hypothesized that the relational self is the core self-structure in women. This theory offers us a different emphasis on the processes of development by assuming that relatedness is the primary and basic goal of development. Miller hypothesized that autonomy develops only within the context of a capacity for relating. As Phyllis Katz, Ann Boggiano, and Louise Silvern (1993) point out with respect to Miller's theory:

> From this perspective even at a very early stage, the infant develops an internal representation of self that reflects a relationship between self and caretakers. The formation of self depends on "being in relation" . . . and a sense of well-being is presumed to occur only as the infant and caretaker move dynamically in an emotional relationship that promotes positive emotional interplay between self and caretaker. Not only does the caretaker attend to the infant but the infant has an effect on both the caretaker and the dynamics of their emotional relationship. The development of the self then is seen in this view as inseparable from a reciprocal ongoing emotional interplay between the self and caretaker. (p. 267)

Nancy Chodorow (1978) also suggested that a woman's capacity for intimacy and friendship has its origin in her relationship with her mother: Because a girl is similar to her mother, she experiences connectedness rather than separation. In each of their relationships, women bring a capacity for reciprocal socialization. For example, a young girl's attachment to her mother helps to facilitate her exploration of her home, the neighborhood, family members, and friends. Simultaneously, the girl's development in independence and assertiveness helps to facilitate the renegotiation of responsibilities and expectations between the girl and her mother. Thus, although relationships contribute to an individual's development, the girl's and woman's development changes these same relationships.

Miller and Chodorow thus believe that empathic competence in a woman stems from her early relationship with her mother. They acknowledged that the self-in-relationship can apply to boys and men as well as to girls and women, but both Miller (1984) and Chodorow (1978) believe that women are more likely to be socialized to "feel as the other feels" (1984, p. 3). Miller and Chodorow also hypothesized that self-esteem for girls and women is derived from feelings that they are part of relationships, and that they nurture as well as receive nurturance from these relationships.

We need to emphasize, however, that most of the research on women's caring has been conducted with white women or with race, class, and ethnicity not being part of the analyses. As Joan Tronto (1987) has commented, minority group members may fit the care perspective of Gilligan, Miller, and Chodorow better than they fit other developmental theories, including theories of moral development. Baldwin (1986), Fairchild (1988), and Mays (1988) described core African American culture as emphasizing basic respect for individuals as well as a commitment to honesty and a respect for the choices of others. LeVine and Padilla (1980) also described Chicano, Eskimo, and Native American children as caring for each other and for the earth. Thus, there exists a possibility of a social—and not solely a psychological—cause for the self-in-relation theory.

There are some costs to caring. The importance women place on relationships may contribute to stress-related illnesses (Russo & Greene, 1993). This is especially true for women who are caring for their dependent children, friends, partners, and aging parents—the **in-between generation.**

Letty Cottin Pogrebin (1987) referred to caring as **feminist friendship.** Feminist friendship "works to help women function in the world as it is while making it better" (p. 285). She also noted:

> You feel it when you notice yourself assuming the best of a woman, not anticipating hostility or suppressing envy. You feel it when you are interested in what a friend thinks—not just about you and your activities but about everything. You feel it when your friends alter your perspective on life, help you sort out your problems, enlarge your goals and help you move toward achieving them, help you see yourself not as one isolated woman treated this way or that but as a vital member of half the human race. (p. 305)

In addition to the influence friends have on our attitudes and behaviors as well as the ways we view ourselves, teachers also contribute to our self-concept and self-worth. We will address the impact of teachers and mentors on girls' and women's self-concept in the next chapter when we discuss the career psychology of women.

NEW TERMS

autonomic egalitarian relationship

clique

compulsory heterosexuality

egalitarian relationship

feminist friendship

in-between generation

modern relationship

network family

self-disclosure

self-in-relation theory

singlehood

syncratic egalitarian relationship

traditional relationship

CHAPTER REVIEW QUESTIONS

1. Define and discuss the following components of friendship: altruism, empathy, and companionship.

2. Describe the pattern of friendships for adolescent girls.

3. Among girls and women who have physical disabilities, how do the disabilities impact their friendship formation?

4. Discuss the importance of support networks for women who are widowed.

5. Discuss some ways that traditional gender-role socialization impedes friendship formation between women and men.

6. Discuss what Lillian Rubin meant when she referred to women and men in romantic relationships as "intimate strangers."

7. Explain what Adrienne Rich meant when she referred to heterosexuality as compulsory.

8. Why do some women choose to remain single throughout their life span?

9. Discuss what Carol Gilligan meant when she noted that intimacy and caring have been devalued, which in turn has led to the devaluation of women.

10. Discuss self-in-relation theory.

SELECTED READINGS

Pogrebin, L. C. (1987). *Among friends: Who we like, why we like them, and what we do with them.* New York: McGraw-Hill.

Rose, S. (1995). Women's friendships. In J. Chrisler & A. Huston Hemstreet (Eds.), *Variations on a theme: Diversity and the psychology of women.* Albany: State University of New York Press.

LEARNING MORE ABOUT . . .

Suggestions for Term Papers and Independent Studies Related to *Women and Intimate Relationships*

Discrimination against voluntarily childless women

Similarities between widows and divorced women in terms of a loss of a relationship

Impact of fairy tales and nursery rhymes on women's development of friendships with women and with men

Promoting cross-race friendships among children and adolescents

Television programs' portrayal of friendships between women and men, e.g., "Friends," "Will and Grace"

Lesbian women's experiences with anti-gay prejudice

TAKING ACTION . . .

on *Women and Intimate Relationships*

Inquire about being a Big Sister or Big Brother to a child or adolescent. Integrate the scholarship cited in this chapter on friendships and caring with your little sister or little brother.

Exercise your caring: Join walks for the cure for diabetes and breast cancer. Help raise money for research for these diseases.

Organize a drive on your campus for obtaining canned food goods to donate to a local city mission, food pantry, or battered women's shelter.

Join local chapters of community organizations, e.g., American Association of University Women, YWCA, YMCA, League of Women Voters. Volunteer your services for fundraising and membership drives.

Join a mentoring program and mentor adolescents in your community.

REFERENCES

Antonucci, T. C., & Akiyama, H. (1987). An examination of sex differences in social support among older men and women. *Sex Roles, 17,* 737–49.

Baldwin, J. (1986). African (black) psychology: Issues and synthesis. *Journal of Black Studies, 16,* 235–250.

Basow, S. (1986). *Sex role stereotypes: Traditions and alternatives.* Monterey, CA: Brooks/ Cole.

Benenson, J., Apostoleris, N., & Pamass, J. (1998). The organization of children's same-sex peer relationships. In W. Bukowski & A. Cillessen (Eds.), *Sociometry then and now: Building on six decades of measuring children's experiences with the peer group. New directions for child development.* San Francisco, CA: Jossey-Boss.

Betz, N. (1993). Women' career development. In F. L. Denmark & M. Paludi (Eds.), *The psychology of women: A handbook of issues and theories.* Westport, CT: Greenwood Press.

Broverman, I., Broverman, D., Clarkson, F., Rosenkrantz, P., & Vogel, S. (1970). Sex role stereotypes and clinical judgments of mental health. *Journal of Consulting and Clinical Psychology, 34,* 1–7.

Bukowski, W., Newcomb, A., & Hartup, W. (Eds.). (1996). *The company they keep: Friendships in childhood and adolescence.* New York: Cambridge University Press.

Caldwell, M. A., & Peplau, L. A. (1982). Sex differences in same-sex friendship. *Sex Roles, 8,* 721–732.

Caldwell, M. A., & Peplau, L. A. (1984). The balance of power in lesbian relationships. *Sex Roles, 10,* 587–599.

Cancian, F. (1986). The feminization of love. *Signs, 11,* 692–709.

Cavanaugh, J. (1998). Friendships and social networks among older people. In I. Nordhus et al. (Eds.), *Clinical geropsychology.* Washington, DC: American Psychological Association.

Chasteen, A. (1994). "The world around me": The environment and single women. *Sex Roles, 31,* 309–328.

Cheng, S., & Chan, A. (1999). Sex, competitiveness, and intimacy in same-sex friendship in Hong Kong adolescents. *Psychological Reports, 84,* 45–48.

Chodorow, N. (1978). *The reproduction of mothering: Psychoanalysis and the sociology of gender.* Berkeley: University of California Press.

Collins, N., & Miller, L. (1994). Self-disclosure and liking: A meta-analytic review. *Psychological Bulletin, 11,* 457–475.

Deaux, K., & Hanna, R. (1984). Courtship in the personals column: The influence of gender and sexual orientation. *Sex Roles, 11,* 363–375.

de Beauvoir, S. (1949/1961). *The second sex.* New York: Bantam.

DeFosier, M., & Kupersmidt, J. (1991). Costa Rican children's perceptions of their social networks. *Developmental Psychology, 27,* 656–662.

Diamond, L., Savin-Williams, C. R., & Dube, E. (1999). Sex, dating, passionate friendships, and romance: Intimate peer relations among lesbian, gay, and bisexual adolescents. In W. Furman et al. (Eds.), *The development of romantic relationships in adolescence.* New York: Cambridge University Press.

Etaugh, C. (1993). Psychology of women: Middle and older adulthood. In F. L. Denmark & M. A. Paludi (Eds.), *Psychology of women: A handbook of issues and theories.* Westport, CT: Greenwood Press.

Etaugh, C., & Malstrom, J. (1981). The effect of marital status on person perception. *Journal of Marriage and the Family, 43,* 801–805.

Etaugh, C., & Petroski, B. (1985). Perceptions of women: Effects of employment status and marital status. *Sex Roles, 12,* 329–339.

Etaugh, C., & Stern, J. (1984). Person perception: Effects of sex, marital status and sex-typed occupation. *Sex Roles, 11,* 413–424.

Fairchild, H. (1988). Curriculum design for black (African American) psychology. In P. Bronstein & K. Quina (Eds.), *Teaching a psychology of people.* Washington, DC: American Psychological Association.

Felmlee, D. (1994). Who's on top? Power in romantic relationships. *Sex Roles, 31,* 275–295.

Filed, D. (1999). Continuity and change in friendships in advanced old age: Findings from the Berkeley Older Generation Study. *International Journal of Aging and Human Development, 48,* 325–346.

Firestone, S. (1971). *The dialectics of sex.* New York: Bantam.

Garnets, L. (1996). In J. Chrisler, C. Golden, & P. Rozee (Eds.), *Lectures on the psychology of women.* New York: McGraw-Hill.

Gilligan, C. (1982). *In a different voice.* Cambridge, MA: Harvard University Press.

Golombok, S., & Tasker, F. (1996). Do parents influence the sexual orientation of their children? *Developmental Psychology, 32,* 3–11.

Goode, E. (1996). Gender and courtship entitlement: Responses to personal ads. *Sex Roles, 34,* 141–169.

Gray, J. (1996). *Mars and Venus together forever.* New York: Harper Perennial.

Gray-Little, B., & Burks, N. (1983). Power and satisfaction in marriage: A review and critique. *Psychological Bulletin, 93,* 513–538.

Green, S., & Sandos, P. (1983). Perceptions of male and female initiators of relationships. *Sex Roles, 9,* 849–852.

Guilbert, D., Vacc, N., & Pasley, K. (2000). The relationship of gender role beliefs, negativity, distancing, and marital instability. *Family Journal Counseling and Therapy for Couples and Families, 8, 124–132.*

Hartup, W. (1998). The company they keep: Friendships and their developmental significance. In M. Hertzig et al. (Eds.), *Annual progress in child psychiatry and child development: 1997.* Bristol, PA: Brunner/Mazel.

Hartup, W., & Stevens, N. (1999). Friendships and adaptation across the life span. *Current Directions in Psychological Science, 8,* 76–79.

Herek, G., & Berrill, K. (1992). *Hate crimes.* Newbury Park, CA: Sage.

Hite, S. (1989). *Women and love.* New York: St. Martin's Press.

Hyde, J. S., & DeLamater, J. (1999). *Understanding human sexuality.* New York: McGraw Hill.

Jourard, S. (1964). *The transparent self.* Princeton, NJ: Van Nostrand.

Katz, P., Boggiano, A., & Silvern, L. (1993). Theories of female personality. In F. L. Denmark & M. A. Paludi (Eds.), *Psychology of women: A handbook of issues and theories.* Westport, CT: Greenwood Press.

Kilbourne, J. (1999). *Deadly persuasion.* New York: Free Press.

Krieger, S. (1982). Lesbian identity and community: Recent social science literature. *Signs, 8,* 91–108.

Kurdek, L. (1999). The nature and predictors of the trajectory of change in marital quality for husbands and wives over the first 10 years of marriage. *Developmental Psychology, 35,* 1283–1296.

Kuttler, A., LaGreca, A., & Prinstein, M. (1999). Friendship qualities and social-emotional functioning of adolescents with close, cross-sex friendships. *Journal of Research on Adolescence, 9*, 339–366.

LeVine, E., & Padilla, A. (1980). *Crossing cultures in therapy: Pluralistic counseling for the Hispanic.* Monterey: Brooks/Cole.

Lim, S. (1998). Linking play and language in Singapore preschool settings. *Early Child Development and Care, 144*, 21–36.

Luria, Z., & Meade, R. G. (1984). Sexuality and the middle aged woman. In G. Baruch & F. Brooks-Gunn (Eds.), *Women in mid-life.* New York: Plenum Press.

Matthews, S. (1986). *Friendships through the life course.* Newbury Park, CA: Sage.

Mays, V. (1988). Even the rat was white and male: Teaching the psychology of black women. In P. Bronstein & K. Quina (Eds.), *Teaching a psychology of people: Resources for sociocultural awareness.* Washington: American Psychological Association.

McGloshen, T., & O'Bryant, S. (1988). The psychological well-being of older, recent widows. *Psychology of Women Quarterly, 12*, 99–116.

McNelles, L., & Connolly, J. (1999). Intimacy between adolescent friends: Age and gender differences in intimate affect and intimate behaviors. *Journal of Research on Adolescence, 9*, 143–159.

Miller, J. B. (1984). *Toward a new psychology of women.* Boston: Beacon Press.

Paludi, M., Paludi, C., & Doyle, J. (in press). *Sex and gender.* (5th ed.). New York: McGraw Hill.

Peplau, L., Rubin, Z., & Hill, C. (1977). Sexual intimacy in dating relationships. *Journal of Social Issues, 33,* 86–109.

Podrouzek, W., & Furrow, D. (1988). Preschoolers' use of eye contact while speaking: The influence of sex, age, and conversational pattern. *Psycholinguistic Research, 17*, 89–98.

Pogrebin, L. (1987). *Among friends.* New York: McGraw-Hill.

Recer, P. (1997, April 4). Studies find children of lesbian couples well-adjusted. *Rocky Mountain News,* p. 36A.

Rich, A. (1980). Compulsory heterosexuality and lesbian existence. *Signs, 5*, 631–660.

Roopnarine, J., Johnson, J., & Hooper, F. (Eds.). (1994). *Children's play in diverse cultures.* Albany: State University of New York Press.

Rose, S. (1995). Women's friendships. In J. Chrisler & A. Huston Hemstreet (Eds.), *Variations on a theme: Diversity and the psychology of women.* Albany: State University of New York Press.

Rose, S. (1997). Friendships and women. In J. Chrisler, C. Golden, & P. Rozee (Eds.), *Lectures on the psychology of women.* New York: McGraw-Hill.

Rose, S., & Roades, L. (1987). Feminism and women's friendships. *Psychology of Women Quarterly, 11*, 243–254.

Roy, R., Benenson, J., & Lilly, F. (2000). Beyond intimacy: Conceptualizing sex differences in same-sex relationships. *Journal of Psychology, 134,* 93–101.

Rubin, L. (1976). *Intimate strangers: Men and women together.* New York: Harper & Row.

Russo, N. F., & Greene, B. (1993). Women and work. In F. L. Denmark & M. A. Paludi (Eds.), *The psychology of women: A handbook.* Westport, CT: Greenwood Press.

Schultz, K. (1991). Women's adult development: The importance of friendship. *Journal of Independent Social Work, 5,* 19–30.

Simon, B. L. (1987). *Never married women.* Philadelphia: Temple University Press.

Stevens, N., & van Tilburg, T. (2000). Stimulating friendship in later life: A strategy for reducing loneliness among older women. *Educational Gerontology, 26,* 15–35.

Tannen, D. (1995). *Talking from 9 to 5: Women and men in the workplace, language, sex and power.* New York: Avon Books.

Tronto, J. (1987). Beyond gender difference to a theory of care. *Signs, 12,* 644–663.

Van-Aken, D. (1999). Exploration of sibling relationships in middle childhood. *Dissertation Abstracts International, 59,* 5623.

Vaughn, B., Azria, M., Krzysik, L., Caya, L., Bost, K, Newell, W., & Kazura, K. (2000). Friendship and social competence in a sample of preschool children attending head start. *Developmental Psychology, 36,* 326–338.

Weissman, D. (1999). Gender of preschoolers' preferred play partners. Children's perspectives. *Dissertation Abstracts International, 59* (12-B), 6518.

NINE

CAREER PSYCHOLOGY
OF WOMEN

IN WOMEN'S VOICES

Certainly it is . . . no longer assumed that women who pursue careers are neurotic, an often-expressed view in prefeminist days.

Martha Mednick and Veronica Thomas

Interventions into women's career development require attack on at least two individual and several societal levels: (1) restoring women's options to them; (2) convincing them that they, like men, not only can but deserve to have it all; (3) working toward continued change in societal institutions such that women have a better shot at both educational and occupational opportunities and equity.

Nancy Betz

Even within our basically achievement-oriented society the anticipation of success, especially in interpersonal competitive situations, can be regarded as a mixed blessing if not an outright threat. Among women, the anticipation of success . . . poses a threat to the sense of femininity and self-esteem and serves as a potential basis for becoming socially rejected. . . . In order to feel or appear more feminine, women...disguise their abilities and withdraw from the mainstream of thought, activism, and achievement in our society. This does not occur . . . without a high price, a price paid by the individual in negative emotional and interpersonal consequences and by the society in a loss of valuable human and economic resources.

Matina Horner

Chapter Outline

Questions for Reflection

1. Why do you believe you do well on exams—are you lucky? Do you study quite a bit? Do you have the ability to do the subject matter?

2. Why do you believe you do not do well on certain exams? Do you lack the ability? Do you not put in the effort it takes to do well on the test? Does the professor not like you?

3. How did you come to select the major field of study that you did? Did you identify this career early on in your adolescence or did you wait until you began attending college?

4. Do you believe you have a strong need to achieve? How does this need express itself in your college classes?

5. What are some barriers you have noticed to your meeting your career goals?

6. What have been some facilitators of your career development?

7. Do you believe you have a "fear of success"? What do you believe this term,"fear of success" means?

8. Have you had a mentor for your career development? If so, what kind of professional guidance did this individual provide you? If not, would you like to have a mentor? For what reasons?

9. What stereotypes do you believe exist with respect to children of employed mothers?

10. Do you believe all women's colleges are beneficial for women's career development? Why or why not?

11. Cite some ways your professors can make women students feel more welcome in their courses—especially courses in the sciences and mathematics.

12. In the next five years where do you see yourself in your career? How do you plan to achieve these goals?

INTRODUCTION: GENDER AND THE EDUCATIONAL SYSTEM

Mills College, located in Oakland, California, has been an all-women's college for over 140 years. In the spring of 1990, the board of trustees announced that declining enrollment and budget problems had left them no choice: Men would be admitted as undergraduate students beginning in August 1991 (men have been admitted as graduate students since the 1930s). Hundreds of women students at Mills College expressed concern over the board's decision. for example:

> I felt like my best friend had died.
>
> It was like the earth fell out from our feet, and we were falling.
>
> We love men. But we want this place to ourselves.
>
> We'll do whatever it takes to reverse the decision.
>
> They can't run a school if they don't have any students. We have the power to close the college.
>
> (Kunen, McNeil, & Waggoner, 1990, p. 63)

Women went on strike; demanded the resignation of the board of trustees' president, Warren Hellman; boycotted classes; wore yellow armbands, anklets, and bandanas to symbolize women's "hostage status"; and put up banners that proclaimed:

WE HAVE BEEN BETRAYED.

A few weeks after the decision to admit men as undergraduate students at Mills College, the board reversed its edict and accepted a plan proposed by alumnae and faculty to increase the budget. Faculty members agreed to teach an extra course a year and to recruit more women students to Mills. Hellman, when announcing the new decision, exclaimed: "All of you have had a lot of banners for us all week. Here's one for you":

Women students protesting Mills College's decision to admit men as undergraduates.

MILLS. FOR WOMEN. AGAIN.

These events at Mills College restimulated a great deal of discussion and empirical research about the value of all women's colleges for women's career development, self-concept, and feminist identity development. Research on women's career development has suggested that the goals of education are translated very differently, leaving lasting effects for girls and women and for boys and men (Betz, 1993; Eccles, 1994). For example, among first- and second-graders, there has been considerable evidence of gender bias in the kinds of jobs children target for their future employment. Third- and fifth-grade girls most often select the occupations of nurse, teacher, and flight attendant; they do not select police officer, truck driver, pilot, and architect (Betz, 1993). Once set, girls' (and boys') range of occupations is difficult to change (Betz, 1993).

Golombok and Fivush (1994) reported that by fourth or fifth grade, approximately 90 percent of positive feedback boys receive from their teachers concerns their academic performance; less than 80 percent of positive feedback for girls is

One sentiment expressed by women students at Mills College in 1990.

for their academic performance. Furthermore, less than 33 percent of the negative feedback boys receive from their teachers is related to their academic performance. More than 66 percent of the negative feedback for girls is related to their academic performance. Golombok and Fivush interpreted these results in the following way:

> From this pattern of praise and criticism, boys may be learning that they are smart, even if they are not very well behaved. Girls, on the other hand, are learning that they may not be very smart, but that they can get rewards by being "good." (p. 173)

When we look at the interface of sex and race, we see that the traditional educational system does not reward girls (and boys) of color (Reid, Haritos, Kelly, & Holland, 1995). Rumet (1999) found that African American boys are the least likely to be discussed favorably in curriculum materials. As Angela Ginorio and her colleagues (Ginorio, Gutierrez, Cauce, & Acosta, 1995) pointed out:

> [Teachers'] expectations were shaped not only by success-related measures such as educational skills but by students' characteristics such as ethnicity and gender. In this case, Latinas who were assertive and independent were expected to be less successful

than other less conforming students. Second, characteristics typically encouraged within the traditional Latina family are not valued by Anglocentric schools. (p. 251)

Teachers' gender-related and race-related messages are reinforced by the curricular materials available at the elementary school level (Odean, 1997; Rumet, 1999; Tepper & Cassidy, 1999). Girls and boys of color are underrepresented in textbooks and readers. Furthermore, the organization of activities in the elementary school classroom contributes to the "hidden curriculum" for girls and boys. Children are asked to form separate lines according to their sex and they are assigned different classroom chores according to their sex (e.g., erasing chalk boards, using audiovisual equipment) (Thorne, 1993). These illustrations of "sex separation" prevent girls and boys from working cooperatively and learning about each other's interests (Haag, 1999).

The American Association of University Women (Haag, 1999) asked approximately 2,000 girls from 38 states the following questions:

What do you think are the most important issues facing teenage girls today?
What do you wish you could change about your school, related to these issues?
What is something that someone has said to you that you wish they hadn't said?
What is something that you know that you think other girls your age need to know?
What would you like to learn from other girls your age?
What is your definition of "sisterhood"?

Responses from the adolescent girls included the following:

I wish in school the teachers would give the students more opportunities to work with and cooperate with other students; that would increase the probability of making new friends for people who are shy and have difficulty in that area. (p. 35)

Asian American, 15 years old

Someone said "Are you in special education?" because I didn't understand something. (p. 59)

African American, 15 years old

I wish people would not make comments about my report card when I receive straight A's. . . . My friends should be happy for me, not demean my accomplishments. (p. 53)

White, 15 years old

The AAUW study also noted that secondary school systems direct girls and boys into different courses by a differential "tracking system" whereby girls are taught to think in terms of becoming nurses, secretaries, and mothers while boys are taught to think about becoming physicians and engineers (also see Miles, 1995; Sadker & Sadker, 1994). Related to this issue is the statistic that women secondary school teachers are rarely found in industrial arts, industry and trade, agriculture, and mathematics (Betz, 1993; Commission on Professionals in Science and Technology, 1992).

For women students in college, gender stereotypes create a "chilly climate" in the classroom and the science laboratory (Betz, 1993; Hall & Sandler, 1982). "Chilling" behaviors include:

Discouraging women's participation in class discussions.
Preventing women from seeking help outside of class.
Dampening career aspirations.
Undermining women's confidence.
Minimizing women's development of collegial relationships with faculty.
Interrupting women in class.

Women who participate in such classes may act or react as though:

Their presence in a given class, department, program, or institution is at best peripheral, or at worst an unwelcome intrusion.
Their participation in class discussion is not expected, and their contributions are not important.
Their capacity for full intellectual development and professional success is limited.
Their academic and career goals are not matters for serious attention or concern (Hall & Sandler, 1982).

A chilly classroom environment may develop when men who are not supportive of feminism are present; it is a relatively rare occurrence in all-women classes (Lippert-Martin, 1992). For example, Lippert-Martin (1992) asked faculty and researchers concerned with classroom climates the following questions:

How do you think the classroom climate for women has changed in the last ten years? Has it improved?
Has women's studies played a role in changing the climate?

TABLE 9.1   *Educational and Workplace Equity?*

- Approximately 95% of jobs in the future will require the use of computers. However, fewer than 33% of students in computer courses are girls and women.
(*U.S. Labor Statistics: JOBS 2000*)

- Women leave science and engineering careers twice as frequently as men.
(*Career Engineering, 1996*)

- Sixteen percent fewer girls than boys report talking to their parents about science and technology issues and careers.
(*National Science Foundation, 1994*)

- Thirty-four percent of high-school-aged girls reported being advised by a teacher not to take senior math.
(*National Science Foundation, 1994*)

- Girls consistently match or surpass boys' achievements in math and science as measured by SATs, achievement tests, and class grades.
(*National Science Foundation, 1994*)

What are individuals—as opposed to institutions—able to do to make a difference for women?

Lippert-Martin obtained responses to these questions from Directors of Women's Studies Programs and administrators at the following campuses: University of Missouri-Columbia, University of Colorado, Lewis and Clark College, Hunter College, Old Dominion University, Temple University, Lesley College, and California State University-Fullerton. Lippert-Martin obtained responses such as the following:

I think there are pockets where (the climate has) changed.

Increasingly, as more women—and especially feminists—are hired as faculty, there will be more of a sensitivity to women students and support for women students in the classroom. I think women's studies classes are kind of an oasis. . . . Lip service is given to diversity, both racial and gender, but in practice things haven't changed that much outside of these pockets.

On the campuses where women have been able or encouraged to take women's studies classes, they are more aware. If they take these courses early, they will tend to be conscious of the climate and try to speak up more. From that point of view, there is much promise.

Women at Mills College wanted to avoid the possibilities of having the classroom become a "masculine" setting for discussion; of becoming silenced; of having sex-related discrimination interfere with their educational process and their vocational development. They heard the voices of other women students around the country:

> Students in one of my classes did a tally and found that male professors called on men more than on women students.
>
> What male students have to say or contribute is viewed as having more importance than what female students have to contribute in class.
>
> You come in the door . . . equal but having experienced the discrimination—the refusal of professors to take you seriously; the sexual overtures and the like—you limp out doubting your own ability to do very much of anything.
>
> What I find damaging and disheartening are the underlying attitudes . . . the surprise I see when a woman does well in an exam—the condescending smile when she doesn't.
>
> My high school girlfriends used to be the brightest and most talkative students in class. When we got together during our first vacation from college, the girls who went to co-ed schools said they hardly talked at all in their classes. I couldn't believe it! I go to [an all-women's college] . . . and women are not at all reticent there.
>
> (Hall & Sandler, 1982)

In this chapter, we will discuss women's achievement motivation and their educational and occupational development. I will include the barriers to women's career choices and the facilitators of women's career development. Let's begin with an overview of the field of career psychology.

REPLACING WOMEN IN THEORIES OF CAREER PSYCHOLOGY

A book entitled *Choosing a Vocation*, written by Frank Parsons and published in 1909, is credited with ushering into psychology the subfield of vocational psychology and career development. The study of women's career development is of more

Students marching on Fifth Avenue, New York City, 1909.

recent origin, however, despite the fact that the field of vocational psychology is more than ninety years old. Psychologists Nancy Betz and Louise Fitzgerald (1987) view this relative neglect of the career psychology of women as being a result of two widely accepted assumptions. The first assumption concerns the **motherhood mandate** (Russo, 1976), or the belief that the primary career roles of women center around domestic and child-care responsibilities. According to Nancy Felipe Russo:

> Characterizing motherhood as prescribed, however, does not adequately communicate the centrality of this behavior to the definition of the adult female. "Being pretty" is also prescribed, but one can compensate for not being pretty (by being a "good mother," for example). It is a woman's *raison d'etre*. It is mandatory. The mandate requires that one have at least two children (historically as many as possible and preferably sons) and that one raise them "well." As long as this situation exists for the vast majority of women in Western society and the world in general, prohibitions may be eliminated and options widened, but change will occur only insofar as women are first able to fulfill their mandate of motherhood. (p. 144)

When women did work outside the home, they were observed to occupy primarily low-level, low-status positions that provided little or no opportunity for advancement and social recognition (Betz, 1993). Women were seen as holding jobs, not building careers. They were considered "individually transient and collectively insignificant due to the level of jobs available to them" (Vetter, 1973, p. 54).

The second widely held assumption about the vocational psychology of women involved the belief that the theories developed to describe men's career development would automatically apply to the description of women's career development (Super, 1957). For example, Donald Super divided individuals' career pathways into five distinct stages:

1. Growth stage (birth–14 years).

2. Exploration stage (15–24).

3. Establishment stage (25–44).

4. Maintenance stage (45–64).

5. Decline stage (age 65 and older).

Super's major concern was with the manner in which individuals searched for an appropriate occupation: playing at various roles and activities in childhood; assessing needs, abilities, and interests in adolescence; and establishing and focusing on the selected vocation in adulthood.

As we discussed in Chapter 3, there is a danger of overinterpretation when considering stage theories. Neither of the above theories takes into account women's unique career patterns. It is unreasonable to accept Super's assumption that all individuals (especially women) go through a single set of stages in one vocational pathway. Women may participate in several jobs before making a major vocational commitment to one of them. Women may change careers at midlife. Or, women may first begin to prepare for a career in midlife. The two theories above do not address the fact that most women have children for whom they are primarily responsible and thus (1) may need or want to take some time out from full-time careers for child rearing or (2) may go to work or school part-time. By having only one career pattern in mind—full-time, uninterrupted work—institutions may close many women out of many careers.

This is especially true of women of color (e.g., Arroyo & Ziegler, 1995). For example, Angela Ginorio and her colleagues (Ginorio et al., 1995) reported that, to obtain an education, Latinas (and Latinos) must overcome several obstacles, including racism, classism, poor preparation, financial need, and an educational system that does not support cultural diversity.

As another example, American Indian women are very conflicted about pursuing a college education (LaFromboise, Choney, James, & Running Wolf, 1995). One reason for their conflict is their difficulty in adapting to the competitive nature of colleges. Another reason is the discouragement they receive from families and friends about continuing with higher education. Many American Indian women report that they feel they are going against their culture by attending college (Landrine, 1995).

Personal and public attitudes toward women's vocational psychology began to change in the late 1960s and early 1970s, signaled and stimulated by the reemergence of the women's movement (Betz, 1993). These attitudinal changes are mirrored in the proportion of women, including women with preschool children, engaged in paid employment outside the home. Since 1970, for example, approximately 6 million women have joined the workforce. Among adult learners, women outnumber men in all age groups, constituting 57 percent of the total. No other age group shows a percentage increase in college enrollment. Older women comprise the largest potential source of students. "Women's place" has thus been extended outside the home to college, graduate school, and the paid labor force (Doyle & Paludi, 1997).

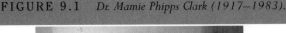

FIGURE 9.1   *Dr. Mamie Phipps Clark (1917–1983).*

"To the world she leaves the importance of the sense of self."

(Robert Guthrie describing Dr. Clark)

Dr. Clark is best known for her developmental studies that helped remove race barriers in education. Dr. Clark founded the Northside Center for Children in New York City in 1946.

The "male as normative" view of vocational psychology has characterized much of psychology as a discipline (see Chapter 1). In the early work on bringing women into vocational psychology, researchers focused on documenting gender differences (Betz & Fitzgerald, 1987). Gender differences observed in vocational psychology include the following (see Betz & Fitzgerald, 1987, for a review of these studies):

- A relatively restricted range of career alternatives is pursued by women, in comparison to a much larger range pursued by men.

- Women continue to be concentrated in female-populated fields where status and market value are low.

- Women are less well represented at each higher degree level.

- Women are more likely than men to be enrolled in public institutions and to attend college on a part-time basis.

- Female-populated professions offer limited careers mobility; women's intellectual capacities are not reflected in their educational and occupational successes; their aspirations are relatively lower than those of men who have comparable ability.

Daryl Bem and Sandra Bem (1970) interpreted many of these gender differences as indicative of the **homogenization of American women:** Women are socialized by family, peers, and teachers to pursue the same careers regardless of their individual aspirations, needs, and abilities. According to this and other research, women's career psychology is predictable not because of their characteristics as individuals, but on the basis of their sex. Furthermore, women's career development has been the product of two sequential decisions: (1) whether they want a career and (2) what occupation or career to pursue.

Vocational psychologists have recognized the need for theory and research focused *specifically* on women's career development rather than on a gender-difference model (Farmer, Wardrop, & Rotella, 1999). The focus is on career choice, not avoidance of male-populated careers. This research may be categorized into **sociopsychological factors** (i.e., personality) and **structural** (i.e., institutional) **factors** that differentially affect women's achievement and the career pathways they follow. Sociopsychological or person-centered issues that have been studied include fear of success and failure, achievement motivation, causal attributions of success and failure, and employed mothers' role strain and job satisfaction. Structural or institution-centered explanations that have been reviewed include evaluations of women's achievement, discrimination in the workplace, the availability of role models and mentors, and gender and sexual harassment.

In the following sections we will summarize the results of some of the research on women's career development and trace the development of research efforts within each of these areas. We will discuss sexual harassment in Chapter 10. Let's start with the sociopsychological factors—specifically, achievement motivation.

SOCIOPSYCHOLOGICAL FACTORS AFFECTING THE CAREER PSYCHOLOGY OF WOMEN

Achievement Motivation

Achievement motivation, as formulated by David McClelland (1961) and John Atkinson (1958), was defined as "competition with a standard of excellence," where winning or doing as well as or better than someone else is of primary concern.

To measure individuals' achievement motivation, McClelland (1961) selected, from the **Thematic Apperception Test (TAT)** (developed by Christiana Morgan and Henry Murray), pictures that he considered portrayals of cultural situations in which behavior related to the achievement motive might be expected to occur. The TAT requires individuals to interpret a picture by telling a story in response to four questions:

1. What is happening? Who are the persons?

2. What has led up to this situation? That is, what has happened in the past?

3. What are the persons thinking and feeling?

4. What will happen next? What will be done?

Psychologists assume that our responses to these questions are governed by our experiences, conflicts, and wishes. Essentially, we project ourselves into the picture and vicariously take the place of a character shown in the picture. In using our fantasy to tell the story, we are displaying our achievement motivation. One of the TAT pictures McClelland selected shows a work situation: Two men are standing by a machine. Here is one story in response to this picture:

Two men are inventing a revolutionary type of machinery. They are brothers working together to fulfill one of their dreams of success as a team. In the past, they have been encouraged to do things together and have been rewarded for doing so. Now in later life they seek rewards of admiration together. Some difficulty has been met, but a solution seems to have been found by one of the brothers, while the other appears to be quite puzzled. The two brothers will continue successfully to solve the problem and create the new piece of machinery. They will be rewarded with praise and some financial success and continue their inventiveness.

(Atkinson, 1958, p. 695)

This story would be scored as suggesting a need or concern for achievement because the reheating of the metal and creating a new piece of machinery implies a desire to move ahead to the ultimate goal. Several categories of achievement themes can be scored in the stories, including an explicit statement about a desire to meet an achievement goal, action taken toward attainment of the achievement goal, thoughts about reaching and/or failing to reach the achievement goal, blocks to meeting the goal, and assistance received in meeting the goal.

McClelland's (1961) initial research using the modified TAT included the following design. In one group of male college students, the writing of stories to the TAT was preceded by a period in which a graduate student (a man) informally gave the participants instructions about the nature of the research, making sure to minimize the number of achievement-motivating cues that might be present in the situation. This condition was referred to as the "relaxed group."

The situation involving a second group of participants, the "neutral group," resembled the first situation in that the researcher conducted himself informally; however, he did not make an effort to minimize the importance of the research. A third group, the "achievement-oriented" group, was given instructions designed to maximize the extent to which achievement cues would affect participants before the writing of the TAT stories. Men in this group were told that the tests predicted creativity and intelligence and that the results from such tests were used to select top governmental officials in Washington.

McClelland reported that men in the achievement-oriented group wrote stories that contained more references to achievement than did those of men in the other two groups, and he claimed that the TAT stories reflected the intensity of the participants' achievement. McClelland's attempts to replicate this finding with women, however, did not reveal similar results. This gender difference was interpreted by McClelland as suggesting that women want to affiliate, not achieve, but subsequent research has questioned this initial interpretation.

For example, Stewart and Chester (1982) discussed the fact that even though the "arousing" achievement instructions did not increase the number of references to achievement in women's stories, the basic level of achievement motivation was higher in women than in men—they wrote stories that contained more achievement imagery in *all* conditions. McClelland and other researchers in the area of achievement motivation could have reformulated their theory and methodology when noting women's results. Instead, they stopped studying women's achievement motivation (Alper, 1974).

Researchers in achievement motivation assumed that only the feminine gender role in this culture constrains achievement. Consequently, they ignored the data suggesting that women are not aroused by traditional achievement manipulations (Stewart & Chester, 1982). Considerable evidence has suggested that women strive for excellence in a wide range of domains (men seem incapable of this breadth). Furthermore, women's need to be a good partner and/or mother may be viewed as fulfilling their affiliative needs, but it also may be viewed as fulfilling their achievement needs—in areas culturally defined as appropriate for women (Doyle & Paludi, 1995). However, this has been rarely studied; sex has been used as the dependent variable rather than as an independent variable.

In critiquing McClelland's conceptualization and measurement of achievement motivation, Janet Spence and Robert Helmreich (1978) developed a self-report measure of achievement motivation, the **Work and Family Orientation Questionnaire (WOFO).** The WOFO contains items dealing with attitudes toward achievement-related activities, the relative importance of work versus marriage as anticipated sources of life satisfaction, and information about respondents' educational aspirations. Items on the WOFO were assigned to one of three scales: work orientation, mastery, and competitiveness. The work factor represents an effort dimension: the desire to work hard and do a good job. The mastery factor deals with preferences for difficult, challenging tasks and for meeting internally prescribed standards of performance. The competitiveness factor reflects the enjoyment of interpersonal competition and the desire to win and do better than others. Spence and Helmreich have reported that, in general, men score higher than women on the competitiveness and mastery subscales of the WOFO, but women score higher on work orientation. They also found that the consequences of achievement striving are similar for women and men.

Gravenkemper and Paludi (1983) suggested that when women and men are asked for subjective definitions of areas of achievement, gender differences disappear. Jean Lipman-Blumen and her colleagues (Lipman-Blumen, Handley-Isaksen, & Leavitt, 1983) described different achievement styles. **Direct achieving styles** are used by people who confront achievement tasks very directly; a director achiever may enjoy winning over competitors or may simply enjoy the thrill of accomplishment. **Rela-**

tional achieving styles are used by people who seek success through their relationships with others—for example, working in collaboration with other people. Women seem to show wide variability in the kind of achieving style they incorporate in their behavioral repertoire.

Motive to Avoid Success?

Matina Horner (1968) introduced the construct "motive to avoid success" in order to "fill a gap" in the understanding of women's achievement. She believed that, in competitive achievement situations, especially those in which important men are present (e.g., prospective dates, boyfriends), women have a motive to become anxious about being successful. Horner believed this motive was present because of an expectation of negative consequences (e.g., loss of femininity, social rejection, and disapproval) as a result of succeeding. As she stated:

> A bright woman is caught in a double bind. In testing and other achievement-oriented situations, she worries not only about failure but also about success. If she fails, she is not living up to her own standards of performance; if she succeeds, she is not living up to societal expectations about the female role. (p. 38)

Horner accepted the psychoanalytic view that motives are developed early in childhood and become relatively stable attributes of personality. Her hypotheses concerning the motive to avoid success may be summarized as follows: Competition against other individuals would engender fear of success because of the affiliative/interpersonal concerns of women.

The traditional socialization of females in North American culture (especially the femininity/achievement incompatibility) engenders fear of success. There is a relationship between motives; there is a perceived threat to affiliative goals when a woman is achievement-oriented, and this in turn would inhibit women's performance.

To test her hypotheses, Horner (1968) administered the opening sentence of a story that was to be completed. Women were presented with the following wording: "After first-term finals, Anne finds herself at the top of her medical school class." Men were given a similar cue except that "John" and "his" were substituted for "Anne" and "her."

Horner (1968) observed differences between women and men in the kinds of responses they made to the opening line. Imagery illustrating the motive to avoid success included negative consequences because of the success; negative affect because of the success; any direct expression of conflict about success; and instrumental activity away from present or future success, including leaving the field for more traditional female-populated work. Women projected more evidence of the motive to avoid success than men did—62 percent (of 90 women) versus 9 percent (of 88 men). Horner reasoned that sensitivity to the sex of the character (Anne or John) served to contribute to women's negative imagery in their stories.

Here are samples of what women wrote:

> Anne starts proclaiming her surprise and joy. Her fellow classmates are so disgusted with her behavior that they jump on her in a body and beat her. She is maimed for life.

> Anne is an acne-faced bookworm. She runs to the bulletin board and finds she's at the top. As usual she smarts off. A chorus of groans is the rest of the class's reply. . . .

> Unfortunately Anne no longer feels so certain that she really wants to be a doctor. She is worried about herself and wonders if perhaps she isn't normal. . . . Anne decides to continue with her medical work but to take courses that have a deeper personal meaning to her.

Horner (1968) also observed that women who projected fear of success performed less well on an anagrams task (i.e., making smaller words from the word "Generation") when they were in competition with men than when working alone. She thus suggested that fear of success acted as a motive and accounted for the major part of the withdrawal of women from higher education and work.

This construct was embraced by psychologists and other researchers concerned with achievement motivation and was renamed "fear of success." It was during this stage in the development of the fear of success construct that a host of correlational studies was published. Horner (1970), for example, found that Radcliffe students who were high in fear of success were most likely to alter their career aspirations in traditionally feminine directions during their college years. Lois Hoffman (1974) correlated fear of success with lifestyle choice. She observed that those women in Horner's initial study who projected fear of success imagery onto a successful woman were more likely than their counterparts to drop out of college, get married, and have many children.

As a final example, Winchel, Fenner, and Shaver (1974) obtained more fear of success responses from women in coeducational schools than from those who attended all-women colleges. However, toward the end of the first decade of research on fear of success, the construct was being questioned. Horner's findings were judged to be not as robust as originally assumed. For example, Lynn Monahan and her colleagues (Monahan, Kuhn, & Shaver, 1974) and Linda Solomon (1975) demonstrated that a cultural interpretation of fear of success is preferable to an intrapsychic one. Their results indicated that both women and men projected more fear of success imagery onto Anne than onto John, suggesting a cultural explanation: "The stereotypes surrounding women's achievements are negative ones, learned and accepted by both sexes" (Monahan et al., 1974, p. 61).

Research subsequent to Horner's original study (1968) has found the content of fear of success stories to be different for women and men. The modal theme of women's protocols appears to be affiliative loss of friends, potential dates, and lovers (Romer, 1974; Sutherland, 1989; Tresemer, 1977), while existential issues surrounding success appear in most men's stories. Part of the definition of gender roles in society involves assumptions about the types of occupations appropriate for women and men. Success in an occupation is valued more when that success is consistent with societal conceptions about the gender role than when it is inconsistent (Pfost & Fiore, 1990; Sancho & Hewitt, 1990). Thus, because Horner's cue depicted "Anne" at the top of her medical school class, it may be hypothesized that protocols written by women reflected concern about success that is "out of place" for women. This "gender-role-inappropriate" hypothesis has also been supported for men when "John's" success occurred in a nontraditional setting such as nursing (Cherry & Deaux, 1975). Thus, the term "medical school," with its numerous connotations, may have been a salient factor in Horner's original study.

Some researchers resolved the inconsistency in results by claiming that fear of success does exist, but the measurement technique had some difficulties. During this period of the research and theorizing on fear of success, several "objective" instruments designed to tap the construct had been developed. In 1984, I reviewed these tests with respect to measurement reliability, validity, and the validity of the fear of success construct. The objective scales did not meet standard psychometric analysis (i.e., they had poor validity, no reliability), and not all researchers conceptualized the fear of success similarly. For example, Horner claimed that the feared negative consequences for success are deviations from social norms and stereotypes. The same theoretical basis underlies Zuckerman and Allison's (1976) fear of success scale. Questionnaires developed by Marice Pappo (1972) and Nina Cohen (1974), on the other hand, are couched in the psychoanalytic approach to fear of success: the feared negative consequences are the defeat of one's defenses against murderous rage or Oedipal success. Some of the objective scales dealt with academic, competitive success; others, with success in general. None of the objective measures is related to Horner's projective technique.

Based on a review of studies subsequent to Horner's original experiment, we can make the following conclusions:

- Inconsistent data exist to support the hypothesis that fear of success is less likely among black women and more likely among white women.

- Fear of success has shown no consistent relationship to ability—"career goals"—in women.

- Inconsistent data exist to support a relationship between fear of success and gender-role identity.

- No reliable age or gender differences in fear of success have been observed.

- Whether fear of success taps a motive or a cultural stereotype is not clear.

The embracing of Horner's findings that women hinder their own achievement most likely illustrated a backlash against early feminist writings—for example, Betty Friedan's *The Feminine Mystique*—that addressed societal devaluation of women.

Causal Attributions for Success and Failure

Let's say that you got an A on your psychological statistics exam. When you think about your grade—a success—what do you believe caused it? Did you study for several hours? Did you work with a study group for many hours? Did you attend and participate in review sessions offered by the professor? Were you lucky? Does the professor like you? Are you "good in math"? What do you believe others will point to as the reason you got an A on your statistics exam? Luck? Ability? Being liked by the professor? Effort? These answers to the question—What caused the A on the statistics exam—are called the **attribution process.**

Bernard Weiner (1972) proposed a **cognitive attribution theory of achievement motivation** to explain the differences between high- and low-achievement individuals. His theory regards the differential persistence of high- and low-achievement persons as due to the attributions they make regarding the causes of success and failure. According to Weiner, high-achievement-oriented individuals take charge of their own achievements; they believe themselves to be the cause of their successes (because of ability and hard work). Low-achievement-oriented persons, on the other hand, attribute their successes to external causes (a teacher's mistake, an easy test) and their failures to internal ones (lack of ability).

Gender and ethnicity differences have been reported in causal attributions for success and failure (e.g., Birenbaum & Kraemer, 1995). The pattern for women was greater externality for success and more internality for failure. Betz (1993), for example, reported that women were more likely to attribute their successes to luck and their failures to low ability. Men's successes and women's failures were attributed to personal dispositions; men's failures and women's successes were attributed to environmental factors.

Meta-analyses of the research in this area (e.g., Frieze, Whitley, Hanusa, & McHugh, 1982) suggest that, for success, men make only slightly more attributions to ability than women do, and women make only slightly more attributions to luck. Explanations for the small effect size in this research concern the manner in which the information was elicited. Was it causally worded (e.g., "To what extent do you think your performance on this task was caused by luck?") or informationally worded (e.g., "How much ability to perform this task do you think you have?")? Women make more luck attributions to causal questions, but not to informational ones.

These results suggest that women need to define achievement for themselves rather than have experimenters impose their own definitions, a topic to which we now turn.

IT'S WOMEN'S TURN TO DEFINE SUCCESS FOR THEMSELVES

In 1986, Jean Fankell-Hauser and I recognized that women differ in the strength of their striving for achievement and in the roles that elicit their striving. Therefore, we believed that women's achievement striving could best be predicted from information about *women's own* specific interests, activities, and aspirations. We developed an **idiographic approach to the measurement of women's success striving.** We accomplished this by using biographical interviewing. This enabled us to identify **facilitators of women's career development,** such as parent(s), peers, and role models.

We interviewed 80 women, 10 each from the following age groups: late teens, 20s, 30s, 40s, 50s, 60s, 70s, and 80s. The mean age was 46.8 years. Our sample included women who were beginning their careers, others who were in the middle of their achievement paths, and some who had been retired. Also included in this sample were women who were employed outside the home and others who were not. We used standardized interview items with each woman, for example:

What, specifically, do you want to accomplish in the next few years?

What specific steps do you plan to take to achieve these goals?

What blocks in yourself will you have to overcome to achieve these goals?

What blocks in the world will you have to overcome to achieve these goals?

How do you feel about the possibility of achieving these goals? Of failing to achieve them?

How do your parent(s) feel about the possibility of your achieving these goals? Of failing to achieve them?

How does your mate feel about your achieving these goals?

How do your children feel about your achieving these goals?

How do your women acquaintances feel about your achieving these goals?

How do your men acquaintances feel about your achieving these goals?

Who (if anyone) are the people (or person) you would like to be like? That is, who are the people you try to model yourself after?

Describe the different role models you've had over the course of your life.

Have you ever been in a situation where you were about to succeed at something and wondered if it was worth it or became afraid of the success or something it might produce?

One theme that emerged from the interview items concerned developmental discontinuities in women's achievement striving. Compared to older women, younger women were more concerned with competitive achievement. Older women (in the 50 to 80 years age groups) reported that their achievement striving increased when they were in the "child launching" phase of their relationships. They reported feeling accepted at that stage by both male and female peers and relatives.

Achievement striving was also likely to be characteristic of women whose parents reinforced and encouraged achievement efforts and who were reared in dual-earner families. These women viewed their relationship with their parent(s) as warmer, closer, more sharing, and more supportive than did other women.

Women voiced their realization that masculine achievement-striving behavior is limited. The biographical interviewing technique did not emphasize the dichotomous acceptance or rejection of achievement. In addition, the technique did not obscure the importance of investigating different types of achievement. Instead, the interviewing approach helped us to explore the personality characteristics that predispose women of several cohorts toward achievement-striving behavior, taking into account the effects of family, friends, and role models. In women's own voices:

A lot has to do with the environment in which I grew up. My parents were never ones to say well you have got to get this grade or we have got to keep up with the Joneses or they never—that was not their frame of reference. I brought home all As one time and they said you aren't doing any work and it's true, I wasn't. Success or failure was never measured in the terms that traditionally people think about—like how much money you make or do you have a car or something. My whole upbringing during this time these things were not measures of success or failure. It was more are you an honest person, do you have respect for others, do you care about others, do you care enough about yourself to educate yourself and to learn things and make a contribution and just be a decent person. That is success and failure, not any of the more traditional measurements. (p. 95)

I've never been afraid of my successes, although I have succeeded at something and wondered if it was worth it. I can work toward a goal and achieve it and then it's done and I'm proud, but something is always missing. I guess I expect fireworks to go off. I like to succeed at something, but then, on the other hand, it seems like after it's done, it was no big deal after all. (p. 94)

(Paludi & Fankell-Hauser, 1986)

Women's responses to these interview items also suggested that structural or institutional factors facilitated or hindered their career development. Let's now discuss some of these structural factors, beginning with performance evaluation.

STRUCTURAL FACTORS AFFECTING THE CAREER PSYCHOLOGY OF WOMEN

Performance Evaluation

A prejudicial belief in overall male superiority was reflected in Philip Goldberg's (1968) research on **performance evaluation.** Women college students in his research evaluated (in terms of persuasiveness, writing style, intellectual depth of article, competence of author) supposedly published journal articles on linguistics, law, art history, education, dietetics, and city planning. For each article, half of the women participants saw a woman author's name (Joan T. McKay) and half saw a man's (John T. McKay). Results indicated that women rated the article more favorably when it was attributed to a man than a woman (even in fields considered sex-appropriate for women). Goldberg's finding that women may discriminate against other women had considerable impact—especially since this study was published during the initial stages of the reemergence of the women's movement.

Several studies quickly followed Goldberg's. Pheterson, Kiesler, and Goldberg (1971), for example, found that men too devalued women's performance. Adolescents and even young children were found to have evaluation biases against women (Etaugh & Brown, 1975).

Deaux and Emswiller (1974) observed that equivalent performances by women and men are not explained by the same attributions. Performance by a man on a masculine task is typically attributed to skill, whereas an equivalent performance by a woman on the same task is seen to be more influenced by luck. Feldman-Summers and Kiesler's (1974) study indicated that men attributed more ability to a male physician than to a female physician. Men also attributed the female physician's success to ease of course and a large amount of effort. Such findings support those of Deaux and Emswiller (1974). As Deaux (1976) pointed out: "Ability still seems to be firmly established as a male virtue" (p. 31). Research suggests a cognitive link between success and masculinity.

Although the devaluation of women is considered to be well established, it has not always been replicated. For example, the male bias observed in the Goldberg study has not been replicated with older women who are not college students (Pheterson et al., 1971). In addition, women are as likely to be evaluated as being just as competent as men when their performance is (1) acknowledged by an authoritative individual (Taynor & Deaux, 1975), (2) judged on explicit criteria (Isaacs, 1981; Jacobson & Effertz, 1974), (3) judged by unqualified experts in the particular field (Ward, 1981), or (4) successful in male-populated occupations or activities (Taynor & Deaux, 1973). Irene Frieze and her colleagues (1982) and Bernard Whitley and his colleagues (Whitley, McHugh, & Frieze, 1986) performed meta-analyses on research on attributional patterns. Their analyses suggested that the magnitude of the gender difference is small.

Perhaps one explanation for the inconsistencies in results concerns individuals' implicit assumptions about femininity and masculinity brought to research settings. For example, Lisa Strayer and I (1985) focused on the interaction of the sex typing (femininity or masculinity) of a task with the sex of the participants in the research. We asked 300 college students (150 women, 150 men) to evaluate an academic article in the field of the psychology of women (considered feminine by college students), politics (considered masculine), or education (considered sex-neutral). Each article had been assigned a woman's name (Joan T. McKay), a man's name (John T. McKay), no name, initials (J. T. McKay), or a sexually ambiguous name (Chris T. McKay).

We found that an article deemed written by a man was valued more positively than if the author was not identified as a man. We also found that women and men made assumptions about the sex of Chris, J. T., and the unnamed author. Eighty-seven percent of the participants attributed an article on politics to a man, and 96 percent attributed the article on the psychology of women to a woman. Explanations given by participants for their decisions about the author's sex centered around stereotypes about femininity and masculinity:

> Men are associated with economics, business, and politics.

> The author seemed to have insight to the woman's feeling and could relate. I don't think a man would have that kind of insight.

> It's by a man—it's very deep and it talks about what men in big business always talk about.

> Male—because the style was abrupt and to the point.

> Had it been female, it probably would have been a little more artistic or dealt more with the effects of the policies on the average American family. (pp. 358–359)

Individuals' assumptions about women and men and about femininity and masculinity are not easily modified in research settings, thus they probably account for the inconsistency in the results of the research on performance evaluation. The sex composition of the group in which the evaluations are made is an important variable. Women in all-women groups endorse more pro-feminist ideas after reading articles by women than do women in mixed-gender groups. This research suggests, therefore, that men in groups trigger negative biases against women.

In work settings, men are rated higher than equivalent women in performing certain tasks and job qualifications. Similarly, women receive lower recognition and economic rewards for their work than men, and lower prestige, knowledge, and expertise are attributed to them as well. Widely accepted stereotypes depict men, but not women, as having the requisite skills and characteristics for managerial and leadership positions. Business professionals indicate a strong preference for male applicants for a stereotypically masculine job, even when similar information on the resumes of women and men applicants had led to perceptions of similar personality traits (Betz, 1993). These stereotypes persist even though gender differences are NOT found in leadership ability or job performance.

When male teachers and employers attribute women's successes to luck rather than skill, women's level of aspiration remains low. Therefore, many women never establish any occupational life plan or prepare themselves for a career.

Success may have different consequences for women, regardless of whether the field of endeavor is traditionally the province of women. How are a woman's and a man's failure explained? Men's successes and women's failures are attributed to personal dispositions; men's failures and women's successes are attributed to environmental factors. As Deaux (1976) suggested, such differences in causal attributions have important consequences:

> For example, if you believe that a person's success is due to ability, you would be more confident in offering that person a job. . . . In contrast, if you believe the person simply lucked out on one occasion, you would probably not have any great confidence in the person's future success. Thus, just as stereotypes may affect performance judgments, so the explanations of these performances may affect future behaviors that can perpetuate the stereotypes of women and men. (pp. 32–33)

Gatekeepers of Women's Careers

The devaluing of women not only influences decisions about abilities and achievements but also tends to devalue female-related activities and topics (Weinstein, 1999). Research conducted on mentoring, for example, suggests that attributions made by male mentors for female proteges are different from attributions they make for their male proteges (DeFour & Paludi, 1992; Fleming, 1996). Male mentors indicated that they perceived a woman's apprenticing herself to them as requiring help—remedial assistance. Male proteges, however, are perceived by male mentors as individuals whose careers need to be developed. This raises a serious paradox, as Marianne LaFrance (1987) has recently commented. As women continue to get the mentoring they need, they will be seen as needing the mentoring they get. Greater male helpfulness is due to definitions of help in terms of heroic and chivalrous acts (Young, 1998). When men with this view are mentoring women, each woman is in a culturally defined relationship vis-à-vis the man. Thus, attributions for the women's success will be external—due to the help of their mentor, a man. This attribution bias also holds true for racially minority women (Carty, 1992). As women noted:

> When we talk about Black issues in class I am called upon, but not at any other time. I am always used as an example. As far as White students go, I am usually ignored if I attend social events.

> When I first came to the department, I was the "token" needed for affirmative action purposes. Now I believe that among Whites I am viewed with suspicion. I also feel some sense of competitive concern among minority men.

> We have no real faculty mentoring or support programs for Black women faculty. What we need is a program similar to the one created for students. Why not a faculty mentor

program for minority faculty? Why not special assistance programs, released time, research grants for minorities and women only?

(Moses, 1988, pp. 3, 14, 16)

Women who work in education, especially ethnic minority women, are viewed as "others," as "outsiders." When women combine lifestyle and vocational roles, they are frequently viewed negatively in at least one (most often, both) sphere. For example, Phyllis Bronstein and her colleagues (Bronstein, Black, Pfennig, & White, 1986) found that male mentors, in their letters of recommendation of female protégés for faculty positions, described the women's family responsibilities as a burden. We need to consider the reactions of individuals reading these descriptions—individuals who will consider which applicant would be more willing to relocate and who would make the most promising and productive colleague. What is also interesting is that none of the women applicants mentioned lifestyle/family status in their resume or cover letters; male mentors, however, mentioned it.

The stereotype-based attributions for women's achievement by male mentors are further illustrated by older women's career development. Mentoring typically occurs during a transitional period in an individual's life. Although some transitions for women and men are alike (e.g., from college to first job), others are not. Transitions that are different include some that older women are much more likely to experience, including transitions from homemaker to full-time worker or from homemaker to college student. These different transitions for women may negatively affect their mentoring opportunities because they seem "out of step" with well-known career transitions for men. That is, a newly divorced 45-year-old woman who is making a transition from full-time homemaking to her first job in business does not resemble either a 22–year-old man who enters business immediately after completing college or a 45-year-old man whose career transition most likely is from mid- to upper-level management. As a consequence of the timing of their transitions, women probably have fewer prospects of finding a mentor willing to invest in them and their "shortened" career in business (Young, 1998).

Thus, in cross-sex mentoring relationships (where the woman is the protégé and the man is the mentor), it may be difficult for a woman to achieve colleague status because of stereotyping of women as helpers and subordinates (Young, 1998). Some men may assume paternal roles with women protégés to avoid sexual rumors and/or involvement. This strategy, however, creates a dependent relationship for women, who are typically inhibited by the mentor from growing out of the relationship and into a more egalitarian one (Fleming, 1996; Young, 1998). Women may need to be especially independent in developing their own style, interests, goals, and achievements if they are to attain full professional status in the eyes of colleagues (Betz, 1993).

Sex Discrimination

As the research on sexual harassment (see Chapter 10) suggests, the progress of women in higher education and in the workforce has long been impeded by **sex discrimination.** Not until 1833 was the first woman allowed admission to a college, Oberlin College in Ohio. But even at Oberlin, a highly progressive institution for its day, women primarily learned the arts and home economics, which were "intended to prepare them for homemaking or teaching" (Deckard, 1983, p. 245). Oberlin College women students were discouraged from pursuing academic programs considered "too strenuous" for women, such as science and commerce, which were areas of study considered suitable "for men only" (Flexner, 1971). Women were required to engage in nonacademic duties:

> Washing the men's clothes, caring for their rooms, serving them at table, listening to their orations, but themselves remaining respectfully silent in public assemblages, the Oberlin "coeds" were being prepared for intelligent motherhood and a properly subservient wifehood. (Flexner, 1971, p. 30)

Faye Crosby (1982, 1984) found that even though women college students and employees reported that they believed women in general are subject to sex discrimination at work, they did not see any discrimination in their own lives.

Increasing numbers of women are employed today—more than ever before—and a large proportion of these women have sole financial responsibility for their families. When it comes to the salaries these women earn, one fact stands out: As a group, women earn significantly less than men. To highlight the wage disparity, the average employed woman must work nearly 8 1/2 days to earn as much as the average employed man earns in 5 days. The disparity is greater when we look at women of color's salaries as compared to men's salaries. When job category, education, and experience are taken into account, there still is a wide disparity. In addition, there are higher admission requirements for women than for men applicants, sex quotas for admission, discrimination in the award of financial aid, and age restrictions on enrollment that constitute age and sex discrimination against women (Betz, 1993).

Jessie Bernard (1988) has characterized the effects of such discriminatory behavior as the **inferiority curriculum,** which contributes to women students' feeling depressed and frustrated and doubting their competency and self-worth. Jo Freeman (1975) described education for women as the **null environment.** A null environment is one that neither encourages nor discourages women—it simply ignores them. The impact of the null environment is to leave women at the mercy of random personal and/or environmental resources to which they have access. As Freeman stated:

> An academic situation that neither encourages nor discourages students of either sex is inherently discriminatory against women because it fails to take into account the differentiating external environments from which women and men students come. (p. 221)

Bernice Lott (1996) also pointed out that men tend to distance themselves from women and that this overt behavior has important social significance:

> Regardless of what it may tell us about feelings and beliefs, interpersonal distancing tells us something about face-to-face discrimination, per se. When one person avoids, withdraws, or distances from another, this behavior directly and clearly denotes separation or exclusion. (p. 61)

In the workplace, research suggests that women in sex-atypical occupations encounter a "glass ceiling" as they work for promotion to more senior-level positions. A "glass ceiling" refers to invisible barriers that prohibit employees (predominantly women and racial minorities) from reaching senior level positions (Maume, 1999; Williams, 1995).

FACILITATORS OF WOMEN'S CAREER DEVELOPMENT

Maternal Employment

One powerful facilitator of women's career development is **maternal employment** (Betz, 1993; Hoffman & Youngblade, 1999). Daughters of employed mothers are more career-oriented (versus home-oriented) than are daughters of full-time homemakers (Gottfried, Gottfried, Bathurst, & Killian, 1999; Hoffman & Youngblade, 1999; Hyde, Klein, Essex, & Clark, 1995). Daughters of employed mothers are also more willing to pursue nontraditional careers than are daughters of full-time homemakers (Hoffman & Youngblade, 1999). Betz (1993) reported that girls socialized by two employed parents were more likely to combine lifestyle and work roles than girls not reared in such families. Thus, maternal employment influences women's career development through its provision of a role model of women's employment and integration of roles (Gottfried et al., 1999). Consequently, girls and women whose mothers are/were employed have less restricted views of gender roles.

Research has also found that employed mothers place considerable emphasis on independence training (Hoffman & Youngblade, 1999). Research with ethnic minority individuals has consistently demonstrated that maternal employment is positively associated with academic achievement (Burchinal, Roberts, Nabors, & Bryant, 1996; Clark-Stewart, 1993; Hoffman & Youngblade, 1999).

Complementing maternal employment, per se, are the effects of the mothers' feelings about work and the nature and quality of the child care received. When children are in high-quality child care, there is no negative impact on their emotional adjustment or their relationship with their mothers (Caruso, 1996). Quality child care has been operationally defined in the following way, according to the American Public Health Association and the American Academy of Pediatrics:

> Child-staff ratios of three to one for children under 25 months, four to one for children 25 to 30 months and seven to one for children 31 to 35 months.

> Group sizes of six for children under 25 months, eight for children 25 to 30 months and 14 for children 31 to 35 months.

> Child-care providers who have formal, post-high school training in child development, early childhood education or a related field for all child-care workers at all ages.

Failure to meet these standards undermines child development (Burchinal et al., 1996; Phillips, Vovan, Kisker, Howes, & Whitebook, 1994).

Women's primary role decisions of career, noncareer work, or homemaking typically do not parallel those of their mothers, but are related to their mother's messages to them (Hoffman & Youngblade, 1999). In addition to mothers' encouragement of their daughters' success is their concomitant lack of pressure toward culturally defined expectations of femininity. Mothers who exert less pressure on their daughters to date, marry, and mother have more career-oriented daughters (Betz, 1993). Mothers who were dissatisfied with the types of jobs available to them might encourage their daughters to achieve more than they themselves had.

Within the United States, the role expectations for girls have many similarities, but they also vary, depending on social class, sexual orientation, and the ethnicity of the family and the surrounding community (Reskin, 1998). Research has suggested greater flexibility and permissiveness in middle-class homes, regardless of ethnicity

(Reid et al., 1995). This flexibility leads to the availability of masculine activity choices for girls. In working-class homes, parents are more concerned that their children adhere strictly to sex-appropriate behavior, as it is stereotypically defined (Reid et al., 1995). Marjorie Hill (1988) noted that lesbian mothers perceived their daughters and sons to be more similar in characteristics than did heterosexual mothers. Lesbian mothers also held less stereotypic ideas relating to the feminine role and encouraged more traditionally masculine role expectations of their daughters (Hill, 1988).

Maternal employment usually benefits the mother herself; research suggests that maternal employment is a boost to the morale of mothers and a buffer against anxieties (Hoffman & Youngblade, 1999). There are, however, stressors related to the integration of family and work roles, as discussed in Chapter 4. For example, the employment of women, particularly those with preschool children, generally necessitates an alternative to parental child care for at least a portion of the workday (Gottfried et al., 1999).

Claire Etaugh and Karen Nekolny (1988) suggested another stressor for employed mothers: the perceptions people hold about mothers who work in addition to caring for children. Read the following description and compare your own views to the participants in Etaugh and Nekolny's study:

> Ann Davis is 36, divorced, and has a one-year-old child. She has a master's degree from the University of Illinois in counseling psychology. She works full time as a counseling psychologist. What do you think about Ann? How would you describe her? (p. 225)

This description was shared with individuals shopping at a mall in Illinois. Variants on this description of Ann included her being married and not working since the birth of her child. Results indicated that employed mothers (especially married mothers) were perceived as more professionally competent than nonemployed mothers. However, employed mothers were perceived as less dedicated to their families and less sensitive to the needs of others than were nonemployed mothers! Etaugh and Nekolny also found that divorced employed mothers were rated as less professionally competent than married employed mothers. Married women were viewed as better adjusted than unmarried women.

Supportive Fathers

Researchers have suggested that fathers play an important role in high school girls' and college women's career choices (Cabrera, Tamis-LeMonda, Bradley, Hof-

---

MEET DR. LUCIA GILBERT

Dr. Lucia Gilbert is Professor of Educational Psychology at the University of Texas at Austin. Her teaching and research focus on various aspects of the psychology of women: role modeling and mentoring, concepts of gender and family life.

Question: What have you concluded from your research on role models and mentors?

Dr. Gilbert's response: Here are some suggestions for women students currently in search of a mentor:

1. Look for someone who holds similar values in areas important to you. For example, if you see yourself as a feminist, seek someone who shares these views. You need to remember that not all women hold feminist views and that not all men do not. Feminism can vary greatly in its personal meaning. Let your mentor have some differences from you without condemning her/him or yourself.

2. Look for someone who is willing and able to enter into a collaborative relationship with you.

3. Seek out possible mentors; don't wait to be picked.

---

ferth, & Lamb, 2000; Lamb, 1999). For example, Margaret Hennig and Anne Jardim (1977) reported that fathers were important as role models and sources of support for their daughters. Fathers' support is more important when girls and women are working in a nontraditional career than when they are choosing a career. Fathers' greatest influence may occur after their daughters select a nontraditional career.

Mentors

Arguments in favor of women **mentors** for women have stressed the importance of women's identification with other women, the significance of the information provided by the woman mentor's behavior, and the positive incentive through women's illustrative success (Fleming, 1996; Young, 1998). Women have been advised to find a woman mentor and to be one to other women. Lucia Gilbert and her colleagues (Gilbert, Gallessich, & Evans, 1983) observed that women graduate students who identified women professors as their mentors viewed themselves as more career-oriented, confident, and instrumental than did women who identified with men professors. Women students paired with women also reported higher satisfaction with their student role than women (or men) students paired with a man.

A feminist perspective on mentoring stresses the reciprocal nature of mentoring relationships (Gilbert & Rossman, 1992). Moore (1984) advocated an emphasis on **womentoring,** which she contends is the sharing of power, competence, self, and differences. Swoboda and Millar (1986) advocated **networking mentoring,** in which two or more women fulfill the roles of mentor and protégé to each other at different times in the relationship. Both approaches are egalitarian rather than hierarchical and are based on a belief in mutual enhancement. The advantages of networking mentoring include: It is open to all women (not just a select few who find someone to mentor them); it has fewer relational problems that stem from intensity; it has greater self-reliance and therefore less resentment by colleagues concerned about favoritism; it provides an opportunity to learn how to mentor; and there are no setbacks related to a mentor's career problems (Young, 1998).

Women faculty (especially untenured women faculty) may have less time available to be mentors. Because they face more structural barriers to career advancement, they must spend considerably more time than their male colleagues performing their jobs and advancing their careers in the academy (Makosky & Paludi, 1990).

Darlene DeFour (1991) noted that, because of time constraints and the number of requests for a mentoring relationship by potential protégés, ethnic minority women may be less likely to mentor. She further noted:

> Minority students are at a disadvantage in forming mentor-protégé relationships due to the small number of minority faculty members. This is not to say that nonminority faculty cannot serve as effective mentors for ethnic students. However . . . nonminority faculty are less willing to initiate mentor-protégé relationships with minority students. (p. 14)

Research by DeFour (1991) and Yolanda Moses (1988) provides compelling evidence of the importance of African American faculty in the retention of African American graduate and undergraduate students. Contact with African American faculty is associated with better academic performance and psychological well-being. Moreover, African American faculty may serve as role models for African American students (DeFour & Hirsch, 1990).

As African American women faculty have noted:

> Because of the paucity of Black professors at my university, I am placed in the dilemma of being all things to all Black students. Note that there are only two other females (in a university of 16,000 students), one in the school of medicine and the other in agriculture—and both . . . have little contact with Black students.

White professors contribute to this problem of overwork for me because they refer Black students who are experiencing difficulties to me. When I first arrived at the university (my first professional appointment), I enjoyed the attention I received. After a short while, however, I realized that the responsibility associated with being the only Black female in my college, and only one of a handful in the university, was overwhelming. I have suffered several instances of burnout and exhaustion. As a consequence I have learned to maintain a less visible profile as a coping and survival strategy.

(Moses, 1988, pp. 15–16)

CAREER COUNSELING

To be effective for women, career counselors need to be aware that the choices women have made concerning their careers may have been constrained by gender-role stereotypes, discriminatory behavior, home-versus-career conflicts, and math anxiety (Farmer et al., 1999; Juntunen, 1996). Miles (1995) noted that school counselors provide little useful career information to high school girls: More than 70 percent of the 600 girls interviewed for this research reported that the career advice they received at school was inadequate or not helpful. Counselors can facilitate women's career development by restoring to women options that societal pressures have taken away from them (Betz & Schifano, 2000). This process can involve several techniques, including (1) encouraging women to make decisions that leave their options open until *they* are ready to reject them for appropriate reasons, and (2) asking women how their beliefs about women and women's roles influence their choices about their careers, and then sharing with them the research on women's vocational development. Betz (1993) and Lupart and Barva (1998) also recommend that counselors introduce adolescent girls to women role models, work with girls to manage anxiety about a career, and provide active support and encouragement to girls' efforts to develop skills and competencies. Counselors need to support and encourage women as they confront barriers to meeting their career goals (Juntunen, 1996).

Other psychologists have focused their work on intervention in adolescent girls' lives so that they will not have negative self-identities as women, students, and employees. For example, Carol Gilligan has worked with adolescent girls at the Emma Willard School in Troy, New York, and at the Laurel School in Cleveland, Ohio. Gilligan (1990) and her colleagues reported that until girls are 11 years old, they typically assert themselves, speak openly about what they are feeling, and accept conflict

FIGURE 9.2   *Dr. Carol Gilligan.*

Dr. Gilligan suggests that adolescent girls encounter a "wall of prohibition." She has developed programs for helping girls feel central to their educational curriculum.

as healthy, as part of relationships. At adolescence, however, girls begin to use statements such as "I don't know." They fear that speaking of their opinions and feelings will anger people; consequently, they keep silent. And they settle for idealized relationships in which all people are "nice" (Pattatucci, 1998). Mary Field Belenky and colleagues (Belenky, Clinchy, Goldberger, & Tarule, 1986) also reported that women whom they interviewed believed themselves to be "voiceless" and "mindless," incapable of learning from authority. Along these lines, Gilligan suggests that adolescent girls encounter a **wall of prohibition.** She noted:

> The struggle girls go through in adolescence has been observed before, but nobody interpreted it the way we do. Psychologists have seen it as a struggle for autonomy. Our work suggests that adolescence is a time of repression for girls. (1990, p. A8)

Gilligan and her colleagues have developed programs for helping women teachers assess their relationships with girls, their own gender-role stereotypes, and the ways in which they themselves had been silenced during adolescence. The goal of the intervention in the lives of adolescent girls is to make girls feel central, not marginal, to education and work. Through writing and performing plays, adolescent girls are learning to explore their skills and be confident in their own perspectives in public.

RETHINKING CAREER PSYCHOLOGY: THE IMPACT OF WOMEN'S WAYS OF LEARNING AND WORKING

The research reviewed in this chapter has suggested new agendas for the vocational psychology of women. The person-centered (or sociopsychological) explanations and the situation-centered (or structural) explanations for women's career development suggest different strategies for improving women's education and employment conditions. The person-centered explanations propose that women can advance by taking courses to make them more assertive or more skilled in conducting meetings or seeking a mentor. Women who "improve" themselves still face hostility on the job, pay inequity, and sex discrimination. Person-centered approaches stress that women should adopt a traditionally masculine approach to problems.

The situation-centered explanations propose different strategies: training managers to use sex-fair rating scales, presenting affirmative action policies appropriately, and eliminating women's token status. Feminist objectives will not be achieved without structural changes in the economy and in society. Of the barriers, the external ones are most important and most serious, yet people often deliberately ignore them and "blame the victim" rather than instituting social change.

We should abandon the expectation that women in the workforce and in education rate highly in both feminine and masculine personality characteristics—independence and dependence, assertiveness and passivity, depending on the situation. Androgyny is not the ideal human situation we thought it to be; it does not lead to degenderizing behavior (see Chapter 4). We should be able to figure out what behavior in the workplace or classroom is ideal for adults, without having to rely on terms such as femininity and masculinity. Androgyny tempts us to believe that the solution to sex discrimination in education and employment lies in changing the individual. Androgyny is not a solution to our present social problems in the area of women's career development.

Areas that are considered successful usually have a masculine bias. Success may be represented by achievement at a prestigious occupation, academic excellence, and other accomplishments that are associated with masculine, heterosexual values. Accomplishments that are associated with traditionally feminine values or lesbian values receive little or no attention. Women may manage a household and children; yet, this kind of accomplishment has traditionally not been studied in light of achievement motivation and work. Traditional educational and occupational policies reflect the separation of work and family life and the societal expectation that mothers remain at home to care for their children (see Chapter 1). There is, thus, a general incompatibility between the school/workplace and family demands; there is also a relative lack of provisions to ease women's integration of these roles (Cleveland, Stockdale, & Murphy, 2000; DeCenzo & Robbins, 1999). These conditions may produce greater potential stress and conflict among student and working mothers, who hold the primary responsibility for child rearing and child care.

BOX 9.1
JOB ANNOUNCEMENT

Requirements:
  Intelligence, good health, energy, sociability, patience
Skills:
  At least 12 different occupations
Hours:
  99.6 hours per week
Salary:
  None
Holidays:
  None; will be required to remain on stand-by 24 hours a day, seven days a week
Opportunities for Advancement:
  None
Job Security:
  None. Trend is toward more layoffs, particularly as employee approaches middle age. Severance pay will depend on discretion of the employer.
Fringe Benefits:
  Food, clothing, and shelter generally provided, but any additional bonuses will depend on financial standing and good nature of employer. No health, medical, or accident insurance, no social security, no pension plan.

(Adapted from Phyllis Chesler: *Women, Money, and Power,* Bantam Books, 1976)

Many universities and businesses have adopted family-oriented policies such as job sharing, flexible work hours, or employer-sponsored day care as an employee benefit. These organizations have found positive ramifications for the schools and businesses as well as for parents, including lower absenteeism, higher morale, positive publicity, lower turnover, child-care hours that conform to work hours, and access to quality infant and child care (Anderson-Kulman & Paludi, 1986; DeCenzo & Robbins, 1999).

The field of career psychology needs to redefine achievement and achievement-related issues in a way that does not keep women's realities and choices invisible. This will be accomplished by affirming values that women bring to education, work, and relationships. We will return to this issue in Chapter 11.

NEW TERMS

achievement motivation

attribution process

cognitive attribution theory of achievement motivation

direct achieving styles

facilitators of women's career development

homogenization of American women

idiographic approach to the measurement of women's success striving

inferiority curriculum

maternal employment

mentors

motherhood mandate

networking mentoring

null environment

performance evaluation

relational achieving styles

sex discrimination

sociopsychological factors affecting achievement

structural factors affecting achievement

Thematic Apperception Test (TAT)

wall of prohibition

womentoring

Work and Family Orientation Questionnaire (WOFO)

CHAPTER REVIEW QUESTIONS

1. Discuss ways in which the goals of education are translated very differently for girls/women and for boys/men.

2. Summarize the literature on girls' and women's use of occupational stereotypes in their career choice.

3. Give examples of behaviors that can contribute to a chilly classroom environment for girls and women. Offer suggestions for eliminating these behaviors.

4. Cite some reasons for the failure of vocational psychologists to have studied women until recently.

5. Discuss some gender-related differences in vocational choice and development.

6. Explain what Sandra Bem and Daryl Bem meant by the "homogenization of American women."

7. Distinguish between sociopsychological and structural factors affecting women's career development.

8. Cite the methodological problems in the early research on achievement motivation.

9. Discuss the critiques of the literature on the fear-of-success construct.

10. What causal attribution patterns do many women use in explaining their successes and failures?

11. Summarize the literature on mentoring for women.

12. Discuss what Bernard means by the inferiority curriculum for girls and women.

13. Summarize the research on facilitators of women's career development.

14. Summarize Gilligan's research with girls' self-concept and self-esteem during adolescence.

SELECTED READINGS

Cleveland, J., Stockdale, M., & Murphy, K. (2000). *Women and men in organizations: Sex and gender issues at work*. Mahwah, NJ: Erlbaum.

Hoffman, L., & Youngblade, L. (1999). *Mothers at work: Effects on children's well being*. New York: Cambridge University Press.

Pattatucci, A. (Ed.). (1998). *Women in science: Meeting career challenges*. Thousand Oaks, CA: Sage.

LEARNING MORE ABOUT . . .

Suggestions for Term Papers and Independent Studies Related to the *Career Psychology of Women*

Impact of same-sex and cross-sex mentors on women's career development

The Glass Ceiling Initiative of the U.S. Department of Labor

On-site day care centers: Impact on mothers' career development and well-being

Pay equity and comparable worth

New legislation on parental leaves

Race discrimination in education and employment

TAKING ACTION . . .

on the *Career Psychology of Women*

Try comparing the "silent language" of your psychology of women class with the "silent language" of another non-women-centered class you are currently taking. Specifically, jot down your impressions in answer to the following questions for each of the two classes:

1. When making general statements about women (or any other group), are the two professors basing these statements on accurate information?
2. Are universal generalizations about any social group, such as "Women don't think geographically," made in class?
3. Is there "humor" in the form of gratuitous remarks that demean or belittle people because of sex or sexual orientation?
4. Do the faculty members avoid using generic masculine terms to refer to both sexes?
5. Do the faculty members:
   a. Give more time to men than to women students?
   b. Pay more attention to men's responses than to women's?
   c. Direct more of their own questions to men than to women?
   d. Assume a heterosexual model when referring to human behavior?

What suggestions would you make to the professors if you had an opportunity to do so?

REFERENCES

Alper, T. (1974). Achievement motivation in college women: A now-you-see-it-now-you-don't phenomenon. *American Psychologist, 29,* 194–203.

Anderson-Kulman, R., & Paludi, M. (1986). Working mothers and the family context: Predicting positive coping. *Journal of Vocational Behavior, 28,* 241–253.

Arroyo, C., & Ziegler, E. (1995). Racial identity, academic achievement, and the psychological well-being of economically disadvantaged adolescents. *Journal of Personality and Social Psychology, 69,* 903–914.

Atkinson, J. W. (Ed.). (1958). *Motives in fantasy, action, and society.* Princeton, NJ: Van Nostrand.

Belenky, M. F., Clinchy, B., Goldberger, N., & Tarule, J. (1986). *Women's ways of knowing: The development of self, voice, and mind.* New York: Basic Books.

Bem, D., & Bem, S. (1970). Case study of a nonconscious ideology: Teaching the woman to know her place. In D. J. Bem (Ed.), *Beliefs, attitudes and human affairs.* Monterey, CA: Brooks/Cole.

Bernard, J. (1988). The inferiority curriculum. *Psychology of Women Quarterly, 12,* 261–268.

Betz, N. (1993). Career development. In F. L. Denmark & M. A. Paludi (Eds.), *Psychology of women: A handbook of issues and theories.* Westport, CT: Greenwood Press.

Betz, N., & Fitzgerald, L. F. (1987). *The career psychology of women.* New York: Academic Press.

Betz, N., & Schifano, R. (2000). Evaluation of an intervention to increase realistic self-efficacy and interests in college women. *Journal of Vocational Behavior, 56,* 35–52.

Birenbaum, M., & Kraemer, R. (1995). Gender and ethnic-group differences in causal attributions for success and failure in mathematics and language examinations. *Journal of Cross-Cultural Psychology, 26,* 342–359.

Bronstein, P., Black, L., Pfennig, J., & White, A. (1986). Getting academic jobs: Are women equally qualified and equally successful? *American Psychologist, 41,* 318–322.

Burchinal, M., Roberts, J., Nabors, L., & Bryant, D. (1996). Quality of center child care and infant cognitive and language development. *Child Development, 67,* 606–620.

Cabrera, N., Tamis-LeMonda, C., Bradley, R., Hofferth, S., & Lamb, M. (2000). Fatherhood in the twenty-first century. *Child Development, 71,* 127–136.

Carty, L. (1992). Black women in academia: A statement from the periphery. In H. Bannerji, L. Carty, K. Dehli, S. Heald, & K. McKenna (Eds.), *Unsettling relations: The university as a site of feminist struggles.* Boston: South End Press.

Caruso, D. (1996). Maternal employment status, mother-infant interaction, and infant development. *Child and Youth Care Forum, 25,* 125–134.

Cherry, F., & Deaux, K. (1975, May). *Fear of success versus fear of gender-inconsistent behavior: A sex similarity.* Paper presented at the annual meeting of the Midwestern Psychological Association, Chicago.

Clark-Stewart, A. (1993). *Daycare.* Cambridge, MA: Harvard University Press.

Cleveland, J., Stockdale, M., & Murphy, K. (2000). *Women and men in organizations: Sex and gender issues at work.* Mahwah, NJ: Erlbaum.

Cohen, N. (1974). *Explorations in the fear of success.* Unpublished doctoral dissertation, Columbia University, New York.

Commission on Professionals in Science and Technology. (1992). *Professional women and minorities.* Washington, DC: Author.

Crosby, F. (1982). *Relative deprivation and working women.* New York: Oxford University Press.

Crosby, F. (1984). Relative deprivation in organizational settings. *Research in Organizational Behavior, 6,* 51–93.

Deaux, K. (1976). *The behavior of women and men.* Monterey, CA: Brooks/Cole.

Deaux, K., & Emswiller, T. (1974). Explanations of successful performance on sex-linked tasks: What's skill for the male is luck for the female. *Journal of Personality and Social Psychology, 29,* 80–85.

DeCenzo, D., & Robbins, S. (1996). *Human resource management.* New York: Wiley.

Deckard, B. (1983). *The women's movement.* New York: Harper & Row.

DeFour, D. C. (1991). Issues in mentoring ethnic minority students. *Focus, 5,* 1–2.

DeFour, D. C., & Hirsch, B. J. (1990). The adaptation of black graduate students: A social networks approach. *American Journal of Community Psychology, 18,* 489–505.

DeFour, D. C., & Paludi, M. A. (1992). The Mentoring Experiences Questionnaire. *Mentoring International, 6,* 19–23.

Doyle, J., & Paludi, M. (1997). *Sex and gender* (3rd ed). Dubuque, IA: Brown.

Eccles, J. (1994). Understanding women's educational and occupational choices: Applying the Eccles et al. model of achievement-related choices. *Psychology of Women Quarterly, 18,* 585–610.

Etaugh, C., & Brown, B. (1975). Perceiving the causes of success and failure of male and female performers. *Developmental Psychology, 11,* 103.

Etaugh, C., & Nekolny, K. (1988, August). *Perceptions of mothers: Effects of employment status and marital status.* Paper presented at the annual conference of the American Psychological Association, Atlanta.

Farmer, H., Wardrop, J., & Rotella, S. (1999). Antecedent factors differentiating women and men in science/nonscience careers. *Psychology of Women Quarterly, 23,* 763–780.

Feldman-Summers, S. A., & Kiesler, S. (1974). Those who are number two try harder: The effect of sex on attributions of causality. *Journal of Personality and Social Psychology, 30,* 846–855.

Fleming, J. (1996). *Who are the proteges? The relationship between mentoring experiences, self-efficacy, career salience, attachment style, and Eriksonian life stage.* Doctoral dissertation submitted to the School of Arts and Sciences, Columbia University, New York.

Flexner, E. (1971). *Century of struggle.* New York: Atheneum.

Freeman, J. (1975). How to discriminate against women without really trying. In J. Freeman (Ed.), *Women.* Palo Alto, CA: Mayfield.

Frieze, I. H., Whitley, B., Hanusa, B., & McHugh, M. (1982). Assessing the theoretical models for sex differences in causal attributions for success and failure. *Sex Roles, 8,* 333–343.

Gilbert, L., Gallessich, J. M., & Evans, S. (1983). Sex of faculty role model and students' self-perceptions of competency. *Sex Roles, 9*, 597–607.

Gilbert, L., & Rossman, K. (1992). Gender and mentoring process for women: Implications for professional development. *Professional Psychology: Research and Practice, 23*, 233–238.

Gilligan, C. (1990). Prologue. In C. Gilligan, N. Lyons, & T. Hanmer (Eds.), *Making connections.* Cambridge, MA: Harvard University Press.

Ginorio, A., Gutierrez, L., Cauce, A., & Acosta, M. (1995). Psychological issues for Latinas. In H. Landrine (Ed.), *Bringing cultural diversity to feminist psychology.* Washington, DC: American Psychological Association.

Goldberg, P. (1968). Are women prejudiced against women? *Transaction, 5*, 28–30.

Golombok, S., & Fivush, R. (1994). *Gender development.* Cambridge: Cambridge University Press.

Gottfried, A., Gottfried, A., Bathurst, K., & Killian, C. (1999). Maternal and dual-earner employment: Family environment, adaptations, and the developmental impingement perspective. In M. Lamb et al. (Eds.), *Parenting and child development in "nontraditional" families.* Mahwah, NJ: Erlbaum.

Gravenkemper, S. A., & Paludi, M. A. (1983). Fear of success revisited: Introducing an ambiguous cue. *Sex Roles, 9*, 897–900.

Haag, P. (1999). *Voices of a generation: Teenage girls on sex, school, and self.* Washington, DC: American Association of University Women.

Hall, R., & Sandler, B. (1982). *The classroom climate: A chilly one for women.* Washington, DC: Project on the Status and Education of Women.

Hennig, M., & Jardim, A. (1977). *The managerial woman.* New York: Anchor/ Doubleday.

Hill, M. (1988). Child-rearing attitudes of black lesbian mothers. In Boston Lesbian Psychologies Collective (Eds.), *Lesbian psychologies: Explorations and challenges.* Urbana: University of Illinois Press.

Hoffman, L. (1974). The employment of women, education, and fertility. *Merrill-Palmer Quarterly, 20*, 99–119.

Hoffman, L., & Youngblade L. (1999). Maternal employment, morale and parenting style: Social class comparisons. *Journal of Applied Developmental Psychology, 19*, 398–413.

Horner, M. (1968). *Sex differences in achievement motivation and performance in competitive and noncompetitive situations.* Unpublished doctoral dissertation, University of Michigan.

Horner, M. S. (1970). The motive to avoid success and changing aspirations of college women. In *Women on Campus 1970: A symposium.* Ann Arbor, MI: Center for Continuing Education of Women.

Hyde, J., Klein, M., Essex, M., & Clark, R. (1995). Maternity leave and women's mental health. *Psychology of Women Quarterly, 19*, 257–285.

Isaacs, M. B. (1981). Sex-role stereotyping and the evaluation of the performance of women: Changing trends. *Psychology of Women Quarterly, 6,* 187–195.

Jacobson, M., & Effertz, J. (1974). Sex roles and leadership. Perception of the leaders and the led. *Organizational Behavior and Human Performance, 12,* 383–396.

Juntunen, C. (1996). Relationship between a feminist approach to career counseling and career self-efficacy beliefs. *Journal of Employment Counseling, 33,* 130–143.

LaFrance, M. (1987). *Paradoxes in mentoring.* Paper presented at the International Interdisciplinary Congress on Women, Dublin, Ireland.

LaFromboise, T., Choney, S., James, A., & Running Wolf, P. (1995). American Indian women and psychology. In H. Landrine (Ed.), *Bringing cultural diversity to feminist psychology.* Washington, DC: American Psychological Association.

Lamb, M. (Ed.). (1997). *The role of the father in child development.* New York: Wiley.

Landrine, H. (Ed.). (1995). *Bringing cultural diversity to feminist psychology.* Washington, DC: American Psychological Association.

Lipman-Blumen, J. (1972). How ideology shapes women's lives. *Scientific American, 226,* 34–42.

Lipman-Blumen, J., Handley-Isaksen, A., & Leavitt, H. (1983). Achieving styles in men and women: A model, an instrument, and some findings. In J. T. Spence (Ed.), *Achievement and achievement motives.* San Francisco: Freeman.

Lippert-Martin, K. (1992). The classroom climate: What has changed, what has made a difference? In Association of American Colleges (Ed.), *On Campus with Women, 21,* 1–5, 10.

Lott, B. (1996). The perils and promise of studying sexist discrimination in face-to-face situations. In M. Paludi (Ed.), *Sexual harassment on college campuses: Abusing the ivory power.* Albany: State University of New York Press.

Lupart, J., & Barva, C. (1998). Promoting female achievement in the sciences: Research and implications. *International Journal for the Advancement of Counseling, 20,* 319–338.

Makosky, V. P., & Paludi, M. A. (1990). Feminism and women' studies in the academy. In M. A. Paludi & G. A. Steuernagel (Eds.), *Foundations for a feminist restructuring of the academic disciplines.* New York: Haworth Press.

Maume, D. (1999). Glass ceilings and glass escalators: Occupational segregation and race and sex differences in managerial promotions. *Work and Occupations, 26,* 483–509.

McClelland, D. (1961). *The achieving society.* New York: Van Nostrand.

Miles, T. (1995, April 25). Girls complaint of "poor" school careers advice. *PA News* (Internet).

Monahan, L., Kuhn, D., & Shaver, P. (1974). Intrapsychic vs. cultural explanations of the fear of success motive. *Journal of Personality and Social Psychology, 29,* 60–64.

Moore, K. (1984). Careers in college and university administration: How are women affected? In A. Tinsley, C. Secord, & S. Kaplan (Eds.), *Women in higher education administration.* San Francisco: Jossey-Bass.

Moses, Y. (1988). *Black women in the academy.* Washington, DC: Project on the Status and Education of Women.

Odean, K. (1997). *Great books for girls.* New York: Ballantine.

Paludi, M. A. (1984). Psychometric properties and underlying assumptions of four objective measures of fear of success. *Sex Roles, 10,* 765–781.

Paludi, M. A., & Fankell-Hauser, J. (1986). An idiographic approach to the study of women's achievement strivings. *Psychology of Women Quarterly, 10,* 89–100.

Paludi, M. A., & Strayer, L. (1985). What's in an author's name? Differential evaluations of performance as a function of author's name. *Sex Roles, 12,* 353–361.

Pappo, M. (1972). *Fear of success: An empirical and theoretical analysis.* Unpublished doctoral dissertation, Teachers College, Columbia University, New York.

Pattatucci, A. (Ed.). (1998). *Women in science: Meeting career challenges.* Thousand Oaks, CA: Sage.

Pfost, K., & Fiore, M. (1990). Pursuit of nontraditional occupations: Fear of success or fear of not being chosen. *Sex Roles, 23,* 15–24.

Pheterson, G., Kiesler, S., & Goldberg, P. (1971). Evaluation of the performance of women as a function of their sex, achievement, and personal history. *Journal of Personality and Social Psychology, 19,* 114–118.

Phillips, D., Voran, M., Kisker, E., Howes, C., & Whitebook, M. (1994). Child care for children in poverty: Opportunity or inequity? *Child Development, 65,* 472–492.

Reid, P., Haritos, C., Kelly, E., & Holland, N. (1995). Socialization of girls: Issues of ethnicity in gender development. In H. Landrine (Ed.), *Bringing cultural diversity to feminist psychology: Theory, research and practice.* Washington, DC: American Psychological Association.

Reskin, B. (1998). Bringing men back in: Sex differentiation and the devaluation of women's work. In K. Myers et al. (Eds.), *Feminist foundations: Toward transforming sociology.* Thousand Oaks, CA: Sage.

Romer, N. (1974). *Sex differences in the development of achievement-related motives, sex role identity, and performance.* Unpublished doctoral dissertation, University of Michigan.

Rumet, M. (1999). Values in the best-selling children's books in the United States, 1990–1997. *Dissertation Abstracts International, 60* (6A), 2031.

Russo, N. F. (1976). The motherhood mandate. *Journal of Social Issues, 32,* 143–153.

Sadker, M., & Sadker, D. (1994). *Failing at fairness: How America's schools cheat girls.* New York: Scribner.

Sancho, A., & Hewitt, J. (1990). Questioning fear of success. *Psychological Reports, 67,* 803–806.

Solomon, L. Z. (1975). Perception of a successful person of the same sex or the opposite sex. *Journal of Social Psychology, 85,* 133–134.

Spence, J. T., & Helmreich, R. (1978). *Masculinity and femininity: Their psychological dimensions, correlates, and antecedents.* Austin: University of Texas Press.

Stewart, A., & Chester, N. (1982). Sex differences in human social motives: Achievement, affiliation, and power. In A. Stewart (Ed.), *Motivation and society.* New York: Bantam Books.

Super, D. (1957). *The psychology of careers.* New York: Harper & Row.

Sutherland, E. (1989). *A follow-up study on achievement-related motivation and behavior.* Unpublished doctoral dissertation, University of Michigan.

Swoboda, M., & Millar, S. (1986). Networking mentoring: Career strategy of women in academic administration. *Journal of NAWDAC, 49,* 8–13.

Taynor, J., & Deaux, K. (1975). Equity and perceived sex differences: Role behavior as defined by the task, the mode, and the actor. *Journal of Personality and Social Psychology, 3,* 381–390.

Tepper, C., & Cassidy, K. (1999). Gender differences in emotional language in children's picture books. *Sex Roles, 40,* 265–280.

Thorne, B. (1993). *Gender play: Girls and boys in school.* New Brunswick, NJ: Rutgers University Press.

Tresemer, D. (1977). *Fear of success.* New York: Plenum Press.

Tresemer, D., & Pleck, J. (1972, April). *Maintaining and changing sex-role boundaries in men (and women).* Paper presented at the Resources for a Changing World Conference, Radcliffe Institute, Cambridge, MA.

Vetter, L. (1973). Career counseling for women. *The Counseling Psychologist, 4,* 54–67.

Ward, C. (1981). Prejudice against women: Who, when, and why? *Sex Roles, 7,* 163–171.

Weiner, B. (1972). *Theories of motivation and attribution theory.* Morristown, NJ: General Learning Press.

Weinstein, M. (1999). What makes a good mentor? The role of mentor flexibility in mentor functions and protégé outcomes. *Dissertation Abstracts International, 59* (12B), 6508.

Whitley, B., McHugh, M., & Frieze, I. (1986). Assessing the theoretical models for sex differences in causal attributions of success and failure. In J. Hyde & M. Linn (Eds.), *The psychology of gender: Advances through meta-analysis.* Baltimore: Johns Hopkins University Press.

Williams, C. (1995). *Still a man's world: Men who do women's work.* Berkeley: University of California Press.

Winchel, R., Fenner, D., & Shaver, P. (1974). Impact of coeducation on fear of success imagery. *Journal of Educational Psychology, 66,* 726–730.

Young, S. (1998). Mentoring of female graduate students by male faculty. *Dissertation Abstracts International, 58* (8A), 3029.

Zuckerman, M., & Allison, S. (1976). An objective measure of fear of success: Construction and validation. *Journal of Personality Assessment, 40,* 422–430.

TEN

GENDER, POWER, AND VIOLENCE AGAINST WOMEN

IN WOMEN'S VOICES

It is only after a great deal of agonizing consideration that I am able to talk of these unpleasant matters to anyone, except my closest friends. . . . Telling the world is the most difficult experience of my life. . . . I may have used poor judgment early on in my relationship with this issue. I was aware, however, that telling at any point in my career could adversely affect my future career. . . . Perhaps I should have taken angry or even militant steps . . . but I must confess to the world that the course that I took seemed the better, as well as the easier approach.

Anita Hill

To win, to be superior, to be successful, to conquer—all demonstrate masculinity to those who subscribe to common cultural notions of masculinity, i.e., the masculine mystique. And it would be surprising if these notions of masculinity did not find expression in men's sexual behavior. Indeed, sex may be the arena where these notions of masculinity are played out, particularly by men who feel powerless in the rest of their lives, and hence, whose masculinity is threatened by this sense of powerlessness.

Diana Russell

Women truly have no safe haven from victimization because they are vulnerable both within and outside their homes.

Mary Koss

Chapter Outline

Questions for Reflection

1. Does discussing sexual victimization make you uncomfortable?

2. Do you believe your campus accurately records the number of sexual assaults that occur to women and men?

3. What do you believe your campus needs to do in order to make students feel safer with respect to sexual assault?

4. What is your campus' policy statement on sexual harassment? What are your campus' investigatory procedures with respect to sexual harassment?

5. Have you participated in training programs on sexual harassment at your college/university?

6. Are there counselors available at your campus for discussing sexual assault and sexual harassment?

7. Do you know of any classmates who are involved in courtship violence? What assistance can you provide them?

8. How do you explain why sexual violence occurs?

9. If you were asked to identify the types of sexual violence that occur on college/university campuses, what would you include in your listing?

10. How would you discuss sexual victimization with your adolescent son? Your adolescent daughter?

SOME WORDS OF SUPPORT

Unlike other topics in the study of the psychology of women, the unit on violence against women is very difficult for students (and the professor) to discuss. We may believe we can distance ourselves from some of the other issues, but this topic touches us emotionally. We probably have either been victimized or we know of family and friends who have been.

Because of the sensitivity of the issues involved in this chapter, I offer these suggestions:

- Monitor your nonverbal communication. Some people may laugh when they are tense or when they are discussing sensitive topics. Laughter should not be permitted during this unit. If you do find yourself smiling or laughing because of discomfort, say something similar to the following: "Sometimes when I am uncomfortable or about to cry I may giggle or smile. Please don't interpret my behavior as meaning that I find the topic silly or stupid. I take it very seriously."

- Permit yourself to cry if you want to or need to. Feel free to leave the class for a break, to compose yourself.

- If you don't believe you can attend class during the discussions of violence against women, inform your professor of your concern and get all the reading assignments that will be required of you for an exam.

- Remind yourself of the statistics concerning incidence of sexual harassment, incest, battering, and rape. These statistics suggest that some women and men in your class may have experienced one or more of these violent acts.

- Contact your counseling center or locate support groups for continuing the discussion of the issues raised in a unit on violence against women.

- Be good to yourself. Take a walk, see a movie, talk with friends. The material in this chapter, as well as in your course, can be stressful.

- If you come to believe that you yourself have been sexually victimized, tell someone you trust immediately.

• Seek support through your campus counseling center or community organizations. Suggestions for this purpose are presented in this chapter.

INTRODUCTION

The statistics are startling: 30 percent of all women are battered at least once in their adult lives. Incidence of sexual harassment among undergraduate women ranges between 30 and 70 percent each year (Paludi, 1996). The incidence is even higher for women in graduate school and in the workforce (Levy & Paludi, 1997). At least 20 percent of women have been a victim of incest sometime in their lives (Courtois, 2000). Between 8 and 15 percent of college women have disclosed they were raped, and at least one-third of battered women have been raped by the batterer.

As Mary Koss (1990) pointed out in her review of the research on violence against women:

> More disturbing than the overall prevalence rates is the proportion of violent incidents that were perpetrated by close friends or family members. Acquaintances of the victim were implicated in up to 49% of child sexual assault; romantic partners were implicated in 50% to 57% of sexual assaults reported by college age and adult women. Family members perpetrated 90% of the physical and sexual assaults reported by psychiatric patients. . . . These data suggest that for women, the U.S. family is a violent institution. (p. 375)

In this chapter we will discuss research on four types of sexual victimization: sexual harassment, rape, incest, and battering. We will also discuss ways we can assist our friends and ourselves with being victimized.

SEXUAL HARASSMENT

For the next few minutes, read the following stories.

Jamie is taking a laboratory course in psychology in her third semester at college. She is having a rather difficult time conducting one experiment and using statistics to analyze her results. She decides to talk with her graduate teaching assistant for the course about her work. While she is discussing the research, her TA suggests that the two of them date. Jamie makes it quite clear that she isn't interested in him romantically. Throughout the remainder of the semester Jamie receives low grades on her research papers. When she asks her TA about his grading system, he replies: "You had your chance."

In her introductory psychology class, Sonia, a Latina, notices that her professor smiles and comments on her appearance as a greeting each morning—and that he does not greet any other student in this way. Before his lecture on contemporary sexual roles and behavior, he remarks to the class, "Sonia can probably help us understand this topic since she has to put up with macho types."

Maria is taking a course dealing with human physiology this semester. Her professor has been discussing anatomy and today brings in slides to complement his lecture. For 25 minutes the class sits through a discussion of male anatomy, complete with slides from *Gray's Anatomy*, a textbook. Following this presentation and class discussion, Maria's professor begins to lecture on female anatomy. He explains that, for lack of time, he will show only a few select slides that illustrate the points he wants to make about female anatomy. Maria at once notices that the slides are nude photos from men's magazines.

(From Paludi & Barickman, 1998)

Do you believe these stories illustrate sexual harassment? Why or why not?

Legal Definition of Sexual Harassment

Title VII of the 1964 Civil Rights Act addresses the workplace in its role as employer and prohibits discrimination based on sex in the terms, conditions, and privileges of employment. **Title IX of the 1972 Education Amendments** prohibits sexual harassment in education.

The **Equal Employment Opportunity Commission (EEOC)** is the governmental agency charged with enforcement of **Title VII.** The EEOC has published guidelines that define sexual harassment as "unwelcome sexual advances, requests for sexual favors, and other verbal or physical conduct of a sexual nature" when any one of the following criteria is met:

- Submission to such conduct is made either explicitly or implicitly a term or condition of the individual's employment.

- Submission to or rejection of such conduct by an individual is used as the basis for employment decisions affecting the individual.

- Such conduct has the purpose or effect of unreasonably interfering with an individual's work or creating an intimidating, hostile, or offensive work environment.

MEET DR. ANNE LEVY

Dr. Anne Levy, a Professor at Michigan State University, teaches law, public policy, and business. Prior to joining the University, Dr. Levy was a judicial law clerk to Michigan Supreme Court Justice Patricia Boyle. Her primary research interests are centered around employment discrimination, especially sexual harassment and the interplay of law and psychology in the management of a diverse workforce.

According to Dr. Levy:

There are few external forces which can impact the success of women in school and the workplace more than an environment in which women are devalued, debased, and made to feel uncomfortable and unwelcome. A serious and comprehensive sexual harassment policy, coupled with effective procedures, which encourage victims to come forward, can solve these problems. When those who teach or work in an institution or business are made to realize that this is a serious and important matter and are given guidance and training as to appropriate behavior and responses, all women can finally approach their school or workplace with a sense of full worth and belonging rather than a sense of daily apprehension.

Two types of sexual harassment are described by the EEOC definition (which has been applied to educational institutions as well): (1) **quid pro quo sexual harassment** and (2) **hostile-environment sexual harassment.** In quid pro quo sexual harassment, an employee is claiming that a supervisor or someone with authority to confer workplace benefits (e.g., hiring, raises, promotions) is offering those benefits in exchange for sexual favors or is threatening to take away economic benefits for failure to comply with the sexual requests. Quid pro quo sexual harassment usually involves a situation between people of differing power positions in the workplace. Examples in an academic setting would be a teacher directly bribing a student with the letter grade of "A" for being sexually cooperative, or denying the student the grade earned because she did not consent to sexual relations with the professor.

Sexual harassment can also occur in the absence of a power differential. In hostile-environment sexual harassment, a coworker may create a work environment for an employee that is hostile, intimidating, and offensive. This coworker is not in a position to offer a bargain in an expressed or implied way, but she or he does set up a climate that interferes with the employee's being able to work. Examples of hostile environment in the workplace or in academic institutions include:

- Unwelcome sexual advances.

- Implied or expressed threat of reprisal for refusal to comply with a sexually oriented request.

- Demeaning or belittling remarks, jokes, slurs, innuendos, or taunting about the sex or body of an employee or student.

- Sexually suggestive objects, books, magazines, posters, photographs, cartoons, or pictures displayed in the work area or in class.

Empirical Definitions of Sexual Harassment

Empirical definitions of sexual harassment are databased and are most generally developed by researchers in the field of human resource management and psychology (Fitzgerald et al., 1988; Paludi, 2000). Empirical definitions are derived from students' and employees' descriptions of their experiences of harassment (Paludi, 2000). The descriptions are then categorized, and the categories are used as the elements of the definition. For example, Frank Till (1980) classified the responses to an open-ended sexual harassment survey of college women and derived the following five categories of generally increasing severity:

1. Gender harassment

2. Seductive behavior

3. Sexual bribery

4. Sexual coercion

5. Sexual imposition or assault

According to Till's research, **gender harassment** consists of generalized sexist remarks and behavior not designed to elicit sexual cooperation but rather to convey insulting, degrading, or sexist attitudes about women. **Seductive behavior** consists of unwanted, inappropriate, and offensive sexual advances. **Sexual bribery** is the solicitation of sexual activity or other sex-linked behavior by promise of a reward (e.g., salary increase, promotion). **Sexual coercion** is the solicitation of sexual activity by threat of punishment (e.g., failure to give a promotion, being fired), and **sexual imposition or assault** includes gross sexual imposition, assault, and rape.

Incidence of Sexual Harassment

Elementary and Secondary School.   In 1993, the American Association of University Women (AAUW) collected incidence rates of adolescents' experiences with sexual harassment. In this study, 1,632 students in grades 8 through 11, from 79 schools across the United States, were asked:

> During your whole school life, how often, if at all, has anyone (this includes students, teachers, other school employees, or anyone else) done the following things to you **when you did not want them to?**
>
> • Made sexual comments, jokes, gestures, or looks.
>
> • Showed, gave, or left you sexual pictures, photographs, illustrations, messages, or notes.
>
> • Wrote sexual messages/graffiti about you on bathroom walls, in locker rooms, etc.
>
> • Spread sexual rumors about you.
>
> • Said you were gay or lesbian.
>
> • Spied on you as you dressed or showered at school.
>
> • Flashed or "mooned" you.
>
> • Touched, grabbed, or pinched you in a sexual way.
>
> • Pulled at your clothing in a sexual way.
>
> • Intentionally brushed against you in a sexual way.
>
> • Pulled your clothing off or down.
>
> • Blocked your way or cornered you in a sexual way.
>
> • Forced you to kiss him/her.
>
> • Forced you to do something sexual, other than kissing.

Four out of five students (81%) reported that they had been the target of some form of sexual harassment during their school lives. With respect to gender comparisons, 85 percent of girls and 76 percent of boys surveyed reported that they had experienced unwelcome sexual behavior that interfered with their ability to concentrate at school and with their personal lives.

The AAUW study also analyzed the data for race comparisons. African American boys (81%) were more likely to have experienced sexual harassment than white boys (75%) and Latinos (69%). For girls, 87 percent of whites reported having experienced behaviors that constituted sexual harassment, compared with 84 percent of African American girls and 82 percent of Latinas.

The AAUW study also suggested that adolescents' experiences with sexual harassment are most likely to occur in the middle school/junior high school years (6th to 9th grade). The behaviors reported by students, in rank order from most occurrences to least occurrences, were:

- Sexual comments, jokes, gestures, or looks.
- Touched, grabbed, or pinched in a sexual way.
- Intentionally brushed against in a sexual way.
- Flashed or "mooned."
- Had sexual rumors spread about them.
- Had clothing pulled at in a sexual way.
- Sexual pictures, photographs, illustrations, messages, or notes were shown, given, or left for them to find.
- Had their way blocked or were cornered in a sexual way.
- Had sexual messages/graffiti written about them on bathroom walls, in locker rooms, etc.
- Forced to kiss someone.
- Called gay or lesbian.
- Had clothing pulled off or down.
- Forced to do something sexual, other than kissing.
- Spied on as they dressed or showered at school.

Like adults, adolescents most frequently experience hostile-environment sexual harassment (Fineran & Bennett, 2000). Students who participated in the AAUW study reported that they experience these behaviors while in the classroom or in the hallways as they are going to class. The majority of harassment in schools is student-to-student (i.e., peer harassment). However, 25 percent of harassed girls and 10 percent of boys reported they were harassed by teachers or other school employees.

Incidence rates similar to the AAUW study were reported by Fineran and Bennett (1999), Strauss and Espeland (1992), and the Connecticut Permanent Commission on the Status of Women (1995).

Karen Bogart and her colleagues (Bogart, Simmons, Stein, & Tomaszewski, 1992) reviewed the sexual harassment complaints brought by students against teachers employed by the Massachusetts Department of Education. Among the complaints they reported were the following:

> A science teacher measured the craniums of the boys in the class and the chests of the girls. The lesson in skeletal frame measurements was conducted one by one, at the front of the class, by the teacher.
>
> The print shop teacher, who was in the habit of putting his arms around the shoulders of the young women, insisted, when one young woman asked to be excused to go to the nurse to fix her broken pants' zipper, that she first show him her broken zipper. She was forced to lift her shirt to reveal her broken pants zipper. (p. 197)

Girls in nontraditional high school programs have reported the following experiences (Stein, 1986, cited in Bogart et al., 1992):

> One female in diesel shop refused to go to lunch during her last two years of shop because she was the only young woman in the lunchroom at that time. When she went to the cafeteria, she was pinched and slapped on the way in and had to endure explicit propositions made to her while she ate lunch.
>
> A particular shop's predominantly male population designated one shop day as "National Sexual Harassment Day," in honor of their only female student. They gave her nonstop harassment throughout the day and found it to be so successful (the female student was forced to be dismissed during the day) that they later held a "National Sexual Harassment Week." (p. 208)

Children and adolescents are likely to experience sexual harassment when they attend schools that, according Sandler and Paludi (1993):

- Do not have a policy prohibiting sexual harassment.

- Do not disseminate the policy or enforce it.

- Do not have training programs for students, teachers, and staff.

- Do not intervene officially when sexual harassment occurs.

- Do not support victims of sexual harassment.

- Do not remove sexual graffiti quickly.

- Do not sanction individuals who engage in sexual harassment.

- Do not inform the school community about the sanctions for offenders.

College/University.   We have seen how adolescents are likely to engage in and to experience **peer harassment,** the sexual harassment of women by their male colleagues, or of women students by men students. Illustrations of peer harassment at the college level include (Association of American Colleges, 1988; Sandler, 2000):

- A group of men regularly sit at a table facing a cafeteria line. As women go through the line, the men loudly discuss the women's sexual attributes and hold up signs with numbers from 1 to 10, "rating" each woman. As a result, many women skip meals or avoid the cafeteria.

- Sexist posters and pictures are placed where women will see them.

- A fraternity pledge approaches a young woman he has never met and bites her on the breast—a practice called "sharking."

Research has indicated that the most serious forms of peer harassment involve groups of men. When men outnumber women, as in fraternity houses and stadiums, or at parties, group harassment is especially likely to occur. Examples of **group harassment** include:

- Yelling, whistling, and shouting obscenities at women who walk by fraternity houses or other campus sites.

- Intimidating a woman by surrounding her, demanding that she expose her breasts, and refusing to allow her to leave until she complies.

- Creating a disturbance outside of women's residence halls.

- Vandalizing sororities.

Darlene DeFour and I (1998) reported that college students, when asked to identify the activities that would be summarized under the heading "Campus Violence," generated the following terms: hazing, rape, assault, battering, emotional abuse, and date rape. The term **sexual harassment** was not mentioned, a surprising finding when the current estimate of sexual harassment of college students by professors approximates 50 percent, ranging from sexual come-ons to sexual coercion (i.e., faculty threatening to lower students' grades for noncompliance with faculty's requests for sexual activity). Students' omission of sexual harassment from a list of behaviors that constitute campus violence indicates the strength of the socialization message: Men should initiate sexual contact in any setting, including a college/university (Fitzgerald & Omerod, 1993). Students' responses also reflect the silence that still surrounds sexual harassment on campuses. Sexual harassment remains a "hidden issue," which is how the Project on the Status and Education of Women referred to it in 1978.

Fitzgerald and collegues (1988) investigated approximately 2,000 women at two major state universities. Half of the women respondents reported experiencing some form of sexually harassing behavior. The majority of these women reported experiencing sexist comments by faculty; the next largest category of sexual harassing behavior was seductive behavior, including being invited for drinks and a backrub by faculty members, being brushed up against by their professors, and having their professors show up uninvited at their hotel rooms during out-of-town academic conferences or conventions.

Dziech and Weiner (1984), and DeFour (1996) suggested that ethnic minority women are more vulnerable to receiving sexual attention from professors. Ethnic minority women are subject to stereotypes about sex, viewed as mysterious, and less sure of themselves in their careers (DeFour, 1996). Thus, although all students are vulnerable to some degree, male teachers and faculty tend to select those who are most vulnerable and needy. For certain student groups, the incidence of sexual harassment appears to be higher than for others (Barickman, Paludi, & Rabinowitz, 1993). For example:

Women of color, especially those with "token" status.

Graduate students, whose future careers are often determined by their association with a particular faculty member.

Students in small colleges or small academic departments, where the number of faculty available to students is quite small.

Women students in male-populated fields, such as engineering.

Students who are economically disadvantaged and work part-time or full-time while attending classes.

Lesbian women, who may be harassed as part of homophobia.

Physically or emotionally disabled students.

Women students who work in dormitories as resident assistants.

Women who have been sexually abused.

Inexperienced, unassertive, socially isolated girls and women, who may appear more vulnerable and appealing to those who would intimidate or entice them into an exploitive relationship.

Fitzgerald and Gelfand (1994) obtained incidence data on sexual harassment among students in the United States and Brazil. Brazilian and U.S. women students reported experiencing a similar degree of gender harassment and sexual coercion. Brazilian women students reported higher mean rates of unwanted sexual attention than U.S. women students. Mecca and Rubin (1999) reported that African American women college students indicated they experienced a high degree of sexual touching. Uhari and colleagues (1994), in their study of sexual harassment among medical students in Finland, reported that most incidents of sexual harassment were of a sex discrimination nature: Women students were denied career opportunities because of their sex. Recently, Gruber and De Souza (2000) offered comparable incidence

---

MEET DR. CAROLE POND

Dr. Carole Pond, Sexual Harassment Officer at The University of Saskatchewan, helped organize the Canadian Association Against Sexual Harassment in Higher Education (CAASHE). CAASHE is an organization of individuals in universities and colleges who work in the area of sexual harassment. According to Dr. Pond, the objectives of CAASHE are:

1. To train new sexual harassment advisors and provide professional development for continuing sexual harassment advisors by organizing an annual conference.
2. To provide a forum at the annual conference for the exchange of information, ideas, and innovations in the area of sexual harassment policy, procedure, and education.
3. To provide a communication network for members.
4. To provide an organizational structure/mechanism at the national level which will collect and distribute information about sexual harassment policies, procedures, and staff organizations in postsecondary institutions in Canada.
5. To publish a newsletter on a regular basis.
6. To provide for research, as possible, at the national level.
7. To issue, from time to time, public statements on issues of national concern with respect to sexual harassment.

rates among students in several countries, including Finland, United States, Turkey, and Japan.

Workplace.   Sexual harassment in the workplace is widespread (Hordes, 2000). For example, the U.S. Merit Systems Protection Board (1981) addressed sexual harassment in the federal workplace and suggested that 42 percent of all women employees reported being sexually harassed. Merit Systems reported that many incidents occurred repeatedly, were of long duration, and had a sizable practical impact, costing the government an estimated minimum of $189 million over the two-year period covered by the research project. Results also indicated that 33 percent of the women reported receiving unwanted sexual remarks, 28 percent reported suggestive looks, and 26 percent reported being deliberately touched. These behaviors were classified in the study as "less severe" types of sexual harassment. When "more severe" forms of sexual harassment were addressed, 15 percent of the women reported experiencing pressure for dates, 9 percent reported being directly pressured for sexual favors, and 9 percent had received unwanted letters and telephone calls. One percent of the sample had experienced actual or attempted rape or assault. Merit Systems repeated the study of workplace sexual harassment in 1987 and reported results that were identical to their 1981 findings.

Research by Barbara Gutek (1985) with women in the civilian workplace reports similar findings: Approximately half the female workforce experiences sexual harassment. Based on telephone interviews generated through random digit dialing procedures, Gutek's results suggested that 53 percent of women had reported one incident they believed was sexual harassment during their working lives, including degrading, insulting comments (15%), sexual touching (24%), socializing expected as part of the job requirement (11%), and expected sexual activity (8%).

Group differences in sexual harassment are common. Louise Fitzgerald and her colleagues (1988), for example, found that women who were employed in a university setting (e.g., faculty, staff, and administrators) were more likely to experience sexual harassment than were women students in the same institution. Gold (1987) reported that her sample of blue-collar tradeswomen experienced significantly higher levels of all forms of sexual harassment (e.g., gender harassment, seductive behavior, sexual bribery, sexual coercion, sexual assault) than did either white-collar professional women or pink-collar clerical women.

LaFontaine and Tredeau (1986) reported similar findings in their sample of 160 women, all college graduates employed in male-populated occupations (e.g., engineering and management). Nancy Baker (1989) studied a sample of 100 women employed in either traditional or nontraditional occupations, where traditionality was defined by the sex distribution in the work group. Baker also divided the traditional group into pink- and blue-collar workers. The pink-collar group included women who were secretaries and clerical workers. The blue-collar group included women who were industrial workers. Baker reported that high levels of sexual harassment are associated with having low numbers of women in the work group. For example, machinists reported a significantly high frequency of all levels of sexual harassment, whereas the traditional blue-collar workers reported very low levels. Clerical women reported experiences that were more similar to those of the traditional blue-collar workers than to those of the nontraditional blue-collar workers. Baker also reported that women in the pink-collar and traditional blue-collar groups encountered just as many men as the machinists during the workday, but were treated differently. These results suggest that as women approach numerical parity in various segments of the workforce, sexual harassment may decline.

This perspective has also been raised by Gutek (1985), who argued that sexual harassment is more likely to occur in occupations in which **"sex-role spillover"** has occurred. Gutek's model suggests that when occupations are dominated by one sex or the other, the sex role of the dominant sex influences (i.e., spills over) the work role expectations for that job. For example, gender stereotypes imply that men should be sexually aggressive and women should be ready and willing to be sex objects. Sexual harassment may occur when these gender stereotypes carry over or spill over into the workplace setting. When individuals act on their thoughts about women and men, they may engage in behavior that is discriminatory. For example, research suggests that women are evaluated less favorably than men for identical performance on a job (Doyle & Paludi, 1995). Men have higher expectations for other men's ability than for women's ability; they attribute women's successful performance on the job to luck, cheating, sexuality, or the fact that someone "likes" them. The causal attribution of "lack of ability" is used by men to describe women's job performance when anything is not perfect (Gutek & Koss, 1993; Levy & Paludi, 1997)

The workplace is not insulated from gender stereotyping. Women employees may be evaluated by their coworkers and supervisors in terms of their sexuality and their performance as sex objects instead of their merit as managers or colleagues. Gender stereotypes are related to the amount of perceived power one has in the workplace. Stereotypes are more commonly used to describe the behavior of those who are seen as having less power in the organization and who occupy lower-echelon positions (Levy & Paludi, 1997).

Magley, Hulin, Fitzgerald, and DeNardo (1999) compared women's and men's experiences with sexual harassment using data from the United States Department of Defense's survey of gender issues. They found that women were more likely to have been sexually harassed than men were in the military. In addition, women experienced sexual harassment in the military more frequently than did men. The impact of sexual harassment (to be discussed below) was more pronounced for women than for men. Furthermore, women who reported sexual harassment always indicated that the perpetrator was a man. For men who said they were sexually harassed, they too indicated that they were more likely to experience the harassment from other men than from women. We'll discuss this later finding in more detail below.

Barak (1997) reviewed incidence data on workplace sexual harassment within several countries, including Australia, Canada, Egypt, Japan, Italy, Portugal, Sweden, Pakistan, Luxembourg, and Mexico. Methodological constraints (e.g., questioning methods, connotative meanings of survey items) made it difficult to compare incidence rates of sexual harassment across countries. However, Barak noted that workplace sexual harassment is a "relatively widespread phenomenon across countries, continents, cultures, languages, and societies . . . the form or the type of sexual harassment being carried out might be different in different countries" (p. 275).

Who Harasses?

Men are more likely to sexually harass than are women. Research suggests that a man who is likely to initiate severe sexually harassing behavior appears to be one who emphasizes male social and sexual dominance and who demonstrates insensitivity to other individuals' perspectives (Zalk, 1996). Men are less likely than women to define sexual harassment as including jokes, teasing remarks of a sexual nature, and unwanted suggestive looks or gestures (Levy & Paludi, 1997). Men are also significantly more likely than women to agree with the following statements, taken from Paludi's (1996) "attitudes toward victim blame and victim responsibility" survey:

Women often claim sexual harassment to protect their reputations.

Many women claim sexual harassment if they have consented to sexual relations but have later changed their minds.

Sexually experienced women are not really damaged by sexual harassment.

It would do some women good to be sexually harassed.

Women put themselves in situations in which they are likely to be sexually harassed because they have an unconscious wish to be harassed.

In most cases, when a woman is sexually harassed, she deserved it.

Sexual harassment, similar to rape, incest, and battering, may be understood as an extreme acting-out of qualities that are regarded as supermasculine in our culture: aggression, power, dominance, and force. Men who harass are not pathological, but they exhibit behaviors characteristic of the masculine gender role in U.S. culture (Zalk, 1996).

Can/Do Women Harass Men?

The research can be summarized as follows (Levy & Paludi, 1997):

1. Women are highly unlikely to date or initiate sexual relationships with their coworkers or supervisors.

2. A small number of men in the workplace setting believe they have been sexually harassed by women. The behaviors that many of these men label as sexual harassment, however, do not fit the legal definition of either quid pro quo or hostile-environment sexual harassment.

3. Men are more likely than women to interpret a particular behavior as sexual. For example, in research by Barbara Gutek, men were likely to label a business lunch as a "date" if it was with a woman manager.

4. The great majority of men report that they are flattered by women's advances, whereas women report feeling annoyed, insulted, and threatened by men's advances.

5. It is rare for a woman to hold the organizational and sociocultural power that would allow her to reward a man for sexual cooperation or punish him for withholding it, even if gender role prescriptions did not ensure that she was extremely unlikely to demand sexual favors in the first place.

It is possible for women to harass men; however, that behavior is unlikely because of both the women's relative lack of formal power and the socialization that stigmatizes sexually assertive women. Many of men's experiences with sexual harassment are with other men. Men may be reluctant to disclose this information because of homophobic concerns.

Impact of Sexual Harassment

Several reports have documented the high cost of sexual harassment to women (Dansky & Kilpatrick, 1997; Munson, Hulin, & Drasgow, 2000; Schneider & Swan, 1994). Louise Fitzgerald and Alayne Omerod (1993) noted that the outcomes of the harassment/victimization process can be examined from three main perspectives: (1) education/work-related, (2) psychological or emotional, and (3) physiological or health-related. Let's review the research findings in each of these perspectives.

Education/Work-Related Outcomes. As a result of sexual harassment, girls and women change career goals, are absent from school or work, and have decreased morale, decreased job satisfaction, performance decrements, and damage to interpersonal relationships at work or school.

Psychological Outcomes. Research has identified the following symptoms reported by victims of sexual harassment: fear, guilt, anger, anxiety, insecurity, frustration, denial, fear of rape, fear of crime in general, decreased self-esteem, withdrawal from social situations, helplessness, depression, and fear of meeting new people.

Physiological Outcomes. The following physical symptoms have been reported in the literature concerning academic and workplace sexual harassment: headaches, sleep disturbances, disordered eating, gastrointestinal disorders, nausea, weight loss or gain, and crying spells. Victims of sexual harassment can exhibit a "post-abuse" syndrome characterized by shock, emotional numbing, constriction of affect, flashbacks, and other signs of anxiety and depression (Fitzgerald & Omerod, 1993; Salisbury, Ginorio, Remick, & Stringer, 1986). These responses are influenced by disappointment in the way others react and by the stress of harassment-induced life changes, such as moves, loss of income, and disrupted work history.

Not all victims of sexual harassment will experience all of these symptoms. The likelihood is great, however, that most victims of sexual harassment experience severe distress associated with sexual harassment. Symptoms also become more pronounced the longer the victim has to endure the harassment (Levy & Paludi, 1997).

What Can We Do?

Let us now summarize each of the issues raised in this section:

• Sexual harassment can be viewed as an abuse of power and a reflection of the low status of students and employees.

- Many individuals cling to the myth that sexual harassment includes only physical assault. In fact, sexual harassment is far more pervasive than sexual assault.

- Sexual harassment, defined as unwelcome sexual advances or requests for sexual favors, also includes other verbal or physical conduct of a sexual nature.

- Research suggests that as numerical parity is reached, sexual harassment may decline.

- Men may experience sexual harassment as well, but the incidence for women is greater than that for men.

- Most victims do not use an externally focused strategy for dealing with sexual harassment.

- Victims of sexual harassment fear retaliation if they confront the harasser.

- Students and employees may not label their experiences as sexual harassment, even when the experiences meet the legal definition of this form of victimization. Consequently, they may not identify their stress-related responses as being caused or exacerbated by the sexual harassment.

- Sexual harassment has a radiating impact: it can affect the learning experiences of all women and men on a campus or in a workplace.

Margaret Mead (as quoted in Dziech & Weiner, 1984) has called for "new taboos" against sexual harassment:

> What should we—what can we—do about sexual harassment on the job? . . . As I see it, it isn't more laws that we need now, but new taboos. . . .
>
> When we examine how any society works, it becomes clear that it is precisely the basic taboos—the deeply and intensely felt prohibitions against "unthinkable" behavior—that keep the social system in balance . . . The complaints, the legal remedies and the support institutions developed by women are all part of the response to the new conception of women's rights. But I believe we need something much more pervasive, a climate of opinion that includes men as well as women, and that will affect not only adult relations and behavior on the job but also the expectations about the adult world that guide our children's progress into that world. What we need, in fact, are new taboos that are appropriate to the new society we are struggling to create—taboos that will operate within the work setting as once they operated within the household. Neither men nor women should expect that sex can be used either to victimize women who need to keep their jobs or to keep women from advancement or to help men advance their own careers. (p. 184)

To effectively deal with sexual harassment, the following responses are recommended (Fitzgerald & Omerod, 1993; Paludi, 1996; Paludi & Barickman, 1991): an *effective policy statement,* an *effective investigative procedure,* and *education/ training programs* for all members of the school or workplace.

In addition to enforcing effective policies, procedures, and training, we need to not view sexual harassment as normative. It is not an expected part of the adolescent life stage (Fineran & Bennett, 1999; Stein, 1995). Secondary school administrators must intervene in sexual harassment for a number of reasons, including to assist adolescents in understanding that they do not have to accept sexual harassment or other forms of sexual victimization.

What to Do If You Are Sexually Harassed

1. Don't blame yourself. It's not your fault.

2. Write down the description of the sexually harassing behavior. Include date, times, circumstances, people present, how you felt.

3. Talk about the incident with someone you trust—a family member, friend, or adviser.

4. Don't hurry into a decision.

5. After you think through the options available to you, if you decide to seek resolution through the school or workplace, contact the individual who has been designated to handle sexual harassment complaints. Read through the policy statement and procedures. Know your rights and responsibilities. Be sure the procedures will be kept confidential.

6. Consider participating in a support group.

7. Be good to yourself! Dealing with sexual harassment is emotionally and physically exhausting. Rest, eat well, exercise, get medical checkups, and spend time with friends and family.

RAPE

For the next few minutes jot down the behaviors in which you engage as you leave campus at night to go to your dorm or apartment. When I ask women students in my class to do this exercise, we have generated the following behaviors:

Call my roommate to tell her I'm on my way back to the dorm.

Call for a campus escort to help me get home.

Take out my mace.

Look behind me and across the street as I walk home.

Look in the backseat of my car before I get into it.

Be sure the lock on my door hasn't been tampered with.

Did you list any behaviors similar to these? How much time each day do you spend in engaging in these activities? Do you find men engaging in these identical behaviors?

Do you believe men engage in these behaviors as well? Why or why not?

If you had to label these behaviors, what would you use? Once again, students in my classes have typically answered "life" or "phobias." In fact, the behaviors are rape-avoidance strategies.

Are you surprised by this label? Would you describe yourself as engaging in rape-avoidance strategies? Why or why not? It may be difficult to use this term to describe our behavior. We typically avoid putting ourselves in the position of a victim. Let's address these issues in more detail as we discuss rape, including acquaintance rape or date rape.

Legal Definition and Incidence of Rape

Rape is legally defined as *nonconsensual oral, anal, or vaginal penetration obtained by force, by threat of bodily harm, or when the victim is incapable of giving consent* (Searles & Berger, 1987). Rape is an act of violence. FBI statistics indicate that approximately 100,000 cases of rape are reported annually in the United States. The high-risk ages for rape are between 13 and 24 years; however, infant girls and middle-aged and older women are also victimized. According to Koss (1993), urban women younger than 35 years of age fear rape more than murder. Statistics suggest that the lifetime possibility that a woman will be raped is between 14 and 25 percent (Koss, 1993). We do not have any absolute statistics for the total annual number of completed or attempted rapes in the United States. We can, however, estimate a 30 percent probability of a woman's being the victim of rape in her lifetime. The enormity of the incidence of rape becomes more staggering when we note the untold numbers of children under 12 years of age who are victims of sexual assault (Finkelhor & Dziuba-Leatherman, 1994). Adolescent and young adult women are in a high-risk range. The risk of rape is so high for African American women that elderly African American women are just as likely to be raped as young white women. A few cultures may be less prone to violent sexual acts by men toward women, but our culture and most others are "rape-prone" cultures (Rozee, 1999). Rape is more common in societies that are characterized by male dominance and by a high degree of violence in general; both are illustrative of an ideology of male aggressiveness (Rozee, 1999).

Rape is one of the most underreported of all serious crimes, in the United States and in other countries (Koss, 1993; Rozee, 1999). Most women refuse to report to proper authorities incidents of sexual violence. For many women, a sense of shame, guilt, or self-blame about their role in the rape assaults (stemming from stereotypes about women's sexuality and control of men's sexuality) may be sufficient to prevent them from pressing charges. Those who do press charges, however, are apt to meet with questions, accusations, and other degrading and humiliating experiences (Rozee, 1999).

When rape victims press charges against their assailants, their life histories—especially their sexual activities—are shared with the public. In many instances, individuals are willing to blame women for the assault rather than the rapist (Koss, 1993). One explanation for the attribution of guilt to the victim rather than to the assailant concerns the **"just-world" hypothesis:** the tendency to blame others for one's misfortunes, or the belief that bad things happen only to those who somehow bring on their own problems or deserve the consequences of their acts. A likely result of such a "just-world" orientation is that, more often than not, the defenders of rapists will try to show that the rape victims "had it coming" because of their actions. With all the barriers preventing the victims of sexual assault from coming forward, it is no wonder that rape continues to be one of the most underreported crimes (Rozee, 1999).

Women in Asian cultures have experienced a high incidence of rape. Mollica, Wyshak, and Lavelle (1987) found that the incidence of rape, as well as other forms of sexual abuse, experienced by Asian refugee women living in Boston approximated 100 percent. Southeast Asian women may not report these attacks to law enforcement personnel because, in their own experiences in their countries, law officers or authorities committed most of the sexual abuse.

Lira, Koss, and Russo (1999) called for rape research and intervention programs to become more culturally sensitive. In their study of Mexican American's definitions of rape, Lira and colleagues (1999) found that remaining silent was a consistent theme among women. This silence contributes to difficulties in accurately assessing the incidence of rape in Latina cultures. Rozee (1999) reported that among the most vulnerable women to rape are immigrant women and refugee women. They are at risk for being raped due to their language differences as well as unfamiliarity with their new culture. They also fear reporting rape because they believe they will be deported (Rozee & Van Boemel, 1989). Holzman (1994) reported that physically challenged women are three times more likely to be raped than physically unchallenged women.

Approximately 6 percent of rape victims are men (U.S. Department of Justice). Pino and Meier (1999) found that men fail to report rape when it jeopardizes their self-identity in terms of masculinity. Thus, failure to report differs by victims' sex: Women are less likely to report rape that did not fit their stereotypical view of rape.

Date Rape

Rape involving a victim who knows or is familiar with the rapist is referred to as **"acquaintance rape."** The United States Department of Justice (1994) estimated that at least 55 percent of rapes are acquaintance rapes, which account for the 90 percent of reported cases involving children under 12. Acquaintance rapes are likely to go unreported for a number of reasons, as we mentioned earlier in this discussion.

On college/university campuses, acquaintance rapes are commonly referred to as **"date rapes."** Psychologist Mary Koss facilitated the *Ms.* national research project on acquaintance rape that was discussed in Robin Warshaw's (1988) book, *I Never Called It Rape.* Koss surveyed 32 college campuses in the United States and found that one in four women surveyed (a total of 3,187 were raped) were victims of rape or attempted rape; 84 percent of women who had been raped knew their attacker; and 57 percent of the rapes happened on dates. Women did not label what had happened to them as rape when it occurred between dating partners, when they had consented to sexual intimacy with the same man on previous occasions, and when minimal violence was involved. Women reported the following:

> I didn't tell anyone. In fact, I wouldn't even admit to it myself until about four months later when the guilt and fear that had been eating at me became too much to hide and I came very close to a complete nervous breakdown. I tried to kill myself, but fortunately I chickened out at the last minute.
>
> There's no way to describe what was going on inside me. I was losing control and I'd never been so terrified and helpless in my life.
>
> I felt as if my whole world had been kicked out from under me and I had been left to drift all alone in the darkness. I had horrible nightmares in which I relived the rape, and others which were even worse. I was terrified of being with people and terrified of being alone. I couldn't concentrate on anything and began failing several classes. Deciding what to wear in the morning was enough to make me panic and cry uncontrollably. I was convinced I was going crazy, and I'm still convinced I almost did.
>
> (quoted in Warshaw, 1988, pp. 67–68)

Thirty percent of the women identified as rape victims in the *Ms.* study considered suicide after the rape, 31 percent sought psychotherapy, 22 percent took self-defense courses, and 82 percent said the experience had permanently changed them. In the year prior to this research, 2,971 college men reported that they had committed 187 rapes, 157 attempted rapes, 327 episodes of sexual coercion, and 854 incidents of unwanted sexual contact. Eighty-four percent of the men who committed rapes did not label their behavior as rape.

This study also found unacknowledged rape victims (i.e., women did not identify what had happened to them as rape when it took place between dating partners, when they had consented to sexual intimacy with this man on previous occasions, and when minimal violence was involved) (Schwartz & DeKeserdy, 1997). Research subsequent to Koss's has found comparable results (e.g., Schwartz & DeKeserdy, 1997). In addition, college students' definition of date rape is not consistent with legal definitions (Sawyer, Pinciaro, & Jessell, 1998). Students' perceptions and attitudes change and become more in line with legal definitions as they participate in training programs on rape awareness (Foubert, 2000).

Psychological Impact of Rape

Rape victims exhibit very high distress levels within the first week (Koss, 1993). This distress peaks in severity three weeks following the victimization, continues at a high level for one month, and then starts to improve three months post-rape (Rozee, 1999). One-fourth of women who are raped continue to experience negative effects several years post-victimization (Hanson, 1990). Rape victims are likely to experience depression, substance abuse and dependence, generalized anxiety, and posttraumatic stress disorder (Koss, Heise, & Russo, 1994).

Koss (1993) reported several persisting conditions that were disproportionately experienced by rape victims: headaches, gastrointestinal disorders, premenstrual symptoms, general pain, pelvic pain, and psychogenic seizures.

Koss (1988) also found that few rape victims seek formal mental health treatment in the immediate aftermath of rape. According to Koss (1993):

> It is understandable that rape victims strongly resist the identity of "psychiatric patient.". . . . Often they hope that the rape will resolve itself if they go back to their normal routine and don't think or talk about it. However, resolution of rape on one's own is difficult because victims face a culture that challenges their credibility and holds them at least partially culpable for the sexual assault against them. (p. 1065)

What Can We Do?

As with sexual harassment and other forms of sexual violence against women, we need to examine the masculine gender role with its prescriptive aggression against women. Aggression and violence are still seen by many as integral to the masculine gender role (Paludi, Paludi, & Doyle, in press). Thus, one way to reduce sexual assault in our society would be to redefine the masculine gender role, incorporating nonaggressive elements.

Several campuses have men's programs that conduct rape awareness education. For example, in Madison, Wisconsin, an organization called Men Stopping Rape offers community educational programs about rape and provides education for middle school, high school, and college students. These programs address ways to define masculinity without including aggressiveness and sexual violence. *Ms.* Magazine (1999/2000) summarizes research from Glasgow and North London universities in which 50 percent of male students believe it is permissible to rape a woman in some circumstances, for example, forcing their wives to have sex, if the man was "so turned on he can't stop," if the woman had "slept with loads of men," or if no one would find out. This research is comparable to studies conducted in the United States (e.g., Malamuth & Check, 1981). Good, Heppner, Hillenbrand, & Wang (1995) reported that masculinity ideology (i.e., a set of beliefs about what men's behavior should be like; see Paludi et al., in press) was the most consistent predictor of college men's violence-supporting beliefs and actions. College men who hold more traditional masculinity ideologies are more likely to endorse rape myths and are more likely to participate in psychological violence than men with more egalitarian masculinity ideologies.

Timothy Beneke (1982) asked men to view rape as their problem too (a view that could be extended to other forms of victimization), because it is men who rape and who collectively have the power to stop rape. Robin Warshaw (1988) argued that "to harness that power, many men will have to rethink their beliefs about women and sex and change their behaviors" (p. 161).

We may believe that women should not fight a rapist because she would be injured more seriously if she did actively resist. Research disputes this belief (e.g., Koss & Mukai, 1993, Zoucha-Jensen & Coyne, 1993). Kleck and Sayles (1990) found that 3 percent of rapes involve any additional serious injury. The rape itself is the most serious injury to women. Rozee (1999) summarized this research on self-defense:

1. Women who fight back and fight back immediately are less likely to be raped than women who do not.

2. Women who fight back are no more likely to be injured than women who do not fight back. In fact, it has been shown that victim resistance often occurred in response to physical attack.

3. Pleading, begging, and reasoning are ineffective in preventing rape or physical injury.

4. Women who fight back experience less post-assault symptomatology due to avoidance of being raped.

5. Women who fought back had faster psychological recoveries whether or not they were raped.

6. Fighting back strengthens the physical evidence should the survivor decide to prosecute for rape or attempted rape. (p. 110)

Warshaw offered the following guidelines (adapted from rape awareness advocates' literature) to help men achieve this goal (1988, pp. 161–164):

1. Never force a woman to have sex.

2. Don't pressure a woman to have sex.

3. Stay sober.

4. Don't buy the myth that a drunken woman "deserves" to be raped.

5. Do not "join in" if a friend invites you to participate in sexual behavior.

6. Do not confuse "scoring" with having a successful social encounter.

7. Don't assume that you know what a woman wants, and vice versa.

8. "No" means "No."

9. Speak up if you feel you're getting a double message from a woman.

10. Communicate with women.

11. Communicate with other men.

Warshaw also outlined specific steps for women to take:

1. You have the right to set sexual limits and to communicate those limits.

2. Be assertive.

3. Stay sober.

4. Find out whatever you can about a new date.

5. Remain in control.

6. Take care of yourself.

7. Trust your feelings.

If you are a friend of a woman who has been raped, there are several important steps for you to take (Warshaw, 1988):

1. Believe her.

2. Listen to her.

3. Comfort her.

4. Reinforce the contention that the rape was not her fault.

5. Provide protection (e.g., a secure place to sleep).

6. Suggest calling a rape crisis center.

7. Encourage her to preserve evidence.

8. Treat her medical needs.

9. Help her to organize her thoughts, but let her make decisions about how to proceed.

10. If you are her lover, with her approval, use appropriate touching and language to reestablish her feelings of worth.

11. Help her get psychological and legal help.

12. Be available.

13. Learn about rape trauma syndrome.

14. Get therapeutic support for yourself.

If you are a victim of rape, I encourage you to follow these suggestions:

1. Believe in yourself! The rape was not your fault.

2. Report the crime. Tell someone you trust—your roommate, parent, friend, professor.

3. Get medical attention immediately.

4. Choose when to report the rape to campus officials and to the police.

5. Give yourself lots of time to recover. If you have to, take some time off from classes and/or work.

6. Seek therapeutic support at the campus counseling center or a local rape crisis center.

7. When you are ready, share your experiences with other women.

INCEST

Legal Definition and Incidence of Incest

Incest is defined as sexual contact between a child and a person considered an ineligible partner because of blood and/or social ties to the child and the child's family (e.g., father, stepfather, mother). Exact prevalence rates of incest are not known; they are difficult to determine since most incestuous experiences are not reported at the time of their occurrence (Lundberg-Love, 1999).

Research on incest has suggested that at least 20 percent of women have been a victim of incest at some time in their lives. Of these women, 12 percent experienced incest before the age of 14 years and 16 percent before the age of 18 years. Most of the abuse is perpetrated by a family member, family friends or acquaintances, relatives, or neighbors—the very individuals who should be protecting children (Lundberg-Love, 1999). The perpetrators of incest are predominantly men, including perpetrators of incest with boys (Courtois, 1988; U.S. Department of Justice, 1994). Girls are more likely to be sexually abused within the family; boys are more likely to be abused by a nonfamily member (Courtois, 1988, 2000). Christine Courtois (1988) stated:

> The child is manipulated by the unequal power in the relationship, that is, by the relationship with the perpetrator on whom she is dependent. The child is further coerced by the perpetrator's strong desire to keep the activity a secret, which has the purpose of minimizing intervention and allowing repetition. (p. 6)

If children do disclose information about the incestuous relationship, they are typically met with disbelief and rationalization of the perpetrator's behavior (Courtois, 1988, 2000). Thus, most girls and boys do not tell.

We may believe that incest occurs more often in families of working-class background, in ethnic minority families, and in rural families, but these beliefs have not been substantiated by research (Lundberg-Love, 1999). Girls in high-income families were more frequently the victims of incest than girls in low-income families. In addition, the percentage of incest victims is comparable across all ethnic groups studied (with the exception of Asian women, who are at a lower risk; Landrine, 1995).

Psychological Impact of Incest

Girls and boys who are victims of incest suffer after effects that are, in many cases, serious enough to warrant therapy continuing into adulthood (Courtois, 2000; Lundberg-Love, 1999). The effects of incest on the victim are serious, despite the fact that the incidents are not typically reported and have been repressed. Incest victims suffer from depression, guilt, anger, and a loss of self-esteem. Adult survivors frequently report suicidal ideation (Saunders, Villeponteaux, Lipovsky, & Kilpatrick, 1992). Nightmares, crying spells, and fear reactions are very common in girls who have been victims of incest. Consciousness-raising groups (see Chapter 4) have been valuable for women who experienced incest (Lundberg-Love, 1999).

In incest victims' own voices:

> For the next 20 years, I will probably continue to walk around and ask other women, "What was your childhood like?" Hearing women say that no one touched them sexually at that young age helps me realize that something in my childhood was really wrong.
>
> I feel empowered by letting him know I am aware that the incest occurred. I feel empowered by the fact that I didn't ask him if he remembered, I just told him. I knew he would deny it. I just wanted to say, "This happened." I did not expect results. Telling him was the total opposite of all that happened—what was invisible is now out in the open.
>
> (Boston Women's Health Book Collective, 1984, pp. 109–110)

Koss (1990) reported that several random community surveys have found that adult women who were victims of incest had identifiable degrees of impairment when compared with nonvictims. For example, 17 percent of adult women who were victims of incest as children were clinically depressed, and 18 percent were considered severely psychoneurotic. In their lifetimes, victims were more likely than nonvictims to have had problems with depression, alcohol and other drug abuse, panic, and obsessive-compulsive symptoms.

What Can We Do?

As parents, teachers, family members, and concerned adults, we all have responsibilities in dealing with incest. Tedisco and Paludi (1996) recommend the following:

1. We must teach children the names for parts of their bodies. Many children do not know the names for their genitals. Parents who are uncomfortable with using the correct language may teach children to refer to "the part of my body that's covered by underwear."

2. When children know the parts of their bodies, we must teach them the difference between "good touch" and "bad touch." Children should be told that a "good touch" makes them feel right, wanted, and cared for, and a "bad touch" is unwanted and does not feel good.

3. We should not encourage children to give unconditional affection. If a child refuses to kiss or hug a relative, that wish should be respected. By encouraging children to give hugs and kisses to everyone, we are giving a message that forced physical contact is acceptable. This message is a dangerous one for children to learn; they may rely on it with someone who may abuse them.

4. We need to be sensitive to changes in children's behavior and attitudes. Children communicate in a variety of ways. We must question why they don't want to be with someone.

5. We must establish an atmosphere of warmth and affection so that children will come to us if something is troubling them.

If you remember incestuous experiences you have had, I encourage you to take the following suggestions:

1. Trust yourself. Believe that the abuse was not your fault.

2. You were not seductive; you did not initiate the incestuous act. You cannot be held responsible for behavior that occurred to you when you were a child.

3. Report the abuse. Tell someone you trust—your roommate, a friend, a professor, a counselor, a member of the clergy.

4. Decide whether you want to report the incest to your relatives. If you do, get support for this encounter—perhaps ask an advocate to come with you.

5. Give yourself lots of time to recover. If you have to, take some time off from classes and/or work.

6. Seek therapeutic support at the campus counseling center or a local rape crisis center.

BATTERING

Incidence of Battering

Despite a considerable amount of publicity about battered women, most **battering** remains a secret, especially within ethnic minority groups (Browne, 1993; Butts Stahly, 1996; Graham & Rawlings, 1999; Ryan, Frieze, & Sinclair, 1999). Walker (1999) reported that the Fourth United Nations International Conference on Women (1996) identified no country that had an absence of domestic violence.

How prevalent is battering? It is difficult to answer this question, because of the private nature of the commission of the act and the hesitancy on the part of many women to seek outside help. For many women (and men), battering is a taboo topic to which they do not admit. Yet, we do have some evidence of the problem via estimates of families that harbor women beaters in their midst.

Battering in dating relationships affects one-third of U.S. college/university students (Ryan et al., 1999). In dating relationships, women experience being pushed, grabbed, or shoved by their male dates. In addition, they report being slapped and having objects thrown at them. They may be stalked by an ex-lover who refuses to accept the end of the relationship (Ryan et al., 1999). Men are more likely than women to view courtship violence as justifiable (Tontodonato & Crew, 1992).

In a national sample of over 2,000 families, Murray Straus, Richard Gelles, and Suzanne Steinmetz (1980) found that one out of every six couples engage in at least one violent act each year. Over the course of a marriage, just over one-fourth of couples will experience marital violence. Straus and his colleagues concluded: "The American family and the American home are perhaps as or more violent than any other American institution or setting (with the exception of the military, and only then in time of war)" (p. 4).

Browne (1993) estimated that a minimum of 4 million women are assaulted by male partners each year in the United States, and between 21 and 34 percent of all women will be physically assaulted by a male intimate during adulthood. We can only speculate how many men abuse their wives emotionally; psychological abuse is destructive, but less visible. The abuse of women is not confined to marriage. Some studies suggest that violence among unmarried couples who live together is even greater than among married couples. Abuse in couples' relationships may include intense criticisms and put-downs, verbal harassment, sexual coercion and assault, physical attacks and intimidation, restraint of normal activities and freedoms, and denial of access to resources (Butts Stahly, 1999).

Impact of Battering

Battered women may stay in a violent relationship because they believe the situation is inescapable or is part of their lot in life. They feel helpless about changing their lives, and they fear that any action they take will contribute to more violence. These fears are justified (Butts Stahly, 1999). Root (1995) reminds us that the insular nature of Asian American families, as well as cultural imperatives to protect the family's honor, contribute to women's remaining silent about battering and other forms of sexual abuse.

Lenore Walker (1989) published a book titled *Terrifying Love: Why Battered Women Kill and How Society Responds.* Her analysis indicates that battered women who kill their abusers share many characteristics with those who do not. They typically have a poor self-image and low self-esteem, and they suffer guilt, believing they are at fault for not making the violent behavior on the part of their batterer cease. Walker explains these common expressions in terms of traditional socialization of girls and women in our culture. In nearly 85 percent of the cases in which a woman is killed by her husband or lover, the police had previously been called to stop domestic violence (Butts Stahly, 1999).

Walker adds to this analysis by suggesting that battered women who kill are different from those who do not, in terms of the perceived danger of their situation as well as the severity of the psychological, sexual, and physical abuse they suffer. Walker notes:

> Eventually, special legal procedures for battered women defendants must be legitimized: procedures that recognize and validate the world view of women as well as of men, procedures that ultimately will allow battered women's voices to be heard. Once battered women are allowed to speak, they will be able to tell their own stories. And to know a battered woman's story is to understand, without a doubt, why she has killed.
>
> Battered women modify their own behavior so as to minimize the violence. However, these attempts may be met with further attacks. Whatever the woman does can be thought of as provocative by the man and thus can cause him to react in a violent way (Walker, 1989).

Power Analyses of Battering: Same-Sex and Other-Sex Battering Relationships

Rather than examining domestic violence from the viewpoint of the individual, we need to look at it from the view of the *imbalance of power* that is normally found between women and men.

While women are more likely to be victims of battering, men may be battered by women (Straus, 1999). Some research has suggested that men are more likely than women to underreport the frequency of and the severity of their violence, considering the culture's stereotypic beliefs about masculinity and power (Crowell & Burgess, 1996; Dobash, Dobash, Cavanagh, & Lewis, 1998). In addition, there has been a distinction noted between men's and women's battering. Women may batter men because of fear (Mason & Blankenship, 1987) or self-defense (Makepeace, 1986) or retaliation (Makepeace, 1986). Women are more seriously injured by and killed by male batterers than men are by female batterers (Dobash et al., 1998; Greenfeld, 1998).

There has been a paucity of research to date on violence in lesbian and gay relationships. Island and Letellier (1991) estimated that approximately 500,000 men are battered by their male partner each year. Lie, Schilit, Bush, Montagne, and Reyes (1991) reported that over 50 percent of the lesbians in their sample had been either physically assaulted, psychologically abused, and/or sexually victimized by their partner. One methodological issue should be noted, however, when reviewing the research on battering in gay and lesbian relationships: Most of the research participants are volunteers; they may not be representative of the gay and lesbian populations.

Renzetti (1992) noted that the incidence of same-sex battering may be similar to that of heterosexual battering. Furthermore, once battering occurs in the relationship, it is likely to recur and become more severe over time. Most victims of same-sex battering do not report the violence, nor do they leave the violent relationship (Renzetti, 1992). They are committed to each other and are involved in partnerships in which leaving would result in substantial financial loss. Renzetti (1996) reported that lesbians do not feel especially welcome at battered women's shelters, which may be ill equipped to handle same-sex battering victims.

Certainly, we should point out that the amount of homophobia that exists in this culture as well as others prohibits lesbian and gay victims of battering to report their experiences to the police. They would have to disclose their sexual orientation to the police if they disclosed the violence. They may resist this disclosure due to their concerns about retaliation to themselves, their family members, and their children (Renzetti, 1996).

Physical and Psychological Impact of Battering

Injuries that battered women receive include bruises, cuts, concussions, black eyes, broken bones, scars from burns, knife wounds, loss of hearing and/or vision, and joint damage. McHugh, Frieze, and Browne (1993) reported that, in the United States, women are more at risk of homicide as a result of battering than from all other categories of causes. Pregnant women who are involved with a violent mate face the risk of severe outcomes for their fetus as well as themselves.

Reactions to battering include shock, denial, confusion, psychological numbing, fear, substance abuse, disturbed sleep, and eating disorders (Browne, 1993). A woman remains in a violent relationship not because she is masochistic, but for several well-founded reasons:

Threats to her life and the lives of her children if she leaves the home.
Fear of not getting custody of her children.
Financial dependence.
Feeling of responsibility for keeping the relationship together.
She still loves the batterer.
The batterer is not always violent.

Why Battering Occurs

We have already addressed the reasons why battering may occur in same-sex relationships. Let's now address battering in heterosexual relationships. Most researchers (e.g., Browne, 1993; Dutton, 1992; Frieze, 1983; Walker, 1999) recognize that the United States is a violence-prone society that has an ambivalent view of the role of violence. Americans decry the violence found in many of U.S. urban settings, yet, as a society, we relish watching violent activities and movies. Our society has a patriarchal social order; men are regarded as absolute rulers in their homes (Walker, 1999). We need to _____ batterers come from homes in which they were b_____ ir fathers beating their mothers.

Batterers have l_____ n other sources—that battering their wives is an e_____ rity. From their use of violence, batterers gain per_____ ol. Batterers are likely to be jealous and possessiv_____ ers' whereabouts and demand to know everything _____ nd at home. Hastings and Hamberger (1988) dep_____ rigid and unstable men who are so self-absorbed that reciprocity and empathy are impossible for them.

Men who batter do not do so continually. Rather, a cyclical pattern of beating is common. Walker (1979) identified three phases within this cycle. In the ***tension-building phase***, there are battering incidents. The woman attempts to avoid escalation of the battering by trying to "calm" her mate and by staying out of his way. Tension builds too high to be controlled by these efforts, and the batterer responds with an ***acute battering incident*** in the second phase. In phase three, the tension from the first two phases is gone and the batterer becomes "charming" toward the woman. He delivers *apologies and promises* to never batter again.

The duration of these phases vary from couple to couple. The level of violence tends to increase both in frequency and severity as the relationship continues over time (Walker, 1999).

Child Witnesses to Battering

Children are often in the middle of domestic violence in a number of ways. Arguments about child-rearing practices and children's behavior precipitate major crises that lead to violent episodes. Although children are not the cause of this violence, many children, like their mothers, blame themselves for the violence because of the sequence of events and the family's inability to examine the real underlying factors (Black & Newman, 2000). Research has estimated that, each year, at least 3.3 million children in the United States, between the ages of 3 and 17 years, are at risk of exposure to their mothers' being battered by their fathers (Walker, 1999). Parents may minimize or deny the presence of children during incidents of wife assault, suggesting that the children were asleep or were playing outside. In interviews, however, children can give detailed accounts of the violent behavior that their parents never realized they had witnessed (Graham & Rawlings, 1999).

Several researchers have noted a significant overlap between wife assault and child abuse. Retrospective accounts from women in shelters reveal that as many as 80 percent of the women recall witnessing their mothers being assaulted by their fathers as well as being assaulted themselves. Children may be at particular risk for witnessing violence during significant periods of the family's history. Pregnancy can be a critical period in relation to wife assault, which can have very serious consequences for women and children. Advanced stages of pregnancy leave a woman less capable of maneuvering to avoid blows or escape attacks; there is also greater secondary risk to the fetus and herself (Black & Newman, 2000). Infants and toddlers add stress for the family and leave women in very vulnerable positions regarding battering. Increased violence is also precipitated by the problems of adolescence (e.g., delinquency, running away) that are associated with children's reacting to years of witnessing their mothers being assaulted by their fathers.

Walker (1992) identified three domains that are affected by psychological damage resulting from domestic violence: (1) what individuals think (cognitive), (2) how they feel (affect), and (3) what they do (behavior). Young children and adolescents who have been victimized and/or who have witnessed their mothers being battered may not be able to verbalize the impact of the abuse on them until much later in their lives. With respect to the cognitive impact, victims of domestic violence initially believe that the victimization is going to stop. When their fathers' behavior escalates, these children, like their mothers, begin to feel out of control, helpless, and powerless in the situation. Subsequent to the batterer's continuing behavior, children and women feel trapped. A sense of learned helplessness sets in—no matter what they do, the victimization will not cease and the home will not be returned to safety.

With respect to the affective impact of abuse, among the emotional reactions reported by victims of battering are anger, fear, anxiety, irritability, loss of self-esteem, feelings of humiliation and alienation, and a sense of vulnerability (Butts Stahly, 1999). In addition, most victims experience an immediate post-victimization generalized distress response characterized as a state of psychological shock (e.g., repeated reexperiencing of the trauma by intrusive waking images or dreams, depression, emotional numbing). Children, like their mothers, may not resolve the immediate distress. Instead, a chronic symptom picture may develop and may persist for a considerable length of time (Walker, 1999).

Finally, with respect to the behavioral impact of battering, children and adolescents try to escape their fathers. Their attempts, however, are frequently met with increased violence and threats that they will be killed, that they will be blamed for the victimization, or that their families will be killed if they attempt to flee one more time (Paludi et al., in press). Homicide is currently one of the five leading causes of child mortality in the United States.

Children will be affected by the behaviors that are modeled, by the trauma they are experiencing, and by the distress of their parents. The adults on whom they must depend for safety and nurturance can offer neither safety nor nurturance. Regardless of whether they are physically abused themselves, the psychological scars they bear from watching their fathers beat their mothers are significant (Black & Newman, 2000; Walker, 1999). They learn to become part of a dishonest conspiracy of silence. They lie to prevent inappropriate behavior, and they learn to suspend fulfillment of their needs rather than risk another confrontation. They live in a world of make-believe.

Being battered has direct implications for a mother's effectiveness as a parent because the vast majority of battered women are primary caretakers for their children. Their role as a parent is demeaned through their victimization, because the dysfunction and disorganization of the home offer little nurturance, support, structure, or supervision for children (Walker, 1999). Children may even be neglected by their mothers, who may be too emotionally and physically abused to help even themselves (Black & Newman, 2000). Children's misbehavior and special needs are at a peak when their mothers' ability to respond to them is at a low point (Black & Newman, 2000).

Battering as a Workplace Concern

Women who leave a battering relationship often mention that they had been close to another individual who gave them information and support. This research finding has led organizations—for example, the Business and Professional Women's Organization—to recommend that employers must respond to the needs of children and mothers, in collaboration with other community agencies.

Employment may provide an escape from the battering, but the workplace offers a reliable site where a batterer can find his victim. Homicide is the most frequent manner in which women employees are fatally injured at work (DeCenzo & Robbins, 1999). Battering annually costs employers more than $200 million in reduced worker productivity, increased turnover, and absenteeism. Approximately 25 percent of women who visit emergency rooms are battered women. They incur more than $70 million in hospital bills annually. Thus, these realities demand that employers take remedial and educational steps to deal with domestic violence and its impact on the workplace, including an effective and enforced policy statement, training programs, and providing counseling through **Employees Assistance Programs** (Paludi & Paludi, 2000). Recommendations for Employees Assistance Programs include: helping women and children to develop a sense of trust and safety in the current environment, helping women and children to foster relationships with appropriate nonviolent male models, understanding women and children's insecurity about their future, and countering any sense of guilt about having caused the violence and/or not being able to prevent the abuse. Trained counselors can offer the following treatment modalities for women and children: behavioral techniques to deal with specific problem behaviors, such as aggression; play assessment and play therapy to encourage preschool children to express feelings about the trauma; individual counseling for children, including specific strategies for creating a better understanding of their reaction to the abuse and their preparation for future violence; and women-children support groups. These services can be integrated with other community agencies (Paludi & Paludi, 2000).

What Can We Do?

A realistic view of battering can be found in the imbalance in power between women and men and the idea that men have a right to dominate women in nearly every social situation. Battering is a symptom of a social system wherein men believe that their will is law—a belief that is supported by the social structures. When men no longer believe they have the right to control women's lives, and when they stop thinking that aggression is part of their masculine mandate, we will see a reduction of domestic violence.

Walker (1999) summarized advocacy programs and intervention programs that have been established in several countries, including Japan, Chile, Russia, Greece, Mexico, Nicaragua, and Argentina. The goal of these programs is to assist women in recognizing and disclosing the battering and to encourage fewer victim-blaming attitudes among family members and friends of the victims.

Fawcett, Heise, Isita-Espejel, and Pick (1999) noted that myths about the causes of battering are common in the Izlacalco community they studied, as does resistence to intervening in family violence. One common phrase reported by women research participants in Fawcett and colleagues' study was "El que mete paz, saca mas" (Whoever tries to make peace gets more than (s)he bargained for). Their research indicated that 66 percent of women in a peri-urban neighborhood in Mexico City had reported being physically abused, 76 percent psychologically abused, and 21 percent sexually abused. Romero and Tolbert (1995) reported similar incidence rates: 61 percent of women attending an outpatient clinic in San Miguel de Allende experienced physical abuse in adulthood. Fawcett and collegues (1999) facilitated an intervention program that included media and a twelve-session workshop to train women as community change agents. The following topics were discussed in the workshops:

Family violence as a community problem
Family violence legislation
Forms of violence
Gender role expectations and violence against women
Female socialization and violence against women
Male socialization and violence against women
The cycle of violence
The personal and social consequences of violence against women
Alternatives available for abused women
Crisis-intervention skills
Institutions that support victims of violence
Community intervention

If you are battered:

1. Do not blame yourself for the beatings.

2. Get medical attention immediately.

3. Consider telling a friend or family member who can be trusted.

4. Decide whether you want to report the battering to the police.

5. Decide whether you want to go to a shelter.

If someone you know tells you she has been battered:

1. Listen to her talk about the violence.

2. Let her know her feelings are valid.

3. Let her cry if she wants.

4. Don't give her advice.

5. When she calms down, try to figure out what she wants from you, and offer information regarding:
   a. A hotline any time of day or night.
   b. Legal counsel/advocacy.
   c. Group counseling.
   d. Individual counseling.
   e. Shelter.

6. Help locate services nearest her.

7. Work with her to determine what she can do right now to give her the kind of life she wants.

A CALL TO ACTION

We must all work together in stopping violence against individuals as a way of life. And, we must work on a redefinition of masculinity that excludes sexual violence. Research has suggested that sexually aggressive men are more likely than nonaggressors to rate themselves as traditional on measures of masculinity (Goodman, Koss, Fitzgerald, Russo, & Keita, 1993; Paludi, 1999). As Myriam Miedzian (1991) concluded:

American boys must be protected from a culture of violence that exploits their worst tendencies by reinforcing and amplifying the atavistic values of the masculine mystique. Our country was not created so that future generations could maximize profit at

---

FREEDOM OF SPEECH

In 1996, actor Woody Harrelson starred in the film *"The People v. Larry Flynt."* The movie centered around Larry Flynt, publisher of *Hustler,* which holds the title of being the largest (in circulation) hard-core pornographic magazine in the world. Promotions for this movie included an interview with Harrelson by Matt Lauer, co-anchor of "The Today Show." Here's a segment from the interview:

> LAUER: You are someone who cares deeply about . . . animal rights. . . . If *Hustler* magazine made its reputation . . . publishing pictures of animals strapped to the bumpers of hunters' cars, would you still have wanted to do this role?
>
> HARRELSON: Well, you know, certainly not.

Gloria Steinem, in an article in *MS.* in March/April 1997, summarized the interview in the following way:

> His [Harrelson's] answer said it all: If Larry Flynt published a magazine that portrayed animals in pain, bound and in chains, with objects shoved up their genitals, being tortured and even murdered—which is how *Hustler* has portrayed women—this movie would almost certainly never have been made. (p. 76)

Steinem also stated:

> Why can feminists speak against anything, from wars and presidents to tobacco companies, yet if we use our free speech against pornography, we are accused, in Orwellian fashion, of being against free speech? . . .
>
> We've made progress in explaining that rape is violence, not sex; that sexual harassment is power, not sex; but not in explaining that pornography, from the Greek work *pornoi,* is about female slaves—the women who were considered the lowest of the low among prostitutes—while erotica, from *eros,* is about sexuality and pleasure.
>
> Fortunately, each of us has the First Amendment right to protest. We don't have to let hate masquerade as love, violence as sex, or Larry Flynt as a defender of our freedom. (p. 76)

---

any cost. It was created with humanistic, egalitarian, altruistic goals. We must put our enormous resources and talents to the task of creating a children's culture that is consistent with these goals. (p. 298)

We also need legislation that will elevate the status of women as well as reduce the social acceptability of abuse directed at them (Goodman et al., 1993; Stevenson,

---

BOX 10.1
ORGANIZATIONS CONCERNED WITH VIOLENCE
AGAINST WOMEN

National Center for the Prevention and Control of Rape
National Institute of Mental Health
5600 Fishers Lane
Rockville, Md 20857

9 to 5
YWCA
140 Clarendon St.
Boston, MA 02139

Equal Employment Opportunity Commission
2401 E Street, NW
Washington, DC 20506

National Coalition Against Domestic Violence
P.O. Box 34103
Washington, DC 20043

National Organization for Victim Assistance
1757 Park Rd. NW
Washington, DC 20010

Violence Against Women Office U.S. Department of Justice
10th and Constitution Ave., NW
Room 5302
Washington, DC 20530

Websites

www.mincava.umn.edu/ (University of Minnesota Center Against Violence and Abuse)
www.dpscs.state.md.us/pct/ccpi/sexi.htm (Sexual Assault Prevention Resources)

1999). This legislation, including the Violence Against Women Act, Drug-Induced Rape Prevention Act, the Interstate Stalking Punishment and Prevention Act and the Sexually Violent Offender Registration Act will be discussed in the next chapter when we address equity, justice, and social change.

NEW TERMS

acquaintance rape
acute battering incident

battering
date rape

Employees Assistance Programs

Equal Employment Opportunity
Commission (EEOC)

gender harassment

group harassment

hostile-environment sexual harassment

incest

just-world hypothesis

peer harassment

quid pro quo sexual harassment

rape

seductive behavior

sex-role spillover

sexual bribery

sexual coercion

sexual harassment

sexual imposition

tension-building stage

Title VII of the Civil Rights Act

Title IX of the Education Amendments

CHAPTER REVIEW QUESTIONS

1. Cite incidence rates of the following forms of sexual victimization of women: sexual harassment, rape, incest, battering.

2. Cite reasons why women who have been victims of sexual violence may be reluctant to report the incidents.

3. Distinguish between quid pro quo and hostile-environment sexual harassment.

4. What is acquaintance rape?

5. Outline the major findings from the *Ms.* Study on Acquaintance Rape.

6. Discuss the psychological impact of incest.

7. Why do men batter women?

8. Discuss the cyclical patterns of battering.

9. Cite the research on same-sex as well as other-sex violence. Explain how a power perspective can be used to interpret same-sex violence.

10. You have been asked to talk with high school students about battering in dating relationships. What would you tell these teens? What topics would you not cover? Why? How would you answer the following questions these students pose to you?

    Are all boys and men violent?

    Do I ask to be beaten? Is it my fault?

    What should I do the first time my boyfriend slaps me?

    Who is going to believe that I, a guy, gets pushed and slapped by my girlfriend?

11. How does a "just-world hypothesis" limit our understanding of sexual violence?

SELECTED READINGS

Paludi, M. (Ed.). (1999*). The psychology of sexual victimization: A handbook.* Westport, CT: Greenwood Press.

Schwartz, M., & DeKeserdy, W. (1997). *Sexual assault on the college campus.* Thousand Oaks, CA: Sage.

LEARNING MORE ABOUT . . .

Suggestions for Term Papers and Independent Studies Related to *Gender, Power, and Violence Against Women*

Cultural beliefs about sexual violence

Counselors' attitudes toward women victims of sexual violence

Expert witness testimony in rape cases

Role of religion in counseling women victims of sexual violence

Children as witnesses in court cases on sexual violence

Supportive men's programs for educating men about sexual violence against women

Developing, for high school teachers, a training module on sexual violence against women

TAKING ACTION . . .

on *Gender, Power, and Violence Against Women*

1. Call or write your state assembly member or state senator about bills that have been introduced in the legislature(s) to deal with violence against women.

   Questions to consider asking:

   a. How long have the bills been under consideration?

   b. Do the bills take into account women who are especially vulnerable to sexual victimization?

   c. Do the bills provide for curriculum development to teach children and adolescents about sexual violence against women?

   d. What support do the legislators need from their constituents regarding the passage of these bills?

   Summarize the research on violence against women and share it with your legislators. Present to your class the information you obtained from your legislators.

2. Try some advocacy on your campus through your women's studies program, campus sexual assault committee or similar group:

   a. Hand out fact sheets on sexual victimization to students.

   b. Hold a vigil for victims of sexual violence.

   c. Work with your local YWCA and plan a "Take Back the Night" march throughout your town.

   d. Place photos of missing children, adolescents, and adults around campus. Contact the National Center for Missing and Exploited Children for information.

   e. Conduct a survey of the incidence of various forms of sexual victimization on your campus. Present the results of the survey to campus administrators. Work with your campus administrators to ensure safety on campus.

   f. Work with your campus administrators to revise your sexual harassment policy statement and investigatory procedures.

REFERENCES

Adams, J., Kottke, J., & Padgitt, J. (1983). Sexual harassment of university students. *Journal of College Student Personnel, 24,* 484–490.

American Association of University Women. (1993). *Hostile hallways: The AAUW survey on sexual harassment in America's schools.* Washington, DC: Author.

Association of American Colleges. (1988). *Peer harassment: Hassles for women on campus.* Washington, DC: Project on the Status and Education of Women.

Bailey, N., & Richards, M. (1985, August). *Tarnishing the ivory tower: Sexual harassment in graduate training programs in psychology.* Paper presented at the annual meeting of the American Psychological Association, Los Angeles.

Baker, N. (1989). *Sexual harassment and job satisfaction in traditional and nontraditional industrial occupations.* Unpublished doctoral dissertation, California School of Professional Psychology, Los Angeles.

Barak, A. (1997). Cross-cultural perspectives on sexual harassment. In W. O'Donohue (Ed.), *Sexual harassment: Theory, research, and treatment.* Boston: Allyn & Bacon.

Barickman, R., Paludi, M. A., & Rabinowitz, V. (1993). Sexual harassment of students: Victims of the college experience. In E. Viano (Ed.), *Victimology: An international perspective.* New York: Springer.

Beneke, T. (1982). *Men on rape.* New York: St. Martin's Press.

Black, D., & Newman, M. (2000). Children: Secondary victims of domestic violence. In A. Shalev et al. (Eds.), *International handbook of human responses to trauma.* New York: Plenum.

Bogart, K., Simmons, S., Stein, N., & Tomaszewski, E. (1992). Breaking the silence: Sexual and gender harassment in elementary, secondary, and postsecondary education. In S. Klein (Ed.), *Sex equity and sexuality in education.* Albany: State University of New York Press.

Bond, M. (1988). Division 27 sexual harassment survey: Definition, impact, and environmental context. *The Community Psychologist, 21,* 7–10.

Boston Women's Health Book Collective. (1984). *The new our bodies, ourselves.* New York: Simon & Schuster.

Browne, A. (1993). Violence against women by male partners: Prevalence, outcomes, and policy implications. *American Psychologist, 48,* 1077–1087.

Butts Stahly, G. (1996). Battered women: Why don't they just leave? In J. Chrisler, C. Golden, & P. Rozee (Eds.), *Lectures on the psychology of women.* New York: McGraw-Hill.

Connecticut Permanent Commission on the Status of Women (1995). *In our own backyard: Sexual harassment in Connecticut's public high schools.* Hartford, CT: Author.

Courtois, C. (1988). *Healing the incest wound.* New York: Norton.

Courtois, C. (2000). The aftermath of child sexual abuse: The treatment of complex posttraumatic stress reactions. In L. Szuchman et al. (Eds.), *Psychological perspectives on human sexuality.* New York: Wiley.

Crowell, N., & Burgess, A. (1996). *Understanding violence against women.* Washington, DC: National Academy Press.

Dansky, B., & Kilpatrick, D. (1997). Effects of sexual harassment. In W. O'Donohue (Ed.), *Sexual harassment: Theory, research, and treatment.* Boston: Allyn & Bacon.

DeCenzo, D., & Robbins, S. (1999). *Human resource management.* New York: McGraw Hill.

DeFour, D. C. (1996). The interface of racism and sexism in sexual harassment. In M. Paludi (Ed.), *Sexual harassment on college campuses: Abusing the ivory power.* Albany: State University of New York Press.

Dobash, R., Dobash, R., Cavanagh, K. & Lewis, R. (1998). Separate and intersecting realities: A comparison of men's and women's accounts of violence against women. *Violence Against Women, 4,* 382–414.

Doyle, J., & Paludi, M. (1995). *Sex and gender: The human experience* (3rd ed.). Dubuque, IA: Brown.

Dutton, M. (1992). Assessment and treatment of PTSD among battered women. In D. Foy (Ed.), *Treating PTSD: Procedure for combat veterans, battered women, adult and child sexual assaults.* New York: Guilford Press.

Dziech, B. W., & Weiner, L. (1984). *The lecherous professor.* Boston: Beacon Press.

Fawcett, G., Heise, L., Isita-Espejel, L., & Pick, S. (1999). Changing community response to wife abuse: A research and demonstration project in Iztacalco, Mexico. *American Psychologist, 54,* 41–49.

Fineran, S., & Bennett, L. (1999). Gender and power issues of peer sexual harassment among teenagers. *Journal of Interpersonal Violence, 14,* 626–641.

Fineran, S., & Bennett, L. (2000, August). *A cross-cultural comparison of peer sexual harassment among high school students in South Africa and the United States.* Paper presented at the International Coalition Against Sexual Harassment Conference, Washington, DC.

Finkelhor, D., & Dziuba-Leatherman, J. (1994). Victimization of children. *American Psychologist, 49,* 173–183.

Fitzgerald, L. F., & Gelfand, M. (1994, August). *Sexual harassment in Latin America: Prevalence and perceptions in Brazil.* Paper presented at the annual conference of the American Psychological Association, Los Angeles.

Fitzgerald, L. F., & Omerod, A. (1993). Sexual harassment in academia and the workplace. In F. L. Denmark & M. A. Paludi (Eds.), *Psychology of women: Handbook of issues and theories.* Westport, CT: Greenwood Press.

Fitzgerald, L. F., Shullman, S., Bailey, N., Richards, M., Swecker, J., Gold, Y., Omerod, M., & Weitzman, L. (1988). The incidence and dimensions of sexual harassment in academia and the workplace. *Journal of Vocational Behavior, 32,* 152–175.

Foubert, J. (2000). The longitudinal effects of a rape-prevention program on fraternity men's attitudes, behavioral intent, and behavior. *Journal of American College Health, 48,* 158.

Frieze, I. (1983). Investigating the causes and consequences of marital rape. *Signs, 8,* 532–553.

Gold, Y. (1987, August). *The sexualization of the workplace: Sexual harassment of pink-, white-, and blue-collar workers.* Paper presented to the annual conference of the American Psychological Association, New York.

Good, G., Heppner, M., Hillenbrand, T., & Wang, L. (1995). Sexual and psychological violence: An exploratory study of predictors in college men. *Journal of Men's Studies, 4,* 59–71.

Goodman, L., Koss, M., Fitzgerald, L., Russo, N. F., & Keita, G. P. (1993). Male violence against women: Current research and future directions. *American Psychologist, 48,* 1054–1058.

Graham, D., & Rawlings, E. (1999). Observers' blaming of battered wives: Who, what, when, and why. In M. Paludi (Ed.), *The psychology of sexual victimization: A handbook.* Westport, CT: Greenwood Press.

Greenfeld, L. (1998). *Violence by intimates.* Washington, DC: U.S. Department of Justice, Bureau of Justice Statistics.

Gruber, J. & DeSouza, E. (2000, August). *Sexual harassment in a cross-cultural context: Results from college students in four countries.* Paper presented at the International Coalition Against Sexual Harassment conference, Washington, DC.

Gutek, B. (1985). *Sex and the workplace.* San Francisco: Jossey-Bass.

Gutek, B., & Koss, M. (1993). Changed women and changed organizations: Consequences of and coping with sexual harassment. *Journal of Vocational Behavior, 42,* 28–48.

Hanson, R. (1990). The psychological impact of sexual assault on women and children: A review. *Annals of Sex Research, 3,* 187–232.

Hastings, J., & Hamberger, L. (1988). Personality characteristics of spouse abusers: A controlled comparison. *Violence and Victims, 3,* 31–48.

Holzman, C. (1994). Multicultural perspectives on counseling survivors of rape. *Journal of Social Distress and the Homeless, 3,* 81–97.

Hordes, D. (2000, August). *The workplace.* Paper presented at the Inernational Coalition Against Sexual Harassment, Washington, DC.

Island, D., & Letellier, P. (1991). *Men who beat the men who love them.* New York: Haworth Press.

Kleck, G., & Sayles, S. (1990). Rape and resistance. *Social Problems, 37,* 149–162.

Koss, M. P. (1988). Hidden rape: Sexual aggression and victimization in a national sample of students in higher education. In A. W. Burgess (Ed.), *Rape and sexual assault.* New York: Garland.

Koss, M. P. (1990). The women's mental health research agenda: Violence against women. *American Psychologist, 45,* 374–380.

Koss, M. P. (1993). Rape: Scope, impact, interventions, and public policy. *American Psychologist, 48,* 1062–1069.

Koss, M. P., Heise, L., & Russo, N. F. (1994). The global health burden of rape. *Psychology of Women Quarterly, 18,* 509–537.

Koss, M. P., Mukai, T. (1993). Recovering ourselves: Frequency, effects, and resolution of rape. In F. Denmark & M. Paludi (Eds.), *Psychology of women: A handbook of issues and theories.* Westport, CT: Greenwood.

LaFontaine, E., & Tredeau, L. (1986). The frequency, sources, and correlates of sexual harassment among women in traditional male occupations. *Sex Roles, 15,* 423–432.

Landrine, H. (Ed.). (1995). *Bringing cultural diversity to feminist psychology.* Washington, DC: American Psychological Association.

Levy, A., & Paludi, M. A. (1997). *Workplace sexual harassment.* Englewood Cliffs, NJ: Prentice-Hall.

Lie, G., Schilit, R., Bush, J., Montagne, M., & Reyes, L. (1991). Lesbians in currently aggressive relationships: How frequently do they report aggressive past relationships? *Violence and Victims, 6,* 121–135.

Lira, L., Koss, M., & Russo, N. (1999). Mexican American women's definitions of rape and sexual abuse. *Hispanic Journal of Behavioral Sciences, 21,* 236–265.

Lundberg-Love, P. (1999). The resilience of the human psyche: Recognition and treatment of the adult survivor of incest. In M. Paludi (Ed.), *The psychology of sexual victimization: A handbook.* Westport, CT: Greenwood Press.

Magley, V., Hulin, C., Fitzgerald, L., & DeNardo, M. (1999). Outcomes of self-labeling sexual harassment. *Journal of Applied Psychology, 84,* 390–402.

Makepeace, J. (1986). Gender differences in courtship violence victimization. *Family Relations, 36,* 383–388.

Malamuth, N., & Check, J. (1981). The effects of mass media exposure on acceptance of violence against women: A field experiment. *Journal of Research in Personality, 15,* 436–446.

Mason, A., & Blankenship, V. (1987). Power and affiliation motivation, stress, and abuse in intimate relationships. *Journal of Personality and Social Psychology, 52,* 203–210.

McHugh, M., Frieze, I., & Browne, A. (1993). Research on battered women and their assailants. In F. L. Denmark & M. A. Paludi (Eds.), *Psychology of women: A handbook of issues and theories.* Westport, CT: Greenwood Press.

Mecca, S., & Rubin, L. (1999). Definitional research on African American students and sexual harassment. *Psychology of Women Quarterly, 23,* 813–817.

Miedzian, M. (1991). *Boys will be boys: Breaking the link between masculinity and violence.* New York: Doubleday.

Mollica, R., Wyshak, G., & Lavelle, J. (1987). The psychological impact of war trauma and torture on Southeast Asian refugees. *American Journal of Psychiatry, 144,* 1567–1571.

Munson, L., Hulin, C., & Drasgow, F. (2000). Longitudinal analysis of dispositional influences and sexual harassment: Effects on job and psychological outcomes. *Personnel Psychology, 53,* 21–46.

Paludi, C., & Paludi, M. (2000, October). *Developing and enforcing an effective workplace policy statement, procedures, and training programs on domestic violence.* Workshop presented at the Domestic Violence as a Workplace Concern conference, Nashua, NH.

Paludi, M. A. (Ed.). (1996). *Sexual harassment on college campuses: Abusing the ivory power.* Albany: State University of New York Press.

Paludi, M. A. (Ed.). (1999). *The psychology of sexual victimization: A handbook.* Westport, CT: Greenwood Press.

Paludi, M. (2000, August). *Contributions from the discipline of psychology to the understanding and prevention of sexual harassment in the workplace and education.* Paper presented at the International Coalition Against Sexual Harassment, Washington, DC.

Paludi, M. A., & Barickman, R. (1991). *Academic and workplace sexual harassment: A resource manual.* Albany: State University of New York Press.

Paludi, M. A., & Barickman, R. B. (1998). *Academic and workplace sexual harassment: A manual of resources* (2nd ed.). Albany: State University of New York Press.

Paludi, M. A., & DeFour, D. C. (1998). Sexual harassment on college campuses. In A. Hoffman, J. Schub, & R. Fenske (Ed.), *Violence on campus.* Gaithersburg, MD: Aspen.

Paludi, M., Paludi, C., & Doyle, J. (in press). *Sex and gender* (5th ed.). New York: McGraw Hill.

Pino, N., & Meier, R. (1999). Gender differences in rape reporting. *Sex Roles, 40,* 979–990.

Renzetti, C. (1992). *Violent betrayal: Partner abuse in lesbian relationships.* Newbury Park, CA: Sage.

Renzetti, C. (1996). The poverty of services for battered lesbians. *Journal of Gay and Lesbian Social Services, 4,* 61–68.

Romero, M., & Tolbert, K. (1995, June). *La consulta externa como oportunidad de deteccion de la vilencia domestica.* Paper presented at the National Council of International Health Conference, Crystal City, VA.

Root, M. (1995). The psychology of Asian American women. In H. Landrine (Ed.), *Bringing cultural diversity to feminist psychology.* Washington, DC: American Psychological Association.

Rozee, P. (1999). Cultural issues in rape. In M. Paludi (Ed.), *The psychology of sexual victimization: A handbook.* Westport, CT: Greenwood Press.

Rozee, P., & Van Boemel, G. (1989). The psychological effects of war trauma on older Cambodian refugee women. *Women and Therapy 8,* 23–50.

Ryan, K., Frieze, I., & Sinclair, H. C. (1999). Physical violence in dating relationships. In M. Paludi (Ed.), *The psychology of sexual victimization: A handbook.* Westport, CT: Greenwood Press.

Salisbury, J., Ginorio, A., Remick, H., & Stringer, D. (1986). Counseling victims of sexual harassment. *Psychotherapy, 23,* 316–324.

Sandler, B. (2000, August). *Peer harassment.* Paper presented at the Ninth Annual Interdisciplinary Congress on Sexual Harassment, Washington, DC.

Sandler, B., & Paludi, M. (1993). *Educator's guide to dealing with sexual harassment.* Washington, DC: Thompson.

Saunders, B., Villeponteaux, L., Lipovsky, J., & Kilpatrick, D. (1992). Child sexual assault as a risk factor for mental disorder for women: A community survey. *Journal of Interpersonal Violence, 7,* 189–204.

Sawyer, R., Pinciaro, P., & Jessell, J. (1998). Effects of coercion and verbal consent on university students' perception of date rape. *American Journal of Health Behavior, 22,* 46–53.

Schneider, K., & Swan, S. (1994). *Job-related, psychological, and health-related outcomes of sexual harassment.* Paper presented at the Ninth Annual Conference of the Society of Industrial and Organizational Psychology, Nashville, TN.

Schwartz, M., & DeKeserdy, W. (1997). *Sexual assault on the college campus: The role of male peer support.* Newbury Park, CA: Sage.

Searles, P., & Berger, R. (1987). The current status of rape reform legislation: An examination of state statutes. *Women's Rights Law Reporter, 10,* 25–43.

Stein, N. (1995). Sexual harassment in school: The public performance of gendered violence. *Harvard Educational Review, 65,* 145–162.

Steinem, G. (1997, March/April). What's wrong with this picture? *Ms.,* 76.

Stevenson, M. (1999). Sexual victimization of women: The congressional response. In M. A. Paludi (Ed.), *Psychology of sexual victimization: A handbook.* Westport, CT: Greenwood Press.

Straus, M. (1999). The controversy over domestic violence by women: A methodological, theoretical, and sociology of science analysis. In X. Arriaga et al. (Eds.), *Violence in intimate relationships.* Thousand Oaks, CA: Sage.

Straus, M., Gelles, R., & Steinmetz, S. (1980). *Behind closed doors: Violence in the American family.* Garden City, NY: Anchor Books.

Strauss, S., & Espeland, P. (1992). *Sexual harassment and teens.* Minneapolis: Free Spirit.

Tedisco, J., & Paludi, M. A. (1996). *Missing children.* Albany: State University of New York Press.

Till, F. (1980). *Sexual harassment: A report on the sexual harassment of students.* Washington, DC: National Advisory Council on Women's Educational Programs.

Tontodonato, P., & Crew, B. (1992). Dating violence, social learning theory, and gender: A multivariate analysis. *Violence and Victims, 7,* 3–14.

Uhari, M., Kokkonen, J., Nuutinen, J., Vainionpaa, L., Rantala, H., Lautala, P., & V'yrynen, M. (1994). Medical student abuse: An international phenomenon. *Journal of the American Medical Association, 271,* 1049–1051.

U.S. Department of Justice (1994, November). *Domestic violence: Violence between intimates.* In Bureau of Justice statistics: Selected findings, Office of Justice programs (NcJ-149259). Washington, DC: U.S. Government Printing Office.

U.S. Merit Systems Protection Board. (1981). *Sexual harassment of federal workers: Is it a problem?* Washington, DC: U.S. Government Printing Office.

U.S. Merit Systems Protection Board. (1987). *Sexual harassment of federal workers.* Washington, DC: U.S. Government Printing Office.

Walker, L. (1979). *The battered woman.* New York: Harper & Row.

Walker, L. (1989). *Terrifying love: Why battered women kill and how society responds.* New York: Harper.

Walker, L. (1992). Traumatized populations: Roles and responsibilities. In E. Viano (Ed.), *Critical issues in victimology: International perspectives.* New York: Springer.

Walker, L. (1999). Psychology and domestic violence around the world. *American Psychologist, 54,* 21–29.

Warshaw, R. (1988). *I never called it rape.* New York: Harper & Row.

Zalk, S. (1996). Men in the academy: A psychological profile of harassers. In M. A. Paludi (Ed.), *Sexual harassment on college campuses: Abusing the ivory power.* Albany: State University of New York Press

Zoucha-Jensen, J., & Coyne, A. (1993). The effects of resistance strategies on rape. *American Journal of Public Health, 83,* 1633–1634.

ELEVEN

THE PSYCHOLOGY OF WOMEN: EQUITY AND SOCIAL CHANGE

IN WOMEN'S VOICES

Let's work toward a culture in which there is a place for every human gift, in which children are safe and protected, women are respected, and men and women can love each other as whole human beings. . . . Then our daughters will have a place where all their talents will be appreciated, and they can flourish like green trees under the sun and the stars.

Mary Pipher

We need to begin to develop a "moral" basis for feminist psychology and its concern with diversity. To do so, we will need to move beyond our laboratory context, where issues of poverty and power are irrelevant. We will also need to leave our comfortable surroundings for much less pleasant realities so that we can better understand healthy coping in dire circumstances.

Rhoda Unger

Chapter Outline

Questions for Reflection

1. Have your opinions about "the psychology of women" changed since participating in this course and reading this textbook? In what ways have they changed or remained the same?

2. Do you believe you will see an eradication of traditional gender roles in your lifetime? Why or why not?

3. In what ways can you work for social change with respect to fair treatment of women and men in the workplace, education, the family?

4. Have any of your friends told you that you have been "different" now that you have taken a course in the psychology of women? Are you less tolerant of sexist comments, advertisements, television programs? Are you more willing to stand up for your rights? Are you more sensitive to the viewpoints of others that may be different from your own? Are you more likely to value women and men?

5. Would you like to take other courses on the psychology of women? Why or why not?

6. Have you found it easy or difficult to integrate the material you have learned in your psychology of women course into other courses in the psychology curriculum? Are professors eager to discuss research on women's lives in courses on personality? Developmental psychology? Abnormal psychology? Statistics? Cognitive psychology? Social psychology?

7. If you had to describe this textbook and course on the psychology of women to a friend, what adjectives would you use? Why?

INTRODUCTION: ERADICATING GENDER ROLES VERSUS VALUING WOMEN AS WELL AS MEN

As we near the end of my courses on the psychology of women, students frequently ask me questions about when I believe gender roles in North American culture will be eradicated. I reply that gender roles will most likely never be eradicated.

My response is very often met with sighs and comments from students such as the following:

> How could all of the work done by feminists never become fully realized?
>
> Why bother fighting for women's rights if it will never happen anyway?
>
> Why work on integrating the scholarship on women into the psychology curriculum if no real changes will ever take place?

These comments reflect the "learned helplessness" frequently experienced by individuals committed to social change as defined by eradicating gender roles—statements frequently made by students at the end of a course on the psychology of women.

Perhaps you too share this frustration. It is obvious from reading this textbook that many of the goals of the early women psychologists have still not been realized. A great deal of the empirical research discussed in this textbook has yielded results similar to research conducted one or two decades earlier. For example, we have not reached pay equity in the workplace; sexual victimization is reaching epidemic proportions; the Equal Rights Amendment in the United States has never been passed. You may also wonder why you yourself should work for human rights issues if you may never see the eradication of traditional gender roles in your lifetime or your children's lifetime. Reading the previous chapter on sexual victimization of girls and women probably contributed to any feelings you may have about hopelessness related to changing gender roles.

I always propose an alternative question to students: **When can we begin valuing women?** This question contributes to much less learned helplessness and more action-oriented activities. The answer to this question is **NOW, IMMEDIATELY.**

For example, we can value women by valuing children and by working toward affordable child care. We can value women by helping them learn about AIDS and other sexually transmitted diseases and encouraging them to take responsibility for their sexuality. In addition, we can value women by acknowledging and respecting their choices about not having or having children. We can value women by respecting a variety of physiques—not only placing value on slender women. We can value women by acknowledging older women's wisdom, caring, and beauty.

We can also value women by redefining constructs typically used in psychological research. For example, an ethic of care needs to be considered an alternative moral theory, not simply a complement to justice theories of moral reasoning (Tronto, 1987). We can also value women by redefining "work" to include child care, housekeeping, and volunteer services. Furthermore, "power" needs to be considered as a "capacity" rather than a "thing" word (Paludi, Paludi, & Doyle, in press), and "women" must include women of color, women from all socioeconomic classes, and ethnic women (Landrine, 1995).

In order to reach these goals, we need to redefine the core elements of the feminine and masculine gender roles (Doyle & Paludi, 1998). The issues of employed mothers and day care and of violence against women provide us with several examples of how we may accomplish redefining these gender roles at the **individual level** (through interpersonal relationships), **institutional level** (e.g., workplace policies prohibiting sexual harassment), and **societal level** (e.g., legislation for stricter penalties for rapists). Let's begin by discussing employed women and child care.

A CLOSER LOOK AT EMPLOYED WOMEN AND CHILD CARE

Throughout this text I have discussed the powerful *motherhood mandate* that exists in North American culture (Russo, 1979). According to this mandate, women should bear children and be primarily responsible for their care. Psychologists made this belief popular with their insistence on mothers remaining at home with their children to ensure the children's optimal development (Clark-Stewart, 1993; Etaugh, 1993). The majority of women with children today, however, work outside the home (Sinacore-Guinn, 1998; Sweeney, 1999). The rate of maternal employment for two-parent families with school-age children is more than 75 percent. African American women with school-age children are more likely to be employed than white or Latinas with children (Vandell & Ramanan, 1991).

Employed mothers constitute a heterogeneous group of women who vary in terms of age, relationship status (e.g., single, divorced, widowed, in lesbian relationships, married), stage in the family life cycle (e.g., number and ages of children), and socioeconomic factors. The reasons for women working outside the home are related primarily to financial needs and self-actualization (Scarr, Phillips, & McCartney, 1989; Sinacore-Guinn, 1998). Families must have two incomes to support them at a level previously achieved by one wage earner. Single, widowed, and divorced women with children *must* work to avoid poverty (Duncan & Brooks-Gunn, 2000). Thus, employment is not always a choice for women; it is a necessity. The research question "Should mothers of young children work?" contains a middle-class assumption that mothers don't have to work but simply want to; that they have a choice. Women have always had to work to support themselves and their families (Betz, 1993).

Employed women with children have also reported wanting to work for the social support, adult companionship, and social networks offered by workplaces. Hoffman (1989) and Hyde, Klein, Essex, and Clark (1995) described employment for mothers as a morale boost and a buffer against stress from family roles. What matters most is how satisfied mothers are with the choices they have made regarding integrating work and family (Barnett & Rivers, 1992; Gilbert, 1994) as well as the support they receive from mates, other family members, and employers.

Research on the impact of maternal employment on children has generally found no negative effects on the children of employed mothers (Caruso, 1996; Sweeney, 1999; Vandell & Ramanan, 1991). In fact, maternal employment appears to have a positive influence on adolescents, particularly daughters. The daughters are more likely to be self-confident, to achieve better grades in school, and to pursue careers themselves (Caruso, 1996). Research with children of color consistently has demonstrated that maternal employment is positively associated with academic achievement (Betz, 1993).

Among infants and preschool children, the nature and quality of the child care received are important factors in determining children's adjustment (Clark-Stewart, 1993). Overall, research on child care has found that when children are in high-quality care, there is no negative impact on their emotional adjustment or their relationship with their mothers (Burchinal, Roberts, Nabors, & Bryant, 1996; Hoffman & Youngblade, 1999; Phillips, Voran, Kisker, Howes, & Whitebook, 1994). Child care has been found to have no negative effects on the intellectual development of children, and it may have a positive impact on children from economically disadvantaged homes (Caruso, 1996). The social behavior of children attending day care has been found to show increases in both positive and negative peer-oriented behaviors (Gottfried, Gottfied, Bathurst, & Killian, 1999; Hoffman & Youngblade, 1999).

Girls and boys in middle childhood who care for themselves after school **("latchkey" children)** also do not suffer the negative consequences once believed to be the case with children of employed mothers (Vandell & Ramanan, 1991). If older children are home rather than with friends in unsupervised activities, they may avoid involvement in situations that may be problematic, including gang activity and drug abuse (Rodman & Cole, 1987). Self-care children have an enhanced sense of independence and competence. Their self-esteem is higher than many children who do not care for themselves after school because they feel they are contributing to the household in significant ways (Hoffman, 1989). The type of after-school care has been found not to be as important as the quality of children's experiences with their families (Vandell & Ramanan, 1991).

We should note that there are significant cultural distinctions in the way preschool children and older children are valued. For example, in Belgium and France, access to preschool is a legal right. In Finland, preschoolers whose parents are employed have day care provided to them. In Russia, state-run *yasli-sads* or preschools are attended by 75 percent of children aged 3 to 7 years. In these countries there is thus a coordinated national policy on child care. In the United States, a coordinated policy does not exist. Rather, decisions about preschoolers' education is left to the states and local school districts. Furthermore, the United States does not have a formal curriculum for teaching preschoolers.

Related to the emphasis on child care concerns women's job-protected leaves from employment. For example, women in France have a job-protected leave of six weeks before childbirth. Women in Italy have a six-month job-protected leave paid at a flat rate that is equal to the average income for women. They also have available to them an unpaid job-protected leave for one year, following this six-month period. In Great Britain, parents whose children were born or adopted after December 15, 1999 are given up to thirteen weeks of unpaid leave over their child's first five years of life.

In the United States, policies on child care and maternal leave are recognizing the need to replace myths with realities about *all* women's "personality" and career goals, as well as about what is involved in caring for infants. For example, there is wide variation in women's responses to the birth process. Some women (especially midlife women) need an extended rest period following delivery if the pregnancy and/or birth was difficult. Some women and their babies require three or more months to adjust to a breastfeeding routine. As Sandra Scarr and her colleagues (1989) commented:

> How long should a maternal leave be for either the mother's or the infant's benefit? Neither a mandatory child care nor a mandatory maternal leave policy suits all families. What we need are equally attractive options so that families can choose how best either to take advantage of quality child care while parents work or to arrange an extended leave for parents, usually the mother, to care for the baby. . . . Until the United States recognizes the rights of women to participate fully in the life of the society, through motherhood, employment, and political life, we will continue to fail to make appropriate provisions for the care of children of working families. (pp. 1405–1406, 1407)

Eighty percent of women in their childbearing years are expected to have children during their career path. The **Family and Medical Leave Act** that went into effect in 1993 mandates that employers must permit female and male employees up to a total of twelve workweeks of unpaid leave during any twelve-month period for one or more of the following reasons:

The birth and care of a newborn child of the employee

The placement with the employee of an adopted child or foster care child

The care for an immediate family member with a serious medical condition

To take medical leave because the employee is unable to work because of a serious medical condition

The Family and Medical Leave Act also states that spouses employed by the same employer are jointly entitled to a combined total of twelve workweeks of family leave for the reasons identified above. However, this might not be a likely choice because most two-income families cannot live on one income for a long time. Employees are guaranteed to return to the same job or one comparable in terms of responsibilities and salary.

VALUING EMPLOYED WOMEN
AND EMPLOYED MOTHERS

Areas of conflict endorsed by employed mothers indicate that managing the household, home cleaning, and caring for sick children are major sources of stress (Bird, 1999; Dempsey, 1999). Other problems include issues with time management, stress, and fatigue. The lack of time appears to be most accentuated in areas that are self-related: community activities, reading, hobbies, and physical fitness (Betz, 1993). Instead of doing everything alone, women need help from other women and from men. Family chores and child-rearing responsibilities are not exclusively "women's work" (Paludi et al., in press).

Traditional occupational policies reflect a separation of family from work life and a societal expectation that mothers remain at home to care for their children. There is a tendency for individuals to believe that equality translates into women being employed. However, working outside the home is not progress if women must also continue with full-time responsibility for housekeeping and motherhood, performing "double duty" or what Hochschild (1989) referred to as the "second shift." Thus, equality of the parenting and housekeeping roles has not been achieved (Gottfried et al., 1999).

There is a general incompatibility between the workplace and family demands, and a relative lack of provisions that would ease women's integration of these roles. Present conditions may be expected to produce greater potential stress and conflict among employed mothers, who still have the primary responsibility for child rearing and child care (Gottfried et al., 1999). Many businesses have adopted **family-oriented policies** such as job sharing, flexible work hours, or employer-sponsored day care as employee benefits (DeCenzo & Robbins, 1999; Frone & Yardley, 1996; Kahnweiler & Kahnweiler, 1992). These organizations report positive ramifications for the businesses as well as for parents: lower absenteeism, higher morale, positive publicity, lower rate of turnover, child care hours that conform to work hours, and access to quality infant and child care (Frone & Yardley, 1996).

Finally, women's salaries need to be addressed. In 2000, the Bureau of Labor Statistics Report identified significant earnings gaps between women and men in most occupations. Women still earn far less than their male co-workers. Women's earnings as a percentage of men's earnings did increase from 62.5 percent in 1979 to 76.5 percent in 1999. But we must recognize the interface between race and sex in this change. The pay gap for African American women and Latinas is much wider. African American women receive 64 cents for every dollar earned by white men. Latinas receive 55 cents for every dollar earned by white men. Like white women, African American women are concentrated in low-paying, stereotypic "feminine" jobs, such as domestic and service jobs. Disparity between women's and men's incomes still exists when job category, education, and experience are taken into account. The salary disparity is in large part linked to the cultural belief that men are the primary "breadwinners" of the family and therefore should earn more than women (Paludi et al., in press).

Some individuals have argued that rectifying the problem of salary inequities between women and men should not come about by enacting new laws or by court action. They believe that allowing the marketplace to determine the worth or value of someone's work is still the best way to solve the problem of wage disparity. Most women who are employed as teachers, nurses, day care specialists, and secretaries are underpaid for the quality and quantity of work demanded of them. Most of these women have sole financial responsibility for their families. Furthermore, who cares for children—a relative, day care center, or nanny—is an important determinant of women's work effort and their net earnings (Maume & Mullin, 1993). If the marketplace determines wages, discriminatory practices against women will continue (Doyle & Paludi, 1998).

ANOTHER LOOK AT VIOLENCE AGAINST WOMEN

In the previous chapter, I discussed the incidence of sexual victimization against women. All types of sexual victimization illustrate how men have more power than women, whether it be physical power, expert power, or power derived from the inequalities in the relationship (Doyle & Paludi, 1997).

Russell (1973) described rape not as the act of a disturbed man, but rather as an act of an overconforming man. According to Russell:

> Rape is not so much a deviant act as an overconforming act. Rape may be understood as an extreme acting-out of qualities that are regarded as super masculine in this and many other societies: aggression, force, power, strength, toughness, dominance, competitiveness. To win, to be superior, to be successful, to conquer—all demonstrate masculinity to those who subscribe to common cultural notions of masculinity, i.e., the masculine mystique. And it would be surprising if these notions of masculinity did not find expression in men's sexual behavior. Indeed, sex may be the arena where these notions of masculinity are most intensely played out, particularly by men who feel powerless in the rest of their lives, and hence, whose masculinity is threatened by this sense of powerlessness. (p. 1)

MacKinnon (1979) defined sexual harassment in a similar way:

> Sexual harassment . . . refers to the unwanted imposition of sexual requirements in the context of a relationship of unequal power. Central to the concept is the use of power derived from one social sphere to lever benefits or impose deprivations in another. . . . When one is sexual, the other material, the cumulative sanction is particularly potent. (p. 1)

I too have focused not on men's attitudes toward women but on men's attitudes toward other men, competition, and power. Many of the men with whom I have discussed sexual harassment often act out of extreme competitiveness and concern with ego, or out of fear of losing their positions of power (Levy & Paludi, in press). They may not want to appear weak or less masculine in the eyes of other men, so they will engage in rating women's bodies, pinching women, making implied or overt threats, or spying on women. Women represent a game played to impress other men (Kimmel, 1994; Paludi & Barickman, 1998).

When men are being encouraged to be obsessionally competitive and concerned with dominance, they are likely to eventually use violent means to achieve dominance (Paludi, 1999). They are also likely to be abusive verbally and intimidating in their body language. Deindividuation is quite common among men who engage in "scoping" (numerically rating women as they walk by in the halls or in the classroom). These men discontinue self-evaluation and adopt group norms and attitudes. Under these circumstances, group members behave more aggressively than they would as individuals (American Association of University Women, 1993; Paludi, 1996).

As I discussed in Chapter 10, girls and women who have been sexually victimized experience an immediate post-victimization distress response (Koss, 1993). The features of this response are fear/avoidance, affective constriction, disturbances of self-concept/self-efficacy, and sexual dysfunction. Several researchers have considered female sexual abuse and assault victims to be the largest group of posttraumatic stress disorder sufferers (Koss, 1993; Rozee, 1999). Koss (1993) reported that repeated violent victimizations leave women less skilled at self-protection, more apt to accept victimization as part of being a woman, and less sure of their own self-worth and personal boundaries. Early victimization in a girl's life may increase the chances of her future victimization (Koss, 1993; Lundberg-Love, 1999; Rozee, 1999). Furthermore, research has suggested that men who batter women are likely to have witnessed their fathers beating their mothers. These men are also more likely to abuse their children (Dutton & Golant, 1995; Graham & Rawlings, 1999; Graham, Rawlings, & Rigsby, 1994; Paludi & Paludi, 2000; Walker, 1999).

VALUING WOMEN

We need to examine the masculine gender role, with its prescriptive aggression against women. Aggression and violence are still seen by many as integral parts of the masculine gender role (Doyle, 1995). Thus, one way to reduce sexual assault in our society would be to redefine the masculine gender role, incorporating non-aggressive elements.

Another controversial change aimed at reducing the number of sexual victimizations would be a campaign against violence-oriented **pornography** (Graham & Rawlings, 1999; Levy, 1999; Pollard, 1995). As Gloria Cowan, Cherly Chase, and Geraldine Butts Stahly (1989) pointed out:

> [Pornography] debases, objectifies, and dehumanizes women and . . . the portrayal of violence and rape mythology reinforces, if not fosters, inequality. (p. 97)

The pornography industry has mainly directed its sales to men (Cowan et al., 1989). A large proportion of the male-oriented pornography that is sold in stores across our country portrays women as victims of physical and sexual assault (Cowan, 1995). Donnerstein and Malamuth have found that men's exposure to violent pornography increases (1) sexual arousal, (2) negative attitudes toward women, and (3) favorable attitudes toward sexual assault (Donnerstein, 1983; Malamuth & Donnerstein, 1982).

One way to reduce the sexual violence against women in our society would be to eliminate such material. However, members of the Attorney General's Commission on Pornography (1986) did not agree that a causal link existed between violence and pornography. Members of the commission raised the issue of each person's **First Amendment rights,** which guarantee freedom of speech. Such opposition, however, misinterprets the Constitution and its intent. As Russell (1993) argued:

> Indeed, there would be a public outcry—and rightly so—if there were special non-pornographic movie houses where viewers could see whites beating up people of color, or Christians beating up Jews, and where the victims were portrayed as enjoying or deserving such treatment. But if it's called pornography and women are the victims, then it is considered sex and those who object that it is harmful to women are regarded as prudes. (p. 11)

Insofar as institutional structures are dominated by traditional masculine perspectives, denial of the nature, extent, and seriousness of sexual victimization will continue. Persistent, comprehensive educational strategies are central to any genuine resolution of the sexual victimization against women that is epidemic in all of our institutions (Paludi, 1999; Stevenson, 1999).

These strategies demand that we all make new norms and not rely on masculine-biased definitions of success, career development, sexuality, and power (Graham & Rawlings, 1999). We must work toward a new ethic that will refuse to blame the victim and that will foster an environment that will be compatible with the needs of wives, mothers, women students, and women employees. What this new ethic requires is earnest work on what the family, the schools, and the workplace would look like if caring was deemed a central value and these institutions could be structured to facilitate caring. This goal will be accomplished when women and women's own experiences are placed in the center of the family, workplace, and classroom—when "power over" is replaced by "power to."

SOME CONCLUDING COMMENTS

A major theme throughout this book on the psychology of women is that we need to value women and women's experiences. Women must be valued in terms of their contributions to society and to the development of children. Likewise, women must value themselves and other women.

I hope that you have derived strength from reading about all of the efforts of psychologists to diminish the barriers of sexual orientation, race, disability, class, ethnicity, and sex. And, I hope you have derived strength from reading about the similarities that women around the world share, as well as the distinctiveness among women. I invite you to work for individual as well as social change. Some ways to accomplish these goals are outlined in Box 11.1. All of these suggestions have a common concern for gender justice.

Gentry (1989) asked us to consider the image of making a quilt in understanding feminist psychology. There are many people working on this quilt. Each person is making one piece of the quilt that will have to eventually be joined with the other parts. Each individual uses different stitching on their piece of the quilt. As the suggestions in Box 11.1 illustrate, we can work for social change on an individual level, through our interpersonal relationships with our mates, parents, friends; on an institutional level, by lobbying to make courses on the psychology of women and gender required courses, not electives, and on a societal level, by lobbying state lawmakers on issues related to sexual victimization, reproductive rights, education, and child care. No one of these suggestions is more important than the other. Indeed, all are needed if we are to complete making the quilt that is the psychology of women. As Gentry (1989) stated:

> Feminist psychology and feminism in general seem to be at the point of trying to piece together the individual parts of a quilt. The overall pattern of the quilt that we want is still emerging. No one knows what equality in a post-patriarchal world will look like. We are beginning to piece the separate parts together—to explore the kinds of stitching to use in connecting the pieces and how to place the separate pieces into the pattern. But we have not stopped questioning the process of quilting itself. . . . (p. 5)

I conclude this book with a statement from a student in one of my courses on the psychology of women:

> I learned so much about women. Women face many issues: discrimination, sexism, prejudices . . . by society. Women need to work together to change how society views us. I learned so much and talked about much of the issues brought up in class to my friends and family. My attitudes have changed toward a lot of things. I got to look at myself, my life, and what I see for the future.

I hope that you will share the ideas presented in this book with your friends, family, and instructors. More importantly, I hope you will share **your own** thoughts about the psychology of women, adding your own unique pieces to the quilt.

BOX 11.1
SUGGESTIONS FOR WORKING FOR GENDER JUSTICE

---

1. Volunteer at an organization that is dedicated to assisting victims of sexual violence, e.g., a battered women's shelter, rape crisis center.

2. Encourage your family and friends who are parents to purchase non-sexist books and toys for their children.

3. Inquire about the health problems women in your family have faced, e.g., diabetes, lupus, cardiovascular disease, arthritis. Locate supportive environments (e.g., self-help groups, women's health centers) for women with these health problems. Determine some precursors of health problems at midlife and beyond, for women in your family. For example, find out how nutrition, vitamins, and exercise affect diabetes, osteoporosis, lupus, etc. Provide this information to the women in your family.

4. Write letters of support to companies valuing men and women in their advertisements.

5. Work on better communication in your sexual relationship. Identify your honest feelings about your sexual relationship. Do you believe you are communicating these honest feelings to your partner? Are you being honest with yourself about these feelings? Practice saying what you want—with no apologies.

6. Lobby your state and federal officials about issues you learned from this textbook and your course, e.g., domestic violence, date rape, reproductive rights.

7. Take other women's studies courses and participate in women's studies events, celebration of Women's History Month in March, Take Back the Night Rallies.

8. Join local chapters of organizations committed to empowering women and men in work, education, and relationships, e.g., American Association of University Women, Zonta International, Planned Parenthood, YWCA, YMCA, Business and Professional Women.

9. Take an Independent Study course and conduct empirical research in an area of your interest in the field of the psychology of women. Share your results at a professional conference and in journal form. Consult with your professor about student presentations at the American Psychological Association Annual Meeting as well as at regional meetings, e.g, Eastern Psychological Association, Midwestern Psychological Association. Also inquire about Psi Chi's sponsoring of student research at professional meetings.

(continued)

10. Write letters to newspaper and television executives regarding the antiwomen messages presented in advertisements, rock music videos and commercials.

11. Begin valuing your physique. Do not harm your body in order to meet some unrealistic image of women or men perpetuated by the media.

12. Assist your campus by offering suggestions on ways to improve upon their sexual harassment policy and procedures. Share the information presented in this textbook with the individual(s) charged with writing the policy statement and investigatory procedures.

13. Hold a week long "Sexual Victimization Awareness Week" at your campus in which you bring in speakers, hold guided discussions, show videos on types of sexual victimization. Encourage the support and participation by faculty and administration in this week of activities.

14. Suggest ways students can facilitate training programs on courtship violence for sororities and fraternities. Inquire about assisting your campus trainers in conducting these training sessions.

15. Vote for political candidates who will value women and men in education and the workplace as well as value children and the elderly.

16. Offer to work on a political candidate's campaign.

17. Write articles for your campus newspaper about gender justice.

NEW TERMS

Family and Medical Leave Act

family-oriented policies

First Amendment rights

individual level of change

institutional level of change

latchkey children

pornography

societal level of change

yasli-sads

CHAPTER REVIEW QUESTIONS

1. Identify three ways you can work toward gender justice on an individual level.

2. Identify three ways you can work for gender justice on the societal level.

3. List ways your campus can benefit from gender justice.

4. Cite myths and realities with respect to employed mothers and child care.

5. To what does "deindividuation" refer? How can we assist boys and men in not adopting a group identity with respect to violence against women?

6. Cite ways redefining gender roles means a revision of the masculine as well as feminine gender role.

7. Contrast the term "rape victim" with the term "rape survivor." What do the terms convey in relationship to women's strength and power?

8. Pretend you have been asked to give a presentation on sexual violence and traditional gender roles to high school-aged girls and boys. What topics would you discuss? Why? What topics would you avoid discussing? Why?

9. Discuss your views about the relationship between pornography and men's attitudes and behavior toward women.

10. Offer some suggestions for a training program for a "parents-to-be" class that will deal with raising children to be non-sexist and egalitarian.

11. To date, psychologists' definitions of justice, equity, power, and social change have been limited. In what ways? Discuss your answer citing relevant research.

SELECTED READINGS

Findlen, B. (Ed.). (1995). *Listen up: Voices from the next feminist generation.* Seattle: Seal Press.

Lorber, J. (1998). *Gender inequality: Feminist theories and politics.* Los Angeles: Roxbury.

Steinem, G. (1994). *Moving beyond words.* New York: Simon & Schuster.

Unger, R. K. (1998). *Resisting gender: Twenty-five years of feminist psychology.* London: Sage.

Wyche, K. (1998). Teaching the psychology of women courses in another discipline: The case of African American studies. *Psychology of Women Quarterly, 22,* 69–76.

LEARNING MORE ABOUT . . .

Suggestions for Term Papers and Independent Studies Related to *Equity and Social Change*

Impact of on-site day care centers at businesses on employed mothers' productivity, job satisfaction, and morale

Impact of family-oriented work policies, e.g., flex time, job sharing, on employed mother's morale, work productivity, and parenting skills

Impact of advertising campaigns on sexual victimization on incidence of sexual assault

Effectiveness of sexual harassment policies and investigatory procedures on incidence of sexual harassment on college campuses

Effectiveness of training programs for men and women on "better communication" on relationship satisfaction

Impact of women's studies courses on the entire academic disciplines

Integration of women of color into psychology of women courses and textbooks

REFERENCES

American Association of University Women. (1993). *Hostile hallways: The AAUW survey on sexual harassment in America's schools.* Washington, DC: Author.

Attorney General's Commission on Pornography. (1986). *Final Report.* Washington, DC: U.S. Department of Justice.

Barnett, R., & Rivers, C. (1992, February). The myth of the miserable working woman. *Working Woman, 2,* 62–65, 83–85.

Betz, N. (1993). Career development. In F. L. Denmark & M. A. Paludi (Eds.), *Psychology of women: A handbook of issues and theories.* Westport, CT: Greenwood Press.

Bird, C. (1999). Gender, household labor, and psychological distress: The impact of the amount and division of housework. *Journal of Health and Social Behavior, 40,* 32–45.

Burchinal, M., Roberts, J., Nabors, L., & Bryant, D. (1996). Quality of center child care and infant cognitive and language development. *Child Development, 67,* 606–620.

Caruso, D. (1996). Maternal employment status, mother–infant interaction, and infant development. *Child and Youth Care Forum, 25,* 125–134.

Clark-Stewart, A. (1993). *Daycare.* Cambridge, MA: Harvard University Press.

Cowan, G. (1995). Black and white (and blue): Ethnicity and pornography. In H. Landrine (Ed.), *Bringing cultural diversity to feminist psychology.* Washington, DC: American Psychological Association.

Cowan, G., Chase, C. J., & Butts Stahly, G. (1989). Feminist and fundamentalist attitudes toward pornography control. *Psychology of Women Quarterly, 13,* 97–112.

DeCenzo, D., & Robbins, S. (1999). *Human resource management.* New York: McGraw Hill.

Dempsey, K. (1999). Attempting to explain women's perceptions of the fairness of the division of housework. *Journal of Family Studies, 5,* 3–24.

Donnerstein, E. (1983). Erotica and human aggression. In R. Geen & E. Donnerstein (Eds.), *Aggression.* New York: Academic Press.

Doyle, J. (1995). *The male experience.* Dubuque, IA: Brown.

Doyle, J., & Paludi, M. (1998). *Sex and gender: The human experience* (3rd ed.). Dubuque, IA: Brown.

Duncan, G., & Brooks-Gunn, J. (2000). Family, poverty, welfare reform, and child development. *Child Development, 71*, 188–196.

Dutton, G., & Golant, S. (1995). *The batterer: A psychological profile.* New York: Basic Books.

Etaugh, C. (1993). Psychology of women: Middle and older adulthood. In F. L. Denmark & M. A. Paludi (Eds.), *Psychology of women: A handbook of issues and theories.* Westport, CT: Greenwood Press.

Frone, M., & Yardley, J. (1996). Workplace family-supportive programmes: Predictors of employed parents' importance ratings. *Journal of Occupational and Organizational Psychology, 69*, 351–366.

Gentry, M. (1989). Introduction: Feminist perspectives on gender and thought: Paradox and potential. In M. Crawford & M. Gentry (Eds.), *Gender and thought.* New York: Springer-Verlag.

Gilbert, L. (1994). Current perspectives on dual-career families. *Current Directions in Psychological Science, 3*, 101–105.

Gottfried, A., Gottfried, A., Bathurst, K., & Killian, C. (1999). Maternal and dual-earner employment: Family environment, adaptations, and the developmental impingement perspective. In M. Lamb et al. (Eds.), *Parenting and child development in "nontraditional" families.* Mahwah, NJ: Erlbaum.

Graham, D., & Rawlings, E. (1999). Observers' blaming of battered wives: Who, what, when and why? In M. Paludi (Ed.), *The psychology of sexual victimization: A handbook.* Westport, CT: Greenwood.

Graham, D., Rawlings, E., & Rigsby, R. (1994). *Loving to survive: Sexual terror, men's violence,and women's lives.* New York: New York University Press.

Hochschild, A. R. (1989). *The second shift.* NewYork: Viking.

Hoffman, L. W. (1989). Effects of maternal employment in the two-parent family. *American Psychologist, 44*, 283–292.

Hoffman, L., & Youngblade, L. (1999). Maternal employment, morale and parenting style: Social class comparisons. *Journal of Applied Developmental Psychology, 19*, 389–413.

Hyde, J., Klein, M., Essex, M., & Clark, R. (1995). Maternity leave and women's mental health. *Psychology of Women Quarterly, 19*, 257–285.

Kahnweiler, W., & Kahnweiler, J. (1992). The work/family challenge: A key career development issue. *Journal of Career Development, 18*, 251–257.

Kimmel, M. (1994). Masculinity as homophobia: Fear, shame, and silence in the construction of gender identity. In H. Brod & M. Kaufman (Eds.), *Theorizing masculinities.* Thousand Oaks, CA: Sage.

Koss, M. P. (1993). Rape: Scope, impact, interventions, and public policy responses. *American Psychologist, 48,* 1062–1069.

Landrine, H. (Ed.). (1995). *Bringing cultural diversity to feminist psychology.* Washington, DC: American Psychological Association.

Levy, A. (1999). The law and workplace sexual harassment. In M. Paludi (Ed.), *The psychology of sexual victimization: A handbook.* Westport, CT: Greenwood.

Levy, A., & Paludi, M. (in press). *Workplace sexual harassment* (2nd ed.). Upper Saddle River, NJ: Prentice Hall.

Lundberg-Love, P. (1999). The resilience of the human psyche: Recognition and treatment of the adult survivor of incest. In M. Paludi (Ed.), *The psychology of sexual victimization: A handbook.* Westport, CT: Greenwood.

MacKinnon, C. (1979). *Sexual harassment of working women.* New Haven, CT: Yale University Press.

Malamuth, N., & Donnerstein, E. (1982). The effects of aggressive-pornographic mass media stimuli. In L. Berkowitz (Ed.), *Advances in experimental social psychology* (Vol. 15). New York: Academic Press.

Maume, D., & Mullin, K. (1993). Men's participation in child care and women's work attachment. *Social Problems, 40,* 533–546.

Paludi, C., & Paludi, M. (2000, October). *Developing and enforcing an effective workplace policy statement, procedures, and training programs on domestic violence.* Presented at the Domestic Violence as a Workplace Concern Conference, Nashua, NH.

Paludi, M. (Ed.). (1996). *Sexual harassment on college campuses: Abusing the ivory power.* Albany: State University of New York Press.

Paludi, M. (Ed.). (1999). *The psychology of sexual victimization: A handbook.* Westport, CT: Greenwood Press.

Paludi, M., & Barickman, R. (1998). *Sexual harassment, work and education: A resource manual for prevention.* Albany: State University of New York Press.

Paludi, M., Paludi, C., & Doyle, J. (in press). *Sex and gender* (5th ed.). New York: McGraw Hill.

Phillips, D., Voran, M., Kisker, E., Howes, C., & Whitebook, M. (1994). Child care for children in poverty: Opportunity or inequity? *Child Development, 65,* 472–492.

Pollard, P. (1995). Pornography and sexual aggression. *Current Psychology: Developmental, Learning, Personality, Social, 14,* 200–221.

Rodman, H., & Cole, C. (1987). Latchkey children: A review of policy and resources. *Family Relations, 36,* 101–105.

Rozee, P. (1999). Stranger rape. In M. Paludi (Ed.), *The psychology of sexual victimization: A handbook.* Westport, CT: Greenwood.

Russell, D. (1993, August). *Rape and the masculine mystique.* Paper presented at the meeting of the American Sociological Association, New York.

Russo, N. F. (1979). Overview: Sex roles, fertility and the motherhood mandate. *Psychology of Women Quarterly, 4,* 7–15.

Scarr, S., Phillips, D., & McCartney, K. (1989). Working mothers and their families. *American Psychologist, 44,* 1402–1409.

Sinacore-Guinn, A. (1998). Employed mothers: Job satisfaction and self-esteem. *Canadian Journal of Counseling, 32,* 242–258.

Stevenson, M. (1999). Sexual victimization of women: The Congressional response. In M. Paludi (Ed.), *The psychology of sexual victimization: A handbook.* Westport, CT: Greenwood Press.

Sweeney, Y. (1999). The evolution of motherhood: Balancing family and work roles during children's school age years. *Dissertation Abstracts International, 59.*

Tronto, J. (1987). Beyond gender difference to a theory of care. *Signs, 12,* 644–663

Vandell, D. L., & Ramanan, J. (1991). Children of the national longitudinal survey of youth: Choices in after school care and child development. *Developmental Psychology, 27,* 637–643.

Walker, L. (1999). Psychology and domestic violence around the world. *American Psychologist, 54,* 21–29.

GLOSSARY

abortion   Ending of a pregnancy and the expulsion of the contents of the uterus.

access discrimination   Discrimination toward individuals who are seeking access to a job or education.

achievement motivation   Individuals' desire to seek out competitive situations where they are likely to succeed and avoid situations where they are likely to fail.

acquaintance rape   Rape by an individual who is known to the victim.

acquired immunodeficiency syndrome (AIDS)   Sexually transmitted disease that destroys the body's natural immunity to infections.

acute battering incident   According to Walker, the second phase of the cycle of battering in which the batterer engages in violence.

adipose tissue   Fat.

adolescence   Period of the life cycle ranging from ages 12 to 21 during which physical and cognitive as well emotional changes occur.

adrenogenital syndrome   Hormonal abnormality.

amenorrhea   Absence of menstruation.

androcentric paradigm   Focus on men and men's issues.

androcentrism   Theories of personality that use boys and men as the prototye for humankind.

androgen   Sex hormones produced by the adrenal glands.

androgynous conception of femininity and masculinity   Femininity is not thought to be composed of personality characteristics that were opposites of masculinity; instead the psychological characteristics of femininity and masculinity are viewed as comprising two independent dimensions that could be separate but could overlap as well.

anorexia nervosa   Eating disorder characterized by three symptoms: self-induced severe weight loss, amenorrhea, and an intense fear of losing control over eating and gaining weight.

anovulatory period   Menstrual cycle during which the ovaries failed to release an egg despite the fact that menstruation occurred.

anti-gay prejudice   Negative attitudes and behaviors exhibited toward lesbians and gay men.

antiprostaglandin drugs   Prescribed for the relief of menstrual cramps.

areola   Dark circular area of skin surrounding the nipple of the breast.

Association of Black Psychologists   Founded in 1968; the major objectives of this organization are to eradicate the myths regarding the psychology of African American women and men as well as to increase the representation of African Americans in the discipline of psychology.

Association for Women in Psychology   Formed in 1969, this association promotes research on women.

autonomic egalitarian relationship   Identified in Peplau's research, a marital pattern referring to an egalitarian relationship in which the wife and husband each exercise power over separate spheres.

baseline mammogram   Initial mammogram.

battering   Partner abuse; intimate violence toward a mate or dating partner.

Bem Sex Role Inventory   Developed by Bem as a measure of individuals' gender role identity.

biculturalism   According to Brown, one element in a lesbian and gay reality; refers to having dominant and minority cultures as part of one's family of origin.

binge-purge syndrome   Bulimia.

bipolar continuum   Femininity and masculinity viewed as opposite sides of a single continuum; not independent dimensions of femininity and masculinity.

Board of Ethnic Minority Affairs   Appointed in 1981 to assist with promoting ethnic awareness in the discipline of psychology.

body (of the uterus)   Main part of the uterus.

body position   Nonverbal behavior in which women tend to sit in a less relaxed way than men; women display a more restricted body posture than men.

Body-Self-Relations Questionnaire   Developed by Jackson and her colleagues, this survey deals with perceptions of physical appearance.

Boston Women's Health Book Collective   Formed in 1969 to teach women about their physical and mental health; published the *New Our Bodies, Ourselves* and *Ourselves Getting Older*.

breast diseases Includes fibrocystic condition and fibroadenomas as well as breast cancer.

breast self-examination Examination of breasts monthly to help detect changes in the breasts, e.g., lumps.

bulimia Eating disorder characterized by episodes of inconspicuous gross overeating that is followed by self-induced purging.

cephalocaudal development Growth trend in which development begins with the brain and head and then works it way down the body.

cervix Lower part of the uterus; next to the vagina.

chilly classroom climate Identified by Hall and Sandler, behaviors that discourage girls and women's participation in classes, e.g., preventing women from seeking help outside of class, dampening career aspirations, undermining women's confidence, interrupting women in class.

cilia Tiny hairlike structure lining the fallopian tubes.

climacteric Menopause.

climax Orgasm.

clique Characteristic of girls' friendships; characterized by three or four girls in which at least two are involved in a close friendship.

clitoral hood Sheath of tissue that passes around the clitoris and is an extension of the labia minora.

clitoris Small, highly sensitive sexual organ in the female that is located in front of the vaginal entrance.

cognitive attribution theory of achievement motivation Proposed by Weiner to explain the differences between high and low achievement individuals as due to the attributions they make regarding the causes of their successes and failures.

coming out Process of acknowledging to oneself and then to other individuals that one is lesbian or gay.

Committee on Women in Psychology Formed in 1973 to serve as a catalyst to the various parts of the American Psychological Association's governing structure.

competency cluster In Rosenkrantz' research, stereotypic characteristics for women and men fell into two clusters, a warmth-expressiveness cluster for women and a competency cluster for men.

compensatory history The historian locates lost or overlooked women to the discipline and places them back in the history of the field.

compulsory heterosexuality According to Rich, women experience compulsory heterosexuality; lesbian relationships need to be viewed along a continuum of woman-identified behaviors that empower women, e.g., sharing, supporting, bonding.

connectedness   According to Gilligan, women view women as relational; caring is an essential feminine attribute.

consciousness-raising groups   Therapeutic support in which the main focus centers on the group members' feelings and self-perceptions.

contagion of stress   Women who live in poverty are likely to experience stressful events occurring to others in their environment as well as the stressors in their own lives.

contribution history   Women's contribution to the field of history are noted.

corpus luteum   The mass of cells remaining after a follicle has released an egg; secretes progesterone.

cortisol   Hormone produced by a fetus's adrenal glands.

cultural sensitivity of psychotherapists   An understanding of clients' behavior in the context of their cultural community.

date rape   Rape by an individual who is known to the victim, especially a dating partner.

decoding   The ability to evaluate other individuals' nonverbal communication.

devaluation of women   Putting down women's work or women's performance.

direct achieving styles   Identified by Lipman-Blumen; used by individuals who confront achievement tasks very directly and enjoy winning over competitors.

distal stimulation   Behaviors such as looking and vocalizing.

divergent meanings of sexuality   Women and men view sexuality differently.

Division of the Psychology of Women of the American Psychological Association   Formed within the American Psychological Association to promote research on women.

double duty   Women working outside the home and doing most of the chores inside the home as well, e.g., housekeeping, as well as the childrearing.

double jeopardy   According to Beale, minority women's participation in a culture that has valued neither women nor nonwhites.

double standard for mental health   Research by Broverman and her colleagues determined that clinicians viewed adult men and adults (sex not specified) in more positive characteristics than they did women.

double standard of aging   According to Sontag, the view that older men are distinguished while older women are unattractive.

double standard of sexuality   A standard in which premarital sexual relationships are considered acceptable for men and unacceptable for women.

dowager's hump A consequence of women's bone becoming more brittle and porous.

Draw-A-Person Test A test developed by Machover that has been used as a measure of individuals' gender role identification.

dysmennorrhea Painful menstruation.

dyspareunia Painful intercourse.

eating disorders Anorexia and bulimia.

egalitarian relationship In Peplau's research, a relationship in which power is shared fairly equally between the partners.

egalitarian role relations Equal time devoted by women and men to housekeeping and child rearing as well as to their careers.

eight stages of man Erikson's theory of personality development across the life cycle.

embryonic period Second stage of prenatal development; lasts from the end of the second week to the eighth week; characterized by rapid growth, the establishment of a placental relationship with the woman, and the early structural appearance of all major organs.

employee assistance programs Specific programs at workplaces designed to help employees with personal problems.

empowerment Supporting individuals in their process of becoming less vulnerable and feeling out of control because of victimization.

encoding Ability to communicate nonverbally.

endometriosis Condition in which the endometrium grows in some place other than the uterus.

endometrium The inner lining of the uterus.

engendering psychology According to Denmark, the field of psychology must cultivate a discipline that is sensitive to issues of gender and diversity.

English language defining women Women's identities being tied to the men with whom they are associated, e.g., father, husband.

English language deprecating women Language that treats women deferentially to men; the use of derogatory terms to refer to girls and women.

English language ignoring women Use of generic pronouns that ignore women.

Equal Employment Opportunity Commission Government agency responsible for enforcing Title VII of the 1964 Civil Rights Act.

estrogen A group of sex hormones.

estrogen replacement therapy Doses of estrogen prescribed for menopausal women.

ethnocentrism   Personality theories that assume identical development for all individuals across all racial, ethnic, and class groups.

ethic of care   Identified by Gilligan, women's morality is viewed as a series of connections based on caring for others rather than a contract between people.

excitement phase   Masters and Johnson's term for the first stage in the sexual response cycle during which physical changes, such as a rise in blood pressure and modified heat rates and breathing, accompany women's psychological arousal.

experimenter bias   Researcher bias; researchers influenced by their cultural beliefs, values, and expectations that may cause a researcher to look at a problem in only one way, while avoiding other possibilities.

external sexual organs   Consists of the clitoris, mons pubis, labia majora, labia minora, and vaginal opening; collectively the female external organs are referred to as the vulva.

facilitators of women's career development   Employed mothers, supportive fathers, mentors, career counseling.

fallopian tubes   Tubes extending from the uterus to the ovary.

Family and Medical Leave Act   In effect since 1993, mandates employers must permit employees up to a total of 12 workweeks of unpaid leave during any 12-month period for child care or care of elderly parents, for example.

Family-oriented policies   Policies adopted by businesses such as job sharing, flexible work hours, or employer-sponsored day care.

female viability   Women have an overall life expectancy that surpasses men at every decade of life, regardless of race; girls have fewer congenital disorders, are less likely to succumb to sudden infant death syndrome, and are less prone to hyperactivity; genetically determined strength.

feminist friendships   Identified by Pogrebin, caring in women's friendships with women.

feminist health care movement for women   Women reclaiming control over their physical health.

feminist therapies   Therapeutic support for women based on a philosophical critique of society wherein women are seen as having less political and economic power than men have and that the bases for women's personal problems are social, not personal.

feminization of poverty   More women than men are living in poverty.

feminization of psychology   Identified by Strickland, the discipline of psychology has more women than men.

fetal alcohol syndrome   Serious growth deficiency and malformations in a child born to a woman who abuses alcohol.

fetal period   Third stage of prenatal development; begins with the ninth week and ends with birth; characterized by the continuous development of major organ systems, with the organs assuming their specialized functions.

fibroadenomas   Lumps that do not fluctuate with the menstrual cycle.

fibrocystic condition   Breast cells retaining fluid.

fillers   Phrases such as "you know," "ah," "uhm" in speech.

First Amendment Rights   Right to free speech.

first generation of American women psychologists   Women psychologists, e.g., Christine Ladd-Franklin, Margaret Washburn, Mary Calkins, who experienced access and treatment discrimination and overcame barriers to women's advancing in psychology to make substantial contributions to the science.

follicles   The capsule of cells surrounding an egg in the ovary.

follicle-stimulating hormone (FSH)   A hormone secreted by the pituitary gland; it stimulates follicle development in females.

follicular phase   The first phase of the menstrual cycle, beginning after menstruation.

fundus   Top of the uterus.

gatekeeper   Individuals who make judgments about individuals' work and who may prohibit them from participating in a certain career or advancing in their career.

gender harassment   Generalized sexist remarks and behavior not designed to elicit sexual cooperation but rather to convey insulting, degrading, or sexist attitudes about women or men.

gender as socially constructed   View of women and men in terms of their position in society.

gendercentrism   Separate paths of life-cycle development are suggested for women and men as a result of the biological differences between them.

gender-role adoption   Individuals' overt behavior that is characteristic of a given sex rather than of stated preferences per se.

gender-role identification   The incorporation of a feminine or masculine role and the actions characteristic of the behavior of a particular role.

gender-role identity   Term used to describe a developmental process that includes gender-role preference, gender-role adoption, gender-role identification, gender-role orientation, and knowledge of sex-determined role standards.

gender-role orientation   Individuals' self-definition as feminine or masculine.

gender-role preference   Individuals' desire to adopt the behavior associated with either women or men, or the perception of such behavior as preferable.

gender-role transcendence   Identified by Garnets and Pleck; women and men transcend rather than merge prescribed gender role characteristics all together.

gender schema theory   According to Bem, children's gender-role acquisition derives from gender-schematic processing as well as a generalized readiness on the part of children to encode information from a variety of socialization agents.

generic pronouns   Pronouns such as "his" that are sometimes believed to represent all persons but actually only refer to men.

germinal period   First stage of prenatal development; characterized by the growth of the zygote and the establishment of a linkage between the zygote and the woman's support system.

gonadotrophins   Hormones released by the pituitary gland.

group harassment   Groups of individuals engaging in sexual harassment, e.g., shouting obscenities at women who walk by fraternity houses or other campus sites; demanding a woman expose her breasts and refusing to allow her to leave until she complies.

heterosexism   Personality theories that assume that a heterosexual orientation is normative and a lesbian and gay sexual orientation is deviant and worthy of change.

homogenization of American women   Identified by Bem and Bem; the belief that women are socialized by family, peers, and teachers to pursue the same career regardless of their individual aspirations, abilities, and needs.

hostile-environment sexual harassment   An environment that is created in the workplace or classroom that is perceived by another as hostile, intimidating, and offensive; e.g., demeaning or belittling remarks, jokes, slurs, innuendos about the sex or body of a coworker or student; sexually suggestive objects, books, magazines, pictures, or photographs displayed in the classroom or work area.

hot flashes   Occurring during menopause, feelings of intense heat in the face, neck, and upper chest that last for a few minutes at a time.

hymen   A membrane that partially covers the vaginal opening.

hypothalamus   Part of the brain that is important in regulating certain body functions including sex hormone production.

hysterectomy   Surgical removal of the uterus.

hysterotomy   A method of abortion used during the second trimester.

idiographic approach to the measurement of women's success striving   Asking women to define success and their career pathways themselves through interviewing methodology.

identity vs. role confusion   Stage 5 of Erikson's personality theory.

identity acceptance   Stage in coming-out process in which the individual states he or she is a homosexual and accepts this sexual orientation rather than tolerates it.

identity comparison   Stage in coming-out process in which the individual believes she or he is a homosexual.

identity confusion   Stage in coming-out process in which the person is confused by same-sex attractions.

identity pride   Stage in coming-out process in which the individual dichotomizes the world into heterosexuals and homosexuals, the latter perceived to be good and important.

identity synthesis   Stage in coming-out process in which the person is able to synthesize public and private sexual orientations.

identity tolerance   Stage in coming-out process in which an individual makes contact with the gay subculture in hopes for affirmation for his or her sexual orientation.

imaginary audience   Identified by Elkind, adolescents feel they are the focus of attention; it is imaginary, however, in that other people are actually not that concerned with the adolescents' thoughts.

in-between generation   Individuals who are caring for their children and aging parents simultaneously.

incest   Sexual activity between close relatives.

independent dimensions   Separate dimensions of femininity and masculinity rather than being opposite ends of a bipolar continuum.

individual level of change   Redefining gender roles at the individual level, e.g., through interpersonal relationships with mates.

inferiority curriculum   According to Bernard, discrimination against girls and women contributes to their feeling depressed and frustrated and doubting their competency and self-worth.

institutional level of change   Redefining gender roles at the institutional level, e.g., developing and enforcing workplace policies prohibiting gender discrimination and sexual harassment.

internal sexual organs   Consists of the vagina, uterus, ovaries, and fallopian tubes.

intimacy vs. isolation   Stage 6 of Erikson's personality theory.

introitus   Entrance to the vagina.

IT Scale for Children   Developed by Brown as a measure of children's gender role preference.

just-world hypothesis   Belief that bad things happen only to these who somehow bring on their own problems or deserve the consequences of their actions.

knowledge of sex-determined role standards   Individuals' concepts and espousal of gender-role stereotypes of both femininity and masculinity.

labia majora   Outer lips; fatty pads of tissue lying on either side of the vaginal opening.

labia minora   Inner lips; thin folds of skin on either side of the vaginal entrance.

lanugo   Growth of downy hair on the body commonly occurring in anorexics.

latchkey children   Term used to describe children who come home from school and take care of themselves; their parent(s) work outside the home and are not there when the children come home from school.

lesbian communities   Networks established to provide mutual support for lesbians.

life expectancy   Average number of years an individual may be expected to live from a given age or from birth.

linguistic sexism   Ignoring women in the English language, defining women and deprecating women through the use of language.

long requests   Incorporating words such as "Please" or "I'd appreciate it if . . ." into one's speech.

lung cancer   Surpasses breast cancer as the leading cause of death for women; rise in lung cancer in women is directly related to the increase in women's smoking cigarettes, with adolescent and young adult women surpassing men in acquiring this habit.

luteal phase   The third phase of the menstrual cycle following ovulation.

luteinizing hormone(LH)   A hormone secreted by the pituitary; causes ovulation in females.

magnitude of gender differences   How large a gender difference really is; relates to practical significance of a research finding.

mammary glands   The milk-producing part of the breast.

mammograms   X-rays for diagnosing breast cancer.

marginality   According to Brown, one element that defines a lesbian and gay reality; refers to the view of lesbians as "others," not belonging to the dominant heterosexual culture.

masculine bias   Defining terms, e.g., achievement, morality, in terms of boy's and men's responses and preferences rather than both men's and women's experiences.

maternal employment   Paid employment of women who have children.

mefenamic acid   Antiprostaglandin drug to help with menstrual problems.

menarche   The first menstruation.

menopause   The gradual cessation of menstruation.

menorrhagia   An excessively heavy and prolonged menstrual flow leads to a temporary state of anemia.

menstrual fluid   Contains cervical mucus, vaginal secretions, cells, mucus, and degenerated endometrial particles in addition to blood.

menstruation   A bloody discharge of the lining of the uterus.

mentor   An individual who guides and supports the career development of another person in professional and personal ways, e.g., providing support on how to incorporate a career and family life.

meta-analysis   Statistical procedure that permits psychologists to synthesize results from several studies in order to measure the magnitude of a difference; a statistical method for conducting a literature review.

midwife deliveries   Deliveries assisted by an individual who is trained as a birth attendant.

Mittelschmerz   Abdominal cramping during ovulation.

modern relationship   Identified by Peplau, type of marriage in which the husband is less dominant and traditional gender roles are somewhat modified.

mommy track   Track at work in which women do not pursue managerial positions or positions that involve travel so that they will be able to take care of their children; not viewed positively by employers as a consequence of negative stereotypes about women integrating work and family.

mons pubis   The fatty pad of tissue under the pubic hair.

moral reasoning   Thought processes involved in deciding moral issues and resolving moral dilemmas, e.g., abortion, stealing for saving an individual's life.

motherhood mandate   Introduced by Russo to describe prescribed role of mother for women in North American culture.

multicomponent approach   Position that gender role stereotypes comprise more than only certain personality traits.

multiple orgasms   Series of orgasms occurring within a short period of time.

myometrium   Middle layer of the uterus.

myotonia   Muscle contraction.

network family   Support group of non-kin.

networking mentoring   Introduced by Swoboda and Millar in which two or more women fulfill the roles of mentor and protégé to each other at different times during their relationship.

nipple   The pigmented tip of the breast.

nonsexist research   Research that values both male and female experiences; research that places value on scholarship that is concerned with the larger society.

nonverbal communication   Communication such as body language, eye contact, smiling, personal space.

null environment   According to Freeman, education for women that neither encourages or discourages women—it simply ignores them.

Office of Ethnic Minority Affairs   Established at the American Psychological Association to assist with promoting ethnic awareness in psychology.

oophorectomy   Surgical removal of the ovaries.

orgasm   An intense sensation that occurs at the peak of sexual arousal and is followed by release of sexual tension.

orgasmic phase   Characterized by a sequence of rhythmic contractions of the orgasmic platform.

orgasmic plateau   Sexual arousal becomes intensified and sexual and muscular tension increases.

orgasmic platform   The thickening of the walls of the outer third of the vagina that occurs during sexual arousal.

osteoporosis   Excessive loss of bone tissue that results in the bones becoming thinner, brittle, and more porous.

ovaries   The paired sex glands in the female that produce ova and sex hormones.

overweight   Weighing at least 20 percent more than the recommended weight on standardized charts.

ovulation   Release of an egg by the ovaries.

ovulatory phase   Second phase of the menstrual cycle.

pectoral muscles   Muscles underlying the breast tissue.

peer harassment   Sexual harassment between two students or two employees where no organizational power differential exists.

pejoration   Words take on negative connotations because of the devaluing of women in general.

penis envy   According to Sigmund Freud, women have a penis envy and consequently a basic sense of inferiority; women resolve the "genital loss" by passively accepting it from a man and bearing children.

performance evaluation   Evaluation of performance, e.g., paintings, articles; the identical performance by women and men is evaluated differently, with work attributed to women being devalued in comparison to the identical work attributed to men.

perimetrium   Outer layer of uterus that forms the cover of the uterus.

personal fable   According to Elkind, adolescents tell themselves a subjective story about their "special qualities," It is frequently translated into a conviction that they are not subject to the dangers suffered by others.

personal space   Amount of space taken around one's body; women tend to take less personal space around their bodies than men; women are also assigned to smaller spaces, e.g., offices.

plateau phase   Masters and Johnson's term for the second phase of sexual response, occurring just before orgasm.

pornography   Sexually arousing literature, art, or films.

poverty   Stressors involved in poverty impact women's depressive symptomatology; inadequate housing, dangerous neighborhoods, and financial concerns are more serious stressors than acute crises.

premenstrual syndrome (PMS)   A combination of severe physical and psychological symptoms that occur in some women prior to menstruating.

prenatal period   Time that elapses between conception and birth; averages about 280 days from the last menstrual period; divided into three stages: germinal period, embryonic period, fetal period.

prepuce   Protective hood of skin covering the glans of the clitoris.

primitive streak   A ridge that is formed by the cells in the central portion of the embryo that thicken.

progesterone   A female sex hormone produced by the corpus luteum in the ovary.

progestin   Synthetic drug prescribed in the 1940s and 1950s that affected female fetuses.

prostaglandins   Chemicals that stimulate contractions of the muscles of the uterus; the likely cause of painful menstruation.

prostaglandin abortion   A method of abortion that is performed in the late second trimester and involves inducing labor by injecting prostaglandins into the amniotic sac.

proximal stimulation   Holding, touching.

proximodistal development   Growth trend characterized by growth away from the axis.

psychological androgyny   Personality pattern wherein an individual combines the socially valued stereotypic characteristics associated with both femininity and masculinity.

puberty   Period of the life cycle during which the body matures from that of a child to that of an adult capable of reproducing.

pubescence   Period of development during which secondary sex characteristics become mature.

pubic symphysis   Center point at which pubic bones join.

publication bias   Publishing research that only conforms to previously accepted findings, e.g., publishing research only focusing on gender differences and not gender similarities.

qualifier   A word or phrase that softens a statement.

qualitative data techniques   Includes structured interviews and focus groups.

quantitative data techniques   Include personality tests, achievement tests.

quid pro quo sexual harassment   Sexual harassment where a supervisor or someone with authority to confer workplace benefits (e.g., hiring, raises, promotions) is offering those benefits in exchange for sexual favors or is threatening to take away economic benefits for failure to comply with sexual requests.

rape   Nonconsenting oral, anal, or vaginal penetration obtained by force, by threat of bodily harm, or when the victim is incapable of giving consent.

reconstruction history   Introduced by Lerner, reconstructing history through perspective of women, not men.

relational achieving styles   Identified by Lipman-Blumen, used by people who seek success through their relationships with others.

reproductive freedom   The ability to choose whether or when to have children; all women's choices are respected and supported.

researcher bias   Researchers are likely to be influenced by their cultural beliefs, values, and expectations; they may look at a psychological issue in only one way, avoiding other possibilities.

resolution phase   Masters and Johnson's term for the last phase of sexual response; the body returns to the unaroused state.

role conflict   Competing roles demanding of women, e.g., having to act "feminine" with loved ones and "masculine" at the office in order to be respected.

role overload   Overly demanding work in which women are employed outside the home and have to perform the majority of childrearing and housework.

RU-486   New pill that produces a very early abortion.

saline-induced abortion   Method of abortion performed in the late second trimester; involves inducing labor by injecting a saline solution into the amniotic sac.

scientific method   Research paradigm that leads to studying human behavior from a linear, predetermined model.

seductive behavior   Unwanted, inappropriate, and offensive sexual advances.

self-disclosure   Introduced by Jourard to describe the sharing of personal or intimate information about oneself with others.

self-in-relation theory   Proposed by Miller, posits that early socialization experiences account for women's communication styles and skills in intimacy.

sex discrimination Discriminatory behavior based on the individual's sex.

sex flush A rash-like condition on the skin that occurs during sexual arousal.

sex role spillover Identified by Gutek; when occupations are dominated by one sex or the other, the sex role of the dominant sex influences or "spills over" the work role expectations for that job.

sexual bribery Soliciting sexual activity by promising a reward.

sexual coercion Coercing sexual activity by threatening punishment.

sexual harassment Unwelcome sexual advances, requests for sexual favors, and other verbal or physical conduct of a sexual nature when (1) submission to such conduct is made either explicitly or implicitly a term or condition of the individual's employment; (2) submission to or rejection of such conduct by an individual is used as the basis for employment decisions affecting the individual; (3) such conduct has the purpose or effect of unreasonably interfering with an individual's work or creating an intimidating, hostile, or offensive work environment.

sexual imposition One type of sexual harassment: assault.

silencing women Through communication in conversations or the media, keeping girls and women from expressing their opinions and feelings.

singlehood Status of individuals who have never been married or are once again single following a divorce, separation, or widowhood.

social eye contact Looking at another individual, which may indicate an expression of affection or interest in developing a more intimate relationship with the other person.

social support networks Individuals who serve very different functions in friendships.

socialization agent An individual or institution that shapes a person's values, beliefs, or behaviors.

societal level of change Redefining gender roles at the societal level, e.g., working for stricter penalties for rapists.

Society for the Psychological Study of Ethnic Minority Issues A division of the American Psychological Association that is devoted to ethnic awareness.

sociopsychological factors affecting achievement Factors such as achievement motivation, causal attributions for success and failure, and fear of failure that impact individuals' career development.

structural factors affecting achievement Factors such as role models, mentors, employed mothers, social policies, and performance evaluation that impact individuals' career development.

substance abuse Use of alcohol or drugs to such an extent that normal functioning is impaired.

sudden infant death syndrome   Death, while sleeping, of apparently healthy infants who cease breathing for unknown medical reasons.

syncratic egalitarian relationship   According to Peplau's research, a marital pattern in which wife and husband wield power and make decisions jointly in all areas.

tag questions   Partly a statement and partly a question.

tension-building stage   Identified by Walker; first phase of cycle of battering in which the woman attempts to avoid escalation of the battering by trying to "calm" her mate and by staying out of his way.

Thematic Apperception Test   Projective test developed by Morgan and Murray that is used to measure individuals' achievement motivation.

therapist bias against women   Includes women being seen for longer periods of time in therapy and prescribed stronger prescriptive medications than men.

Title VII of the Civil Rights Act   Prohibits discrimination in getting access to and once individuals are at employment based on sex, race, color, religion, national origin.

Title IX of the Education Amendments   Prohibits discrimination, including sexual harassment in education.

traditional relationship   According to Peplau's research, a marital relationship in which the husband is more dominant than the wife; both partners maintain traditional gender roles.

treatment discrimination   Discrimination experienced by individuals when they are at their employment, e.g., not being promoted to a senior level management position because of sex or race.

Turner's syndrome   Abnormal sex chromosome pattern in which the second X chromosome is either defective or missing.

unaroused states   State prior to excitement phase and following resolution phase of the sexual response cycle identified by Masters and Johnson.

uterus   Organ in the female in which the fetus develops.

vacuum aspiration   A method of abortion that is performed during the first trimester.

vagina   Organ in the female into which the penis is inserted during intercourse and through which a baby passes during the birth process.

vaginal barrier   Approximately 8 to 10 centimeters long and tilts slightly backward from the bottom to the top; at the bottom it opens to the vaginal opening.

vaginal lubrication   As the level of sexual arousal increases, lubrication enters the vaginal walls because of the vasocongestion that develops in the pelvic area.

vaginal mucosa   Inner layer of the vaginal wall.

value-laden approach to research   Research that is embedded with a culture's all-pervasive antifeminine and androcentric worldviews.

variability hypothesis   Studied by Hollingworth, the assertion that women are less variable among themselves than are men.

verbal communication   Includes use of fillers, tag questions, long requests, and qualifiers in one's speech.

voting method   Counting method used by Maccoby and Jacklin in documenting gender differences.

vulva   The collective term for the external genitals of the female; includes the mons, clitoris, inner and outer lips, and vaginal and urethral openings.

wall of prohibition   According to Gilligan, adolescent girls encounter a wall of prohibition in which girls are repressed and silenced in classrooms and their relationships.

warmth-expressiveness cluster   Cluster women tended to exhibit in Rosenkrantz's research on sex-determined role standards.

within-group variability   Amount of variability within a particular group, e.g., women; women differ among themselves more than they do between themselves and men.

woman-based theory of personality   Personality theory that addresses issues from the perspective of women's experiences.

women's history in psychology   Subfield of women's history in response to the neglect of women's contributions to psychology.

womentoring   Sharing of power, competence, self, and differences in a mentor-protégé relationship.

Work and Family Orientation Questionnaire (WOFO)   Self-report measure of achievement motivation developed by Spence and Helmreich.

X chromosome   Sex chromosomes of a genetically normal female consist of two X chromosomes.

Y chromosome   Sex chromosomes of a genetically normal male consist of one X and one Y chromosome.

yasli-sads   Preschools in Russia.

zygote   The fertilized egg.

Author Index

Subject Index